Ethical Leadership

For David
RMM

For Mindy, Zoe, and Anna Marie
SJW

For Jack, Finn, and Henry
AKP

Ethical Leadership

A Primer

Edited by

Robert M. McManus

McCoy Professor of Leadership Studies and Communication, McDonough Center for Leadership and Business, Marietta College, Ohio, USA

Stanley J. Ward

Dean of Capstone Studies and Director of the Center for Action Research, Claremont Lincoln University, California, USA

Alexandra K. Perry

Clinical Ethicist, OhioHealth, Ohio, USA

Edward Elgar
PUBLISHING

Cheltenham, UK • Northampton, MA, USA

Cover image: Beth Nash
Cover design: Tina Ullman

Published by
Edward Elgar Publishing Limited
The Lypiatts
15 Lansdown Road
Cheltenham
Glos GL50 2JA
UK

Edward Elgar Publishing, Inc.
William Pratt House
9 Dewey Court
Northampton
Massachusetts 01060
USA

A catalogue record for this book
is available from the British Library

Library of Congress Control Number: 2018944037

Printed on elemental chlorine free (ECF)
recycled paper containing 30% Post-Consumer Waste

ISBN 978 1 78811 035 8 (cased)
ISBN 978 1 78811 037 2 (paperback)
ISBN 978 1 78811 036 5 (eBook)

Typeset by Servis Filmsetting Ltd, Stockport, Cheshire

Printed and bound in the USA

Contents in brief

SECTION II

Full contents

Contributors

Editors

Robert M. McManus is the McCoy Professor of Leadership Studies and Communication at the McDonough Center for Leadership and Business at Marietta College, Ohio. He is the co-author of *Understanding Leadership: An Arts and Humanities Perspective* (Routledge, 2015). His work has appeared in the *Journal of Leadership Studies* and he served as a section editor for *Leadership in Complex Worlds* (Jossey-Bass). McManus has also served as the Chair of the Leadership Education Member Interest Group of the International Leadership Association. He regularly teaches classes on the foundations of leadership, organizational leadership, theories and models of leadership, and global leadership. He is an award-winning educator and has traveled extensively teaching on leadership in global contexts. His forthcoming book, *Leadership and Communication: Theory and Practice*, will be released in 2021 (Routledge). McManus holds a Ph.D. in Communication as well as a Master of Business Administration.

Alexandra K. Perry is a Clinical Ethicist at OhioHealth, working at Grant Medical Center and Doctor's Hospital in Columbus, Ohio. She was also the 2017–2018 Fitzgerald Executive-in-Residence at Marietta College. She holds a master's in Education and a Doctorate in Philosophy and Pedagogy from Montclair State University, and trained in Clinical Ethics at INTEGRIS Health in Oklahoma. Previously, she was an Assistant Professor of Ethics and Leadership at the McDonough Center for Leadership and Business at Marietta College, and also worked for the sections of Adolescent Medicine, Pediatric Hospital Medicine, and Pediatric Palliative Care at the University of Oklahoma. She also spent time during her dissertation fellowship working with Japanese physicians on issues related to clinical ethics, including a nationally funded project on organ donation and transplantation. Dr. Perry has published academic articles on leadership and medical ethics, and is the editor or author of four books relating to ethics: *Ethics and Neurodiversity* (Cambridge Scholars Publishing, 2013), *The Moral Philosophy of Bernard Williams* (Cambridge Scholars Publishing, 2013), *New Perspectives in Japanese Bioethics* (Cambridge Scholars Publishing, 2015), and *Paper Cranes and Mushroom Clouds* (Cambridge Scholars Publishing, 2016). Currently,

Dr. Perry is writing a series of articles on advanced care planning for terminally ill children in state custody and is also working on a book focused on leadership in healthcare.

Stanley J. Ward holds a Ph.D. in Leadership Studies and serves as both the Dean for Capstone Studies at Claremont Lincoln University (Claremont, California) and the Director of CLU's Center for Action Research, which promotes an action research model based on mindfulness, dialogue, and collaboration that lead to positive social change. Dr. Ward previously served as an instructor and interim dean for the university's Ethical Leadership program. Outside of his work in academia, Dr. Ward is founder and principal at Influence Coaching, providing both individual and team leadership development. His development model uses a variety of coaching and assessment tools to help leaders and teams maximize their strengths, correct their liabilities, and make peace with weaknesses. He is also a member of both the International Leadership Association and the International Coach Federation.

Contributors

J. Michael Cervantez is an Assistant Professor of Philosophy at Crafton Hills College. He is also the Chair of the healthcare concentration for the Master's of Organizational Leadership program at Claremont Lincoln University. He holds a Ph.D. in Philosophy from the University of Tennessee-Knoxville. His areas of focus, as an educator, are in logic, critical thinking, ethics, bioethics, social justice issues, philosophy, and religion. As a scholar, he has published articles in journals and books on topics in ethics, political philosophy and religion. In addition to teaching and writing, he has done volunteer work as a clinical ethicist and chaplain.

Austin Council is a doctoral student at the University of Florida in the Department of Agricultural Education and Communication in Gainesville, Florida. Austin is also a teaching assistant and frequently assists in teaching undergraduate leadership courses. Austin was previously a middle school social studies teacher in Alachua, Florida before pursuing his Ph.D. His current research concentration is the relationship between the virtue of humility and leadership, more specifically, how leaders develop and cultivate humility for effective leadership. Austin holds a master's degree in history from the University of Florida and is seeking a doctorate degree in agricultural education and communication with a concentration in leadership.

Benjamin P. Dean serves on the university faculty of The Citadel, in Charleston, South Carolina, where he is an Associate Professor in the Tommy and Victoria Baker School of Business and a former head of the Department of Leadership Studies. He holds a Ph.D. in Organizational Leadership, and teaches in organizational development, human resources, and business law and ethics. His certifications include Senior Professional in Human Resources (SPHR), and the Senior Certified Professional certification by the Society of Human Resources Management (SHRM). He is a licensed attorney and certified mediator, having actively practiced in business law and civil litigation, and served on the White House staff as Assistant Counsel to the President. He has extensive organizational and global experience, and has worked in over thirty countries. He has authored journal articles and text-book chapters on organizations, leadership, law, and online education. He speaks and consults in leading organizational change and in human capital development.

Gavin G. Enck is Director of Clinical Ethics for INTEGRIS Health in Oklahoma City. He oversees the Clinical Ethics Consultation Services and co-Chairs the INTEGRIS Baptist Medical Center's adult and pediatric ethics committees. Enck also co-created the Central Oklahoma Bioethics and Palliative Care Consortium. Enck is a selection committee member for the University of Oklahoma's Medical College Patricia Browne Biomedical Ethics Award and a co-facilitator of OU Medical School's Clinical Ethics course. He is a reviewer for the *American Journal of Hospice and Palliative Medicine* and his academic publications focus on clinical ethics and the ethics of pharmaceutical neuroenhancement, appearing in *American Journal of Bioethics* and *Medicine, Healthcare and Philosophy*. Prior to his current position, he completed a Clinical Ethics Post-Doctoral Fellowship at the M.D. Anderson Cancer Center at the University of Texas, Houston. Enck holds an MA from Ohio University and a Ph.D. from the University of Tennessee in Philosophy.

Beth A. Pauchnik is the Managing Director, General Counsel and Chief Administrative Officer of INTEGRIS Health in Oklahoma City. Pauchnik has served in numerous leadership positions throughout her journey from bedside nurse to managing director. During her professional career, she has focused on improving corporate leadership via self-awareness. To facilitate developing self-awareness, she co-created and teaches a course at the INTEGRIS Leadership Institute and is working on *Anatomy of Awareness*, a forthcoming book on self-awareness in leadership. Additionally, Pauchnik teaches courses on healthcare law, ethics and leadership in advanced degree programs at the University of Central Oklahoma. She holds a Juris Doctorate in Law as well as a Bachelor of Science in Nursing.

Stephanie Raible is an Assistant Professor of Social Entrepreneurship at the University of Delaware, with dual affiliations within the Department of Human Development & Family Sciences and Horn Entrepreneurship. Stephanie has also held faculty appointments at Claremont Lincoln University, University of Minnesota Duluth, Social Entrepreneurship Akademie, Global Entrepreneurship Summer School, and Chestnut Hill College. She is a former Fellow of the Robert Bosch Foundation Fellowship Program, Visiting Fellow of the Deusto International Tuning Academy, and member of the BMW Responsible Leaders and Transatlantic Core Groups. Stephanie teaches social entrepreneurship, organizational leadership, creativity and innovation, cultural organization management, and responsible business topics. She has been an active member of several nonprofit, professional associations, and alumni organization boards in North America and Europe. She is currently a doctoral candidate in Organizational Leadership at Northeastern University and holds two master's degrees from the University of Pennsylvania and from the Institute of Education, London and University of Deusto.

Maribeth Saleem-Tanner is the Director of Civic Engagement at the McDonough Center for Leadership and Business at Marietta College, Ohio. In this role, she oversees programs focused on nonprofit capacity building, campus community engagement, and student leadership development, and teaches classes on project planning, nonprofit board leadership, facilitation and deliberation, and innovative leadership. She has over a decade of experience working professionally in community-based nonprofits, and continues to be actively engaged in the sector as a board member, consultant, and volunteer. She holds an MA in conflict transformation with a concentration in peacebuilding and development from the Center for Justice and Peacebuilding at Eastern Mennonite University in Harrisonburg, Virginia, as well as a BA in English and creative writing from Pomona College.

Phyllis Huckabee Sarkaria is a human capital executive, coach, and adviser and serves on the teaching faculty at Claremont Lincoln University. Before starting her consulting practice, Sarkaria was Vice President, Human Resources for Quidel Corporation, a leading manufacturer of medical diagnostic tests, where she oversaw the company's global HR strategy and programs for more than 12 years. In addition to human resources, Sarkaria has held financial analysis, strategic planning, and government affairs roles in industry, approaching leadership and ethics issues as an outcome-driven practitioner. Sarkaria earned a BBA in Finance and an MBA, both from Texas Tech University, and an MA in Ethical Leadership from Claremont Lincoln University. She holds SPHR, SHRM-SCP, CCP, and CEBS certifications, taught Extension courses in HR at the University of California, San Diego for almost a decade, and has spoken on a variety of topics at regulatory, leadership, and human resources forums.

Lavina Sequeira is an Assistant Professor of Philosophy at Felician University (NJ). She is also an Adjunct Professor for the Educational Foundations at Montclair State University (NJ). She is the co-editor of *Inclusion, Diversity, and Intercultural Dialogue in Young People's Philosophical Inquiry* published by Sense Publishers (2017). Her main research interests are in the field of educational philosophy and immigrant education. Her current interdisciplinary research projects focus specifically on the intersections between racial/ethnic/academic identity and dialogical self of immigrant and minority youth. She teaches courses in the areas of educational foundations, ethics, and critical reasoning. She holds an Ed.D. in Pedagogy and Philosophy from Montclair State University.

Matthew Sowcik is an Assistant Professor of Leadership Education and the Coordinator of the campus-wide Leadership minor in the Department of Agricultural Education and Communication at the University of Florida. He teaches courses such as Leadership Development, Fostering Innovation Through Leadership, Groups and Teams, Organizational Leadership, and Developing Tools for a Changing World for undergraduate and graduate students. Sowcik's research specialization is in humility and the creation of leadership development programs. Aside from his teaching, research and administrative duties, Sowcik has developed and offered leadership trainings for companies like eBay, Mohegan Sun Casino, AssuredPartners, La-Z-Boy, and numerous other small to large banking, engineering and community based organizations. Sowcik also currently serves as a consultant to *The New York Times*, focusing on the newspaper's educational programming for leadership studies faculty and students. He was the lead editor for the book *Leadership 2050: Critical Challenges, Key Contexts and Emerging Trends*, which was a collaborative effort with the International Leadership Associations Building Leadership Bridges book series (Emerald Group, 2015). In addition to the book, Sowcik has published numerous papers influencing the way we think about leadership evaluation and assessment.

James N. Thomas is the Senior Pastor at First Baptist Church in Fayetteville, Georgia. His fields of interest include evangelical theology, servant leadership, and Christian discipleship. He currently serves on the teaching faculty of The Bonhoeffer Project, a national, multi-denominational Christian ministry challenging pastors and ministry leaders to become disciple-making leaders in their organizations. He is also a teaching member of Project 70, a Brazilian Church Planting Partnership in Santa Caterina, Brazil and is a recurring guest lecturer at the Korean Baptist Theological University/Seminary in Daejeon, South Korea. He holds a Bachelor of Arts in Religion from Baylor University, a Master of Arts in Religious Education from

Southwestern Baptist Theological Seminary in Fort Worth, Texas, and a Ph.D. in Leadership Studies from Dallas Baptist University.

Stephen C. Trainor is Head of Curriculum and Faculty Strategy at the Google School for Leaders. He also serves as Visiting Associate Professor of Managerial Ethics at the Naval Postgraduate School and as Teaching Faculty in Organizational Leadership at Claremont Lincoln University. Trainor served over 30 years on Active Duty in the U.S. Navy and was the first Permanent Military Professor of Leadership at the U.S. Naval Academy, where he also served as Director of Leadership Education and Development. Upon military retirement, Trainor served as Executive in Residence at the Soderquist Center for Leadership and Ethics at John Brown University. His current research focuses on complexity leadership, teamwork and culture and his work has appeared in *Armed Forces & Society* and *Current Sociology*. Trainor currently serves on the editorial board of *The Journal of Character & Leadership Integration* at the U.S. Air Force Academy. He holds a Ph.D. in Sociology as well as master's degrees in International Affairs and National Security Studies.

Stephanie Varnon-Hughes is the Director of Cross-Cultural and Interfaith Programs at Claremont Lincoln University, and an award-winning teacher and interfaith leader. She hosts a wide-ranging podcast series focusing on religion and culture called *In Times Like These*, and was a co-founder and editor-in-chief of *The Journal of Inter-Religious Studies*, a peer reviewed journal, and its sister publication, *State of Formation*, an online forum for emerging religious and ethical leaders. Her book, *Interfaith Grit: How Uncertainty Will Save Us*, focuses on everyday tools for embracing diversity. She holds a Ph.D. from Claremont Lincoln University, an MA and S.T.M. from Union Theological Seminary and her undergraduate degrees are in English and Education from Webster University.

Foreword

As the world becomes increasingly interconnected, our leaders face complex challenges that do not have simple answers. Figuring out solutions requires ethically grounded leadership. It is always surprising (at least, to me) to see that amid so many books on ethics, and even more on leadership, there are few of them that actually bring the two together in a consistent and intentional way.

Ethics and leadership are often presented as separate tracks. Introductory texts on ethics may make references to ethical dilemmas that leaders face, but these books tend to focus primarily on the ethical models (such as utilitarianism, ethical egoism, and other such theories). Conversely, leadership texts may make references to ethical challenges, but they are still focused mainly on leadership. It is left up to the aspiring leader to glean the golden nuggets of wisdom from one or the other, at times accidentally.

This book is actually about 'ethical leadership,' merging *ethical thinking* and *ethical doing*. When we look at the leadership theories through the lens of ethical models, we can see that the separateness of the two tracks is actually artificial. They are part of the same process. We want our leaders not only to think about ethics, but also engage in the practice of ethical conduct.

I particularly like the word 'primer' in the title – from the Latin word (*primus*) for 'first.' If you are getting ready to do something, a primer becomes your first step in the process. In this case, before you go out into the world and practice ethical leadership, it will serve you well to explore how these two tracks intersect.

In 2015, Robert McManus and I published a book entitled *Understanding Leadership*, in which we offered the Five Components of Leadership Model. The model was developed through many years of teaching at the McDonough Leadership Program at Marietta College. It helps our students see leadership as a *process*. The model focuses on the relationship between leaders and followers as they pursue common goals. Many leadership definitions focus on those three components, as if the relationship takes place in a vacuum, but our model adds two other critical components – context and cultural norms.

Context can be understood both at the organizational and societal levels. Human activities shape structures that can either constrain or enable certain types of human relations. The fifth component was added as a circle around the other four to express the idea that cultural norms affect the leader–follower relationship, the types of goals that are pursued, and the organizational/societal context. In other words, the values that we hold dear shape the leadership process.

McManus and I then took the five components and connected them to leadership theories, using an arts and humanities approach. I am delighted to see that the Five Components of Leadership Model can be applied so effectively to the study of ethical leadership, as well. Each component of the model – leaders, followers, goals, context, and culture – provides the ethical lens through which we can evaluate leadership theories – such as authentic leadership, as well as the other leadership theories and models contained in this book.

In our book *Understanding Leadership*, McManus and I drew attention to the wise words of John W. Gardner, who counsels against acting without first understanding. The same applies here. Before our leaders go out and practice ethical leadership, they must first think deeply about the way ethical models connect to leadership perspectives. This is not solely an intellectual exercise. It should be grounded in the desire to be thoughtful when choosing an ethical path.

Another great benefit of this primer is the use of a liberal-arts approach to ethical leadership. As we see the value of a liberal-arts education being contested in the halls of government, particularly at the national level, it is reassuring to see how a liberal-arts approach can enhance our understanding of complex issues. Practitioners – including the political leaders who have questioned the value of the liberal arts – will be well served by integrating the approach used by the authors in their own thinking about ethical leadership.

This volume builds on the tradition of the Humanities. It provides a holistic approach, exploring ethical leadership as 'a way of being,' as opposed to the utilitarian approach of seeing ethical leadership merely as a means to an end. The former invites a deeper understanding of ethical leadership as an ongoing challenge that merits a more sophisticated perspective, which is adroitly presented in the coming pages.

Every chapter ends with questions for application and discussion. They are an invitation for the reader to explore the ways in which each chapter connects to their personal experiences in the field. This book serves, therefore, as an accessible resource that can be used both by students of leadership, as well as practitioners, who seek to understand how ethical approaches connect to leadership theories. Enjoy it!

Gama Perruci
Dean, McDonough Leadership Center
Marietta College
Marietta, Ohio

Acknowledgments

No book has ever been published without a number of gracious people lending their support. That is *especially* true of this book. First, we must acknowledge our contributors. They grasped our vision for developing an accessible text that truly merged the fields of leadership and ethics. In many ways, producing a book of this kind *is an act of leadership*. We could not have asked for a group of more dedicated followers who truly came alongside us as partners as we sought to reach the common goal of delivering the book you now hold in your hands.

We must also be sure to thank our home institutions and their leaders, Janet Bland, Gama Perruci, and Bill and Judy Ruud at Marietta College; Eileen Aranda at Claremont Lincoln University, and the administrators at INTEGRIS Health and OhioHealth. We so appreciate their support in this endeavor.

We want to be sure to mention a few other folks that helped us along the way: Linda Roesch for her technical assistance; The Marietta College Faculty Publishing Group and, specifically, David Brown for their helpful comments on the early drafts of the manuscript; Beth Nash, Tina Ullman and Ryan Zundell for their outstanding art and design work; the manuscript reviewers at Edward Elgar and the attendees at our session at the International Leadership Association annual conference in Brussels, Belgium for their helpful feedback; Alan Sturmer, the Executive Editor at Edward Elgar, for believing in our vision, Catherine Cumming, the desk editor, as well as Sarah Cook, Erin McVicar, and Caroline Kracunas also at Edward Elgar for their guidance and support in the final stages of this project.

We also thank our friends and families who supported us in countless ways as we toiled to bring this project to completion. To all of these kind and generous people, we offer our deepest gratitude.

Finally, we would like to posthumously thank Mr. David Lincoln, who passed away as we were finalizing the manuscript for this book. Mr. Lincoln was the founder and generous benefactor behind Claremont Lincoln University, and we hope that our text is a contribution to his vision for promoting ethical leadership.

Section I

In Section I, readers will find the five components of leadership applied to ten different ethical models. We selected these models based on what we believed to be their influence – either explicit or not – on how leaders think today. We also chose models we believed were necessary primary material for students who wished to go deeper into the literature surrounding ethics and leadership.

Our discussion starts with Kantianism and utilitarianism because of their influence on the other ethical models we discuss. We then go into discussions of virtue ethics, ethical egoism, universal ethics, cultural relativism, divine command theory, social contract theory, justice as fairness, and the common good. As readers progress through the chapters, we ask that they keep in mind how these different models often have similar fundamental concerns, yet they have different implications for the five components of leadership.

Readers will also find a variety of case studies in this section. We will take a look at leadership examples from professional sports, international business, public health, politics, religion, medical technology, immigration, mental health, and climate change. Our hope is that by drawing from such a broad selection of settings, readers can visualize how the phenomena of 'ethical leadership' can be expressed in public, private, and social sectors.

1

Introduction

Human beings have asked questions about ethics and leadership for millennia, and each new generation returns to these questions seeking answers in the context of their own leadership challenges. Stan was reminded of this fact while perusing the special collections of Marietta College and examining the personal papers of an early settler in the Ohio territory who also served with George Washington during the American Revolution. Among his possessions was a textbook on soldiering. The book's introduction began by describing various professions available and how all of them contributed to a greater benefit for all of society. Later, the text addressed how soldiers should respond when they feel that their commanding officer had mistreated them. These discussions were reminiscent of concepts like 'the greater good' and 'followership' that are featured in this text. Though specific terms like 'the greater good' and 'followership' may have been foreign to a book published in 1776, the concepts were still present.

What is leadership?

Academic work and the life of the mind is not merely about recording and transmitting information. Rather, it also includes asking critical questions and doing our best to find answers to those questions. Sometimes the answer to those questions may be 'I don't know' or 'I need to find more information.' Yet, even in arriving at an inconclusive answer, the learner benefits by discovering new information and new perspectives. Similarly, readers will note that we use a series of framing questions to move through each of the models we cover here. In a sense, the overarching question for the book is 'What is ethical leadership?' One might object that asking questions does not provide clarity for ethical dilemmas and that both leaders and followers desperately desire such clarity. We suggest that asking questions helps bring forward the fact that ethical decision-making requires the leader to take a step back from the presenting problem and consider what is at stake. Only then can the leader begin to answer the age-old ethical question, 'What is the right thing to do?' By the time readers have worked through our text, they may not have a definitive answer to the overall question of our book, but they will be able to formulate a robust response that considers many of the nuances of leadership across a variety of situations.

If we are going to discuss questions about ethical leadership, we should probably start with a fundamental question – what exactly is 'leadership'? Leadership is more than just stellar individual performance. One might be a 'leader' in a particular field (meaning a top performer), but that does not mean the individual exhibits positive 'leadership.' We can make an argument that influencers can unquestionably produce impressive quantities or qualities of work, yet the way they get those results, and sometimes the secondary consequences of those results, are utterly disastrous. Our book defines leadership as a process that includes the work of leaders and followers accomplishing a goal in a particular context, all while being influenced by cultural values and norms. This model encourages a broader perspective regarding the many elements of the leadership experience – components that extend far beyond just the individual leader. That is not to diminish the importance of individual leaders, as our case studies include examples of individual excellence and failures at such; but the excellence in question involves much more than just individual leaders accomplishing their personal goals.

The original impetus for this project is from Rob and Stan's teaching together in the Master of Ethical Leadership program at Claremont Lincoln University. Stan observed that the course texts often focused primarily on ethics *or* primarily on leadership, and he wanted a text that could provide a definite bridge between the two. He was looking for a text that had a strong mix of both ethical thinking and ethical doing, written in such a way that students who were new to both ethics and leadership could come away with a framework that would support future study, reflection, and above all, action. In short, he wanted a text that would help students appreciate how different ethical models worked, provide guidelines on applying those models, and illustrate what that looked like in the 'real' world. Further, because questions related to ethics and leadership have been part of the human experience for millennia, he wanted a text that explicitly drew on the history of the ideas that impacted ethics as well.

Those motivations carried forward into the creation of *Ethical Leadership: A Primer*. Here we offer our readers – presumed to be upper-level undergraduate or graduate students – an introductory text that is intended to be learner-friendly while still rooted in the history of ideas. By linking the concepts with case studies and specific action recommendations, our book combines both *ethical thinking* and *ethical doing* for leaders. As Rob and Stan began to work on the text, they realized the need for additional expertise in ethics. That's when Rob's colleague, Alex Perry, joined the team of editors. So, for every chapter, Alex, Rob, and Stan attempted to edit with an eye for ethics, leadership studies, and practitioner concerns.

For professors reviewing our text, we suggest that it could work as a singular text for an ethical leadership class, or that it could complement other introductions to leadership such as Robert M. McManus and Gama Perruci's *Understanding Leadership: An Arts and Humanities Perspective* (Routledge, 2015) or Peter Northouse's *Leadership: Theory and Practice* (Sage, 2018). Likewise, it would pair well with Craig Johnson's *Meeting the Ethical Challenges of Leadership* (Sage Publications, 2001), and Terry Price's *Leadership Ethics: An Introduction* (Cambridge University Press, 2008). We hope that this textbook represents the best parts of a liberal arts education, with its emphasis on the history of ideas, critical exploration, and application to human problems. Given how the liberal arts continue to look for ways to prove their relevance in higher education, we believe that we have drawn from that approach to create a resource for leadership programs in technical schools and state universities as well as liberal arts colleges.

The five components of leadership

In an effort to provide a consistent reference point in our discussion of ethics and leadership, we will make use of Gama Perruci's Five Components Model, which was later developed in McManus and Perruci's *Understanding Leadership*.[1] In their text, McManus and Perruci explain that they understand leadership as a process, 'instead of simply the heroic ability of leaders,[2] and that it should be viewed as a *purposeful interaction*.'[3] Such an approach is especially helpful in an ethical leadership text because it does not place the entire emphasis for ethical success or failure on the individual leader, but rather by emphasizing the *leadership process* we can consider the many layers of a leadership event. As leadership studies grow in their appreciation for factors outside of the individual leader, this model becomes even more helpful. Let's briefly consider each component of the model.

The leader

As one would expect in a leadership text, we start our model and consideration with the individual leader. Though in some cases, we find several people or even an entire organization may engage in the role of 'leader.'

The follower

It has been observed that if a leader does not have followers, then that person is simply 'going on a walk.' So, followers are a crucial part of the leadership equation. Here we consider those who are working with the leader (and sometimes *against* the leader) to accomplish a specific goal.

The goal

The third component of a leadership system is what the leaders and followers are trying to achieve – the goal. In its purest expression, leadership 'success' or 'failure' has been viewed as 'goal achievement.' Here we will go beyond a definition of leadership that is just about getting things done *by looking at how those goals are accomplished* as well as the broader context and culture in which those goals are accomplished.

The context

Leadership does not occur in a vacuum, and it is not a thought experiment. Rather, leadership is tied to a real location in both time and space, and that context includes considerations that are part of a leadership event. We will find that behaviors viewed as ethical in one context may not work directly in another context.

The culture

Leaders must also be aware of the forces at work that go beyond the immediate interactions of leaders, followers, and goals within a specific location. There are cultural values, norms, *zeitgeists* and larger belief systems that also impact the leadership process. Discussing ethics and distinguishing between the five components can be tricky, because all ethical systems are making claims about values and norms, and thus tapping into what we label as 'culture.' Yet, as we review different ethical and leadership models, we will find that some systems seem to judge the appropriateness of a leadership event with a particular emphasis on factors such as the actions of the leader, the relationship with followers, the 'rightness' of a goal, or sometimes the demands of a particular context.

The definition of leadership that we will be using throughout this book then is this: '*Leadership is the process by which leaders and followers work together toward a goal (or goals) within a context shaped by cultural values and norms.*'[4]

Figure 1.1 The Five Components of Leadership Model

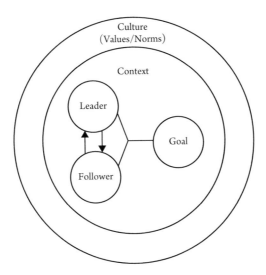

The nuances of 'ethical leadership'

To appreciate the complexities of a question like 'What is ethical leadership?', let's consider the disbanding of the President's Club in Great Britain in 2018. The organization was famous for its all-male, black-tie charity dinner which required the servers to be attractive females in revealingly short, black dresses. Guests at the event included prominent members of British society who were raising funds for children's hospitals in London. Over the 33 years of the organization's existence, it had raised over 20 million pounds ($28 million USD).[5] These esteemed guests engaged in fondling servers, asking servers to sit in their laps and dance on the table, and in some cases even propositioned sex. When an undercover reporter posed as a server and recorded the event, then later released video footage and described her experiences, the news of the event – especially during the same historical moment as the #MeToo movement – resulted in such public outcry that the club permanently disbanded. In the meantime, charities who had received money from the group rushed to both return the money and distance themselves from the group.[6]

Simply put, the President's Club was an example of 'men behaving badly' in the midst of raising money for good causes. Now for some ethical analysis: a strictly utilitarian approach might argue the behavior was part of charity work – so while the behavior might seem reproachable, it's the results that matter most. A counter-argument would argue 'how' you get the results is just as important as the results themselves. Thus, no matter how much money was raised for charity, there was no excuse for these men's behavior and the entire event was ethically reprehensible.

Who is right? Both are making an ethical claim about how wealthy and powerful men are allowed to behave. Our text asks similar questions about behavior, though we are also expanding our concept and examples of leadership to include more than just wealthy and powerful men.

So if we use our Five Components Model to analyze the President's Club example, we find an organization where the goal is to raise money for charities. The 'leaders' in this case seem to be the event organizers, and the 'followers' are the attendees and servers. So far, so good. We have a group of people working together to raise money for a good cause.

The problem arises when we look at the context and cultural values at work in the event. The specific context is an event where women are objectified. To make this more problematic, all this occurs during a time when customs of sexual behavior are being challenged by the #MeToo movement and powerful men are being called out for just such objectifying behavior. So, while a strict utilitarian might argue that the good done by the President's Club outweighed the bad behavior of the men present at the dinner, the Kantian perspective – which emphasizes the importance of respect for persons – would quickly dismiss such thinking as sophistry and balderdash.

The President's Club example is also helpful because it demonstrates that one doesn't need the formal title of 'leader' to demonstrate 'leadership.' Here, a female reporter endured hours of crude behavior in order to bring a negative situation to light. In doing so, she worked with her newspaper and the readers of that paper to accomplish a goal – and the impact of her work became increasingly significant as her article spread.[7]

Explaining our structure

Although we have several contributors to our text, we adopted a consistent structure to use throughout the book. *Ethical Leadership: A Primer* is divided into two major sections. The first section focuses on ethical models and uses the five components of leadership as a lens for understanding and applying the ethical model in a leadership setting. The second section then looks at popular leadership models that purposefully invoke ethical implications and also views those models through the lens of the Five Components Model.

Section I: Ethical models

The first section of our book focuses on ethics models: Kantianism, Utilitarianism, Virtue Ethics, Ethical Egoism, Universal Ethics, Cultural

Relativism, Divine Command, Social Contract, Justice as Fairness, and The Common Good. For those who wish for a preview of the contents of those chapters, we suggest they take a look at Table 17.1 in the conclusion of our book. That table lists the ethical models, the questions we use to frame each chapter, which parts of the five components of leadership we believe are emphasized in those models, and the case study that accompanies the chapter.

Because we don't assume our readers have previous training in ethics, we keep the discussion focused at an introductory level appropriate for university work. We chose ethical models based on what we observed as common models both in the study of ethics and models that we see being applied in the world of leadership. We hope our selected models represent both a thoughtful and practical selection process. By exploring these models and their impact on different components of leadership, we believe leaders can be more intentional with how they approach ethical thinking and ethical doing.

Section II: Leadership models

We then take a look at some popular leadership models that claim an intentional ethical component: Authentic Leadership, Servant Leadership, Followership, Transformational Leadership, and Adaptive Leadership. Like Section I, we don't assume prior knowledge of these leadership models. So, our hope here is to help readers become more intentional in how they approach their own leadership challenges, with an emphasis on being ethical leaders.

At the end of Section II, we will offer a conclusion that provides a summary overview of the ideas contained in our text, and we will make some final observations of the themes that developed as we applied the five components to ethical leadership. After reading our text, readers should be well prepared to dive into more nuanced discussions of ethical leadership as well as take intentional action in their own leadership roles.

For both Section I and Section II, we follow a similar outline where each chapter contains the following elements.

Framing question

We start each chapter with a framing question. The question highlights what the ethical or leadership model asks those practicing leadership to consider. Our goal for the question is to provide an introductory hook that brings forward the key concerns of each ethical or leadership model. As leadership educators, we hope these rudimentary questions will help with the scaffolding process that is needed when learning new content. The chapter then works to answer that question, essentially hanging information on that introductory hook. Direct questions promote new levels of both self- and situational-awareness for leaders. We hope these basic questions do the same for students who read our text.

Timeline

We hope that readers will sense the 'gravitas' of ethics and leadership by seeing how humanity has been wrestling with many of these questions for centuries (if not millennia), and how leaders are still wrestling with them today. We provide a visual representation of significant works addressing the ethical or leadership model, alongside the events of our case studies. Our timelines purposefully connect the history of ideas and the historical events of case studies, showing how these ideas still matter.

History and major concepts

The history and major concepts we provide here are not an exhaustive discussion by any means. Instead, we have asked ourselves, 'What are the essential concepts that would benefit leaders when they attempt to apply ethical models in leadership?' For some of our ethical and leadership models, there is a well-established literature trail to follow. For others, we offer a more practice-oriented discussion. As part of our primer, we also define key terms in this section.

Five components analysis

When we initially considered writing a primer for ethical leadership, we wanted to find a bridge that helped connect the ethical models and leadership models. To help ethics and leadership 'speak' with each other, we consider the implications of a particular ethical or leadership model for the component parts of leadership. To help readers sort out the differences between these models, we also asked ourselves which components seemed to receive particular attention in each model. For example, in our discussion of the President's Club as perceived by utilitarian or Kantian views, we saw that both perspectives emphasized the goal, yet they had different conclusions of what those goals should be – the overall benefit of a leadership event versus how people should be treated. We admit to simplifying concepts here for the sake of accessibility, yet we strove to do so in a way that did not simplify to the point of total absurdity.

Part of what makes this text a contribution to the field of leadership studies is our attempt to provide a visual representation of how ethics and leadership engage each other, where we consider the interplay of multiple factors. When visualized this way, we hope that readers will gain both a renewed appreciation for why ethical leadership is so demanding as well as a better sense of where they need to direct their energies when engaging in ethical leadership.

Case study

Because we are concerned with both 'ethical thinking' and 'ethical doing,' each chapter describes a real-world event and analyzes that event against the concerns of a particular ethical or leadership model. We start with a narrative about the case and then consider the case through the lens of the Five Components of Leadership Model.

Summary and concluding remarks

As we close each chapter, we will return to the framing question and attempt to provide a summary response that includes some action steps. Those suggestions will be broad enough to apply in a variety of circumstances, but still be actionable and measurable, with an emphasis on behaviors.

Discussion questions

True to our intent of creating a teaching text, we include questions designed for either personal reflection or classroom discussion.

Additional resources

Consistent with the fact that our book is a 'primer' that can only offer a 'first word' in the conversation between ethics and leadership, we also offer suggestions for additional resources that students can use as they continue to study these topics.

The problem of pronouns

The presence of women in the labor force has increased over the last fifty years, and so has the presence of women leaders in a variety of fields.[8] Likewise, the field of leadership studies continues to grow beyond exclusively Western perspectives. While our text strives to provide a variety of leadership examples, our cases were chosen because of their ability to illustrate the ethical or leadership models at hand, rather than cases that would provide a full representation of gender and ethnic diversity in leadership. Similarly, readers will find both masculine and feminine singular pronouns referencing individual leaders throughout the text; this is at the discretion of our contributors. We chose to follow this practice rather than rely on a generic singular 'they.' Please know that the decisions were pragmatic and grammatical, and not intended as a slight against leaders of any gender or ethnic identity.

NB: Not the last word

The abbreviation *NB* stands for the Latin phrase, *nota bene*, which we can translate to be 'note well.' The initials are used to highlight information that is important, though not necessarily the focus of the issue being discussed.

So here we offer our *nota bene* at the end of our introduction. Once again, we return to the fact that our text is offered as a 'primer.' By definition, it is not an exhaustive source for leadership ethics. And its opinions are limited to the perspectives and skills of the individual writers and the team of editors who compiled the text. Because we represent a diversity of backgrounds and organizations, not all the contributors necessarily agree with each other's conclusions. And because we are filtering all our cases through a particular ethical or leadership lens, not all the nuances of a particular case will be expressed. With that in mind, we offer only a 'first word' in the conversation about ethics and leadership. Knowing that there is much more work to be done, we invite reviewers and researchers to continue the work by returning to these cases with additional resources and viewpoints. Thus, we offer *Ethical Leadership: A Primer* to our readers as a tool for launching their own conversations about ethical leadership, and we hope that the material herein empowers meaningful leadership conversations that lead to vital leadership action.

As a final comment, we return to what we think makes the humanities tradition so helpful – it focuses on the consistent challenges we face as human beings. So we hope that, if nothing else, our readers come away with this marked conclusion: ethical leaders *and followers* who read this text – our world continues to need both your ideas and your practice.

? **DISCUSSION QUESTIONS**

Before reading this introduction, how did you define leadership?
How does that definition compare to what the authors of this text suggest about leadership?
In your understanding of leadership, how important are factors outside the leader?
How do you recognize when leadership is 'ethical'?

ADDITIONAL RESOURCES

R.M. McManus and G. Perruci, *Understanding Leadership: An Arts and Humanities Perspective*, New York: Routledge, 2015.
McManus and Perruci provide a representative work both for the Five Components Model and for how a liberal arts approach to leadership studies can be beneficial to further understand the leadership process.

J.T. Wren, R. Riggio, and M.A. Genovese (eds), *Leadership and the Liberal Arts: Achieving the Promise of a Liberal Education*, London: Palgrave Macmillan, 2009.
This collection of chapters from different contributors examines both the contributions that leadership studies can make to general education and how the liberal arts contribute to leadership studies.

K. Grint, *Leadership: Very Short Introduction*, Oxford: Oxford University Press, 2010.

and

S. Blackburn, *Ethics: A Very Short Introduction*, Oxford: Oxford University Press, 2010.
These short books offer an accessible starting point for the study of leadership and ethics.

NOTES

1 The Five Components Model was originally referred to as 'The McDonough Model' in reference to its origins at the McDonough Center for Leadership and Business at Marietta College. Gama Perruci presented the model in 'Leadership education across disciplines: The social science perspective,' *Journal of Leadership Studies*, vol. 7 no. 4, 2014, 43–7. The model was further refined and developed in McManus and Perruci's *Understanding Leadership: An Arts and Humanities Perspective*, New York: Routledge, 2015.

2 McManus and Perruci, ibid., p. 13.

3 McManus and Perruci, op. cit., p. 17.

4 McManus and Perruci, op. cit., p. 15. In the first edition of McManus and Perruci's book, the adjective 'environmental' was part of the definition – '. . .within an environmental context. . ..' This adjective caused readers some confusion. The definition has been updated to simply read 'context' in the second edition of McManus and Perruci's work, which will be published by Routledge in 2019. We have used their updated definition of leadership throughout this book.

5 R. Pérez-Peña, 'Britain's "most un-p.c. charity" will shut down,' *New York Times*, January 24, 2018. Online, https://www.nytimes.com/2018/01/24/world/europe/uk-presidents-club-dinner.html (accessed March 13, 2018).

6 Pérez-Peña, ibid.

7 M. Marriage, 'Men only: Inside the charity fundraiser where hostesses are put on show,' *Financial Times*, January 23, 2018. Online, https://www.ft.com/content/075d679e-0033-11e8-9650-9c0ad2d7c5b5 (accessed March 13, 2018).

8 For example, see U.S. Department of Labor, '50 years later: Women, work and the work ahead,' *Women's Bureau*. Online, https://www.dol.gov/wb:pcswinfographic.pdf (accessed March 14, 2018).

2

Kantianism

J. Michael Cervantez

 **FRAMING QUESTION**

What is the moral duty of leaders and followers?

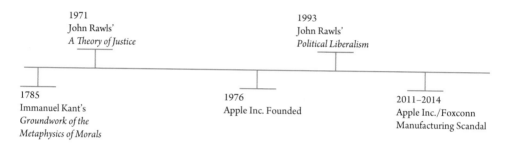

1971
John Rawls'
A Theory of Justice

1993
John Rawls'
Political Liberalism

1785
Immanuel Kant's
*Groundwork of the
Metaphysics of Morals*

1976
Apple Inc. Founded

2011–2014
Apple Inc./Foxconn
Manufacturing Scandal

Figure 2.1 Timeline of major works on Kantian ethics in relation to the chapter case study

Kantian ethics, unlike most other ethical theories, owes its name and reputation to one thinker. Sometimes referred to as Kantian moral theory or simply Kant's ethics, Kantian ethics takes its name from the influential eighteenth-century Prussian philosopher, Immanuel Kant.[1] Kant is regarded as one of the foremost theorists in the Western intellectual tradition. His work remains prominent to this day. His many philosophical contributions are frequently esteemed alongside significant thinkers such as Plato, Aristotle, René Descartes and David Hume. Though Kant was interested in many areas of philosophical and scientific inquiry, it is his unique contributions to ethics that are the most enduring aspects of his work. In this chapter we will examine Kantian ethics and position them within the Five Components of Leadership Model. We will then apply them to a case study surrounding Apple Computer and their manufacturing standards in Asia.

History

Kantian moral philosophy originated with the publication of Kant's *Groundwork of the Metaphysics of Morals* and to a lesser extent the publication of the *Metaphysics of Morals*. It should be noted, however, that the *Metaphysics of Morals* was first published separately in two parts as the *Doctrine of the Right* and the *Doctrine of Virtue*. Both appeared as separate publications sometime in 1797 before being compiled into one volume at a later date.[2] In any event, Kant's *Groundwork* has proven the more influential of the two.

In addition to the texts mentioned here, *The Critique of Practical Reason*, *Anthropology from a Pragmatic Point of View* and various other essays have also contributed to, and provided augmentations of, Kant's ethics. However, it is the *Groundwork of the Metaphysics of Morals* that remains the most widely read and studied text on Kant's moral philosophy. Since the publication of *Groundwork*, the influence of Kantian ethics has been remarkable. To this day, Kant's ethics, along with utilitarianism and virtue ethics, continues to dominate contemporary debates around ethical theory and remains one of the leading moral theories among academics.

In recent years, the most noteworthy champion of Kant's ethics has been the late moral and political philosopher John Rawls, who we will discuss later in Chapter 10. Rawls' *A Theory of Justice* and *Political Liberalism* are replete with allusions to Kant's moral philosophy. Most importantly, Rawls' emphasis on justice as fairness seems, to some extent, inspired by Kant's emphasis on personal autonomy and moral agency. Samuel Freeman points out that there is a clear Kantian interpretation of justice as fairness. It 'relies upon the Kantian conception of moral personality' and 'interprets the principles of justice as an expression of the moral powers of agency and practical reasoning. It plays a central role in [Rawls'] congruence argument.'[3] A survey of Rawls' work will demonstrate the importance of Kant's philosophy to the development of his own ideas. In particular, many Kantian conceptions will ultimately provide the basis for Rawls' Kantian Constructivism, which is prominent throughout his work.

Major concepts of Kantian ethics

Turning our attention back to Kant, and more specifically Kant's ethics, we find a number of concepts deserving attention. This section begins with a discussion of good will and what Kantians mean by 'acting out of duty.' After this, we will undertake an important introduction to Kant's categorical imperative. Together, these ideas form the foundation of a Kantian moral framework.

Good will and acting out of duty

At the core of Kant's ethics is an important question: 'What gives an action moral value?' Why is an action a moral action as opposed to another sort of action? Is there something that makes an action morally significant?

The Kantian answer to this question can be clarified by contrasting it with the utilitarian response.[4] According to the utilitarian – or consequentialist – views of morality, it is the consequences of our actions that are morally significant. An action is morally good when it produces a good outcome. Mark Timmons puts it this way: right actions should be understood primarily in terms of the value and utility of an action's consequences when compared to alterative actions. In short, 'An action is right if and only if (and because) its consequences would be at least as good as the consequences of any alternative action that the agent might instead perform.'[5] So, when two or more potential actions are considered, the morally good action is the one that produces the most utility (utilitarianism) or the more desirable consequences (consequentialism).

On this view an individual's motives are irrelevant. Why one chooses to act as they do is unimportant. Morality is not a matter of moral motives, but favorable outcomes. Per John Stuart Mill, 'He who saves a fellow creature from drowning does what is morally right whether his motive be duty or his hope is being paid for his trouble.'[6] So, while utilitarian ethicists hold this view, this attitude is misguided according to Kantian moral philosophy.

Kant maintains that an action is morally praiseworthy only when it is done with the right motive. Kant refers to this as 'good will.' Good will, he maintains, is the only thing that is good without limitation.[7] In Kant's language 'a good will is good not because of what it effects or accomplishes [not] because of its fitness to attain some proposed end, but only because of its volition, that is, it is good in itself.'[8] That is to say, the good will (that is, a good motive or intention) is primary. Why? Because our 'good will' is in our control. The consequences of our actions are out of our control. What will happen because of our actions is not something we can reasonably foresee at the time. To tie morality to something outside of our control is in effect to take morality out of a person's hands and make it a matter of chance. This idea is what Bernard Williams and Thomas Nagel have famously dubbed 'moral luck.' If an action happens to produce good results, then it was morally good. If it turns out that our actions generated bad results, then those actions were immoral.[9] For Kant, this is fundamentally mistaken. Unpacking the reasons why is important for having a complete and accurate picture of Kantian ethics.

First and foremost, morality comes down to our motives. Did we act with a good will? Did our actions have good intentions? We might summarize Kant on this point saying that having a good will is doing what is right just because it is right and for no ulterior motives. Kant famously refers to this as 'acting out of duty' or 'acting from duty.' It is our *duty* to do the right thing simply because it is the right thing.

To illustrate, consider Kant's well-known example of a shopkeeper who always charges her customers a fair price. In such a case, Kant imagines there are three possible motives for why the shopkeeper might always act fairly. First, the shopkeeper might always charge a fair price because it's good business. Most people would likely agree that there is nothing wrong with this rationale. At the same time, we might say that there is something not quite right about it either. There should be something more to ethics than merely good business.

Second, Kant considers the possibility of the shopkeeper being a naturally fair-minded individual. Being a fair person is just their moral temperament. Cheating a customer would keep them up at night. So, they do the right thing because they do not want an immoral action on their conscience. Again, there is nothing wrong with this rationale. In fact, having a moral conscience is a good thing. However, Kantian ethics challenges us at this point by insisting that ethical principles are more than merely the way I happen to feel about something. Kantians insist that ethics must be more than what happens to be good for an individual or organization.

This idea brings us to Kant's third consideration. He contends that the shopkeeper could choose to be fair to their customers not merely because it's good business and just because they happen to be so inclined but because being fair is their moral imperative. For Kant, therefore, leaders and organizations ought to be motivated to do good not merely because it is good for their bottom-line and not simply because they like to help people, but because this is their moral duty.

In sum, a moral agent ought to have the right motivation when acting. The right motivation for Kant is acting in accordance with one's duty as dictated by our moral imperatives. This raises another important question: 'How can we determine our moral imperatives?' When can we be sure that we are acting out of duty? The answer to this question lies in what Kantians call the 'categorical imperative.'

The categorical imperative

Central to Kant's ethics is the idea of a categorical imperative. The idea behind the term 'categorical' is something that is unconditional or unqualified and without exception. The meaning behind 'imperative' is, of course, a rule, requirement or command of some kind. Thus, putting these two concepts together, a categorical imperative is an absolute moral requirement. For Kant, therefore, morality is best understood as a moral law or rule that must be performed and to which there is no exception. In short, ethics is an absolute moral law. As such, Kant preferred to characterize the categorical imperative 'as an objective, rationally necessary and unconditional principle that we must always follow despite any natural desires or inclinations we may have to the contrary.'[10]

Kantian ethics maintains that our moral duties are derived from these absolute moral imperatives. There are several formulations of Kant's categorical imperative. The two most essential formulations equip the Kantian with their most important moral principles. The first moral principle underscores the moral duty always to respect humanity. The second moral principle is equivalent to a moral test for determining when any proposed action becomes a moral duty. We will now briefly consider each of these principles.

Always respect humanity

One formulation of the categorical imperative is sometimes called the Respect for Humanity Principle. Kant asks us to consider what constitutes proper treatment of persons. He concludes that we ought to 'Act in such a way that you always treat humanity, whether in your own person or in the person of any other, never simply as a means, but always at the same time as an end.'[11] This suggests that at the most fundamental level, morality is about treating human beings with respect.

With this moral principle, Kant brought the notion of respect to the center of moral philosophy for the first time. Respect, per Kantian ethics, amounts to respecting a person's autonomy. It is honoring a person's ability to set his or her own goals and be self-governing. As such, human beings should never be regarded as objects to be used or exploited. Human beings are autonomous moral agents and must be treated as 'ends in themselves' and not as a mere means to an end.[12] Kant believed that 'it is the presence of the self-governing reason in each person that . . . offered decisive grounds for viewing each as possessed of equal worth and deserving of equal respect.'[13]

Always act in accordance with the universal law

Another formulation of the categorical imperative is referred to as the Universal Law Principle. Kantian ethics holds that we should 'always act in such a way that the maxim of your action can be willed as a universal law of humanity.' Or, put otherwise, 'Act as though the maxim of your action were by your will to become a universal law of nature.'[14] The heart of Kant's language here is that individuals must only act in a way that they could will for everyone. In other words, before making a moral decision one should ask, could (or should) my action be a universal law for everyone to follow. By 'maxim' Kant means an action that we are putting to the test. If a leader was considering sidestepping an inconvenient organizational policy, for example, then they should first formulate a maxim: it is permissible to circumvent the policy in question. This is the action (that is, the maxim) being put to the test. To determine the morality of the maxim, ask if it could be universalized for all to follow. Could the action in question become a universal moral law?

This principle is a way to test whether our actions or choices are morally coherent and consistent. We typically think that everyone has the same moral obligations. No one should cheat. We all should keep our word. It's never right to steal from your employer and so forth. Following these ethical norms is the right thing to do. No exception. So, making an exception for yourself or justifying an exception to a moral requirement is fundamentally wrong. What's fair for one person, morally speaking, is fair for everyone. Saying that everyone else ought to adhere to company policy but that this requirement doesn't apply to you, is unfair. In this way, Kantian ethics gives us a handy moral principle. Just ask yourself, would I want my action or behavior in this situation to become a universal law for others to follow?

Critiques of Kantian ethics

Kantian ethics is not without its problems or its critics. There are two main problems that must be addressed. First, there is the relevance of consequences in moral decision-making. Second, there is the question of moral exceptions. Each of these critiques is briefly explored in this section.

What about the consequences?

One significant critic of Kantian ethics was John Stuart Mill. Mill and his predecessor Jeremy Bentham are regarded as the founding fathers of modern Utilitarianism.[15] Utilitarianism has proven to be one of the most formidable challenges to Kant's ethics. For this reason, the debate between Kantianism and Utilitarianism has given opportunity for Kantian moral philosophers to clarify their ideas. Kantian ethics typically emphasizes human dignity and are, thus, often pitted against the utilitarian ideal of maximizing utility. Utilitarians typically criticize Kantians on the grounds that Kantians do not worry enough about the consequences of their actions.

This is a longstanding critique of Kant's ethics. It goes as far back as Bentham and Mill and is clearly expressed in a classic text *The Definition of the Good* written by A.C. Ewing. Ewing maintains 'it is hard to believe that it could ever be a duty deliberately to produce less good when we could produce more.'[16] Ewing is essentially invoking the utilitarian principle of maximizing utility. When it is feasible for a moral agent to do more good rather than less, it is an agent's duty to produce the better outcome. In other words, Ewing wonders whether it is ever morally justified to intentionally produce less good than we could have as a result of our actions.

As a duty-based moral system, Kantian ethics emphasizes moral obligations over utility. Kantians are primarily interested in identifying and acting in accordance with our moral imperatives. There is no significance given to the results of our actions. In fact, Kantians concede that following our moral duties could generate less desirable consequences and, thus, less good as a result. Nevertheless, adhering to our moral duties, as identified by the categorical imperative, is the essence of morality for Kantians. This might be a difficult conclusion for some.

Notwithstanding, Kantian ethics insists that morality is not about maximizing utility. As such, Kantian ethics precludes moral agents from engaging in certain actions. Some actions are so morally appalling – such as torture or exploitation – that they should never be morally permissible. This is true even if they could generate better consequences. It is certainly conceivable that under the right circumstances torture might maximize utility. Think of a case in which a terrorist, if tortured, would reveal vital information – information that could save thousands of lives. Even still, Kantians insist that we ought to draw moral lines and never cross them. Torture, for example, crosses a moral line by treating a human being as a means to an end; it is, thus, off the table as a moral option no matter how favorable the outcome. Adherents of Kantian ethics insist that Kant's categorical imperative provides the necessary moral safeguards we need to protect people and their fundamental rights.

No exceptions?

Kantian ethics is sometimes referred to as an 'absolutist' moral theory. This is because Kant's ethics follows from his categorical imperative. As noted, the categorical imperative generates absolute moral duties. Consequently, the nature of Kant's categorical imperative is such that moral duties are unconditional requirements. This raises the question: 'Are there no exceptions to these moral requirements?'

For Kantian ethics, the answer is 'no.' Ethics imposes on the moral agent absolute moral rules that must be followed without exception. Leaders always ought to tell the truth. Managers should never mistreat their employees. Cheating is under no circumstances a good idea. These are unquestionable moral duties and thus, cannot be sidelined for the sake of convenience, expedience or the greater good. As some Kantians say, 'Being a moral agent, then, means guiding one's conduct by "universal laws" – moral rules that hold, without exception, in all circumstances.'[17]

It is sometimes believed, however, that every good rule has an exception. Moral rules, therefore, should be no exemption. As a rule, leaders should tell the truth and not cheat, for example. But there will undoubtedly be occasions where lying or cheating may seem necessary in the course of leading others and guiding a successful organization. In combat situations, military leaders for example are regularly confronted with difficult moral dilemmas. Obvious examples of this involve saving a subordinate's life. If a lie could save a subordinate, shouldn't the moral rule to *always tell the truth* be suspended?

To be sure, this is a difficult challenge for Kantians. Perhaps, there are resources within Kantian ethics to deal with this worry. It seems plausible to suppose that Kantian ethics could universalize moral exceptions. For instance, if there is a genuine circumstance where lying or cheating is morally conceivable, then we ought to be able to universalize those examples. That is to say, as a moral rule, when moral duties conflict – such as telling the truth verses saving a life – moral agents ought to adhere to the greater duty. W.D. Ross' duty-based moral theory would refer to such actions as one's 'all-things-considered-duty.' It is unclear whether Kantians would permit such a moral rule, but it is not unreasonable to think that they could.

Five component analysis

Now that we have a better understanding of Kantianism, let's look at it in light of the Five Components of Leadership Model presented in Chapter 1.

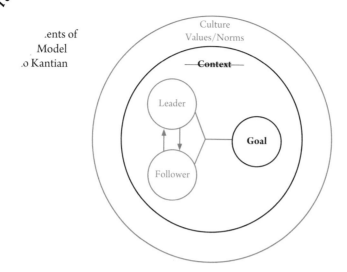

Kant's categorical imperatives provide a highly practical and effective strategy for determining the morally right action. Adhering to Kant's moral principles ensures that leaders maintain a healthy respect for all stakeholders. The respect for humanity principle, therefore, will safeguard leaders and their organizations against inadvertently exploiting followers, partners or other interests. Above is an illustration of the importance of the *leader* to the Five Components of Leadership Model when viewed through the lens of Kantian ethics.

As illustrated in the model depicted here, *Kantian ethics focuses on the goal of leaders and followers upholding their moral duty to behave ethically regardless of the surrounding contextual and cultural factors.* Kant's universal law principle can ensure that leaders and followers hold fast to their integrity when making difficult moral decisions. By putting proposed actions to the test, leaders and followers can practice critical self-reflection. This sort of moral reasoning will act as a check on one's intended decisions and actions. By carefully thinking about and testing our proposed actions, leaders and followers can mitigate moral shortcomings by removing possible moral blind spots, confronting biases and otherwise compelling people to examine their actions. Here are five practical ways that Kantian ethics can help leaders and followers make morally sound decisions.

First, it is important for leaders as well as followers to understand that they have moral duties. Their duties do not change as a matter of position or power. Whether one is in a position of influence or in a support role, we all have absolute moral requirements. Kantian ethics expects individuals to perform and honor their duties without deviation. In doing so, leaders and followers will fulfill Kant's universal law principle. For example, leaders have the moral duty always to be forthright and honest to their subordinates. Consider a situation where it is in the personal interest of a leader to misrepresent the truth. Suppose, for example, that one's organization is anticipating a downturn and jobs are at stake. No doubt some leaders will want to sidestep this issue with their subordinates. But what's their moral duty? If it is relevant to their followers' well-being, leaders should disclose this information to them as a matter of respect. A Kantian ethical framework implies that leaders, among other things, have the responsibility always to demonstrate deference for others. This includes being forthright with leaders and followers even when doing so is difficult. Recall that moral duties are, according to Kantian ethics, categorical imperatives – absolute, unchanging moral requirements.

Kant's universal law formulation of his categorical imperative implies that leaders and followers ought to see it as their moral duty to honor their professional responsibilities and obligations. For example, this would imply not calling in sick when this is only a ploy; not taking items from their organizations for personal use without permission; not violating company policies for the sake of convenience; not handling company time inappropriately and so forth. In short, it is imperative for leaders and followers to always adhere to their moral duties even when it is not in their personal interest to do so. The universal law formulation of Kant's categorical imperative mandates that persons only act in a way that they can consistently will for others as well. So, since neither leaders nor followers could consistently will a lack of professionalism for others, then it is their duty to always act with professional integrity as well.

Second, neither leaders nor their followers are, morally speaking, superior to the other. Kantian ethics coheres with McManus and Perruci on this point (see Chapter 1). Understanding followers as equally important as leaders in one's conception of leadership is a significant moral advancement. For example, leaders ought to respect the rights of followers, while followers must take moral responsibility for their actions. In this way, the respect for humanity principle applies equally to those in authority and subordinates. This entails that the well-being of followers matters as much as that of leaders. This point has obvious application when considering the issues of recognition, individual worth, compensation, working conditions and so on.

Third, to the point of working conditions, Kantian ethics has practical implications for organizational working environments. To the extent that it is the responsibility of leaders to care about the working conditions of their organizations, leaders should strive for safe and healthy working conditions for their followers. Why? Applying Kant's respect for humanity principle entails that the dignity and value of workers are upheld. Workers are not mere commodities or machines. They are persons and must be treated as such. Thus, followers should not be subjected to physically or psychologically hazardous working conditions. Leaders are largely responsible for regulating working conditions. Consequently, leaders must ensure working environments are safe, healthy and well regulated. The case study considered below takes up this point in greater detail.

Fourth, the leader–follower relationship is built upon reciprocal respect. Followers, as well as leaders, deserve deference and equal consideration. In some industries, managers may have a tendency to exploit their subordinates. They might pressure them to work longer hours or perform extra duties not specified in their job description. The balance of power certainly leans in favor of leaders in these circumstances. Thus, rather than pressure or intimidate employees into additional responsibilities, Kantian ethics demands that leaders ought to be sensitive to the needs and expectations of their subordinates. Rather than resort to tactics involving fear, ridicule or shame, leaders ought to engage in more relational building efforts. For example, leaders ought to treat followers as persons who appreciate (and deserve) a little consideration and courtesy. Accolades and recognition go a long way in fostering mutual respect. In their book *The Leadership Challenge*, James Kouzes and Barry Posner suggest that recognition should be personalized. In their words, recognition is about stepping 'into the shoes of other people and asking yourself, "what do I wish other people would do to celebrate and recognize my contribution?" Let your answer to this question guide your own behavior with others.'[18] Such actions are consistent with the respect for humanity formulation of Kant's categorical imperative.

Finally, leaders and followers should see it as their moral duty to work toward the mutual benefit of the other. As stated above, the relationship between leader and follower is reciprocal. Each works for the mutual benefit of both leader *and* follower (and, of course, other stakeholders as well). To be sure, leaders should receive proper benefits for their contributions. And, as a matter of consistency, followers ought to receive a proportional benefit for their labors. Consider the issue of CEO compensation. According to some studies, average CEO pay is over 300 times that of the average employee's pay. In some cases, this disparity is over 800 times more than workers.[19] This is not healthy for the leader–follower relationship in any organization nor is it morally justified under a Kantian analysis.[20] It clearly fails to value subordinates as an end in themselves. Instead, it seems to use workers only as a means to an end. This leads us to the goal.

Leaders and followers inevitably work toward some end or goal. The best-case scenario here is for leaders and followers to work together to develop and achieve organizational goals. To be sure, leaders and followers each play distinct roles in developing and achieving goals, but the point is that organizational goals are what Kouzes and Posner call 'finding a common purpose.'[21] Leaders and followers need to see their work as a joint endeavor. 'What this requires is finding common ground among those people who have to implement the vision [of the organization. A leader's] constituents want to feel part of the process.'[22] Kouzes and Posner go on to say 'nobody really likes being told what to do or where to go, no matter how right it might be. People want to be a part of the vision development process.'[23] The idea of 'a common goal' speaks to the Kantian notion of autonomy. Leaders and followers want to have ownership when pursuing and implementing goals. Thus, leaders honor the personal autonomy of their followers by finding ways for their constituents to work toward a common vision and common goal.

A separate point related to goals needs to be stressed. A Kantian moral framework insists that formulating organizational goals must cohere with absolute moral duties and not deviate from these morals for the sake of maximizing utility. If an organization's goal requires justifying immoral means for the sake of some desired end, such an action must be deemed impermissible. For example, consider the issue of sweatshops.

Some multinational corporations see it as morally justified to outsource their labor to developing countries. Outsourcing labor cuts costs and often sidesteps cumbersome regulations and policies. Notwithstanding, if outsourcing labor means treating people like human cogs in a machine, then it is morally unacceptable. For example, if compensation is not fair, safety conditions are not adequate, or human rights are violated in the process then the practice is not morally justified regardless of the economic benefits. Again, consistent with Kantian ethics, the formulation and implantation of organizational goals must (1) be for the mutual benefit of leaders and followers; and (2) always demonstrate respect for humanity. Thus, leaders should ensure the fair treatment of their followers and never exploit or take advantage of them.

There is a growing trend among businesses to see ethical practices as an important part of their financial success. Good ethics is often seen as good business. To be sure, to some degree, this is a good thing. Social and environmental responsibility should be an important part of any organization's model. Nevertheless, Kant's ethics would invite us to question the motive behind this growing trend.

Behind much of the philanthropy – and in particular 'green' campaigns – might be an ulterior motive. For example, some companies are putting the pressure on their customers to 'go paperless' and no longer receive a paper bill in the mail. Why? Some corporations contend that their customers should go paperless because it's good for the environment. But is that their true motive? Certainly, going paperless would save more trees, and in some ways this is acting socially responsibly. However, do these companies actually care about the environmental impact of using so much paper? Or, is the real incentive to go paperless their bottom line? Paperless bills will save their company money. Is this their real motivation? If so, then why be disingenuous and play the ethical card? The answer is that good ethics is often seen as good business. However, Kant reminds us that organizations should be driven not just by the bottom line, but also by good will. To be sure, environmental considerations are important. The point is not that we shouldn't 'go green', rather the idea is that my motive to 'go green' ought to be sincere.

Finally, Kantian ethics maintains that the specific context or cultural values and norms do not alter one's moral duties. Morality is a matter of categorical imperatives. As such, ethical norms are not changed as a matter of particular situations or cultural circumstances. Both the respect for humanity and the universal law principles hold fast. Their application is the same for leaders and organizations in business as well as the nonprofit sector; and is the same in Europe, South America, the Middle East or anywhere else in the world.

Cultural relativism argues that morality is determined by cultural context. It is the culture that decides what is moral. (We will feature this ethical approach in Chapter 7.) For example, many cultures forbid same-sex relationships and so discriminate against gay men and women in employment. If cultural relativism is correct, then there is nothing, in principle, morally wrong with this discriminating policy. After all, on this view, the culture decides moral principles. Notwithstanding, Kantian ethics disagree. Kant's theory has the moral resources to oppose discriminatory policies. Again, according to Kant's respect for humanity principle, everyone deserves to be treated with dignity and respect no matter their sexual orientation, and for that matter, regardless of their gender, ethnicity, religion or age. The implications of Kant's ethics are emphatic on this point. Leaders have a moral duty to regard all persons with fairness, justice and deference.

Having discussed the core concepts of a Kantian ethical framework and provided examples of how these moral ideals apply in the context of leadership, it is time to turn our attention to a case study. The case study will contextualize Kantian ethics within a real-world situation. The case focuses on a tragic leadership failure. The subject of the case study is Apple and its operating practices in overseas markets. As we will see, the main moral failure, in this case, was not putting human rights and welfare over and above profits. Individuals, it would seem, were used as a means to an end, rather than treated as ends in themselves. There are important leadership principles to gain from this unfortunate case.

CASE STUDY

Kantian ethics applied to Apple Inc.

Organizations like the Human Rights Watch, Human Rights First, International Federation for Human Rights, Global Rights and the UN Human Rights Committee are committed to monitoring and protecting the rights of individuals around the globe. One organization, in particular, has led the charge in this endeavor. Since 1961 Amnesty International has existed to 'protect people wherever justice, freedom, truth and dignity are denied.'[24] Their objective is to expose human rights violations and to educate the public on the ethical treatment of persons. The importance of their work has not gone unnoticed. In 1977 the organization received the Nobel Peace Prize for its groundbreaking work on behalf of human rights.

The most widely accepted document on the subject of human rights is the UN Declaration of Human Rights. (We will examine this document a bit more closely in Chapter 6.) The declaration outlines 30 foundational rights. These rights are said to belong to individuals in virtue of their humanity. No leader or state, government or corporation ought to have the power to violate the inherent dignity of human beings. In particular, Article 23 addresses the individual's right to work. It states that 'Everyone has the right to work, to free choice of employment, *to just and favourable conditions of work. . .*' (emphasis mine). The UN Declaration of Human Rights was published in 1948. Nevertheless, serious human rights violations committed by leaders and their multinational corporations persist to this day.

Fortunately, the labor practices of many multinational corporations have been increasingly scrutinized in recent years. Companies such as Nike, Walmart, Apple, Samsung, Dell and others have each come under fire for their apparent human rights violations in offshore factories.[25] As recently as 2016, Amnesty International documented 'hazardous conditions in which artisanal miners, including thousands of children, mine cobalt in the Democratic Republic of the Congo' in order to supply technology companies like Apple, Samsung and Microsoft with raw materials to power their 'mobile phones, laptop computers, and other portable electronic devices.'[26] To their credit, some companies, like Apple, tried to right their wrongs.

CASE STUDY *(continued)*

Figure 2.3 The Five Components of Leadership Model applied to the Apple case study

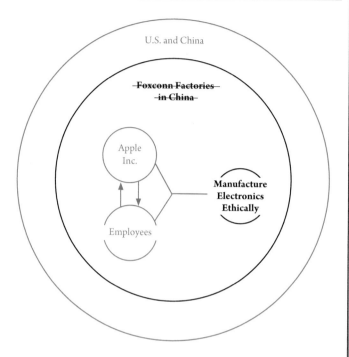

In 2005, Apple created a Supplier Code of Conduct to ensure that the 'working conditions in Apple's supply chain are safe, that workers are treated with respect and dignity, and that manufacturing processes are environmentally responsible.' The code developed by Apple's top executives (including Steve Jobs and Tim Cook) maintained that 'Apple's suppliers are obligated, in all of their activities, to operate in full compliance with the laws, rules and regulations of the countries in which they operate. This Supplier Code of Conduct goes further, drawing upon internationally recognized standards, in order to advance social and environmental responsibility.' The code went on to say that, 'Apple suppliers must uphold the human rights of workers, to treat them with dignity and respect as understood by the international community' and that 'suppliers must be committed to creating safe working conditions and a healthy work environment for all of their workers.' In short, Apple boasted that its company was 'committed to the highest standards of ethical conduct when dealing with workers, suppliers, and customers.'[27] Above you can find a modified version of the Five Components of Leadership Model to illustrate the leadership process in relationship to our case study.

CASE STUDY *(continued)*

Apple and workers' rights violations

Despite its noble code of conduct, Apple's leadership has repeatedly failed to live up to its ethical responsibilities to its workers. A year after Apple created its code of conduct, *The New York Times* reported that a 'British newspaper, *The Mail on Sunday*, secretly visited a Foxconn factory in China, where iPods were manufactured, and reported on workers' long hours, push-ups meted out as punishment and crowded dorms.'[28] Foxconn is one of the world's largest electronics manufacturers, and at the time it made Apple products. Because of the findings at the Foxconn factory, Apple ordered an audit. According to *The New York Times*, by 2011 Apple had inspected 396 facilities and those audits found 'consistent violations of Apple's code of conduct.'[29] Between 2007 and 2011 for example, Apple found that employees regularly worked more than 60 hours a week, worked more than six days in a row, and more seriously, its factories hired 15-year-olds, falsified records and uncovered numerous improper safety precautions. It was not uncommon for workers at Foxconn factories to spend 12 hours a day, six days a week in the plant. As per *The New York Times*, one banner hanging at a Foxconn factory admonished workers to 'Work hard on the job today or work hard to find a job tomorrow.'[30]

Other BBC journalists found similar abuses. In a shocking 2014 article titled 'Apple Failing to Protect Chinese Factory Workers,' the *BBC* uncovered that at a factory in Shanghai exhausted workers were falling asleep on their 12-hour shifts. An undercover reporter was hired in this factory to make parts for Apple computers. They were forced to work 18 days in a row even after repeated requests for time off.[31] On the basis of these and other abuses, one former Apple executive with firsthand knowledge of the audits and factories said, 'If you see the same pattern of problems, year after year, that means the company's ignoring the issue rather than solving it.'[32] In short, according to at least one executive, there was a leadership problem at Apple when it came to respecting workers' rights in foreign factories.

The seriousness of these problems manifested in 2011 when a Foxconn factory in Chengdu exploded. Again, according to *The New York Times*, two weeks before the explosion, a Hong Kong advocacy group drew public attention to the Chengdu plant for a problem with aluminum dust and published a report warning of unsafe conditions. The group even managed to videotape workers at this factory covered with tiny aluminum particles. 'Occupational health and safety issues in Chengdu are alarming,' the report read. 'Workers also highlighted the problem of poor ventilation and inadequate personal protective equipment.'[33] The full report was sent to Apple and it was received without response.

Dust, especially aluminum dust, is a severe safety hazard. *The New York Times* reported 'In 2003, an aluminum dust explosion in Indiana destroyed a wheel factory and killed a worker. In 2008, dust inside a sugar factory in Georgia caused an explosion that killed 14.'[34] So, leaders at Apple were well aware of the danger of these working conditions. Nevertheless, nothing was done to alleviate the unsafe conditions at the Foxconn factory.

CASE STUDY *(continued)*

And, on the morning of May 13, 2011, the factory exploded, killing three people and injuring fifteen others. Many Chinese families and factory workers believe that leaders at Apple were remiss and acted with disregard for the workers' health. Nicholas Ashford, an occupational safety expert, who is now at MIT, said that this is an example of 'gross negligence . . . If it were terribly difficult to deal with aluminum dust, I would understand' he said, 'but do you know how easy dust is to control? It's called ventilation. We solved this problem over a century ago.'[35] Ashford seems to put his finger on the root of the problem saying, 'what's morally repugnant in one country is accepted business practices in another, and companies take advantage of that.'[36]

Applying a Kantian ethical framework brings clarity to this problem. In addressing how, this section will conclude by briefly returning to the Five Components of Leadership discussed above. Our goal here is to see how these components apply to the above case and in so doing, gain some valuable moral insight.

As we turn our attention to the Five Components of Leadership Model, it is important to look at leaders and followers and see what we can learn from the Apple case. For starters, the Apple case demonstrates why it is especially critical for leaders to know and appreciate Kantian ethics. In particular, Kant's Respect for Humanity Principle implies that leaders are morally responsible for how their workers are treated. Once again, this means that leaders, if necessary, ought to go beyond the local laws to promote worker welfare.

The moral standard stated here is strengthened by considering Apple's financial success. When we consider the financial means at Apple's disposal, it becomes evident that leaders in positions of influence not only *ought* to do more to help workers' welfare in their factories, they, in fact, *can* do more. In 2016, *Forbes* ranked Apple as the most valuable company in the world. Its estimated market value topped $530 billon. Thus, given the vast resources at Apple's fingertips, it would be a moral outrage for workers' welfare to not be given sufficient attention.

The Foxconn factory explosion was at least partially the result of dangerous working conditions. The poor ventilation and abundant aluminum dust found at the Foxconn factory were known safety hazards. *The New York Times* reported that a year before the Foxconn factory explosion, '137 workers at an Apple supplier in eastern China were injured after they were ordered to use a poisonous chemical to clean iPhone screens.'[37] In all these instances, it is the workers who were the most vulnerable stakeholders.

Kantian ethics compels leaders to protect human persons, but especially vulnerable human persons. Consequently, if conditions put workers' welfare in jeopardy, it is the moral responsibility of leaders and corporations (like Apple) to do everything they can to improve conditions. 'A failure to implement appropriate safeguards means that employers are treating their employees as disposable tools rather than beings with unique dignity.'[38] For this reason, 'Ethicists, business people, and labor leaders with widely divergent views on a number of issues can agree on a minimum set of health and safety standards that should be in place in factories in the developing world.'[39]

CASE STUDY (continued)

To be sure, the leadership failure at Apple was in monitoring and ensuring that their standards were being met. Apple's code of conduct clearly identified workers' welfare as a priority. In fact, Apple's policies went further than this claiming that 'suppliers must uphold the *human rights of workers*, to treat them with *dignity and respect* as understood by the international community' and that 'suppliers must be committed to *creating safe working conditions and a healthy work environment for all of their workers*' (emphasis mine). Leaders at Apple were clear that they were 'committed to the *highest standards of ethical conduct when dealing with workers*, suppliers, and customers' (again, emphasis mine). Nevertheless, failure to properly implement an effective way to monitor and ensure their standards was at least partially to blame for the Foxconn explosion. Thus, it is not enough to have a code of conduct; corporations must have an effective means for following through on ensuring the proper treatment of their workers in accomplishing their goal.

With regards to the leadership context, there is an equally compelling Kantian mandate. You might remember that Kant's Universal Law Principle holds that we should 'always act in such a way that the maxim of your action can be willed as a universal law of humanity.' Or, put differently, 'Act as though the maxim of your action were by your will to become a universal law of nature.'[40] It is not likely that Apple could universalize a policy that permits disregard for worker safety. Rather, if properly applied, Kant's moral principle would ensure that leaders and organizations are mindful of their impact upon employees. This is true whether or not local laws or policies require doing so. Why? Protecting and maintaining worker safety is in everyone's interest. As a matter of moral principle, therefore, worker safety and considerations ought to go beyond local laws.

Finally, let's consider the cultural values and norms. In this case, Apple's moral duty went beyond local laws and customs. In an insightful essay published in *Business Ethics Quarterly*, Denis Arnold and Norman Bowie summarize this moral problem by saying that it is:

> Partly due to the fact that many of the labor practices in question are legal outside North America and Europe, or are tolerated by corrupt or repressive political regimes. Unlike the recent immigrants who toil in the illegal sweatshops of North America and Europe, workers in developing nations typically have no recourse to the law or social service agencies. Activists have sought to enhance the welfare of these workers by pressuring [multinational corporations] to comply with labor laws, prohibit coercion, improve health and safety standards, and pay a living wage in their global sourcing operations.[41]

Arnold and Bowie go on to argue that the ethical framework provided by Kantian ethics and especially its emphasis on human dignity 'provides a clear basis for grounding the obligations of employers and employees.'[42] Respecting the dignity of workers requires that if multinational corporations choose to outsource their labor to contractors, then they have a moral obligation to not only adhere to local laws but also to respect the human rights of their workforce throughout their supply chain. The duty of fulfilling these moral obligations falls squarely on those in leadership.

CASE STUDY *(continued)*

From a Kantian perspective, Apple's moral shortcomings in this case provide an opportunity to discuss the goal component of leadership. Consider: Why shouldn't multinational corporations merely obey local laws? Why suppose companies have some greater goal? Namely, some greater social responsibility to their workers (and the environment) than what is strictly dictated by law? Kantian ethics has the moral resources to address these questions generally and the issues of workers' welfare and environmental responsibility in particular.

First, think about the issue of workers' welfare. Recall Kant's Respect for Humanity principle. Kant asks us to consider what constitutes proper treatment of persons. He concludes that we ought to 'Act in such a way that you always treat humanity, whether in your own person or in the person of any other, never simply as a means, but always at the same time as an end.'[43] So, following Kant here, organizational goals must include provisions for respecting the autonomy, welfare and rights of workers. Consider the very practical explanation of this principle given by Michael Santoro:

> Multinational corporations are morally responsible for the way their suppliers and subcontractors treat their workers. The applicable moral standard is similar to the legal doctrine of *respondeat superior*, according to which a principal is 'vicariously liable' or responsible for the acts of its agent conducted in the course of the agency relationship. The classic example of this is the responsibility of employers for the acts of employees. Moreover, ignorance is no excuse. Firms must do whatever is required to become aware of what conditions are like in the factories of their suppliers and subcontractors, and thereby be able to assure themselves and others that their business partners don't mistreat those workers to provide a cheaper source of supply.[44]

Consequently, it is not enough for leaders and their corporations to simply make following the law their goal; they must also be mindful of other important moral considerations.

Summary and concluding remarks

What then is the moral duty of leaders and followers? For those who wish to follow Kant's ethics, the leader's actions must be motivated first and foremost by 'good will.' To qualify as acting out of 'good will,' leaders must make sure they always respect humanity and act in a way that is consistent with universal law. The moral requirement to always 'act out of duty' was explained with reference to two important Kantian principles. First, leaders must, without exception, respect humanity. Additionally, leaders should act in accordance with the universal law. In so doing, leaders will ensure that they adhere to their moral duties.

So how can this perspective work practically in an organization? Both leaders and followers will have to be clear on just what is required for 'respect' as well as the values that are non-negotiable and represent universal law. In sum, it may be helpful to return to the framing question at the outset of this chapter. In introducing Kant's ethics, we asked: what is a leader's moral duty? According to a Kantian moral framework, the answer to this question is now clear. The leader's actions and decisions ought to be motivated by 'good will,' where 'good will' is the guiding intention to always act out of duty – to always do the right thing. Why? Because it is a leader's absolute moral imperative.

? DISCUSSION QUESTIONS

According to Kantian ethics, is it morally appropriate for the leaders of multinational corporations to outsource labor to developing countries? Why or why not?

Do the leaders of multinational corporations have a responsibility to go beyond local laws or policies in order to safeguard the welfare of their employees? Justify your answer.

What leadership principles or theories could have been implemented to mitigate Apple's shortcomings in the Foxconn case?

Was the Foxconn case a failure of ethical leadership or some other shortcoming?

What sorts of moral standards would you include in your organization's code of conduct? Be specific.

How would you recommend that leaders monitor and ensure compliance with their code of conduct?

ADDITIONAL RESOURCES

N. Bowie Norman, *Business Ethics: A Kantian Perspective*, New York: Cambridge University Press, 2017.
This book applies Kantian ethical principles to contemporary business practices. It aims to demonstrate how corporations can maintain both institutional integrity and professional success.

C.M. Korsgarrd, *Creating the Kingdom of Ends*, Cambridge: Cambridge University Press, 1996.
This text outlines an influential reading of Kantian ethics. This interpretation of Kant's philosophy emphasizes the teleological and practical nature of his ethics.

O. O'Neil, *Acting on Principle: An Essay on Kantian Ethics*, Cambridge: Cambridge University Press, 2013.
This book takes Kant's idea of a categorical imperative seriously and aims to guide the reader toward a proper application and understanding of this concept in practical ethical decision-making.

NOTES

1 Kantian ethics is a type of deontological ethical system. Deontological ethics (or deontology) is a rule- or duty-based ethical system. Though Kant's ethics is rightly classified as a form of deontological ethics, it is by no means the only form.
2 See I. Kant, 'Groundwork of the Metaphysics of Morals', in Mary Gregor (ed.) *Cambridge Texts in the History of Philosophy*, Cambridge: Cambridge University Press, 1785/1997, p. xxxii.
3 S. Freeman, *Rawls*, New York: Routledge, 2007, p. 474.
4 It has become standard in the academy to compare and contrast utilitarianism (or consequentialism) with

Kantian ethics. The dissimilarities between the two are striking. Thus, it is informative to distinguish one from the other. A complete introduction to utilitarianism is discussed elsewhere in this volume.

5 M. Timmons, *Disputed Moral Issues*, New York: Oxford University Press, 2014, pp. 6–7.

6 J.S. Mill, *Utilitarianism*, 2nd edn, Indianapolis, IN: Hackett Publishing Company, Inc., 2002, p. 18.

7 Kant/Gregor, op. cit., p. 7.

8 Kant/Gregor, op. cit., p. 8.

9 For more about the concept of 'moral luck' see the following influential sources: B. Williams, *Moral Luck*, Cambridge: Cambridge University Press, 1981; and T. Nagel, 'Moral luck,' in Daniel Statman (ed.) *Moral Luck*, Albany, NY: State University of New York Press, 1993, pp. 57–71.

10 R. Johnson and A. Cureton, 'Kant's moral philosophy,' *The Stanford Encyclopedia of Philosophy*, Spring 2017 edn. Online, https://plato.stanford.edu/archives/spr2017/entries/kant-moral/ (accessed April 17, 2017).

11 Kant/Gregor, op. cit., p. 37.

12 Kant/Gregor, op. cit., p. 37.

13 Johnson and Cureton, op. cit.

14 Kant/Gregor, op. cit., p. 31.

15 As stated above, utilitarianism along with key figures associated with this theory are explored in greater detail elsewhere in this volume (see Chapter 3).

16 A.C. Ewing, *The Definition of Good*, London: MacMillan, 1947, p. 188.

17 J. Rachels and S. Rachels, *The Elements of Moral Philosophy*, 8th edn, New York: McGraw-Hill Education, 2014, p. 131.

18 J. Kouzes and B. Posner, *The Leadership Challenge*, San Francisco: Wiley, 2012, p. 286.

19 See, for example, M. Krantz, '9 CEOs paid 800 times more than their workers,' *USA Today*, August 5, 2015. Online, http://www.usatoday.com/story/money/markets/2015/08/05/ceos-paid-many-times-more/31148137/ (accessed February 6, 2017).

20 With respect to organizational health see C. O'Reilly, T. Pollock, and J. Wade, 'Overpaid CEOs and under-paid managers: fairness and executive compensation,' *Organization Science* vol. 17 no. 5, 2006, 527–44.

21 Kouzes and Posner, op. cit., p. 116.

22 Kouzes and Posner, op. cit., p. 116.

23 Kouzes and Posner, op. cit., pp. 116–17.

24 See Amnestyusa.org (accessed April 17, 2017).

25 For example, Nike has been identified on numerous occasions for its human rights violations. See M. Wilsey and S. Lichtig, 'The Nike controversy,' Online, https://web.stanford.edu/class/e297c/trade_environment/wheeling/hnike.html (accessed April 17, 2017).

26 'Democratic Republic of Congo: "This is what we die for": Human rights abuses in the Democratic Republic of Congo power the global trade in cobalt,' *Amnesty International*, January 19, 2016. Online, https://www.amnesty.org/en/documents/afr62/3183/2016/en/ (accessed April 17, 2017).

27 To reference Apple's 'Supplier code of conduct' see https://images.apple.com/supplier-responsibility/pdf/Apple-Supplier-Code-of-Conduct-January.pdf (accessed April 17, 2017).

28 C. Duhigg and D. Barboza, 'In China, human costs are built into an iPad,' *New York Times*, January 25, 2012. Online, http://www.nytimes.com/2012/01/26/business/ieconomy-apples-ipad-and-the-human-costs-for-workers-in-china.html (accessed April 17, 2017).

29 Duhigg and Barboza, ibid.

30 Duhigg and Barboza, op. cit.

31 R. Bilton, 'Apple "Failing to protect Chinese factory workers,"' *BBC*, December 18, 2014. Online, http://www.bbc.com/news/business-30532463 (accessed April 17, 2017).

32 Bilton, ibid.

33 Duhigg and Barboza, op. cit.

34 Duhigg and Barboza, op. cit.

35 Duhigg and Barboza, op. cit.

36 Duhigg and Barboza, op. cit.

37 Duhigg and Barboza, op. cit.

38 D. Arnold and N. Bowie, 'Sweatshops and respect for persons,' *Business Ethics Quarterly*, 13, 2003, p. 617.

39 Arnold and Bowie, ibid.

40 Kant/Gregor, op. cit., p. 31.
41 Arnold and Bowie, op. cit., p. 609.
42 Arnold and Bowie, op. cit., p. 610.
43 Kant/Gregor, op. cit., p. 37.
44 Arnold and Bowie, op. cit., p. 612.

3

Utilitarianism

Robert M. McManus and Alexandra K. Perry

FRAMING QUESTION

How do leaders create the greatest good for the greatest number?

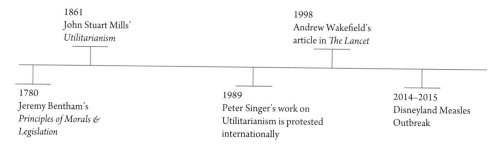

Figure 3.1 Timeline of major works on utilitarian ethics in relation to the chapter case study

Each moral act can be divided into two parts: *action* (or inaction), and the *consequences* brought about by the action. Ethical theories use different evaluative tools to make judgments about the relative morality of action and inaction. Utilitarianism takes a distinct approach; the subject of its evaluation is the consequences of various actions, its evaluative tool is utility. At its core, utilitarianism asks the question: Which action maximizes utility and minimizes harm for the greatest number of people?

Throughout this chapter, we will examine utilitarian ethics and the implication the approach has upon leadership. We will consider major utilitarian philosophers and the various ways they have approached and refined the idea, as well as investigate utilitarianism's major concepts and critiques. After we apply the Five Components of Leadership Model to utilitarian ethical theory, we will 'put the theory on its feet' by applying it to the debate regarding vaccinating children for common diseases. Throughout our time together, we hope to see the benefits, liabilities and implications for leaders using this popular approach to ethical practice.

History

Jeremy Bentham first proposed utilitarianism as a moral principle in his book *An Introduction to the Principles of Morals and Legislation*. The roots of utilitarianism, however, can be traced to the ancient world. Aristippus, a student of Socrates and a contemporary of Plato, first popularized hedonism – the ancient Greek principle that proposed individual happiness ought to be the primary aim of human life.

Aristippus' view of hedonism was epistemological skepticism at its core. He believed that all knowledge was sensory, and therefore there was no universal truth or knowledge. For this reason, the goal of the individual should be to maximize pleasurable sensations and minimize painful sensations.[1] The challenge, Aristippus believed, was for each individual to be in control of their own pleasure, and to avoid those pleasures that would in the long run lead to pain. From this challenge unfolded the hedonistic ethical view: Follow the law so as not to experience the consequences of law-breaking; act justly so as to reap the pleasures that result; be good to friends because of the friendliness you will likely experience in return. Similar to utilitarianism, Aristippus' hedonism evaluated the consequences of each action in order to assess its moral worth, however the evaluative tool was not utility, but rather immediate *individual* pleasure. Epicurus, an ancient Greek philosopher who lived in the third century BCE, popularized the idea of hedonism by shifting its focus to moderation. To Epicurus, maximizing happiness meant that happiness must be sustained, and therefore the goal of the individual should be to live a peaceful life free from fear.[2]

Non-Western roots

While the ancient Greeks were developing schools of Hedonism, non-Western thinkers were also developing early forms of utilitarianism. Chinese Mohist thinkers, whose work is traced back to the fifth century BCE, developed an ethical view that also sought to maximize happiness.[3] Unlike hedonism, the Mohists' focus was not on the individual, but on the happiness of the community writ large. Mohist consequentialism held that the most important factors for human welfare were population growth, material goods, and social 'order,' which referred to times of peace and the avoidance of warfare.

Maximizing these goods, the Mohists believed, would improve the welfare of all humans. This benefit to the individual by way of the collective offers a glimpse of utilitarian theories that were to come later, but the emphasis on the welfare of the collective sets Mohism apart from other consequentialist theories.

Some scholars have argued that Buddhism is the converse to utilitarianism.[4] While utilitarianism focuses on the maximization of pleasure, Buddhism aims to reduce or eliminate suffering. Both goals end up in roughly the same place: A world where pleasure outweighs pain, and an ethical appraisal system that calculates pleasure over pain in order to assess its efforts toward a goal (maximizing pleasure in utilitarianism, and minimizing suffering in Buddhism).

Utilitarianism

Utilitarianism certainly has roots in both ancient Greek philosophy and in non-Western thought, but its approach is distinct from these ethical frameworks because its goal is much further-reaching. The aim of utilitarianism is two-fold: *maximize utility* for the *greatest number* of people. When Jeremy Bentham wrote *An Introduction to the Principles of Morals and Legislation* he argued that it is the second part of this goal – that utility has to be maximized *for the greatest number of people* – that made it important to be both an ethical framework and a legal framework.[5] Bentham believed that his 'greatest happiness principle,' which is what he called his utilitarian calculus, would eventually be a complete legal system. He wrote, 'nature has placed mankind under the governance of two sovereign masters, pain and pleasure. It is for them alone to point out what we *ought* to do, as well as to determine what we *shall* do.'[6]

Bentham developed a calculus to determine an ethical course of action, which he called the felicific calculus. The felicific calculus included circumstances that ought to be considered when determining the moral value of any specific action. These circumstances included duration, purity, extent, certainty, remoteness, and fecundity. The units of currency in felicific calculus were hedons (positive ethical worth), and dolors (negative ethical worth). In addition to being a philosopher, Bentham was an economist whose work focused on improving social welfare, so it is no surprise that his ethical framework borrows from the language and theory of economics.

In the early nineteenth century, Jeremy Bentham became close friends with the British historian James Mill. Bentham's work influenced Mill, who wrote on utilitarianism in publications such as the *Philanthropist* between 1808 and 1818 before his most famous book, *The History of British India*, was published. At the time Mill had a young son, John Stuart Mill, who would grow up under the influence of his father and Bentham. Mill was taught exclusively at home in his early years, and learned Greek, Latin, economics, science, and mathematics from Bentham and his contemporaries. It would be J.S. Mill who would propel the development of Bentham's utilitarianism forward.

In 1863 J.S. Mill published his work *Utilitarianism,* in which he outlined a clear and concise development of Bentham's ethical theory. Responding to critics of Bentham who claimed that utilitarianism was unrefined, or simply a form of hedonism, Mill made a distinction between lower levels of pleasure, which are typically derived from physical stimuli, and higher-level pleasures, which were more intellectual or moral by nature. Mill's most famous quote in *Utilitarianism* reads:

> It is better to be a human being dissatisfied than a pig satisfied; better to be Socrates dissatisfied than a fool satisfied. And if the fool, or the pig, are of a different opinion, it is because they only know their own side of the question.[7]

Mill's utilitarianism maintained the foundation of ethical appraisal that Bentham laid, but his distinction between levels of pleasure is what contemporary utilitarians have argued sets the theory apart from its hedonistic predecessors.

Over the past century, two philosophers have been fundamental to the continued evolution of utilitarianism, R.M. Hare, and Peter Singer. Hare, whose career spanned the mid- to late-twentieth century, continued the work of Mill, but with an eye toward the growing emphasis on language in philosophical theory. Hare's work included *The Language of Morals* and *Moral Thinking,* and in both he outlined the underpinning linguistic and cognitive conventions to moral thinking. Hare developed the term *preference utilitarianism,* which takes into consideration both the universalizability and prescriptive nature of moral terms, and leads to a form of utilitarianism that maximizes the satisfaction of the preferences of the majority of people.

Singer, a student of Hare at Oxford, did not make significant contributions to the theory of utilitarianism, but rather to its application. Singer's career began as the field of applied ethics was beginning to formalize. While philosophers had a long tradition of contribution to ethical theory, there had been a separation of philosophical theory and application for much of the twentieth century. Applied ethicists were beginning to get involved in various rights movements, and to make contributions to areas such as medicine, art and business. Singer quickly became the most prominent utilitarian voice in applied ethics, and sought to live a lifestyle consistent with a utilitarian framework in order to serve as an example of the theory's practicality. His work is controversial for the boundaries that he draws around the scope of his appraisal. Singer has been an outspoken advocate of animal rights, arguing that if animals can feel pain, they ought to be considered in a strict utilitarian calculus.[8] Singer has also taken controversial positions on subjects such as donating the majority of one's money to the poor, giving up cars, and euthanizing disabled infants, all on utilitarian grounds.[9]

Major concepts of utilitarian ethics

The idea that what is ethical is what maximizes good for the greatest number of people is quite intuitive, and has certainly gained traction since Bentham first popularized utilitarianism. Actually measuring the consequences of an action in order to determine whether it is moral, however, is quite complicated. Calculating the scope of those consequences is yet more complicated, as is understanding how those consequences are best weighted in order to do an overall appraisal of the relative harms and benefits brought about by an action. Bentham, Mill and the contemporary utilitarians each approached these questions in slightly different ways. This section will highlight these major concepts in utilitarianism with an eye toward the value of utilitarianism for leaders, before discussing the major challenges to utilitarianism in the following section.

Utilitarian calculus

The fundamental question of utilitarianism is daunting: How can a leader measure the consequences of an action in order to determine whether it is right or wrong? Bentham's felicific calculus was the first formalized attempt at addressing this question.

The felicific calculus attempted to quantify the moral value of an action by assigning each hedon (pleasure value) and dolon (pain value) a worth of 1. In the end, a leader's assessment should be based on whether the number of hedons outweighs the number of dolons. For each hedon and dolon, the leader is told to consider its duration, certainty and intensity, in addition to the number of those who will be affected, the probability that the sensation is pure and will not lead to a sensation of the opposite kind, and the time-frame in which the result will occur. If that sounds like an overwhelming task, Bentham has a device intended to make it easier to remember:

Intense, long, certain, speedy, fruitful, pure – Such marks in pleasures and in pains endure. Such pleasures seek if private be thy end: If it be public, wide let them extend. Such pains avoid, whichever be thy view: If pains must come, let them extend to few.[10]

The attempt to *quantify* moral value was not a central theme in John Stuart Mill's work on utilitarianism. Mill instead turned his sights to the differences in *quality* between different pleasures. Mill believed that lower-level pleasures and pains included those actions that brought about primarily physical sensations. For example, eating or taking a walk would be considered primarily lower-level pleasures, while the experience of falling in love or saving a life would be higher-level pleasures because they have intellectual and moral qualities to them. Likewise, stubbing a toe would be a lower-level pain, while heartbreak would be a higher-level pain.

Though Mill and Bentham placed the emphasis on different elements of the evaluative process, they both agreed that the most ethical course of action is the one that brings about the greatest amount of good for the greatest number of people.

For example, the leader of a corporation might use a utilitarian calculation when trying to decide which supplier to award a contract to when building a new office space. Using Bentham's calculus, the leader might consider all of the people who might be affected by her decision. She would likely consider the cost of each bid, the time that each supplier might take, the effect on her employees, the implications for her stockholders, and so on. Weighing the options, she would likely select the supplier whose product would maximize the happiness of the greatest number of people. In doing so, Bentham would argue that she has done what is morally correct.

Mill would want the leader to take her consideration a step further by balancing not just the potential happiness with the potential unhappiness, but also by deliberating over the weight that she is giving to each consideration in her calculus. For Mill, the temporary inconvenience of employees who are anxious to move into their new office space would be far outweighed by a consideration of the social practices of the supplier that the leader chooses. Mill would want her calculus to emphasize the environmental policies of each company, to consider whether the bids have come from businesses with a history of discriminatory practices, and so on. Because these factors have an intellectual and moral element to them, Mill would say that they are higher-level pleasures than the factors relating to the employees' immediate comfort. How is one to distinguish lower- from higher-level pleasures? Mill's advice is to watch educated citizens and to concern ourselves with the pleasures that they focus on, using the things they consider as 'good' to be the standard that guides our actions.

Defining the scope of evaluation in utilitarianism

A more difficult question for utilitarians is the question of where the boundaries of evaluation should fall. Bentham and Mill both emphasized that their ethical framework was not akin to the Mohists' hedonism in that the goal of utilitarianism is *not* the overall well-being of society, or even all individuals. Still, utilitarian boundaries are not drawn as narrowly as the ancient hedonists might have drawn them, with the individual residing by his or her lonesome within their confines. Utilitarian thinkers have consistently maintained that the scope of utilitarian consideration should be all individuals who the decision will affect.

Utilitarianism is inherently non-discriminatory. Bentham's famous decree 'each to count for one and none for more than one,' is the true goal of utilitarianism. Each individual affected by a particular decision should count as one, regardless of his or her status or standpoint. Still, utilitarianism struggles to define which individuals are worthy of inclusion. How is one to know at the outset of a decision how far the effects of that decision will be felt?

More recent utilitarians like Peter Singer often consider just this question in their evaluation of contemporary moral issues. For Singer, the most salient example of this dilemma is the question of animal rights.[11] Singer has argued extensively that non-human animals ought to be considered as humans in the appraisal of any ethical question of which they are the subject. For Singer, this means that it is unethical to consume animal products, to warehouse animals in zoos or other facilities designed for human entertainment, or to hunt for sport. If animals can feel pain, why shouldn't they be considered in an ethical system that measures levels of discernible pleasures and pains? Singer coined the term 'speciesism' in response to this concern. He argues that ignoring the pain of animals on the basis of their species is discriminatory in the same way that someone might be racist, sexist or homophobic. Would the leader in the example above need to also consider the possible harm to animals that might come from her choosing one supplier over another? Or would she be acting ethically as long as she considered her employees, their families, her stockholders and the consumers that her business serves?

Critiques of utilitarian ethics

Utilitarianism can be a very practical way for leaders to make ethical decisions. The theory prompts the leader to consider his followers and the goal that they are working toward together in order to decide what is right. Ideally, it also prompts the decision-maker to engage those who might be impacted by the decision at hand in order to determine which option will maximize happiness for those impacted. Still, utilitarianism faces some unique challenges and critiques.

Recent elections in many democratic countries worldwide illustrate what might be the most pressing challenge for leaders attempting to use utilitarianism to guide their ethical decision-making. Many of these elections highlighted the incongruent desires of citizens within the same political boundaries. With many elections resulting in poll numbers close to 50 percent for each candidate, it is fair to ask how a leader might act ethically according to utilitarianism. How can a leader maximize happiness for the greatest number of his or her followers if those followers each want very different things? The happiness that some followers feel as a result of a moral decision is always going to come at the expense of the happiness of other followers. Does the happiness of the majority always outweigh the suffering of the minority? This section will look at some of these challenges to utilitarianism, and will also highlight differences between utilitarianism and deontology, which is commonly viewed as its contrasting theory.

The role of the minority

The most pressing challenge to utilitarianism is the question of the rights of the minority. As a theory, utilitarianism aims to maximize happiness for the *greatest number of people*, but this aim at best ignores the desires of the minority, and at worst allows for the moral permissibility of actions that directly cause harm to the minority.

In his lectures on justice, moral philosopher Michael Sandel uses the example of organ donation to highlight this point. Imagine there are five patients, Sandel asks the audience, and each one is in need of a different organ transplant. It might take years for each of these individuals to become transplant recipients if they are listed on the organ transplant waitlist, and subject to the same lottery methods as other organ recipients. It's likely that most of the five, if not all five, would not survive the wait. Sandel then asks the audience to imagine that there is a healthy person in the next room. Why couldn't we simply sedate that person, procure their organs, and provide transplants to each of the other five.[12]

A straightforward and simple utilitarian calculus might allow for this. Five people benefit from the action, while one suffers. Clearly the appraisal would have to be more complex than this: there are families to consider, the likelihood of each organ's suitability and chance for failure, and so on. The details can be shifted in thousands of different ways in order to influence the calculation and weigh the relative harms and benefits.

The criticism is simple, however: Why doesn't that healthy patient have the right to keep his own organs and his life? The fact that he is in the minority does not seem to negate the fact that he has the right to remain free from harm. At an intuitive level something just *seems* wrong about allowing someone to die for the sake of the majority. And it need not be a matter of life and death in order to serve as a hefty criticism to utilitarian theories. Don't all individuals deserve happiness whether they fall in the majority or the minority?

Limits to the consideration of consequences

A second major criticism of utilitarianism is that it is impossible to understand all of the potential consequences of an action, and that it is certainly impossible to consider each one before making an ethical decision. If I am driving down the highway tonight and see a family struggling to get their car to start on the side of the road, I will quickly have to make a decision about whether or not to stop to help them. It seems insensible for me to consider the effect that this might have on my own family, my ability to sleep well tonight, and the implications for my colleagues if I am late arriving to work. In the time I will have to make that decision, I will likely consider my own safety and the safety of the family stuck on the side of the road. My ability to consider more than that is limited by the lack of time that I have, and my own lack of ability to truly understand how far-reaching the effects of my action might be.

Axel Gosseries, a Belgian moral philosopher, uses the example of the production of baby food to illustrate this point. Manufacturers often produce baby food that has a shelf life of a few years.[13] This means that children who aren't even born at the point of their production – perhaps not even conceived – will consume much of the baby food in those jars. Still, we regulate the safety and quality of baby food despite the fact that those who might be harmed by it are simply hypothetical beings. We likely consider the rights of these future humans because of the immediacy of their future existence as well as our manufacturing norms, but how often do we have to consider harms to future generations? How often do we have to consider harms to the deceased? Do we need to consider those on the periphery of our decisions? Utilitarianism has trouble addressing these questions.

Mill anticipates this challenge by limiting our obligation to the consideration of only those immediately and actually affected by our decision at hand. Still, even this qualification raises questions as it tries to address them.

Inherent moral value

Deontology, the moral theory that is most commonly viewed as the contrast to utilitarianism, takes as its central tenet the idea that actions have inherent moral value without regard to their consequences. Immanuel Kant, the eighteenth-century German philosopher whose work is viewed as the foundation of deontology, used a principle called the 'Categorical Imperative' to determine whether an action is right or wrong. (For more on Kant see Chapter 2.) This principle holds that moral laws are intrinsically good, and that all reasonable people will agree on their worth.

The deontological challenge to utilitarianism is that it disregards this intrinsic moral value of certain actions, favoring instead an ends-justify-the-means appraisal. Utilitarianism leaves room for actions such as lying, stealing, and even murder to be viewed as ethical as long as they maximize the happiness of the greatest number of people. Bentham and Mill dismiss this criticism. Both theorists argue that in a society that follows utilitarian moral principles, certain actions will always be unethical because they will not maximize happiness overall. This means that murder, for example, would always be unethical under utilitarianism because it is theoretically impossible for it to maximize happiness overall.

Five component analysis

Taking utilitarianism's major concepts and critiques into consideration, let's now see how the theory applies to the Five Components of Leadership Model.

As we see in Figure 3.2, *utilitarian ethics focuses directly upon the goal and context highlighted in the Five Components of Leadership Model.* However, that does not mean that utilitarian ethics does not also speak to the other leadership components. Utilitarian ethics places a great deal of responsibility on

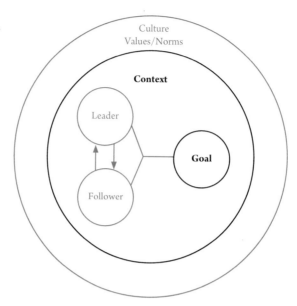

Figure 3.2 The Five Components of Leadership Model applied to utilitarian ethics

leaders and their decision-making. Unlike ethical egoism that is introduced in Chapter 5 in which a leader makes a decision based upon what is best for him or her personally, utilitarianism forces the leader to consider himself or herself *as only one of many stakeholders*. Unlike Machiavelli's famous 'ends/means' calculus that states the ends justifies the means if it preserves the individual's position and power,[14] utilitarian ethics forces the leader to consider the greatest good for the greatest number of people. The 'greatest good' may not be beneficial for the leader personally. Likewise, the leader may not find himself or herself in the company of the 'greatest number of people'; indeed, the leader may be a part of the minority. Thus, utilitarian ethics forces leaders to hold to a high ethical standard for themselves and carefully consider their motivations and reasoning when making a decision.

For example, consider an American politician who receives a large donation from the National Rifle Association (NRA), a U.S. advocacy group for gun owners, for his political campaign. Let's say the politician is from a district that has witnessed a large number of gun-related deaths – perhaps even a mass shooting. Let's also say a bill is introduced to the legislature that would place new restrictions on the purchase of guns in the politician's district. Should the politician vote for the proposed measure? What is the greatest good? What is the greatest number of people? Some may argue that the politician should vote *for* the bill to protect the lives of the people in his district. They would argue this is the greatest good for the greatest number of people. Contrarily, others may argue that the politician should vote *against* the bill to protect the rights of the people in his district to purchase and own guns. They may argue that even if some people use guns to commit murder and terrible crimes, to deny people a right guaranteed by the Unites States' constitution would be detrimental to their other freedoms in the long run. If the politician votes for the bill he runs the risk of alienating one of his key donors and a portion of his constituents, which may mean he might lose in the next election. If he votes against the bill he may be accused of succumbing to special interests and the protection of his own career rather than serving his constituents, in which case he may also lose the next election. What is he to do? Utilitarian ethics would say the politician must take himself out of the equation and only consider what he believes to be the greatest good for the greatest number of people regardless of his personal consequences. This is a tall order, but it is what is required if the politician is to truly follow the mandate utilitarian ethics stipulates.

Followers must also consider their motivations when considering what is the greatest good for the greatest number of people. They must also be able to look past their immediate interests and immediate gratification to consider what may be right for the larger majority. Consider recycling. We all enjoy the benefits of petroleum products, from the gasoline we use in our vehicles to get us from one place to another, to the water bottles we use to quench our thirst on a hot summer's day. These conveniences are simply a part of our modern society. However, rarely do we consider the impact these little conveniences have upon others – including the natural environment, non-human animals, and even future generations. Don't we have an ethical obligation to consider these aspects and the impact our actions have on others?

For a more specific example, consider the great Pacific garbage patch that lies between the West Coast of the United States and Japan. This area of the ocean contains billions of pieces of debris and plastic, much of which cannot even be seen by the naked eye. These particles float in the top portion of the water column and are ingested by marine life, often leading to their death. Many of these particles are used to produce exfoliating soaps and scrubs so popular in the West – little particles of plastic that give us softer and smoother skin. Is it really necessary to have softer skin at the expense of marine life and the ability of future generations to enjoy the benefits and beauties of the sea? Even if our leaders do not provide the regulation to prohibit such particles to be used in our beauty and hygiene products, isn't it incumbent upon the vast majority of followers to consider the impact their actions will have on others and the environment? Utilitarianism answers this question unequivocally – yes! Followers must also consider what is the greatest good for the greatest number, even at the expense of their own convenience and comfort.

Perhaps the most relevant aspect of the Five Components Model as it relates to utilitarian ethics is the goal. Utilitarian ethics falls under the umbrella of teleological ethics – that is, that branch of ethics that considers the ends – or the consequences – of actions. From a normative perspective, what is right or what is wrong is dependent upon the outcome of our actions. For example, consider Second World War Germany. Nazi soldiers come knocking at your door and ask if you are hiding Jewish people in your attic – and indeed you are. Some interpretations of Kantian ethics would say that you are obligated to tell the truth; you must act upon the maxim that you would want to be the law. If you don't want other people to lie to you, then you must not lie to other people; that is your duty. Thus, Kantian ethics falls under the umbrella of deontological or duty-based ethics. According to Kantianism, if the Nazis find and harm the people hiding in your attic, *they* are morally responsible for their actions – not you. However, utilitarianism looks at the *ends* rather than the *means* to that end. If telling the truth would mean that the people hiding in your attic would be taken to concentration camps and face torture and death, *then the morally correct thing to do would be to lie*. In this case, the greatest good – saving a life – far outweighs one's moral obligation to tell the truth. From a normative perspective, what is right or wrong depends upon the outcomes of an action. This is the core of utilitarian ethics as it relates to the Five Components Model – the goal is of utmost importance.

Although the goal is the most important aspect in understanding how utilitarian ethics relates to leadership, the context is also very important. What might be morally honorable in one situation may be morally reprehensible in another. Again, we might use a wartime example to understand this aspect of the theory. In a time of war, killing the enemy is considered the right thing to do. If your commanding officer (in this case, your leader) gives you the order to shoot – you shoot. This is especially true if you and your fellow soldiers are in immediate danger of being killed, and if the cause for which you are fighting is just. However, what should the soldiers do if the context changes and there is no immediate danger. This is precisely what happened in the My Lai Massacre during the war between the United States and Vietnam.

In 1968, during the Vietnam police action, the U.S. Charlie Company came across the village of My Lai in Northern Vietnam. Although there was no threat to the soldiers in the village, and no enemy was ever found, Lieutenant William Calley gave orders to his company to shoot and kill the civilians in the village, including old men, pregnant women, children and even infants. The solders raped an untold number of young girls and women, opened machine gun fire on trapped children, and burned the village to the ground. In the end, more than 500 Vietnamese civilians were killed.[15] All is *not* fair in love and war. Even though the soldiers may have been given orders to shoot 'the enemy,' in the context of the peaceful village, the leader and the followers committed an atrocity. This is a horrible reminder that context matters. Utilitarianism does not give its proponents a license to act unscrupulously.

Finally, we consider cultural values and norms. As we will see in Chapter 7, different cultures may, indeed, hold various values and norms that may deem certain actions ethical in one culture and unethical in others. However, this is not to say that there are not guiding principles that are valued across cultures, such as we will see in Chapter 6 where we will discuss universal human values. Just because racial discrimination is permitted in one culture does not make it permissible for a person to take a laissez-faire 'when in Rome' attitude to racial discrimination when traveling abroad. Ethicists also note that some cultures may have better reasons than others for their practices and ethical concerns.[16] Regardless, the motivating considerations for utilitarianism is what is the greatest good for the greatest number of people, regardless of cultural customs and mores, and that is why its primary concerns are placed in the domains of the goal and the context on the Five Components of Leadership Model. Let's now see how utilitarian ethics plays out in a specific situation. For that we turn to our case study.

CASE STUDY

The anti-vaccine movement and public health

Science and Pseudoscience are at odds when it comes to the idea of a cause and cure for autism spectrum disorders. This is not a clear-cut case of science squaring off against the popular media, conducting shouting matches across the Internet, newspaper and academic journal boundaries as one might expect in such a situation. Why? The heroes and villains of this problem, and there are plenty, simply don't fall clearly into these categories. Science, in this case, has its share of villains, while the media has its share of heroes.

One of the clearest villains in the case of autism and misinformation is Andrew Wakefield, a former physician and surgeon at Britain's well-known Royal Free Medical School, who published a paper in 1998 connecting autism to a vaccine for measles, mumps and rubella (MMR) that is commonly given to toddlers.[17] Wakefield was certainly not the first researcher to propose a cause or cure for autism, but he is the more commonly known. Soon after Wakefield's article was published, news of it began to spread, and parents of

CASE STUDY *(continued)*

autistic children began to seek his help. If the cause of autism had been found, surely it could be cured and new cases could be prevented. Wakefield spent close to six years in the limelight, and became the golden boy of parents seeking a cure for their autistic children.

While Wakefield may have won over parent and advocacy groups, many scientists and physicians remained skeptical. They watched, and began to protest, as Wakefield conducted more trials on autistic children, going so far as to send autistic children to the United States where he could more easily order investigative spinal taps. His proclamations about the ills of vaccines created an anti-vaccine movement that sparked several public health crises.[18] To be fair, Wakefield wasn't the only one promoting the idea that vaccines caused autism. U.S. politicians, such as Robert. F. Kennedy and Dan Burton, claimed that Thiomersal, a mercury-based preservative commonly found in childhood vaccines, caused autism, and held congressional hearings to prove their point. Over the course of a few years, Thiomersal was removed from many vaccines.[19] Wakefield and other anti-vaccine advocates clearly seemed to be the heroes.

The fall from hero-like status, it seems, can happen as quickly as the ascension to it. Within a few years of Wakefield's article in *The Lancet*, and the onset of the sensational anti-vaccine movement, the scientific community grew more skeptical. First, a five-year-old autistic boy in Pennsylvania died of heart failure while undergoing chelation therapy, which some claimed to rid the body of the heavy-metal toxins such as mercury.[20] Later, during the 2007 omnibus hearing, physicians challenged anti-vaccine experts to account for the fact that there was no increase in autism rates in Minamata Bay, Japan, where, in the 1950s, a chemical plant was known to have dumped high levels of mercury, causing damage to humans and animals. They didn't have one case of autism in the community.[21] In the U.K., Andrew Wakefield wasn't faring much better. Put under the microscope, his study began to show some major problems. Wakefield had neglected to acknowledge competing interests in the project, including the fact that parents of autistic children had paid him a large sum of money to conduct his study. Further scrutiny showed many more ethical conflicts with Wakefield's study, including that he had paid for blood samples from children who attended his son's birthday party, which may have skewed his results; that he had run invasive tests on children without approval from the proper ethics board; that he had marketed products to parents of autistic children based on his purported findings; and, perhaps most damning, reports from research assistants that he had falsified data.[22]

In March 2004, ten of the thirteen co-authors of Wakefield's article published a retraction of the study in *The Lancet*,[23] however it wasn't until February 2010 that *The Lancet* would go on to publicly retract Wakefield's research. This retraction came on the heels of a report of over 100 pages released by Britain's General Medical Council (GMC), on 28 January 2010, which declared that Wakefield's work on autism and the MMR vaccine was unethical.[24] The final blow came for Wakefield in May 2010 when the GMC barred him from practicing medicine in Britain.[25]

CASE STUDY *(continued)*

Pseudoscience had its day in court, and lost. The defeat had little effect, however, on the damage that had been done. Scientists and the autistic community denounced Wakefield left and right, but many parents and media outlets paid no attention.[26] Recent studies have linked autism to genetics, but as of yet, no clear consensus over this exists.[27] Another extensive study on autism's relation to various environmental factors to date was published in 2010 and showed that there was no link between vaccinations and autism.[28]

Regardless of the multiple studies that have debunked Wakefield's research and have proven that there is no link between vaccinations and autism, many parents still elect not to vaccinate their children or to delay their children's vaccinations until they are older out of fear their children may develop autism. This poses a problem because failing to properly vaccinate weakens what scientists refer to as 'herd immunity.'

Although there are various uses of the term, basically, herd immunity is that level of immunity to a disease present in a large group of people that protects those who are not immune to the disease from becoming ill and further transmitting the illness to others. As more and more people choose not to have their children vaccinated, there is an increase in other children contracting the disease and passing it on to others.

A classic example of the weakening of the herd immunity was the Disneyland Measles outbreak in 2014–2015.[29] Between December 2014 and February 2015 close to 150 people in the United States, Mexico, and Canada contracted the disease. Many of these patients had visited the Disneyland theme parks in California. In the Disneyland outbreak, the researchers estimated that the vaccination rate 'might have been as low as 50% and no higher than 86%.'[30] Because measles is so contagious, between 96 percent and 99 percent of the population must be vaccinated to provide herd immunity.[31] In addition, some people cannot be vaccinated for measles, such as infants and those with compromised immune systems. The elderly are also susceptible to the disease. Even then, about three percent of the population who are vaccinated may still be vulnerable to contracting the disease. Researchers determined that the disease spread so far and so rapidly because many of the parents visiting the park had elected not to vaccinate their children with the widely available MMR vaccine.[32] And lest one thinks that contracting measles is not a big deal, consider that measles can lead to hospitalization and secondary infections, encephalitis (swelling of the brain) and even death. Regardless of the clear and present danger not vaccinating children poses, many parents still refuse to do so.

This trend has motivated many pediatricians to stop accepting patients who refuse or delay vaccinations for their children out of concern for their other patients and the general public's health. In response to this trend, The American Association of Pediatrics released a clinical report in 2016 stating:

> The decision to dismiss a family who continues to refuse immunization is not one that should be made lightly, nor should it be made without considering and respecting the reasons for the parents' point of view. Nevertheless, the individual pediatrician may consider dismissal of families who refuse vaccination as an acceptable option.[33]

CASE STUDY *(continued)*

Figure 3.3 Five Components of Leadership Model applied to the anti-vaccination movement and the public health case study

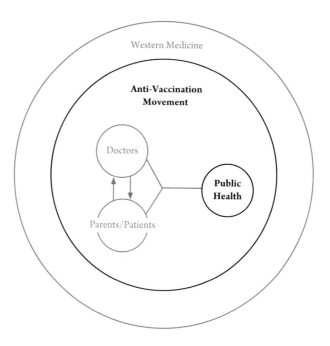

But is it ethical for doctors to refuse to see a patient and therefore punish the child for a decision made by the child's parents? Enter utilitarianism.

From a utilitarian perspective, doctors refusing to take on patients whose parents refuse or delay vaccinations can be justified ethically as they seek the greatest good for the greatest number of people. As we apply this scenario to the Five Components of Leadership Model (see Figure 3.3), we can see that in this case the leaders are identified as the doctors. The followers are their individual patients and their parents or guardians. The goal is to have a healthy child free of disease. The context is the anti-vaccination movement. And the cultural values and norms are those that are influenced by industrialized nations, which values the benefits of modern medicine.

In this case the doctor (the leader) may choose to deny treatment to patients whose parents (the followers) refuse or delay to vaccinate their children. From a utilitarian standpoint, this action is ethically justifiable as the doctors seek the greatest good (protection from disease for the child) for the greatest number of people (the public). It is a classic utilitarian argument. In this case, the doctors are also considering the health of the child they refuse to see. The doctors' hope is that by refusing to take the child on as a patient it will force the parents to reconsider, thus, protecting the child as well as the public health.

CASE STUDY *(continued)*

As we saw earlier, followers must also have the greatest good for the greatest number of people in mind when they pursue the common goal of protecting their child. They must be willing to research the evidence that dispels their notions that vaccinations may harm their child by causing autism. They must also be willing to pursue the greatest good for the greatest number of people and not rely on herd immunity to protect their child, essentially relying on other parents' willingness to vaccinate their children. As we saw in the Disneyland example earlier, between 96 percent and 99 percent of people must choose to vaccinate to keep the herd immunity in place. If too many parents choose not to vaccinate their children for measles, the herd immunity quickly breaks down. Followers (in this case the parents) must also take responsibility to care for the greatest good for the greatest number of people and not take the 'free ride' the herd immunity can bestow upon them or their children.

But why would parents refuse to vaccinate their children if all the research indicates that vaccinations are safe for the vast majority of people? Don't they have the best interest of their children in mind? Of course they do. A healthy child is the common goal for both the parents and the doctor. However, the context in this case is what makes this situation problematic.

Because of the misinformation that is present in the context, parents who are opposed to vaccines are convinced they are doing what is best for their child. This brings us back to the ethical responsibility of doctors to listen to these parents' concerns and seek to provide them with enough information and assurance that their child is not at risk for receiving the vaccine. It is noteworthy that in the same report mentioned above that suggested dismissing patients whose parents refused to vaccinate, the American Association of Pediatrics admonished doctors to listen to their patients' concerns acknowledging they share a common goal. The AAP writes:

> It is important to present this safety information in a nonconfrontational dialogue with the parents while listening to and acknowledging their concerns. Misconceptions should be corrected, because both parents and pediatricians are in agreement in wanting the best for the children's health and well-being.[34]

This brings us back to the heavy responsibility utilitarian ethics places on leaders to act ethically regardless of their personal stake in the matter. It would be very easy for doctors to simply deny treating patients whose parents refuse to vaccinate, but utilitarian ethics forces them to go the extra mile to try to persuade and convince these parents of the importance of vaccination for their child as well as the rest of society.

At least in the industrialized world, modern medicine is valued as a means to help individuals and society to live happier and healthier lives. Some would say that the doctors have an ethical responsibility to take on patients and provide medical care regardless of their parents' choice not to vaccinate. Why should a child be punished for his or her parent's

CASE STUDY *(continued)*

decision, regardless of how misinformed that decision may be? That may be; however, this argument is informed more by deontological ethics than utilitarian ethics. Contrarily, another cultural influence on this debate is the distrust of science and personal relativism that is such a part of post-modern culture. The reasons for this distrust may range from economic to religious factors, but regardless of the reasoning behind it, it plays into the cultural values and norms that are affecting the discussion of vaccination. Yes, doctors must take the prevailing cultural values and norms into account when addressing this pressing leadership challenge. However, they must still do what they believe is going to be the best for the greatest number of people given the information at their disposal.

Summary and concluding remarks

This chapter explored the ethical theory of utilitarianism, and the framing question: 'How can leaders create the greatest good for the greatest amount of people?' Generally speaking, utilitarian theories answer this question by determining which action can maximize happiness and minimize harm for the greatest number. For leaders, this approach to ethical leadership would entail being reflective about the choices that he or she might make in order to analyze which choice might bring about the greatest good for his or her followers. Applying utilitarianism to the issue of vaccine refusal highlighted some of the challenges that leaders might face in taking this approach to ethical leadership.

How then do leaders create the greatest good for the greatest number? Utilitarian leaders consider both their immediate actions and the consequences of those actions. Similar to the common good, the area of concern for these leaders goes beyond themselves and their immediate circle of concern to how the secondary consequences of their actions affect all who are influenced by their leadership. To make this happen, leaders must look beyond the immediate goal and consider both the positive and negative consequences of that goal for their larger communities. In the end, leaders considering a utilitarian approach to understand the ethical dilemmas with which they are faced must first consider their ultimate goal and the surrounding context to know how to act to bring about the greatest good for the greatest number of their followers.

DISCUSSION QUESTIONS

Consider the Kantian critique of utilitarianism. Is there a danger to defining 'right' and 'wrong' based on the happiness of the majority?

How does utilitarianism differ from hedonism, the theory that everyone should do what makes them happy?

Is it ever ethical for parents to refuse vaccines for their children?

The case study presents medical professionals as leaders in the vaccine case. How would the case differ if we defined the media as having a leadership role? What would that role look like, and what obligations would the media have?

How would leaders and followers work together toward a common goal of decreasing vaccine refusal? Focus specifically on the relationship between the leaders and followers.

How might leadership related to vaccine reform differ in a culture that did not have modern medicine, or in a culture that viewed medicine as authoritative and patients as lacking autonomy?

ADDITIONAL RESOURCES

P. Singer, *The Most Good You Can Do: How Effective Altruism is Changing Ideas about Living Ethically*, New Haven, CT: Yale Press, 2015.
Singer offers an analysis of the application of utilitarianism to contemporary ethical challenges such as vegetarianism and charitable giving.

M. Sandel, *Justice: What's the Right thing to do?* New York: Farrar, Straus, and Giroux, 2008. Sandel considers utilitarianism as an approach to ethical decision-making and compares it to alternatives such as Kantianism and Virtue Ethics.

NOTES

1 K. Lampe, *The Birth of Hedonism: The Cyrenaic Philosophers and Pleasure as a Way of Life*, Princeton, NJ: Princeton University Press, 2014.

2 Lampe, ibid.

3 C. Fraser, *The Philosophy of the Mòzǐ: The First Consequentialists*, New York: Columbia University Press, 2016.

4 B. Contestabile, 'Negative utilitarianism and Buddhist intuition,' *Contemporary Buddhism: An Interdisciplinary Journal*, vol. 15 no. 2, 2014, 298–311.

5 J. Bentham, *The Collected Works of Jeremy Bentham: An Introduction to the Principles of Morals and Legislation*, J.H. Burns and H.L.A Hart (eds), New York: Oxford/Clarendon Press, 1789/1996.

6 Bentham in Burns and Hart, ibid., p. 11.

7 J.S. Mill, *Utilitarianism*. Originally published in 1861. See J.S. Mill, *Utilitarianism*, Project Gutenberg, February 22, 2004. Online, https://www.gutenberg.org/files/11224/11224-h/11224-h.htm (accessed February 15, 2018).

8 P. Singer, *Animal Liberation*, New York: Harper Collins, 1975.

9 For example, see P. Singer, 'Voluntary euthanasia: A utilitarian perspective,' *Bioethics*, vol. 17 no. 5–6, 2003, 526–41.

10 Bentham, op. cit., p. 38.

11 P. Singer, op. cit.

12 M. Sandel, *Justice: What's the Right Thing to Do?* New York: Farrar, Straus and Giroux, 2008.

13 A. Gosseries, *Intergenerational Justice*, Oxford: Oxford University Press, 2009.

14 N. Machiavelli, *The Prince*, N.H. Thompson (trans.), New York: Dover Thrift, 1532/1992, pp. 20–3.

15 For more information see History.com Staff, 'My Lai massacre,' *History.com*, 2009, A+E Networks. Online, http://www.history.com/topics/vietnam-war/my-lai-massacre (accessed February 17, 2018).

16 M. Velasquez, C. Andre, T. Shanks, and M.J. Meyer, 'Ethical relativism,' *Markkula Center for Applied Ethics*,

August 1, 1992. Online, https://www.scu.edu/ethics/ethics-resources/ethical-decision-making/ethical-relativism/ (accessed February 17, 2018).

17 A.J. Wakefield, S.H. Murch, A. Anthony et al., 'Ileal-lymphoid-nodular hyperplasia, non-specific colitis, and pervasive developmental disorder in children,' *The Lancet*, vol. 351, 1998, 637–41.

18 P. Offit, *Autism's False Prophets: Bad Science, Risky Medicine, and the Search for a Cure*, New York: Columbia University Press, 2008.

19 J. Burns, 'British medical council bars doctor who linked vaccine with autism,' *New York Times*, May 24, 2010. Online, http://www.nytimes.com/2010/05/25/health/policy/25autism.html (accessed February 14, 2018).

20 E. Harroll, 'Doctor in MMR-autism scare ruled unethical,' *Time*, January 29, 2010. Online, http://content.time.com/time/health/article/0,8599,1957656,00.html (accessed February 14, 2018).

21 Offit, op. cit.

22 Harroll, op. cit.

23 S. Murch et al., 'Retraction of an interpretation,' *The Lancet*, vol. 363, 2004, 75.

24 The Editors of *The Lancet*, 'Retraction – Ileal-lymphoid-Nodular hyperplasia, non-specific colitis, and pervasive developmental disorder in children,' *The Lancet*, vol. 375, 2010, 445.

25 Burns, op. cit.

26 Offit, op. cit.

27 See K.C. Van Meter et al., 'Geographic distribution of autism in California: A retrospective birth cohort analysis,' *Autism Research*, vol. 3 no. 1, 2010,19–29; N. Micali, S. Chakrabarti, and S. Fombonne, 'The broad autism phenotype: Findings from an epidemiological survey,' *Autism*, vol. 8 no. 1, 2004, 21–37; and L. Carroll and M. Owen, 'Genetic overlap between autism, schizophrenia, and bipolar disorder,' *Genome Medicine*, vol. 1 no. 10, 2009. Online, https://genomemedicine.biomedcentral.com/articles/10.1186/gm102 (accessed February 14, 2018); and K.E. Towbin et al., 'Autism spectrum traits in children with mood and anxiety disorders,' *Journal of Child and Adolescent Psychopharmacology*, vol. 15 no. 3, 2005, 452–64.

28 Van Meter et al., ibid.

29 J. Zipprich et al., 'Measles outbreak – California, December 2014–February 2015,' *Morbidity and Mortality Weekly Report*, February 20, 2015, Atlanta: Centers for Disease Control and Prevention. Online, https://www.cdc.gov/mmwr/preview/mmwrhtml/mm6406a5.htm (accessed February 15, 2018).

30 M.S. Majumder, E.L. Cohn, S.R. Mekaru et al., 'Substandard vaccination compliance and the 2015 measles outbreak,' *JAMA Pediatrics*, vol. 169 no. 5, 2015, 494–5. Online, https://jamanetwork.com/journals/jamapediatrics/fullarticle/2203906 (assessed February 15, 2018).

31 Majumder et al., ibid.

32 Majumder et al., op. cit.

33 K.M. Edwards and J.M. Hackell, 'Countering vaccine hesitancy,' *American Academy of Pediatrics Clinical Report*, August 2016. Online, http://pediatrics.aappublications.org/content/early/2016/08/25/peds.2016-2146 (accessed February 15, 2018).

34 Edwards and Hackell, ibid.

4

Virtue ethics

Matthew Sowcik and Austin Council

FRAMING QUESTION

What virtues should a leader possess to act ethically?

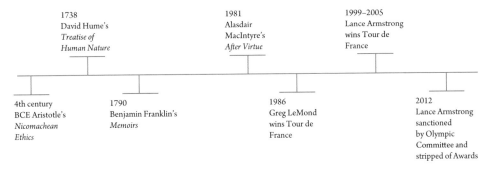

Figure 4.1 Timeline of major works on virtue ethics in relation to the chapter case study

In Benjamin Franklin's memoirs, he points out that his troubled childhood, multiple failed business ventures, and his overall gloomy disposition eventually caused him to leave home at an early age.[1] Disappointed with where his life was heading, Franklin decided to create a list of twelve virtues that he would aim to live by each day. His list included: temperance, silence, order, resolution, frugality, industry, sincerity, justice, moderation, cleanliness, tranquility, and chastity.[2]

As the story goes, Franklin took the list to a well-respected Quaker friend who said, 'Ben, are you serious? Because you sure aren't any of these things now.' Franklin, who was indeed very serious about practicing these virtues, assured his friend that, although he didn't currently possess any of these virtues, he someday would. His friend responded, 'Ben, if you are serious about this endeavor, you will need to add a thirteenth virtue – humility. Because you don't have any.' Franklin thought about his friend's advice and decided to, indeed, add a thirteenth virtue to his list – the virtue of humility.

From that point forward, Franklin began to reshape his life. Every day he would read his list of virtues, and each week he would practice exercising a different virtue on his list. He would go on to become one of the most industrious, prosperous and self-actualizing inventors, politicians and statesmen in the history of the United States. In his autobiography, Franklin mentions that near his death he was reviewing the story of how he came about his list of virtues, and wrote that he had come to feel solidarity with each of his twelve virtues. However, when he pondered the thirteenth virtue, he realized that he was nowhere near humble.[3]

One has to wonder if this act of denying his own humility might actually be the only proof you need to believe that Franklin was, indeed, humble; however, there are other examples of Franklin's humility helping him to achieve some of his most outstanding accomplishments. On the top of this list was the speech he gave on the final day of the Constitutional Convention in Philadelphia. Knowing how important it was to reach a consensus concerning the Constitution of the United States he said:

> I confess that there are several parts of this constitution which I do not at present approve, but I am not sure I shall never approve them: For having lived long, I have experienced many instances of being obliged by better information, or fuller consideration, to change opinions even on important subjects, which I once thought right, but found to be otherwise. It is therefore that the older I grow, the more apt I am to doubt my own judgment, and to pay more respect to the judgment of others.[4]

Some suggest that it was this humility displayed by Benjamin Franklin, and not some 'near-divine insight of the individual delegates,' that was the reason for the success of the Constitutional Convention.[5]

Benjamin Franklin is just one example of many distinguished leaders throughout history who have practiced virtue ethics to achieve great outcomes. However, as author John Steinbeck suggests, 'We value virtue but do not discuss it. The honest bookkeeper, the faithful wife, the earnest scholar gets little of our attention compared to the embezzler, the tramp, and the cheat.'[6] As leadership emerged as a field of study, scholars paid little attention to virtue and ethics. However, this quickly changed when we in the field encountered the embezzler, the tramp, and the cheat. Today, the study of ethical leadership has exploded due to our increased exposure to all kinds of corruption and scandal. The case studies featured in this book, drawn from the fields of sports, medicine, politics and business are just a few illustrations of the way leaders' ethical failings have informed our current understanding of leadership.

In this chapter, we will first take a broad view of the topic of virtue ethics, and then go into depth concerning one virtue in particular – humility. At the end of the chapter, we will present a case study that explores the role of virtue, and specifically humility, in addressing ethics and leadership in the world of professional cycling. As a result of our discussion here, we hope that you will have a better grasp of the role virtue ethics plays in the leadership process, and specifically the importance for leaders to have humility.

History

Definitions of 'virtue' usually relate to a person's demeanor or disposition to act in a particular way that most people would see as decent and upright.[7] The most notable philosopher in the study of virtue ethics is Aristotle. He proposed in his *Nicomachean Ethics* that an ethical person should demonstrate *many* virtues, but identified the four cardinal virtues as prudence, temperance, courage and justice.[8] Virtue ethics, according to Aristotle, focuses on moral and ethical *activity* or *action*, not how someone decides to act or behave morally.[9]

Aristotle's framework of virtue ethics emphasized the importance of the 'good society' and the 'good life.' His writings on virtue ethics focus on the choices and decisions individuals make and how they move to their 'final good end,' or the Greek word *telos*, which means 'complete.'[10] To reach this end, a person must align him or herself with the practicing of virtues and make the effort to obtain 'happiness,' or the Greek word *eudaimonia*. To achieve happiness, an individual must actually practice these virtues. In sum, Aristotle's virtue ethics focuses on the process of a person acting virtuously to reach wholeness or completeness, and in so doing, achieving happiness.

But Aristotle was not the only philosopher to emphasize the importance of leaders practicing virtue. The concept is found in Eastern and Western religions and wisdom traditions, and its trajectory spans thousands of years and across various cultures. For example, in ancient Egypt, the term *Ma'at* was the traditional notion of truth, justice, harmony, balance, order, reciprocity and righteousness.[11] In the Jewish tradition, the Hebrew phrase *middot tovot* refers to positive virtues, such as wisdom, humility, kindness, compassion, righteousness, integrity and tranquility that offer a strong and principled direction for living out our lives. In devoting oneself to these virtues, one can 'spiral upward' and begin to be in unison with God's wishes and desires for humanity.[12] Similarly, Hinduism outlines several virtues in the *Bhagavad Gita*, some of which include fearlessness, purity, service with love and the control of one's senses.[13] Buddhism tells its adherents to follow the Eight-Fold

Path by practicing right understanding, thought, speech, action, livelihood, effort, mindfulness and concentration. By practicing these virtues, Buddhists believe seekers can find enlightenment. Taoism proposes that its followers nurture the 'three treasures' of compassion, simplicity and humility.[14] For Confucius, virtue was seen as attaining one's full 'potential.'[15] Specifically, he viewed virtue as attempting to achieve excellence in our interactions with others.[16] In Christianity, the three main virtues a person should exemplify are 'faith, hope, and love, the greatest of which is love.'[17] Finally, Islam speaks of virtue in the Qu'ran as *Ma'ruf*, or things that are celebrated and well-known. These virtues include traits and behaviors such as honesty, sincerity, politeness, perseverance, determination and courage.[18] In short, religions and wisdom traditions all over the world encourage their followers to practice virtue ethics in order to achieve a good life and have done so for millennia.

In the last several hundred years, notable philosophers such as René Descartes, Immanuel Kant, and Friedrich Nietzsche have all weighed in on the concept of virtue. Coming from a pragmatic point of view, French philosopher Descartes defined virtue as using one's free will to exercise good.[19] According to Descartes, virtue was 'a firm and constant resolution to carry out to the letter all the things which one judges to be best, and to employ all the powers of one's mind in finding out what these are.'[20] According to Kant (whom you read about in Chapter 2) virtue was 'what is unqualifiedly good . . . not an end-state such as pleasure or the performance of certain atomic acts in conformity to rules, but a state of character which becomes the basis for all of one's actions.'[21] German philosopher Nietzsche explained that to flourish in life we must not merely find quiet gratification, but we should continuously be overcoming and strengthening ourselves.[22] These philosophers have made an impact on how we understand virtue ethics today, and we can see this in contemporary philosophers who are once again calling on societies to esteem and individuals to practice virtue.

One of the most influential contributors to the revival of the study of virtue ethics is Alastair MacIntyre.[23] MacIntyre defines virtues as '. . . dispositions not only to act in particular ways but also to feel in particular ways. To act virtuously . . . is to act from inclination formed by the cultivation of virtues.'[24] In other words, MacIntyre, in agreement with Aristotle, views virtuous activity and behavior as something that is crafted over the course of a person's life and must be developed. Where MacIntyre differs from Aristotle is in the implications of virtues for all human beings. According to MacIntyre, the cultivation of virtues does not suggest that there might be a unifying state of being or 'a good life' that is for all individuals at all times.[25] MacIntyre notes that people's diverse experiences in various sorts of communities play a significant role in determining their journey of virtue development.[26] In other words, the cultivation of virtues to achieve *eudaimonia* on the way toward *telos* is not universal for all human beings and depends on the context of each person's past experiences and the community from which they came.

Contemporary thinking has also seen the notion of virtue ethics infiltrate the fields of psychology and, as we mention later in the chapter, leadership. According to Peterson and Seligman, historically, psychology has mainly focused on the patient as a passive vessel 'responding to stimuli.'[27] However, current researchers have suggested a shift in thinking toward positive psychology by developing certain characteristics and virtues that could lead a person to live a healthier, more stable existence.[28] All of the historical and contemporary paradigms of virtue ethics mentioned here relate the concept to an inner perspective of moral character and reference a sort of trajectory in one's life, that of reaching a state of authenticity. However, before addressing the impact virtue ethics has on leadership, let's explore some of the major concepts found throughout the study of the idea.

Major concepts of virtue ethics

Virtue ethics is one of the major approaches to addressing normative ethics, or the ethical standards that address what is morally right and wrong. Different than other approaches to normative ethics, like those focusing on duty and obligation or the consequences of one's actions, virtue ethics emphasizes virtuous traits that develop into good habits of character leading one to live an honorable or 'good life' and have 'good' moral character.

Character

Virtue ethics, distinguishing itself from many other ethical approaches, focuses on the *disposition of character* within the person as they perform an action.[29] If you take into account one of Franklin's thirteen virtues, such as silence, it is easy to see the different approaches and why it is important to consider virtues when defining ethical standards. For example, if a friend of Benjamin Franklin were to approach him and begin to gossip about a common friend, there would be three possible ethical options based on virtue ethics. First, Franklin could feel obligated to the friend and the friend's feelings, which would require that he join in on the gossip. Looking at just the consequences of his actions, if he gossips and the person he is gossiping about finds out about it, he was certainly less than honorable based on the outcome. However, if he does not gossip and the gossiping friend feels betrayed, then that is equally less honorable based on this outcome. It is clear, then, that Franklin needs to rely on his second of the thirteen virtues, 'silence,' to determine what to do. This silence would ensure that no matter what the obligation or outcome, Franklin would be operating out of good moral character.

Practicing virtue

This leads us to the question, 'How does one practice virtue?' Virtues and moral capacities are believed to be developed and learned through practice.[30] Individuals, including leaders, can be taught by their family and communities to be morally upright human beings. Furthering these assertions, Besser and Slote explain, '. . . the emphasis both in ancient and recently revived virtue ethics has been on acquired/developed human character at the personal level, on what it is to become a virtuous person.'[31] Using this framework, virtue ethicists would suggest that one must react to a scenario like a skilled artisan who instantly understands what to do in a situation without explicitly having to apply rules.[32] This decision in a person's response would come from the temperament to act by acquiring and expressing virtues. It is helpful to better understand the differences between the different components of normative ethics and how virtues are developed if we dig deeper into a single virtue. Although there are numerous virtues we could choose to explore further, humility, Franklin's thirteenth virtue, will provide us with the perfect opportunity to discuss how virtues impact leadership.

Isolating one virtue, humility, will allow us to focus on how a leader might consider virtue as an ethical framework for leadership. The virtuous leader would not isolate one single virtue, but in this chapter we focus on humility as a means to highlight the ethical approach. Humility is an important virtue for leaders, and – as mentioned earlier – it is also valued cross-culturally, which makes it a prime virtue for leaders of diverse groups.

The virtue of humility

Now that we have a basic understanding of the importance of virtue and virtue ethics, let's explore one particular virtue as a means to better understand the relationship between virtue ethics and leadership. In recent years, research on ethical leadership has begun to move toward incorporating virtues in both leadership theory and practice, with humility leading the way in this arena. However, what exactly does it mean to be humble? Virtue ethicists, theologians, psychologists, scholars and practitioners have long debated the definition of humility. In this chapter, it is not our intent to provide one 'correct' definition of humility, but rather to present a variety of perspectives, viewpoints and opinions on this virtue, including our own.

As we noted earlier, historically religious traditions such as Hinduism, Buddhism, Taoism, Judaism, Christianity and Islam, among others, have emphasized the importance of virtue; not the least of these is the virtue of humility. For example, in the revered Hindu writings of the *Bhagavad Gita*, humility is viewed as one of the most important virtues.[33] An individual's ability to comprehend their place in the universe, along with one's relation to all things, reduces someone's view of himself or herself and 'confirms that one is only a part of an integrated whole – no more important, valuable or significant than any other part.'[34] In Buddhism, humility is a core virtue, and an essential characteristic of a person's path to enlightenment.[35] For someone to show kindness for others, understanding their similar dilemma, and at the same time move toward the awareness that 'the self' is an imaginary notion in the midst of the coexistence of all lives and activities, is 'essentially a Buddhist concept of humility.'[36] In Judaism, humility is seen as one of the pillar virtues of the faith.[37] In the *Tanakh*, in the books of Psalms and Proverbs, the 'fear of the Lord,' which is known as the uppermost virtue, is paralleled to humility and 'reverence before God.'[38] The New Testament, a cornerstone surrounding Jesus of Nazareth's teachings and the stories of his life, reiterates humility.[39] For example, in the book of John, Jesus assumes the position of a servant when he washes the feet of his disciples the night before he is crucified. Humility is also a foundational piece to practicing Islam. In his discussion about humility, Tariq Ramadan in *Western Muslims and the Future of Islam* writes that within the Islamic tradition there are different states of human life, those of innocence and responsibility.[40] He goes on to argue, 'By marrying the two states of innocence and responsibility, humility is the state that allows the human being to enter into its humanity. Humility is the source of ethics.'[41] Great leaders such as Mahatma Gandhi dedicated their lives to 'modesty, humility, and sacrifice;'[42] and Mother Teresa of Calcutta once said, 'Humility always radiates the greatness and glory of God. Through humility we grow in love. Humility is the beginning of sanctity.'[43]

Yet, our modern-day world actually encourages *pride*, not humility. When attempting to place fault for social misfortunes such as drug abuse, alcoholism, and violence, our contemporary culture blames low self-esteem.[44] The drive to revere self-esteem conjures up images of self-help books and public initiatives. Individuals now celebrate pride as tolerable and worthy of praise, whether it manifests itself in overestimating one's positive qualities or being overconfident about one's self.

Though pride can lead to an overall sense of well-being and happiness, it also has its pitfalls, namely, an imbalance of self-awareness. When we continually focus on ourselves in a positive way, we can easily overlook the dangers that surround us. Neuroscientist Tali Sharot suggests our over-optimistic view about our future life may positively impact our health (less anxiety and stress), however, being overconfident about our health can actually be toxic. According to Sharot, 'Underestimating risk may reduce precautionary behavior such as safe sex, attending medical screenings or buying insurance ... It could potentially promote harmful behaviors such as smoking, overspending, and unhealthy eating.'[45] It is important to note that the pride we are referring to in this chapter is hubristic pride, which is derived from the Greek word *hubris* meaning 'exaggerated pride or self-confidence.'

Hubristic pride is in stark contrast to authentic pride, which, according to Tracy and Robbins is derived from 'specific goals and accomplishments or goal attainments and is often focused on the efforts made towards the goal. Hubristic pride, on the other hand, is related instead to more global beliefs about abilities and strengths, as reflected in statements such as "I do everything well" or "I am naturally talented."'[46] What should we do to counteract this dangerous imbalance of overconfidence and high self-esteem as characterized by hubristic pride? For us, the obvious answer would be a healthy dose of humility.

However, there have often been negative connotations associated with humility.[47] Sometimes a humble person can be viewed as feeble and submissive, lacking self-confidence and self-admiration.[48] Others might connect humility with disgrace, provoking images of shame, embarrassment or disgust with one's self. Despite these differing views, more recent research on the topic encourages a picture of humility that does not include self-disparagement. Contemporary research on science, humility and positive psychology has shed new light on how we can begin to define humility, which reframes our perception of this important construct and provides hope for its future in research and education. In an analysis of current literature, scholars have identified a number of humility's essential qualities, such as: an accurate (not misjudged) sense of one's capabilities and successes; the skill to acknowledge one's shortcomings, flaws, spaces in knowledge, and limitations (often with a suggestion of a 'higher power'); openness to new ideas, opposing information and guidance; keeping one's talents and triumphs in perspective, a generally low focus of the self or an ability to 'overlook the self'; and, an admiration for the worth of all things, as well as the many diverse ways that people and things can contribute to our world.[49]

With this said, there is a difference between humility and modesty, which primarily refers to the moderate estimation of one's distinctions or accomplishments.[50] Contrary to humility, modesty is more of a socially positioned virtue – a way of exhibiting one's self that can result from situational demands and difficulties. Humility, contrarily, involves an inclination to see the self accurately, including both faults and inadequacies. Humble people will not intentionally misconstrue information in order to protect, fix, or validate their own persona.[51] For humble individuals, there should be no stride toward arrogance, and no passionate craving to view or present themselves as being better than they really are. As French philosopher Michel de Montaigne once noted, 'If we mount us on stilts, well and good, for on stilts it is our own legs we walk on; and we sit upon the highest throne in the world, yet we sit upon our own tail.'[52]

As we continue to advance a common definition of humility, we would like to suggest a few factors that are present in much of current literature on this idea. First, most definitions of humility discuss an accurate awareness and acceptance by the individual. This proper perspective allows individuals to see experiences in their lives as neither better or worse than they are, but with a great deal of accuracy and clarity.

An additional consideration when defining humility is the different contexts in which the proper perspective takes place. The most commonly represented meaning of humility is 'an accurate view of oneself.' This includes one's ability to assess the strengths and limitations of one's character without exaggeration, leading to increased self-awareness. The next vital context in which to apply proper perspective is in one's relationship with others. This includes having an accurate perception of the relationship one has with others, which provides a leader the opportunity to see the inherent value of others including the strengths that others bring to the relationship and task.

The final context that the literature addresses is the awareness of one's place in the larger world. This focus on the broader environment allows the individual to connect back to their role in the grander system and away from self-preoccupation. It is the proper perspective or balance of competing forces like being both inward and outward focused or realizing both one's importance and insignificance. This leads to the definition of the term we will utilize for this chapter: '*humility is a proper perspective of oneself, one's relationship with others and one's place in the larger environment.*' It is also important to note that much of the leadership development industry and field of leadership education begins by using assessment tools to help clients or students develop an accurate perception of themselves. Resources such as

360 feedback surveys, StrengthsFinder, personality inventories and similar instruments are all trying to create insight for the leader by refining his or her sense of self – both their abilities and weaknesses.

This chapter has focused on defining virtue ethics and its relation to humility and leadership. We have painted the concepts of virtue ethics and humility in a positive light, providing that a person who leads a virtuous life and practices humility can have a constructive impact on his or her relationship with leaders, followers and the organization as a whole. We have discussed a variety of religious traditions, historical perspectives and contemporary scholarly views associated with virtue ethics and, specifically, humility, which have highlighted the importance of these universal concepts and their many facets.

Critiques of virtue ethics

In the spirit of true humility, there must also be space provided to address the critiques and criticisms of both virtue ethics and humility. The next section is committed to outlining common criticisms related to these concepts. It is important to provide a brief overview of the critiques often associated with this ethical approach, to balance the assertions we have made.

Unobtainable and elitist?

One major criticism related to virtue is the perception that the notion is demanding and elitist, reserved only for the privileged few.[53] Discussing why virtue might be difficult for disadvantaged groups of people, Ethicist Barbro Fröding explains, 'The virtuous life can appear very hard and it may take time to grasp that this is the best life available and, as such, the most rational choice. As a result, the quality of upbringing and the society around us, as well as the laws, are key to the successful development of virtue.'[54] Fröding is asserting that, although the virtuous life is what we should strive to work towards, and is the logical decision based on the intrinsic benefits it provides, some populations have more difficulty developing a life of virtue than others. This, of course, is based on a variety of circumstances including upbringing and socio-economic status, to name a few. Consider the example of a person whose parents spend time teaching them the steps towards a virtuous life along with placing them in educational environments that reinforce these teachings. From this perspective, one could argue that this person's opportunities to develop a virtuous life makes it easier than someone who did not have these advantages. This viewpoint lends itself closely to another critique of virtue ethics, namely, the situationist point of view.

The situationist perspective

A major philosophical view that frequently clashes with virtue ethics is the situationist perspective. According to this critique, evidence about people's unique personality traits, views, outlooks, morals or past conduct is not as beneficial for defining what they will do as much as 'information about the details of their situations.'[55] In essence, one could imagine that if a person possesses a certain character attribute (like kindness), they would act in congruence (kindly) in different settings that are comparable to the related (kind) manner. However, under trial or experimental circumstances, an individual's actions are not found to be cross-circumstantially stable.[56]

Take, for example, the Milgram Experiment conducted by psychologist Stanley Milgram at Yale University in the 1960s. (We will circle back to the Milgram Experiments when we talk about followership later in this volume.) Participants of the study were designated as 'teacher' and 'learner.' The teacher was given the power by the experimenters to shock a learner with incremental levels of gradually higher voltage if he or she answered a question incorrectly – it was revealed at the end of the experiment that the shocks were fake.[57] The point of the experiment was to see how far a person is willing to progress in an objective and measurable situation in which he or she is ordered to inflict increasing amounts of pain on a victim (that is, the 'learner').[58] Despite frequent protests and criticisms by the 'learners,' of the forty volunteers in the experiment, twenty-five obeyed the orders of the experimenter to the end, punishing the victim until they reached the most severe shock able to be administered.[59] Despite the fact that some of the 'teachers' were hypothetically kind people, in a situation where their virtues were tested, the majority of them behaved in a manner that was all but virtuous. This leads us to the final critique, which examines how difficult it is to objectively identify a virtuous human being.

Who is virtuous?

Another difficulty with respect to virtue is how one goes about determining who is virtuous? When we place our attention on the *qualities of a person* rather than the *qualities of an act*, it becomes extremely difficult to know with any confidence if a person really is virtuous.[60] Similarly, an additional critique on virtue comes from a consequentialist perspective regarding the motivation behind the virtues themselves.[61] These critiques have revolved around how many people can actually become virtuous based on their upbringing and lived experience; the situationist perspective, which challenges the consistency of character-traits in different situations; the question of measurement and identification of who is virtuous; and lastly, what makes the motivations behind a virtuous being moral or immoral?

Critiques of the virtue of humility

Now that we have considered some of the major critiques of virtue ethics in general, let's take a closer look at the critiques about humility as a virtue. Despite our brief examination of humility as a positive quality, there are also limitations to this idea.

Good for nothing?

The Scottish Enlightenment philosopher David Hume disapproved of humility, which he considered to be one of the 'monkish virtues,' characterized by 'having no purpose' and not contributing to self-satisfaction, advancement or value:[62]

> Celibacy, fasting, penance, mortification, self-denial, humility, silence, solitude, and the whole train of monkish virtues; for what reason are they everywhere rejected by men of sense, but because they serve no manner of purpose; neither advance a man's fortune in the world, nor render him a more valuable member of society; neither qualify him for the entertainment of company, nor increase his power of self-enjoyment? We observe, on the contrary, that they cross all these desirable ends; stupefy the understanding and harden the heart, obscure the fancy and sour the temper. We justly, therefore, transfer them to the opposite column, and place them in the catalogue of vices; nor has any superstition force sufficient among men of the world, to pervert entirely these natural sentiments.[63]

By calling them 'monkish virtues,' Hume asserts that these virtues carry no benefit for the individual choosing to pursue them. In the case of humility, Hume echoes what many philosophers, academics and researchers believe to be its greatest downfall: the risk of humbling oneself or losing oneself so much that the self is lost entirely and the individual is left without the ability to advance him or herself. In essence, humility can be viewed as a sign of feebleness and submission, effectively hindering growth because the interest of the self is gone. Aside from being critiqued as not valuable, humility may be faulted as not being clearly defined, or lacking uniformity and agreement with its definition.

Too many definitions

A common criticism of humility is the multiple definitions for the concept. For example, according to one scholar, 'One obstacle in humility research involves varying definitions of the construct. For many, humility simply means holding oneself in low regard.'[64] Similarly, another definition describes humility in correlation with low self-esteem.[65] Alternatively, other scholars provide a more constructive, pragmatic approach to humility by explaining, 'Humility also involves accurate self-awareness of strengths and weaknesses, which allows humble individuals to acknowledge and take into account their limitations and inadequacies, especially when confronted by others who believe differently.'[66] When you start examining the virtue of humility, it becomes apparent that there is still no uniform consensus on how the concept is defined, leaving much room for debate among scholars and practitioners. Numerous viewpoints must be taken into account and the research on this particular virtue is still evolving. Along with the lack of clarity around the definition is another tangible critique of humility, the question of measurement.

Overconfidence and the measurement problem

When discussing the psychology of humility, one scholar explains, 'Biased self-assessments also distort managerial judgment. When groups are comparable, most people consider their own group superior.'[67] Other scholars also comment on this criticism by asking, 'To what extent can we trust a person who reports that he or she is modest or humble?'[68] Another fundamental question surrounding humility is whether the idea is more favorable toward disposition or situation. Essentially this criticism asks the question, 'Is humility at the core of one's personality or is it something acted upon in any given situation?'[69] In sum, the majority of the criticisms and critiques revolving around the notion of humility pertain to how the construct almost serves no purpose toward self-satisfaction or personal value, the concept has a wide range of competing definitions, lacks clarity surrounding measurement, and questions humility's relationship to a person's disposition or a particular situation.

Five component analysis

Now that we have a more complete understanding of virtue ethics and, specifically, the virtue of humility, let's take a closer look at how these ideas apply to the Five Components of Leadership Model described in Chapter 1. Remember, in Chapter 1, the editors defined leadership as 'The process by

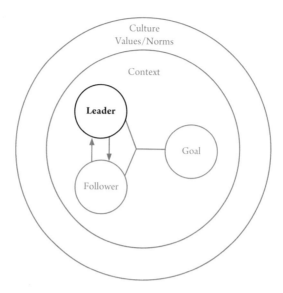

Figure 4.2 The Five Components of Leadership Model applied to virtue ethics

which leaders and followers develop a relationship and work together toward a goal (or goals) within a context shaped by cultural values and norms.'[70] We will now take some time to examine the role of virtue ethics in each of these components.

As we can see in Figure 4.2, *virtue ethics centers squarely upon the leader.* It can be argued, especially when positional aspects of leadership come into play, that leaders often have more authority, control and power than their followers. With this increased power comes increased ethical responsibility. Leaders with power and control have additional expectations placed on them to be sensitive to how their leadership impacts their followers' lives. They also have the responsibility to establish positive expectations of the work environment. While all of us have an ethical responsibility to treat others as we would like to be treated, leaders have a unique responsibility because they 'set the bar' for their followers and organizations and have a greater opportunity to influence others in meaningful ways.[71]

Even though it may be true that 'with great power comes great responsibility,' leaders often fail to live up to this expectation. Sometimes, with great power comes an increased sense of self-worth and overconfidence, and many times leaders start to believe that the rules do not apply to them. This narcissism often prevents leaders from asking for help, being open to new ideas or – at its worst – engaging in unethical behavior that hurts their followers. The virtue of humility has been shown to mitigate this power and counterbalance the narcissism of leaders.[72] As Owens, Wallace and Waldman suggest

'Narcissistic leaders may not be doomed to fail and may not necessarily need to abandon their strong agentic tendencies if they can instead allow these tendencies to be tempered by counterbalancing characteristics.'[73] One of the counterbalancing characteristics the authors are describing is humility and is critically important to the leader's success. The impact of virtues does not impact the leader alone, because leadership is a relational process, virtues like humility can have a significant impact on the followers.

But virtues are not an exclusively leader-centric proposition. The role of the follower in both leadership and virtue ethics is critical to the moral conduct of both the leader and the follower. As Kouzes and Posner point out in their book *The Leadership Challenge*, 'Leadership is a relationship between those who aspire to lead and those who choose to follow. It's the quality of this relationship that matters most when we're engaged in getting extraordinary things done.'[74] The authors go on to say, 'Humility is the only way to resolve the conflicts and contradictions of leadership. You can avoid excessive pride only if you recognize that you are human and need the help of others.'[75]

Humility impacts the leader–follower relationship in two significant ways. If leaders have a proper perspective of the relationship with their followers, as Kouzes and Posner suggest, then leaders are more inclined to see their followers as individuals first and employees – or any part of an organizational chart – second. Virtuous leaders see themselves at the same level as their followers. It is often when a leader perceives himself or herself as 'better' or 'special' in comparison to others that problematic ethical issues surface.

The second major way humility impacts the leader–follower relationship is the modeling of the virtue. When leaders are operating out of virtue, it naturally encourages the follower to behave in the same manner as the leader. Instead of an oppressive, top-down 'leader knows best' environment, the follower is empowered to act for the good of achieving the common goal. If a leader operates from a place of virtue – for example, by demonstrating humility – it becomes an invitation to the follower to actively engage with others and also manifest virtue. By establishing shared virtues, the leader and follower co-create an environment where shared values and beliefs govern how people behave in the context.

If we take a look back at the beginning of the chapter and Franklin's thirteen virtues, it is easy to see the influence virtues can have on leader/follower goals. Virtue ethics provides leaders and followers with an avenue toward setting goals based on 'good' ethical intention, not simply on the outcome of the goal. In this case, the leader and his or her followers can establish a set of virtues that will drive both decision-making and goal setting. These virtues then can be used throughout the environment to help others to both set and justify their ethical decisions on a common set of virtues.

Some could argue that different contexts may require different virtues to be successful. A virtue, like humility for example, may be perceived as a strength in certain contexts and a liability in others. Research conducted by Exline and Geyer found that when participants were reporting on whether humility was a strength in particular social roles, there were perceived distinctions between the importance humility played in different positions. The researchers noticed, 'people were more likely to see humility as a strength in social roles that specifically emphasized virtue or positive social relationships. They were less decisive about whether humility would be a strength in roles that might require assertion, leadership, or entertainment value.'[76] Two additional contexts which can have an impact on people's perspective of the role different virtues play in social roles like leadership are the historical and future contexts. Even though individuals were currently less decisive about whether humility was a strength in leadership, this is not to say that perception will not be different in the future. Often what helps to change perceptions in the current contexts is the last component of the Five Components of Leadership Model – cultural values and norms.

Given the definition of virtue ethics and the practical components of the concept, it is important to question whether or not it is possible to agree on a universal, cross-cultural list of core virtues. The answer may be eye opening. According to Peterson and Seligman, 'a surprising amount of similarity across cultures strongly indicates a historical and cross-cultural convergence of six core virtues: courage, justice, humanity, temperance, transcendence and wisdom.'[77] Rushworth Kidder also identifies several common virtues that leaders seem to hold across cultures.[78] Many of these virtues – and specifically the virtue of humility – were also highlighted at the beginning of this chapter when discussing the place of honor humility holds in many of the world's religions and wisdom traditions. These are just a few examples of how the five components of leadership are impacted by virtue ethics and humility.

Now let's take an in-depth look into a specific case study that draws out these different components and emphasizes their relationship to the virtue of humility.

CASE STUDY

A tale of two cyclists[79]

Greg LeMond

Against the backdrop of the Eiffel Tower, Laurent Fignon, a French road bicycle racer, began the grandest pursuit in the Tour de France, the final stage. 'The Professor,' as Fignon was called, would be defending the coveted yellow jersey from his major challenger, an American cyclist. However, it was already assumed due to the dramatic time difference between the leader and challenger that Fignon would have an easy victory. In fact, French newspapers had already begun preparing the following day's paper with Fignon's victory covering the front page.[80]

The American, who had been in this spot before and who had come out victorious, was using the newest science to help him perform better than the other cyclists, including Fignon. However, at the beginning of this race, he was assuredly not considered a favorite and some suggested that the best he could hope for was to make it into the top-twenty. Nevertheless, after 2,000 miles, it was clear that the race would come down to a photo finish. What made this so extraordinary was the hardship that the American cyclist had to overcome to just be in the race. Many people considered him a hero just for coming back from the adversity he faced over the past two years, but here he was about to win another Tour de France. The American cyclist, Greg LeMond, would go on to win the 1989 Tour de France and beat Fignon by only eight seconds.

Five years earlier, in 1984, LeMond was in his first Tour de France and finished third in support of the team leader, who happened to be no other than 'The Professor,' Laurent Fignon.[81] In 1985, LeMond switched teams and was asked to humbly support team captain Bernard Hinault win his fifth Tour de France. After playing his role as 'dutiful lieutenant,' LeMond finished second. However, due to his service, Hinault promised to repay LeMond by helping him win the following year.[82]

In 1986, Greg LeMond would go on to win his first Tour de France becoming the first American to achieve the distinction. Though, it did not come without its fair share of controversy. Bernard Hinault, who had promised to support LeMond a year earlier, decided he was interested in winning again and competed with LeMond throughout the entire race. When a reporter asked Hinault the reason he consistently attacked his teammate, LeMond, he replied, 'Because I felt like it . . . If he doesn't buckle, that means he's a champion and deserves to win the race. I did it for his own good.'[83]

Then in 1987, LeMond would have to overcome several life-altering adverse experiences. First, he fell off a bike and fractured his left wrist. Then, while recovering from the injury in the United States, he was out hunting and was accidentally shot by his brother-in-law. LeMond almost died, entering the hospital with 10–30 pellets inside of him and losing 65 percent of his blood volume.[84] When returning for surgery a few months later to address obstruction due to adhesions, he asked the doctor also to take out his appendix so he could use that as the excuse for the operation. Without this excuse, some would have raised

CASE STUDY *(continued)*

questions about his recovery and LeMond's team would have more than likely moved on without him. In 1988, Greg started his road to recovery with numerous shotgun pellets still in him, including five in his liver and three in the lining of his heart.[85]

Unfortunately, that was not the only obstacle that LeMond had to overcome during his triumphant return to cycling greatness. In 1988, he learned that his team was doping and decided to change teams for fear that he would be pressured to use performance-enhancing drugs. He purposefully made the decision to move from one of the strongest teams in the sport to a brand-new team, with no track record, in keeping with his values.

The rest, as they say, is history. LeMond won the 1989 Tour de France by knowing as much as anyone about cutting edge nutrition and aerodynamics, including the advantage he gained by utilizing new aero bars and an aero helmet. It has been suggested that these tools may have given LeMond up to a minute advantage over Laurent Fignon in the final time trial. After the win, LeMond went on to gain tremendous stardom including signing, at that point in time, the richest contract in the sport's history. In 1989 Greg LeMond was named 'Sportsman of the Year' by *Sports Illustrated*, which was the first time a cyclist received the honor.[86] He would go on to repeat his win as the Tour de France champion the following year.

Thinking back on his life, LeMond recognized that the sport had changed because of performance-enhancing drugs and it was difficult for him to keep up. In hindsight, he said, 'Something had changed in cycling. The speeds were faster and riders that I had easily outperformed were now dropping me.'[87] Finally, in 1994, he was told that if he was unwilling to use performance-enhancing drugs, he would be unlikely ever to win another race.[88] Greg LeMond would win his last major race, the Tour du Pont, in 1992, because of his choice to not use performance-enhancing drugs.

Lance Armstrong

In 1992, Lance Armstrong started to compete on the biggest stages in cycling. In the first few years, he would go on to win a number of races including the Fitchburg-Longsjo Classic in 1992, the UCI World Road Race Championships in 1993, the Tour du Pont in 1995 and a few different stages in the Tour de France.[89] He was certainly recognizable at this point, but not at the level of stardom he would later come to enjoy.

There are many similarities in the careers of Lance Armstrong and Greg LeMond. First, they were both American cyclists trying to achieve success in a sport that had been dominated by Europeans. Both cyclists, during the peak of their careers, had to overcome incredible amounts of adversity. For LeMond, it was the gunshot and subsequent surgeries; for Armstrong, it was stage three advanced testicular cancer. By October 1996, when the announcement was made that Armstrong was diagnosed with cancer, it had advanced to his abdomen, lungs and lymph nodes.[90] Doctors would go on to discover a cancerous tumor on his brain as well, and, at this point, only gave him a 40 percent chance of survival.[91] Amazingly, in February 1997 Armstrong was declared cancer-free, and two years later, like LeMond, came back to win the Tour de France.

CASE STUDY *(continued)*

Starting in 1999, Armstrong would go on to win the next seven Tour de France races and become the most celebrated sports icon in all athletics. Like LeMond, who parlayed his stardom into sponsorship deals with Trek bicycles, Armstrong was signed by some of the most successful companies in the world including Nike, Anheuser-Busch, and Oakley. Additionally, in an effort to give back, both cyclists started charities using their success and stardom to achieve a positive impact for others. LeMond, who was sexually abused as a child, became a founding board member of the charity 1in6, which provides support for men who have been impacted by sexual abuse.[92] Armstrong, who also selected a cause that personally impacted him, started the LIVESTRONG foundation, whose mission is to 'improve the lives of people affected by cancer, now.'[93] However, like Armstrong's career in cycling, his endorsements and his foundation were significantly more successful than those of LeMond.

Paths cross

It is not difficult to imagine that the only two American champions of the Tour de France would have eventually crossed paths; however, it is how their paths crossed that was surprising. In 2001, LeMond was one of the first to publicly criticize Armstrong for the relationship he kept with Dr. Michele Ferrari, who was well-known in the cycling world for distributing performance-enhancing drugs.[94] LeMond said, 'When Lance won the prologue to the 1999 Tour, I was close to tears, but when I heard he was working with Michele Ferrari, I was devastated. In the light of Lance's relationship with Ferrari, I just don't want to comment on this year's Tour. This is not sour grapes. I'm disappointed in Lance, that's all it is.'[95]

These words of criticism from LeMond were not well received by Armstrong, those in the sport of cycling, and the general biking community. Trek Bicycle Corporation, who sold LeMond's bike, eventually dropped him suggesting that the increased disappointment from the bicycle buying community due to the controversy significantly impacted sales. Due to his views on Armstrong and performance-enhancing drugs in the sport of cycling, LeMond was ostracized by those in the sport. At a ceremony honoring past Tour de France champions, event organizers pressured LeMond to sit in the bleachers and not participate with the other former winners.[96] However, incidents like this did not deter LeMond from knowing his place in the overall context of cycling and passionately speaking up for what he believed was right and morally good for the sport.

Armstrong spent the next 11 years vehemently denying the allegations that he was using performance-enhancing drugs, at times suing those who suggested he was taking these substances. He went on to win the Tour de France every year from 1999 to 2005. However, in 2012 the U.S. Anti-Doping Agency (USADA) filed doping charges against Armstrong, and later that year released their report claiming Armstrong lead 'the most sophisticated, professionalised and successful doping program that sport has ever seen.'[97] Also that year, UCI (*Union Cycliste Internationale*) stripped Lance Armstrong of all his wins as far back as 1998 and banned him from cycling.

CASE STUDY *(continued)*

Shortly thereafter companies like Nike, Anheuser-Busch and Oakley terminated their contracts with Armstrong. It was also during this time that Armstrong decided to step down as chair of the LIVESTRONG foundation.[98] It wasn't until the following year, in an interview with Oprah Winfrey, that Armstrong admitted to taking performance-enhancing drugs. In the interview, Oprah asked Armstrong the question, 'What was, for you, the flaw or flaws that made you willing to risk it all?' He answered, 'I think this just ruthless desire to win. Win at all costs, truly. Served me well on the bike, served me well during the disease, but the level that it went to, for whatever reason, is a flaw.'[99]

As the evidence started to surface about Armstrong, the public learned that lying, doping and drug trafficking was just the beginning of his abuse of power. Armstrong used all his resources to destroy the lives of those who stood in his way. In some cases, he, or others he knew, would leave threatening emails to persuade past teammates to keep quiet, such as telling former teammate Frankie Andreu, 'I hope somebody breaks a baseball bat over your head.'[100] These intimidation tactics happened over and over again. Armstrong also forced teammates to use performance-enhancing drugs if they wanted to remain on his team.[101] If for any reason someone crossed Armstrong, he would use all his networks and resources to make sure the individuals never worked in the sport of cycling again.

Greg LeMond was at the top of Armstrong's list of people who had crossed him and needed to be punished. After LeMond started questioning Lance's relationship with Dr. Ferrari, he began abusing LeMond, making calls threatening that he could find ten people who would vow that LeMond used performance-enhancing drugs. These were not idle threats; Armstrong offered $300,000 to a former teammate to claim they saw LeMond use the drugs.[102] Finally, it has been suggested that it was Armstrong, and not the decline of sales, that pressured Trek Bicycle Corporation to drop LeMond. LeMond was far from perfect, but he knew what was morally right. In this particular case study, it is easy to make the argument that LeMond did not take action because it was his obligation to get involved. By the time Armstrong was tied to doping, LeMond had been out of cycling for a number of years. Additionally, it was also not tied to an outcome that LeMond acted the way he did. Instead, the initial outcome was becoming blacklisted from the sport.

Since Armstrong was stripped of his victories from 1998 to 2010, this makes LeMond the only American cyclist to ever win the Tour de France. In December of 2012, LeMond was vindicated for his comments concerning Armstrong and could have easily ridden off into the sunset, turning his back on the sport that just a few years earlier did the same to him. However, LeMond went right back to work, trying to use his leadership and popularity to advocate for changes that would positively impact the future of cycling. LeMond, knowing that the world of cycling needed leaders with wisdom, courage, integrity and temperance called for the head of the *Union Cycliste Internationale* to resign from his post.[103] Additionally, LeMond stated that he would take up the position himself if it were necessary, adding, 'It is now or never to act. After the earthquake caused by the Armstrong case another chance will not arise. I am willing to invest to make this institution more democratic, transparent and look for the best candidate in the longer term.'[104] Greg LeMond

CASE STUDY *(continued)*

Figure 4.3 The Five Components of Leadership Model applied to the Greg LeMond and Lance Armstrong case study

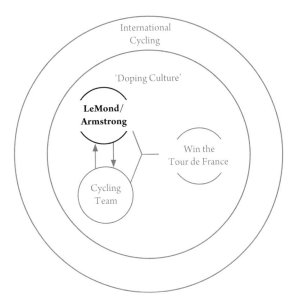

did not have to run for president of UCI. However, his support of Brian Cookson helped Cookson defeat the incumbent. LeMond said of Cookson, 'I feel confident after meeting Brian that his interest is to bring honest and transparent leadership to a sport that so desperately needs it.' He continued, 'My hope is Brian will be the one to bring all interested parties together to once and for all do what was needed to be done years before, find solutions, both short term and long term, and to make it a priority that cycling comes first, not the other way around.'[105]

Reviewing the elements of the case study from an ethical lens, one can easily see the contrast between Lance Armstrong and Greg LeMond concerning the use of performance-enhancing drugs. Both cyclists were exposed to 'doping' culture, both experienced adversity, and both competed at the highest level of their sport. However, their leadership in the midst of crisis was quite different. The question is, how do we consider virtue ethics, and specifically humility, as a part of the lens in which to view these two narratives? These stories provide context to the lives of these two athletes. One can see the differences in their responses; one centering around virtue and humility and the other focusing on self-adulation and arrogance. LeMond displayed overt humility – as well as the virtues of courage, honesty and temperance – in the midst of a firestorm of criticism from fellow cyclists, the professional cycling organization, and even bicycling enthusiasts. Despite being threatened by Armstrong, LeMond fought for cycling and uncovered the lack of ethics and integrity that was a part of the sport. Additionally, when it turned out that LeMond's accusations were entirely true, he once again acted in a virtuous way, and

CASE STUDY *(continued)*

instead of gloating, he used his international reputation to put pressure on cycling to reform.

How does each cyclist measure up in terms of humility? LeMond chose to see himself, his colleagues, and the world of professional cycling from a proper perspective. Understanding Armstrong's relationship with Dr. Michele Ferrari, LeMond knew the long-term impact this would have on the sport of cycling. The decisions made by LeMond placed the sport and others ahead of his own well-being. On the other hand, Armstrong's response to the investigation was anything but humble, from the first accusation to the USADA's eventual ruling, Armstrong only focused on himself. One example of this is on November 10, 2012, Lance tweeted 'Back in Austin and just layin' around. . ..'[106] A picture embedded in the tweet featured Armstrong in his home laying on a couch below a wall featuring his seven Tour de France jerseys, despite the fact that all of his titles had recently been stripped at the conclusion of the USADA investigation.[107]

Summary and concluding remarks

To summarize what has been discussed in this chapter, we refer back to the original framing question: What virtues should a leader possess to act ethically? Though there is not a uniform list that has been agreed upon, we have argued in this chapter that leading with virtue – or having the disposition to act in a more moral way – can have positive impacts on the leader, his or her followers, the goal, the context and the culture. Specifically, we highlighted the virtue of humility as having particular importance in leadership. By providing a very broad historical and contemporary overview of virtue ethics and the virtue of humility, how these pieces fit in to the larger Five Components of Leadership Model, and a case study examining two of the most famous cyclists of all time bringing everything together, it is our hope that you will begin to look at leadership through a more virtuous, ethical and humble lens.

? **DISCUSSION QUESTIONS**

How would you define 'virtue' or 'humility' specifically for a leader? Which specific leaders illustrate these qualities?

In what situations would humility be considered a strength for a leader? In what situations might it be seen as a weakness?

Given the many challenges faced by organizational leaders today, why should they spend time thinking about something as difficult to measure as 'virtue'?

Can you think of any past leaders who seemed to completely lack virtue? What were the outcomes of their leadership?

Can you think of any leaders who seemed to be particularly virtuous? What were the outcomes of their leadership?

What virtues do you think are important for successful followers to develop?

Think of a time in your life where you were put in a situation that required virtuous behavior in order to achieve a positive outcome. What was this experience like from a leadership standpoint?

Think of a time in your life where you were put in a situation that needed virtuous behavior but you did not behave virtuously. Why did you choose to behave as you did?

How can leadership educators and practitioners begin to develop virtue in their followers? What kinds of steps need to be taken?

ADDITIONAL RESOURCES

D. Brooks, *The Road to Character*, New York: Random House Press, 2015.

Brooks offers an approachable take on what it means to develop character. He uses a concept called 'eulogy virtues' that is based on virtue ethics but simplified and applicable to everyday life.

S. Angle and M. Slote, *Virtue Ethics and Confucianism*, New York: Routledge, 2013.

This is an edited volume of different works comparing virtue ethics to the ethical traditions in Eastern thought.

A. MacIntyre, *After Virtue: A Study of Moral Theory*, 3rd edn, Notre Dame, IN: University of Notre Dame Press, 2007.

MacIntyre explores the history and concepts of moral philosophy and calls for a renewal of its importance in contemporary society.

NOTES

1   B. Franklin, *The Autobiography of Benjamin Franklin*, New York: P.F. Collier & Son, 1790/1909, p. 474.
2   Franklin, p. 80.
3   'Ethics, virtues, and values: Knowing what matters most,' U.S. Department of State. Online, https://www.state.gov/m/a/os/64663.htm (accessed August 10, 2017).
4   D. Borchert, *Embracing Epistemic Humility: Confronting Triumphalism in Three Abrahamic Religions*, Lanham, MD: Lexington Books, 2013, p. 190.
5   S. Briggs, 'Intellectual humility: What happens when you love to learn – from others,' InformED, April 18, 2015. Online, https://www.opencolleges.edu.au/informed/features/intellectual-humility/ (accessed August 10, 2017).
6   J. Steinbeck, *Travels with Charley: In Search of America*, New York: Penguin, 1962/2012, p. 14.
7   J. Annas, 'Virtue ethics,' in D.C. Copp (ed.), *The Oxford Handbook of Ethical Theory*, New York: Oxford University Press, 2009, p. 2.
8   Aristotle, Nicomachean Ethics Books 3.6–5.2.
9   M. Calkins, *Developing a Virtue-Imbued Casuistry for Business Ethics*, New York: Springer 2014, p. 73.
10 Calkins, ibid., p. 73.
11 L. Delpit and P. White-Bradley, 'Educating or imprisoning the sprit: Lessons from ancient Egypt,' *Theory Into Practice*, vol. 42 no. 4, 2003, 283–8.
12 K.M. Olitzky and R.T. Sabath, *Striving Toward Virtue: A Contemporary Guide for Jewish Ethical Behavior*, New York: KTAV Publishing, 1996.
13 A.K. Sinha and S. Singh, 'Virtues of wise leaders: Message from the Bhagavad Gita,' *Purushartha: A Journal of Management, Ethics, and Spirituality*, vol. 6 no. 2, 2013, 1–13.
14 S. Mitchell, *Tao te Ching*, New York: HarperPerennial, 1998, Chapters 39, 61, and 66.
15 J. Santiago, 'Confucian ethics and the *Analects* as virtue ethics,' *Philosophical Ideas and Artistic Pursuits in the Traditions of Asia and the West: An NEH Faculty Humanities Workshop* 2008. Online, https://dc.cod.edu/nehscholarship/8/ (accessed February 14, 2018).
16 Santiago, ibid.
17 1 Corinthians 13:13, English Standard Version.

18 A. Al-Maududi, *The Islamic Way of Life*, revised edn, K. Murad and K. Ahmad (eds), Leicestershire, UK: The Islamic Foundation, 1967/1986.

19 L. Alanen and F. Svensson, 'Descartes on virtue,' Hommage à Wlodek: Philosophical Papers Dedicated to Wlodek Rabinowicz, T. Røonnow-Rasmussen, B. Petersson, J. Josefsson, and D. Egonsson (eds), Lund University, 2007. Online, http://www.fil.lu.se/hommageawlodek/site/papper/Alanen&Svensson.pdf (accessed February 17, 2018).

20 N. Naaman-Zauderer, *Descartes' Deontological Turn: Reason, Will, and Virtue in the Later Writings*, Cambridge: Cambridge University Press, 2010, p. 183.

21 R.B. Louden, 'Kant's virtue ethics,' *Philosophy*, vol. 61 no. 238, 1986, 473–89, p. 477.

22 F.W. Nietzsche, *Beyond Good and Evil*, New Delhi: Prabhat Prakashan, 1886/2017.

23 P.E. Murphy, 'Character and virtue ethics in international marketing: An agenda for managers, researchers and educators,' *Journal of Business Ethics*, vol. 18 no. 1, 1999, 107–24.

24 A. MacIntyre, *After Virtue: A Study in Moral Theory*. London: Bloomsbury, 1985, p. 175.

25 G. Moore, 'Corporate character: Modern virtue ethics and the virtuous corporation,' *Business Ethics Quarterly*, vol. 15 no. 4, 2005, 659–85.

26 Moore, ibid.

27 C. Peterson and M.E. Seligman, *Character Strengths and Virtues: A Handbook and Classification*, New York: Oxford University Press, 2004, p. 315.

28 Peterson and Seligman, ibid.

29 R. Hursthouse, *On Virtue Ethics*, New York: Oxford University Press, 1999.

30 Peterson and Seligman, op. cit.

31 L.L. Besser and M. Slote (eds), *The Routledge Companion to Virtue Ethics*, New York: Routledge, 2015, p. 259.

32 Annas, op. cit.

33 E. Woodruff, D.R. Van Tongeren, S. McElroy, D.E. Davis, and J.N. Hook, 'Humility and religion: Benefits, difficulties, and a model of religious tolerance,' in Chu Kim-Prieto (ed.), *Religion and Spirituality Across Cultures*, Dordrecht: Springer, 2014, pp. 271–85; D.V. Jeste, and I.V. Vahia, 'Comparison of the conceptualization of wisdom in ancient Indian literature with modern views: Focus on the Bhagavad Gita,' *Psychiatry: Interpersonal and Biological Processes*, vol. 71 no. 3, 2008, 197–209.

34 Woodruff et al., ibid, p. 273.

35 J.A. Weinstein, 'Humility, from the ground up: A radical approach to literature and ecology,' *Interdisciplinary Studies in Literature and Environment*, vol. 22 no. 4, 2015, 759–77.

36 Weinstein, ibid, p. 767.

37 Woodruff et al., op. cit; R. Green, 'Jewish ethics and the virtue of humility,' *The Journal of Religious Ethics*, 1973, 53–63; D.M. Nelson, 'The virtue of humility in Judaism: A critique of rationalist hermeneutics,' *The Journal of Religious Ethics*, 1985, 298–311.

38 Woodruff et al., ibid, p. 272.

39 Woodruff et al., op. cit.

40 T. Ramadan, *Western Muslims and the Future of Islam*, New York: Oxford University Press, 2003.

41 Ramadan, ibid, p. 18.

42 J.H. Harvey and B.G. Pauwels, 'Modesty, humility, character strength, and positive psychology,' *Journal of Social and Clinical Psychology*, vol. 23 no. 5, 2004, 620–3, p. 621.

43 M. Teresa, *The Joy in Loving: A Guide to Daily Living*, New York: Penguin/Compass, 2000, p. 59.

44 Peterson and Seligman, op. cit.

45 T. Sharot, 'The optimism bias,' *Current Biology*, vol. 21 no. 23, 2011, R941–R945, p. 4.

46 J.L. Tracy and R.W. Robins, 'Show your pride: Evidence for a discrete emotion expression,' *Psychological Science*, vol. 15 no. 3, 2004, 194–7; and J.L. Tracy and R.W. Robins, 'Emerging insights into the nature and function of pride,' *Current Directions in Psychological Science*, vol. 16 no. 3, 2007, 147–50.

47 J.P. Tangney, 'Humility: Theoretical perspectives, empirical findings and directions for future research,' *Journal of Social and Clinical Psychology*, vol. 19 no. 1, 2000, 70–82; and J.P. Tangney, 'Humility,' in C.R. Snyder and S.J. Lopez (eds), *Handbook of Positive Psychology*, New York: Oxford University Press, 2002, pp. 411–19.

48 Peterson and Seligman, op. cit.

49 Tangney, 2000 and 2002, op. cit.

50 Peterson and Seligman, op. cit.

51 Peterson and Seligman, op. cit.

52 Cited in E. Dowden, *Michel de Montaigne*, Philadelphia: JP. Lippincott, 1905, p. 256, Online, https://archive.org/details/micheldemontaig00dowdgoog (accessed February 18, 2018).

53 B. Fröding, *Virtue Ethics and Human Enhancement*, Dordrecht: Springer, 2012.

54 Fröding, ibid, p. 62.

55 R. Kamtekar, 'Situationism and virtue ethics on the content of our character,' *Ethics*, vol. 114 no. 3, 2004, 458–91, p. 458.

56 Kamtekar, ibid.

57 S. Milgram, *Obedience to Authority: An Experimental View*, New York: Perennial Classics, 1974.

58 Milgram, ibid.

59 Milgram, op. cit.

60 R.B. Louden, 'On some vices of virtue ethics,' *American Philosophical Quarterly*, vol. 21 no. 3, 1984, 227–36.

61 Besser and Slote, op. cit.

62 Cited in V. Tiberius, 'Wisdom and humility,' *Annals of the New York Academy of Sciences*, vol. 1384 no. 1, 2016, 113–16, pp. 113–14.

63 Tiberius, ibid.

64 Tangney, 2000, op. cit., p. 71.

65 P.A. Knight and J.I. Nadel, 'Humility revisited: Self-esteem, information search, and policy consistency,' *Organizational Behavior and Human Decision Processes*, vol. 38 no. 2, 1986, 196–206.

66 D.R. Van Tongeren, J.D. Green, T.L. Hulsey, C.H. Legare, D.G. Bromley, and A.M Houtman, 'A meaning-based approach to humility: Relationship affirmation reduces worldview defense,' *Journal of Psychology and Theology*, vol. 42 no. 1, 2014, 62–9, p. 63.

67 D.G. Myers, 'The psychology of humility,' in R.L. Herrmann (ed.), *God, Science, and Humility: Ten Scientists Consider Humility Theology*, Philadelphia: Templeton Foundation Press, 2000, pp. 153–75, p. 172.

68 Peterson and Seligman, op. cit. p. 406.

69 Tangney, 2000, op. cit.

70 R. McManus and G. Perruci, *Understanding Leadership: An Arts and Humanities Perspective*, New York: Routledge, 2015, p. 15.

71 P.G. Northouse, *Introduction to Leadership: Concepts and Practice*, Thousand Oaks, CA: Sage Publications, 2017.

72 B.P. Owens, A.S. Wallace, and D.A. Waldman, 'Leader narcissism and follower outcomes: The counterbalancing effect of leader humility,' *Journal of Applied Psychology*, vol. 100 no. 4, 2015, 1203–13.

73 Owens et al., ibid, p. 1203.

74 J.M. Kouzes and B.Z. Posner, *The Leadership Challenge: How to Make Extraordinary Things Happen in Organizations*, 5th edn, San Francisco: Jossey Bass, 2012, p. 26.

75 Kouzes and Posner, ibid, p. 26.

76 J.J. Exline and A.L. Geyer, 'Perceptions of humility: A preliminary study,' *Self and Identity*, vol. 3 no. 2, 2004, 95–114, p. 104.

77 Peterson and Seligman, op. cit., p. 36.

78 R.M. Kidder, 'Universal human values: Finding an ethical common ground,' *Public Management*, vol. 77 no. 6, 1995, 4–9.

79 Much of the information in the case study can be obtained from the sources cited here: R. Albergotti and V. O'Connell, *Wheelmen: Lance Armstrong, The Tour de France, and the Greatest Sports Conspiracy Ever*, New York: Penguin, 2013; G. Andrews, *Greg LeMond: Yellow Jersey Racer*, Boulder, CO: Velo Press, 2016; *ESPN Films 30 for 30: Slaying the Badger*, documentary, J. Dower (Director), ESPN Films/Team Marketing, 2014; *Stop at Nothing: The Lance Armstrong Story*, A. Holmes (Director), Indie Rights, 2017; J. Macur, *Cycle of Lies: The Fall of Lance Armstrong*, New York: Harper, 2014; R. Moore, *Slaying the Badger: LeMond, Hinault and the Greatest Ever Tour de France*, New York: Random House, 2012; D. Walsh, *Seven Deadly Sins: My Pursuit of Lance Armstrong*, New York, Simon and Schuster, 2013.

80 G. Le Roc'h, 'Tour's shortest final gap deprived Fignon of third win,' Reuters.com, August 31, 2010.

Online, https://www.reuters.com/article/us-cycling-fignon-timetrial/tours-shortest-final-gap-deprive d-fignon-of-third-win-idUSTRE67U3GD20100831 (accessed February 18, 2018).

81 E.M. Swift, 'An American takes Paris pushed to the limit by Bernard Hinault, Greg LeMond (in yellow) rode to a historic win in the Tour de France,' Sports Illustrated Vault.com, August 4, 1986. Online, https://www.si.com/vault/1986/08/04/113757/an-american-takes-paris-pushed-to-the-limit-by-ber nard-hinault-greg-lemond-in-yellow-rode-to-a-historic-win-in-the-tour-de-france (accessed February 18, 2018).

82 Swift, ibid.

83 Moore, op. cit.

84 United Press International, 'Cyclist LeMond stable after hunting accident,' *Sun Sentinel*, April 21, 1987. Online, http://articles.sun-sentinel.com/1987-04 21/sports/8701250625_1_patrick-blades-dr-sandy-beal-hunting (accessed February 18, 2018).

85 E.M. Swift, 'Le Grand LeMond,' Sports Illustrated Vault.com, December 25, 1989. Online, https://www.si.com/vault/1989/12/25/121301/le-grand-lemond-greg-lemond-1989-sportsman-of-the-year-rewrote-his-own-legend-with-a-heroic-comeback-and-a-magnificent-finish-in-the-tour-de-france (accessed February 18, 2018).

86 Associated Press, 'LeMond is honored as Sportsman of Year,' *Los Angeles Times*, December 24, 1989. Online, http://articles.latimes.com/1989-12-24/sports/sp-2094_1_greg-lemond (accessed February 18, 2018).

87 G. LeMond, 'The art of peaking for the Tour de France,' July 2, 2010. Online, http://www.cyclingnews.com/blogs/author/the-art-of-peaking-for-the-tour-de-france-1/ (accessed February 18, 2018).

88 LeMond, ibid.

89 Lance Armstrong Biography. Biography.com. Online, https://www.biography.com/people/lance-armstrong-9188901 (accessed February 18, 2018).

90 Armstrong, ibid.

91 Armstrong, op. cit.

92 'Greg LeMond and LeMond fitness line up for September 17 Echelon Gran Fondo,' 1in6.org, September 5, 2011. Online, https://1in6.org/2011/09/greg-lemond-and-lemond-fitness-line-up-for-september-17-echelon-gran-fondo/ (accessed February 18, 2018).

93 'Our Mission,' Livestrong.org. Online, https://www.livestrong.org/who-we-are (accessed February 18, 2018).

94 'Drugs issue refuses to go away due to winner's Ferrari links,' The Guardian.com, July 29, 2001. Online, https://www.theguardian.com/sport/2001/jul/30/cycling.cycling1 (accessed February 18, 2018).

95 Ibid.

96 T. Brown, 'Greg LeMond moves forward after "12 years of hell,"' StarTribune.com, March 15, 2015. Online, http://www.startribune.com/oct-26-2014-greg-lemond-breaks-his-silence/280231442/ (accessed February 18, 2018).

97 W. Fotheringham, 'Timeline: Lance Armstrong's journey from deity to disgrace,' The Guardian.com, March 9, 2015. Online, https://www.theguardian.com/sport/2015/mar/09/lance-armstrong-cycling-doping-scandal (accessed February 18, 2018).

98 Fotheringham, ibid.

99 ESPN Staff, 'Lance Armstrong interview highlights,' ESPN.co.uk, January 18, 2013. Online, http://en.espn.co.uk/cycling/sport/story/188831.html (accessed February 18, 2018).

100 M. O'Keeffe, C. Red, T. Thompson, and N. Vinton, 'Victims of Lance Armstrong's strong-arm tactics feel relief and vindication in the wake of U.S. Anti-Doping Agency report,' NYDailyNews.com, October 26, 2012. Online, http://www.nydailynews.com/sports/more-sports/zone-lance-armstrong-bully-dow nfall-article-1.1188512 (accessed February 18, 2018).

101 O'Keeffe et al., ibid.

102 O'Keeffe et al., op. cit.

103 M. Seaton, 'Is Greg LeMond the right choice to challenge for the UCI presidency?' The Guardian.com, December 3, 2012. Online, https://www.theguardian.com/sport/blog/2012/dec/03/greg-lemond-cycling-uci-presidency (accessed February 18, 2018).

104 Seaton, ibid.

105 S. Stokes, 'Triple Tour de France winner Greg LeMond backs Brian Cookson in UCI Presidential battle,'

Velonation.com, August 31, 2013. Online, http://www.velonation.com/News/ID/15372/Triple-Tour-de-France-winner-Greg-LeMond backs-Brian-Cookson-in-UCI-Presidential-battle.aspx#ixzz4caiYiasN (accessed February 18, 2018).

106 M.E. Hambrick, E.L. Frederick, and J. Sanderson, 'From yellow to blue: Exploring Lance Armstrong's image repair strategies across traditional and social media,' *Communication & Sport*, vol. 3 no. 2, 2015, 196–218.

107 Hambrick et al., ibid.

5

Ethical egoism

Gavin G. Enck, Beth A. Pauchnik and Alexandra K. Perry

 **FRAMING QUESTION**

What is self-interested leadership?

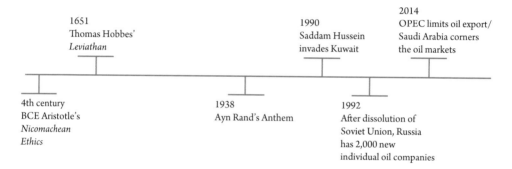

Figure 5.1 Timeline of major works on ethical egoism in relation to the case study

Does leadership based on self-interest necessarily end poorly? When illustrating ethical egoism, we might be drawn to the worst-case examples of self-interested leadership, such as the notorious fraudulent stockbroker Bernie Madoff. Mr. Madoff's decisions in running a financial organization were based on self-interest, either to increase his own profits or to cover his fraud. Yet, cases like Mr. Madoff's are extreme. Leaders acting out of self-interest occur regularly and seldom are as obvious and outrageous as a leader committing fraud.

While not all leadership based on self-interest results in harm, it seems that actions based on self-interest frequently hurt followers, the goal, the context, and even the broader encompassing culture. Ethical egoism helps to clarify what it means for a leader to make a decision based on self-interest and, in turn, map out the ways these decisions impact the other components of leadership.

To illustrate ethical egoism, let's start with a thought experiment. Eric and Nicole are at a company holiday party. Both want a holiday cookie; yet, due to a catering error, there is only one holiday cookie remaining. Eric loves cookies and eating it will satisfy his hunger and make him happy. Nicole also wants the cookie; but, unlike Eric, she is extremely hungry because she has not eaten all day. As an ethical egoist, Eric deliberates on what is the morally right action in this situation. Eating the cookie will maximize his self-interest physically and psychologically – he's hungry and he likes cookies. Despite Nicole being hungry, allowing her to have the last cookie diminishes Eric's self-interests. Therefore, since eating the cookie maximizes Eric's self-interest, it is the morally right action for him to eat the cookie.

However, the interests of others need not – in principle – be excluded from an agent's deliberation. Because well-being is composed of internal and external elements, there are overlapping and deep connections between a person and other people's interests. Returning to the thought experiment, let's re-examine Nicole's hunger as a consideration in Eric's deliberation. Imagine, for example, that Nicole is Eric's supervisor. Eric knows Nicole is hungry and allowing her to have the only cookie will make her happy. Making Nicole happy is conducive to improving their working relationship. Developing this relationship is likely conducive to Nicole promoting Eric at work. Thus, Nicole's hunger may be a relevant consideration in Eric's deliberation. In this situation, giving Nicole the cookie may be the right action for Eric because it will likely maximize his self-interest.

Although Nicole promoting Eric is obviously a benefit, it is far from obvious that maximizing self-interests always requires considering the interests of others as an instrumental benefit to one's well-being. What if Eric and Nicole not only work together but also are best friends. Seeing Nicole hungry causes Eric to be unhappy, diminishing him psychologically. Giving Nicole the cookie could be in Eric's self-interest because doing so makes Nicole happy, which makes him happy. Due to the psychological and relational benefits to well-being, Eric could be morally justified in giving Nicole the cookie. Again, Nicole's hunger has a relevant role as a consideration in Eric's deliberation.

Now let's apply ethical egoism to a broader situation in which a leader has to make another kind of choice. Suppose a leader – in this case, the president of a company – has an opportunity to enter into a multi-million-dollar agreement between her company and another company that happens to be owned by a member of her company's board of directors. At the same time, a vendor for her company offers her the use of a vacation cabin in Colorado.

In the first situation, the leader benefits psychologically and socially by entering into a financially lucrative transaction with a board member, likely because the board member will no doubt protect her job. In many corporate situations, it is a company's board that oversees the CEO or president. This board has the ability to hire, fire, or sanction the president. While this transaction is initially only lucrative to the board member, it is also likely that the organization and followers may benefit in the long term. The whole organization could potentially benefit from the new business, helping to benefit the followers as well as the leaders reaching the common goal of building the company's business. But, this may take one or two years to play out. If this were to occur, the leader then has aligned her interests with the followers' interests and the goal.

However, when the interests of the leader differ from the interests of the organization, it is likely that outcome may benefit the interests of the leader, but not necessarily the interests of anyone else. Consider the vendor's offer of the vacation cabin. The president may benefit psychologically and socially by obtaining the cabin, but the followers don't benefit in any way and the offer does not help the leader or the followers reach their goal of building the company's business. In the first instance, the president's decision to partner with her board member might be justified; in the second instance it may not, yet both are motivated by ethical egoism. Now that we understand the basics of ethical egoism a bit better, let's take a quick look at the history of the idea.

History

Ethical egoism is the view that a person should always (morally) act to improve his or her own self-interest. Although ethical egoism is often dismissed as a legitimate ethical theory, it has a significant and persistent history. Consider that Aristotle's account of eudemonism, happiness or human flourishing discussed in Chapter 4, rests on self-interest. A person strives to attain virtue because it is best for his or her self-interest to be virtuous – not the best interest of others.[1]

Two millennia later, Thomas Hobbes famously posed life in a state of nature is 'solitary, poor, nasty, brutish, and short.'[2] Hence, according to Hobbes, because human judgment is so easily misguided, a person ought to focus more on his or her own self-interests. In many cases, being misled by our emotions and desires harms our self-interest. Consider overeating, for example. The food might taste delicious at the moment, but overeating may cause harm to one's own long-term self-interests and health.

It is important to note that *ethical egoism is not psychological egoism.* Psychological egoism is a *descriptive claim* that human motivations for action are based on self-interest. Ethical egoism differs from psychological egoism because it makes a *normative claim* in the domain of morally right or wrong actions. Ethical egoism maintains that to act morally a person *ought to* behave in his or her own self-interest. Outside of morality, ethical egoism makes no claims about human motivations for action.

Now, for much of the last century ethical egoism has been advanced through the writings of twentieth-century author Ayn Rand.[3] Rand held that the basis of morality is self-interest. Since human beings are rational creatures, we should use our rational capacities for determining our self-interests. According to Rand, since the basis of morality is self-interest and reason defines a person's self-interest, a person has a rational responsibility to pursue and fulfill these interests.

While Rand's view is a form of ethical egoism, it is better understood as rational egoism. Rational egoism is the view that it is always rational for a person to act in ways that promote his or her self-interest.[4] Although ethical egoism and rational egoism are closely connected, they are making two distinct claims. Ethical egoism, again, *makes a normative claim in the domain of morality about how people should act in regards to right and wrong actions.* Rational egoism *makes a claim about human rationality;* that is, it is always *rational* to act in one's self-interest. The reason the focus is on ethical egoism and not rational egoism is that while one should always morally act to improve his or her own self-interest, failing to do so is not invariably irrational. For the purposes of this chapter, the focus is on ethical egoism, not on rational egoism.

This section has outlined the history of ethical egoism and in doing so distinguished it from psychological and rational egoism. The following section details an account of ethical egoism as a normative ethical theory.

Major concepts of ethical egoism

In the field of moral philosophy, normative ethics focuses on offering theoretical justifications for how people *ought to act.* In offering theoretical justifications, an ethical theory provides a theory of right action, which is a way to evaluate and categorize actions as being morally right (the action is required or permitted) or wrong (the action is forbidden).[5]

To illustrate, let's examine the ethical theories of consequentialism and deontology. Consequentialism – also referred to as utilitarianism and addressed in

Chapter 3 – argues that a person should act to promote, increase, or create the best state of affairs (outcomes) for the greatest number of people. A person's action is morally right if it creates the best outcome for the greatest number of people and is morally wrong if it does not. On the other hand, deontology contends, regardless of the possible beneficial outcomes, a person's action must be constrained by certain considerations, such as treating human beings as autonomous agents who are ends in themselves. People should never be treated simply as a means to an end.[6] (This concept is covered in detail in Chapter 2.)

Now, unlike consequentialism or deontology, ethical egoism holds that a person should always act to improve his or her own self-interest. However, as one scholar notes, defining self-interest is of fundamental importance since, ultimately, it not only justifies why people should act in their self-interest but also determines which actions are morally right or wrong.[7]

While self-interest often is regarded as referring to a range of things – such as utility, the satisfaction of preferences, happiness, and pleasure – in this chapter it refers to a person's well-being. A person's well-being is comprised of physical, psychological, social, and relational elements.[8] Physical health is not the only significant element of well-being. Under normal conditions, most people consider psychological health and happiness, living in a community or family, and being engaged in relationships with others as being as important. The advantage of stipulating self-interest in regard to well-being is that human beings value and care about it. Moreover, as a decision-making model, it allows for the broadest range of considerations to be included in an agent's deliberation.

With self-interest defined, ethical egoism argues that a person should always act to improve his or her physical, psychological, social, or relational elements because a person values and cares for them. As a theory of right action, ethical egoism holds that an action is morally right *if and only if* it maximizes an agent's self-interest and wrong if it does not.[9] An action is *morally right* (required or permitted) if and only if it benefits physically, psychologically, socially, and relationally the person acting and is *morally wrong* (forbidden) if it diminishes an agent physically, psychologically, socially, or relationally.

Critiques of ethical egoism

Whether as an ethical theory or decision-making model, ethical egoism faces several general criticisms. In this section, we begin by examining and responding to the theoretical criticism of ethical egoism as an ethical theory.

Table 5.1 Concepts related to ethical egoism

Concept	Authors	Summary
Psychological Egoism	Thomas Hobbes	Human judgment is easily misguided, so we must focus on our self-interest. (Descriptive)
Rational Egoism	Ayn Rand	Since the basis of morality is self-interest and reason defines a person's self-interests, a person has a rational responsibility to pursue those interests.
Ethical Egoism	Also seen in Hobbes	A person *should* act in his or her own self-interest. (Normative)
Consequentialism	John Stuart Mill	A person should promote, increase, or create the best state of affairs for the greatest number of people.
Deontology	Immanuel Kant	Regardless of the possible benefits, a person's actions must be constrained by certain considerations.

Next, we will consider the practical criticism of ethical egoism as a decision-model for leadership. Although ethical egoism is theoretically defensible as an ethical theory, the critiques of ethical egoism in practical leadership decision-making are far more damning.

As an ethical theory, the central criticism of ethical egoism is that the standard for determining the morality of an action is strictly contingent on whether it benefits the self-interest of the person acting. The concern is that basing the morality of an action on a person's self-interest gives license to too many repugnant actions. For example, whether the self-interest of a person acting is benefited determines whether his or her stealing or murdering would be morally right. That morality for ethical egoism is only a matter of advancing one's own interests strikes many as simply objectionable. In addition, it has a difficult time accounting for the things that people value and care most about, for example, friendship. Per ethical egoism, friendship is only valuable if it advances a person's self-interest. A notion of friendship solely being about promoting one's self-interest goes against the basic notion that friendship is about mutual affection. But note, it is incorrect to think that a person who regards friendship as being about the pursuit of self-interests completely misunderstands what it means to act as someone's friend.

Ethical egoism's endorsement for a morality of advancing a person's own self-interests raises legitimate concerns. However, comparison with other ethical theories illustrates that these concerns do not warrant an outright dismissal of ethical egoism as an ethical theory. First, it is not clear why basing a decision on self-interest always makes such a decision objectionable. The assumption is that self-interest and morally right actions are mutually exclusive. But this assumption goes too far and may discount a morally right action that also happens to be in a person's own self-interest.

Second, ethical egoism is not unique in endorsing actions that many regard as being morally repugnant. Consequentialism and deontology have also been criticized as endorsing repugnant actions as being morally right. For consequentialism, creating the best outcome for the greatest number of people may result in the tyranny of the majority; whereas for deontology, always respecting humans as autonomous agents who should be free to make their own decisions may entail constraining helpful actions that may result in immensely beneficial outcomes.

Finally, even if ethical egoism did have difficulty accounting for positive values such as friendship – or even values such as love, affection, and community – it is not evident that deontology and consequentialism do that much better. For deontology and consequentialism, respectively, friendship is governed by duties to respect another autonomous agent or by a person creating the best outcome for you and the greatest number of other people.[10] Nonetheless, neither of these ethical theories accurately encapsulates what it means to be someone's friend.

The practical criticism of ethical egoism as a decision-making model for leaders is far more damaging. Again, examples like Bernie Madoff spring to mind, but leadership motivated by self-interest is seldom this obvious; usually, the actions taken play out in far subtler but equally destructive ways. While leadership based on ethical egoism does not always end poorly, the chances of an action based on self-interest being incompatible with the interests of the other components of leadership are inevitable.

Although a leader's actions based on ethical egoism may not have a poor outcome in the short-term, in the long-term these actions often affect a leader's credibility. Consider the previous examples of a leader making a multi-million-dollar deal with a board member's company and choosing to use a vendor's vacation cabin in Colorado. While the former decision may be profitable for the followers and the goals of the larger organization and the latter was not, they both affect a leader's credibility. Credibility is integral to the trust and support a leader has with followers. In both situations, it is likely, if not inevitable, that rumors about the leader's motivations for acting will start to spread throughout the organization. The followers will not only be suspicious of this leader's past actions but may perceive all future actions as solely motivated by the leader's own self-interests. Hence, the leader's credibility is gradually eroded. When the leader's credibility is harmed, the entire context surrounding the leader, follower, and the goal becomes toxic because the followers no longer trust that the leader's decisions are consistent with the interests of the organization. This toxicity, in turn, may apply to the larger cultural values and norms in which business operates, as can be seen by the general distrust many have of 'big business.' This is why, in the long-term, leadership based on self-interest often ends poorly.

Five component analysis

In this section, we use McManus and Perruci's Five Components of Leadership Model to outline the way that ethical egoism addresses leadership and its various components.[11]

Imagine that Jill is the President of Company-A and reports to the board of directors. Jack is the Chairperson of the board of directors for Company-A. Although not employed by Company-A, Jack is President of the largest and arguably the best advertising company in the state, Company-B. Company-B is a widely respected, but admittedly expensive, advertising company that delivers an exceptional product.

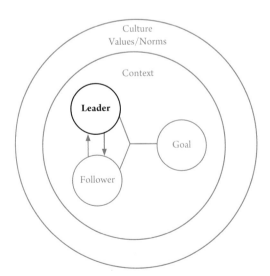

Figure 5.2 The Five Components of Leadership Model applied to ethical egoism

During Jack's tenure as Chairperson of the board, Jill, on behalf of the organization, entered into a multi-million-dollar contract for advertising and marketing services. Jill suggests that by taking an aggressive marketing stance, Company-A stands to increase its market share. However, Company-A's organizational policy requires all contracts have a comparative data review. This policy analyzes the potential expenses and returns on investment of a contract and demands that a service contract reflects fair market value determined by a comparative data review.

However, Jill instructs the Vice President and others responsible to execute this contract without a comparative data review. After the contract is signed, Jill is indifferent to objective data that reflects much lower annual advertising spend for organizations of similar size to Company-A. In fact, Jill's internal reaction to those voicing these concerns is that this contract has solidified her status as President because the contract benefits Jack, Chairperson of the board. Furthermore, she sends clear messages to the employees directly involved in the execution of the contract that anyone who pushes the matter further might find their job is in jeopardy.

According to ethical egoism, a leader should act in a way that maximizes his or her own interests. This mandate means Jill would have been justified in instructing the Vice President to move forward on the contract with Jack's company without conducting a comparative data review. Egoism allows for leaders to act in a self-interested way, and this is what Jill has done in this case. This does not mean that a leader should disregard his or her followers' interests all together. Indeed, in cases where respecting the welfare of followers is in the best interest of the leader, then a leader would be acting in accordance with ethical egoism if they considered the welfare of the followers. The key element of the analysis, however, is the motivation behind the leader's actions; an egoist leader would act in a way that maximized his or her own benefit.

So what is the role of followers in ethical egoism? We know that they can serve to influence a leader if assuaging the followers is in his or her own best interest, but what is the experience for followers within the framework of ethical egoism? Again, let's consider the case of Jill. Imagine that over the ensuing five years, Company-A pays 6–9 million dollars each year for advertising services from Company-B. The comparative data indicates that Company-A exceeds the amount its competitors spend on advertising by over 500 percent. Yet, during this period, Company-A's market share exponentially increases. In part, this is due to the television commercials and weekly quarter-page newspaper advertisements created by Company-B. At the end of a five-year period, this increase in market share results in extensive profits for Company-A.

While this contract generated profits for Company-A, it caused great distress during this period for executives in numerous departments. Executives were struggling to obtain capital and there were scarce operational resources. Moreover, during this time, many employees utilized an anonymous call line to register complaints about Jill's reasons for implementing the contract, Jack's blatant conflict of interest as Chairperson of the board, and the internal financial difficulty it caused other executives or department leaders. In the end, no formal actions or investigations were taken against Jill or Jack. The board of directors turned a blind eye to the exorbitant expense and failure to follow procedure by rationalizing that the profits made up for it. While profits for the company are tremendous, morale is lower than it ever has been, and many talented employees have left the organization.

The role for followers within the framework of ethical egoism is to serve to motivate the leader to act ethically by demonstrating the ways in which it would be to his or her benefit. In Jill's case, despite the fact that her company's profits were good, morale among her followers was poor because her followers sensed that her decision was purely driven by self-interest. The followers likely caused Jill to question her decision by highlighting the distress that was created by the contract. Though Jill probably wouldn't have been motivated to change her decision because of the inherent difficulty caused by the contract, if she continued to lose qualified employees, or her company's reputation was damaged, she might act differently because of the impact that this would have on her.

Per ethical egoism, Jill entering into a multi-million-dollar contract was morally right since it benefited her well-being. This action resulted in relational and social benefits for Jill because it solidified her position as President and insured her job security. Moreover, by increasing market share and profits, Jill benefited by an increase in salary.

However, despite this action being morally right according to ethical egoism, it resulted in several problems for her followers and organization. To begin, this decision was not made on behalf of the interests of the organization's goal. Although it is in the best interest of the organization to increase its market share, Jill's motivation for the contract and pushing it through was not in the interests of the organization. Jill's self-interest in preserving her own job resulted in a total disregard for the organization's goal.

Now, an ethical egoist (or Jill) might respond that this decision *was* in the interests of the company because, in the end, it resulted in profits. Yet, if the intention and outcome of Jill's actions are examined, both are troublesome. Jill's action intended to benefit her own well-being by solidifying and securing her position, not to increase Company-A's market share and profits. Thus, while the outcome may have been profitable, her intentions were not aligned with the interests of the organization and that is a problem. Five years and many millions of dollars later, the transaction resulted in increased financial profits. However, during that time, the culture created at Company-A was one of distrust of Jill's ongoing decision-making motives.

Concerning the outcome, it is relevant to notice that Jill's action resulting in a profitable financial outcome is merely a matter of luck. Without a comparative data review, neither Jill nor Company-A had any evidence for believing that this contract would have resulted in increased market share and profits. This lack of evidence suggests the outcome was simply fortuitous for Jill, which, combined with her intentions, diminishes the merit she deserves for increasing Company-A's market share and profits.

In ethical egoism, the leader in accordance with his or her self-interest defines the goal. Egoism also assumes that followers will have their own goals that are motivated by their own interests, and therefore the leader often has to work to ensure that there is no conflict between goals. In the case of Jill, her goal to maintain her position within the company was complementary to the goal of the company to increase its profits. It conflicted, however, with the followers' goals to work for a leader they felt acted ethically, and to have adequate resources for their projects. Jill's interests may have been better served by spending time to make sure that her goal aligned with that of the followers' goals to provide more competent leadership. Ethical egoism can be a successful approach to leadership if the goal is truly a common one and shared by the entire leader–follower community.

Egoism, perhaps more than other approaches to leadership, relies on established rules and policies to provide safeguards to a leader's actions. Company policies exist for many reasons. Beyond what is required by law and compliance, policies establish standards all employees, including leaders, are expected to follow. Inconsistent application of the policies results in differing treatment of employees despite established standards. These policies also allow for the assessment and evaluation of leadership. A leader who violates company policies creates a double standard. Leaders who think they should not be held to the same standard as all other employees lack awareness of the negative impact their actions have on the organizational context.

Egoism can also be, and often is, tempered by the overall values and norms that exist within a larger community. Jill's followers were upset not only by the fact that she violated company policies, but by the fact that she challenged the community's sense of integrity and values. The followers expected Jill to act in a way that they believed to be moral, rather than in a way that was ethically justified by her own self-interest. Jill's actions indicate that she, rather clearly, failed to provide leadership for her followers and her organization. First, Jill's decision to push the contract forward to benefit her own well-being indicates she failed in her role as leader in managing Company-A's interests. Second, Jill's failure to follow standardized processes created the appearance of two sets of rules and standards: if you are in a leadership role you may or may not have to follow this organization's rules or standards; if you are not in a leadership role you must follow the organization's rules or standards. Third, by subverting the organization's policy requiring comparative data in service contracts, Jill undermined her credibility. A loss of credibility is often devastating to a leader. Without credibility, a leader cannot fulfill the vision for the organization's future. Employees who have lost trust in their leader are unlikely to put energy and effort into carrying out plans to establish the leader's visions. Finally, in setting her plans, authorizing decisions, or delegating projects or actions, Jill never attempted to align employees' interests with the organization's interests. Specifically, even after the contract was pushed through, rather than attempting to align the employees' interests with her action, she actively worked to suppress her followers by ignoring their complaints. In doing this, Jill purposely ignored both the interests of the employees and organization.

It is clear that Jill's actions and leadership failures will inevitably hurt Company-A. Despite the outcome ultimately being profitable, Jill's decision and actions eroded her credibility as leader and harmed her organization. During this five-year period, executives were unable to secure capital and operational resources for their departments, widespread employee vocal dissent was ignored, and employees left the company due to the toxic culture created by Jill's actions. In short, although the outcome may have been fortuitous, the means to the end were ethically suspect.

In order to take a closer look at what egoism would look like as an approach to ethical leadership, we will focus on the case of the international hostility over petroleum in the late twentieth and early twenty-first centuries.

CASE STUDY

International hostilities over petroleum

Prior to the 11 September 2001 attacks on the U.S., the world had been experiencing a 20-year long decline in oil prices. The end of the '2nd oil shock' price spike in 1980 – the result of both Iran and Iraq curtailing their oil production to almost nothing at the outset of the war against each other – resulted in stable and reliable production levels of oil in the OPEC nations. Concurrently, countries in the western hemisphere such as Mexico and Venezuela greatly expanded their oil productions and exports and emerged as competitors on the global market. The Soviet Union became the world's top oil producer during the 1980s, while Americans enjoyed a new surge in domestic oil production from the Alaskan and the North Sea wells.[12] All of this added up to a glut of oil surplus throughout much of the decade, and oil prices fell to below $10 per barrel.[13]

This downward trend remained relatively stable until, on 2 August 1990 the military forces of Iraq, led by the dictator Saddam Hussein, moved into the neighboring nation of Kuwait and within two days of intense fighting seized control of the Kuwaiti government and annexed it for Iraq. Hussein claimed that Kuwait was now 'the nineteenth province of Iraq.' Among the reasons cited to justify the invasion, Hussein claimed that Kuwait had been stealing Iraqi oil through slant well drilling and that Kuwait's overproduction of oil had been hurting Iraq's revenues in the petroleum market.[14] It was also suspected that Iraq needed a way to repay the $80 billion debt it owed the U.S., which it had borrowed to pay for its war against Iran in the 1980s.[15] Regardless of the reasons, Hussein's objective for annexing Kuwait was abundantly clear to everyone. To quote Daniel Yergin, 'An Iraq that subsumed Kuwait would rival Saudi Arabia as an oil power, with far-reaching impact for the rest of the world.'[16]

The Iraqi occupation of Kuwait would only last for about seven months before a coalition of 36 nations led by the U.S. liberated Kuwait's capital and drove the Iraqi military into a full retreat. Among the coalition members was the Soviet Union, whose president, Mikhail Gorbachev, said that they would stand shoulder to shoulder with the United States throughout the operation. To place this point in context, the Berlin Wall – the Soviet Union's symbol of Cold War hostilities and isolation toward the West that had endured since the 1960s – was demolished just eight months before the Iraqi invasion of Kuwait. Its aftermath had been the focus of world politics until the Gulf War crisis happened. This temporary alliance between the two major world powers of the time would prove to be an early bellwether of policy changes toward the West for the Soviet Union, which was very soon to be dissolved and would reemerge as the Russian Federation.

Before the coalition forces were able to complete Iraq's withdrawal from Kuwait, Hussein decided that he would try to cause as much damage to the region's oil production as possible – and by extension the world's petroleum market. He imposed a 'scorched earth' policy on Kuwait's oil wells as his forces retreated into Iraq. As the soldiers were leaving Kuwait, they set fire to nearly 800 oil wells, which caused some of the worst environmental damage the world had ever seen. This was in addition to the six million barrels of oil that was also

CASE STUDY (continued)

deliberately dumped into the Persian Gulf – which remains the largest oil spill in history – in an attempt to combat an anticipated coalition marine assault, which never came. All told, more than six million barrels of oil per day were destroyed by the Iraqis – much more than what Kuwait was producing per day, and even more than what the country of Japan, Kuwait's biggest customer at the time, was importing from them per day. It took more than ten months from the time the first fires were lit in January 1991 until the last fire was put out in November of the same year. All told, the fires burned through about one billion barrels of oil and left 85 percent of all Kuwaiti oil fields inoperable.[17]

As great as the environmental and economic damage to the nation of Kuwait, the Persian Gulf region and the global petroleum market were, the implications for leadership in the Middle East were perhaps the most drastic consequence of this conflict. The United States-led coalition forces had decided not to oust Saddam Hussein from his position of power over Iraq and instead anticipated that having been weakened and humiliated by his defeat, he would succumb to rival opposition within his own government and be overthrown by his own people. This, of course, did not happen, and Hussein managed to remain in power throughout the 1990s and on into the early twenty-first century. Despite this political miscalculation, several of the desired outcomes from the war were still achieved in unexpected ways. Yergin summarizes these outcomes nicely within two separate passages:

> Mideast politics, which so often bedeviled security of supply, was no longer a threat. In the decade that followed the Gulf crisis, it seemed that the Middle East was more stable than before the war and that oil crises and disruptions were things of the past. No longer was there the Soviet Union to meddle in regional politics, and the outcome of the Gulf crisis and the weight of the United States in world affairs looked like an almost sure guarantee of stability. All this was a positive and powerful indication of the world that seemed to be ahead. It might not have happened had Saddam not gone to war.[18]

This new environment was one that fell more in line with the era of globalization. This meant the industry became increasingly privatized and less regulated by national governments. The industry was now more integrated with the rest of the nation's economies, and nations were in turn further interconnected and dependent upon one another. This may not have been the intended outcome of the Gulf War; nevertheless, it served as a catalyst to make it possible. Still, none of this would have happened had it not been for one other major political event which also occurred in the same year as the Gulf War: the end of the Soviet Union.

On Christmas Day 1991, then Soviet president Mikhail Gorbachev announced to his nation that he would be stepping down from his office, and the Soviet Union would cease to exist by the beginning of the following year. In his speech, he said, 'we have a lot of everything – land, oil and gas and other natural resources – and there was talent and intellect in abundance. Yet we lived much worse than developed countries and keep falling

CASE STUDY (continued)

behind them more and more.'[19] Such statements would have been unimaginable as recently as even the year before, as the Soviet Union had been closed off to the outside world for much of the twentieth century. Those in the inner circles of the government, however, knew for several years that the end was coming. The economic and industrial system the Soviets had been using for over half a century was established by Joseph Stalin and centered around a philosophy of self-sufficiency and independence, and as a result was very slow to generate revenue from the export of their most valuable of resources: oil and natural gas. It took the Soviet Union well into the 1960s to begin trading oil in the global market, and until the 1970s before they were trading natural gas. Moreover, these commodities remained their only significant revenue streams of international commerce. The powerful Russian oil magnate Vagit Alekperov once said, 'Crude oil along with other natural resources were nearly the single existing link of the Soviet Union to the world for earning the hard currency so desperately needed by this largely isolated country.'[20]

The new Russian Federation's main competitive advantage was in their vast reserves of both oil and gas resources – by the time of the Soviet Union dissolution, the oil fields of their western Siberia region were producing eight million barrels per day, enough to rival the world's top producer, Saudi Arabia. This level of production was enough to account for a full two-thirds of Russia's total revenue in the 1990s. Thus, the interests of the oil and gas sectors of Russia's economy 'drove the bus' when it came to making any major policy decisions about the nation's welfare. The needs and interests of those heading the ministries of oil and gas production were always placed ahead of all others, and those leaders would often take on a mafia-like persona by hearing requests from and granting favors to the other less fortunate government sectors suffering through their own respective budget crises. Time and again, Russian oil and gas revenues were called upon to do the heavy lifting for the Soviet economy, usually in the form of staving off an impending budget emergency for an essential function of society such as agriculture or police. Without that money, the Soviet Union faced severe shortages in providing some basic services to its citizens – famine, social instability, and even the breakdown of law and order all became distinct possibilities. Thus, the Soviets were faced with the double edges of the petroleum sword: its income enabled the country not just to survive but thrive and progress as a whole while burdened with an economy otherwise insufficient for meeting its own needs. At the same time, the stability (or at least the appearance of it) provided by the petroleum money became the country's crutch and further enabled the Soviets to keep putting off real investments and reforms into modernizing its infrastructure. The economist Yegor Gaidar, who would briefly serve as Russia's acting prime minister in 1992, observed this phenomenon:

> The hard currency from oil exports stopped the growing food supply crisis, increased the import of equipment and consumer goods, ensured a financial basis for the arms race and the

CASE STUDY *(continued)*

achievement of nuclear parity with the United States and permitted the realization of such risky foreign policy actions as the war in Afghanistan.[21]

All of these expenses would eventually snowball into an overwhelming mountain of debt and insolvency. Hampered by antiquated technology and organizational structures, the state-run Soviet oil and gas business just could not compete with the vertically integrated multination corporations of the West. When the Soviet Union finally disbanded and the new Russian Federation began at the beginning of 1992, it started an anarchic free-for-all of acquiring and protecting the infrastructure and real estate formerly held by the government. It was estimated, at one time, nearly 2,000 separate production companies arose from the various regions of petroleum reserves within Russia – though most were from the fields of western Siberia – and many of them were busy trying to claim and steal resources from one another unjustly. No one really knew who owned much of the oil they were all vying for, and this confusion gave rise to a profitable black market for anyone who could manage to sell Russian oil for hard currency.[22] The Russian companies greatly valued having 'cash in hand' since there was very little confidence at the time in the stability of the banking industry.

This instability was, at least in part, brought to an end by the privatization of the oil industry. The reconstruction of the industry in Russia was based on the adoption of the vertical integration model used by the capitalist countries of the west, and Russia quickly returned to profitable levels of production. In fact, the modernization of the organizational structure and industry practices in Russia ultimately resulted in Russia becoming one of the top oil-producing countries in the world, thereby transforming the twenty-first-century global landscape of the oil and gas industry.

The coinciding of peace and stability brought about in the Persian Gulf following the first Gulf War along with the reconstruction of the Russian oil and gas industry in the image of Western models made the 1990s the period of greatest petroleum production in the century. The price of gasoline consequently dropped to some of the comparatively lowest levels of the century. With oil and gas being so cheap and abundant, little effort was put into researching and developing alternative energy systems. Renewable resource technology such as photovoltaic solar, wind turbine, geothermal, and biomass suffered in obscurity throughout the decade. The current scope of adoption for these sources remains disappointingly small, and only in recent years has there been sufficiently renewed interest in them to generate enough implementation for renewable energy to register as contributing to meet the global energy demands. Some may argue that what brought renewable energy systems back into serious consideration was the major defining event of the geopolitical landscape for the twenty-first century thus far: the 11 September terrorist attacks on America and subsequent second Gulf War in Iraq. These events did indeed give rise to similar conditions reminiscent of the previous Gulf War in regards to a spike in oil prices (this time lasting for several years, though) and renewed fears about the security and reliability of oil from the Middle East.

CASE STUDY (continued)

Figure 5.3 The Five Components of Leadership Model applied to the energy markets case study

Both Iraqi leader Saddam Hussein and Russian leadership after the dissolution of the Soviet Union exhibited a leadership style that is predicated on ethical egoism. The contrast between the two very much shows the way in which the leader–follower relationship and a common goal can be impacted by the leader in an egoist framework. These two examples also offer a good case for the analysis of this approach to leadership as understood through the Five Components Model.

For an egoist leader, ethics and self-interest are necessarily tethered together. The moral choice is the one that serves the interest of the leader and the goal that he or she intends to work toward. This ethical framework places a lot of accountability on the leader to choose an ethical goal independently of the leadership relationship. While there is a mandate that leaders act ethically, the justification of the goal can take many forms, and there is no balance of the leader's authority. In the case of Saddam Hussein and 1990s Russian leadership, we see the contrast between a leader whose goal did not coincide with the interests of his followers and a leader whose interests *happened to* coincide with the interests of his followers. This is a crucial point in ethical egoism: the leader's interests and goals may happen to align with the interests or goals of his or her followers, but this is happenstance and not a requirement or consideration of the theory.

In this case, Saddam Hussein's invasion of Kuwait was not in line with the interests of any of the followers, in fact, it was harmful to their interests. Hussein aggressively and violently took over another country and in some cases enslaved its citizens, taking hostages and creating a refugee crisis. The Russian leadership, in contrast, sought to profit by acquiring real estate and the rights to oil and gas reserves writ large, and in doing so created a prosperous economic era for the citizens of Russia. Still, the egoist ethic prevented Russia

CASE STUDY *(continued)*

leadership from thinking about the long-term stability of the investments that they were making. While petroleum can be profitable, the boom and bust cycle that it experiences is not always conducive to the long-term stability of an economy. Russia faced this reality in recent years when countries like Saudi Arabia possessed an almost limitless supply of crude oil and began to export it at a price point that was unprofitable for countries like Russia or the United States. The lack of development of sustainable and environmentally friendly energy sources is also an unfortunate consequence of the Russian attempt to become the world's largest producer and exporter of oil. In this case, the interests of leadership coincided with the goals of followers, though strictly by coincidence, and only for a relatively short time.

The goal for these leaders was to grow their respective country's economic means by asserting power over oil reserves. In both cases, the goal was mainly self-interested. The more prosperous the country, the better the leaders' lifestyles would be. In the case of Saddam Hussein, very little of the money earned through the invasion of Kuwait ever circulated through the economy. The goal of an egoist leader is always going to be tied to his or her own self-interest. The leader's own moral justification of that goal is also important. For Hussein, the invasion of Kuwait was ethically justified based on his belief (or purported belief) that Kuwait had engaged in stealing Iraqi oil through slant drilling, despite the fact that there was no evidence of this.

The context of the foreign conflicts over oil was possible only because of the nature of oil as a commodity. Oil has an extremely high value, but it is difficult to measure before it is acquired and processed. Hussein was able to justify his invasion of Kuwait based on the belief that they might be slant drilling and stealing oil from reserves below Iraq. This claim would have been difficult to prove or disprove based on how difficult it would be to measure the oil reserves before drilling. The relative instability of the political landscape in the Middle East also allowed for Hussein to take over Kuwait with only a grassroots resistance. This is a common theme in egoist leadership – often the followers have relatively little power and the context is already unstable. This political instability was also true of the Russian rush for oil. It occurred only after Gorbachev stepped down and the Soviet Union was dissolved, which made land available that had previously belonged to the state. The value held by these leaders was self-interest above all, and the engagement of their followers in a common goal was not a norm.

Summary and concluding remarks

This chapter began by asking what self-interested leadership looks like. Through a series of examples, we explored that question with an eye toward understanding whether ethical egoism can be an effective (or even a possible) framework for leadership. The biggest challenge to this idea is that ethical egoism fundamentally ignores followers in identifying a goal.

In the absence of a common goal, is it possible that ethical egoism is simply not a foundation for leadership? The answer to this question really depends largely on the composition of the leader's interest. Even in the egregious cases that we explored, such as that of Saddam Hussein, the leader justified his or her actions not simply by self-interest, but by the perception of an action that would benefit others. Hussein claimed that he was defending the Iraqi people. Jill, in our earlier example, justified her actions by looking at the company's overall profitability and success. Some egoist leaders might view their followers' interests as so inextricably intertwined with their own that they are very concerned about a common goal. Imagine a Robin Hood-esque leader stealing from the rich to give to the poor. The common goal is to improve the well-being of the poor. Robin Hood might justify an otherwise unethical action by considering himself a leader who is acting in harmony with this goal. However, you could also question whether Hussein was really a leader, rather than a tyrant. So, what *does* leadership based on self-interest look like? Well, it depends on the leader.

? DISCUSSION QUESTIONS

Think of a recent decision you have made. How much was self-interest a relevant consideration? If not, why not; if so, how so?

Can ethical egoism be considered a foundation for leadership if it does not always rely on a common goal?

With what elements of ethical egoism do you agree?

With what elements of ethical egoism do you disagree?

This chapter stated that the practical criticism of ethical egoism suggests it is not a good decision-making model for leaders. However, might this claim be wrong? If yes, how so?

Could Saddam Hussein be considered a leader? Can he be considered a good leader?

ADDITIONAL RESOURCES

A. Rand, *The Virtue of Selfishness*, New York: Signet, 1964.
This book succinctly summarizes Rand's egoist arguments in a more direct form than her fictional novels, such as *Anthem, Atlas Shrugged, The Fountainhead*, although her novels are more memorable and often referenced as testimonies to her objectivist philosophy.

For more on Ayn Rand's ethical egoism, see her 1959 interview with Mike Wallace. Online, https://www.youtube.com/watch?v=HKd0ToQD00o.

T.L. Price, *Understanding Ethical Failures in Leadership*, Cambridge: Cambridge University Press, 2006.
This is a good resource to explore more about the potential implications of egoist leadership.

NOTES

1 R. Crisp, 'Hedonism Reconsidered,' *Philosophy and Phenomenological Research*, vol. 73 no. 3, November 2006, 619–45.
2 T. Hobbes, *Leviathan*, Edwin Curley (ed.), Indianapolis: Hackett, 1651/1994.

3 A. Rand and N. Branden, *The Virtue of Selfishness: A New Concept of Egoism*, New York: New American Library, 1964.

4 S. Kagan, *Normative Ethics*, Boulder: Westview Press, 1998.

5 D. Reidy, 'The right and the good,' in A. Besussi (ed.), *Philosophy and Politics: Methods, Tools, Topics*, Burlington, VT: Ashgate Publishing, 2013.

6 I. Kant, *Groundwork of the Metaphysics of Morals*, Mary Gregor (ed.), Cambridge: Cambridge University Press, 1997.

7 K. Burgess-Jackson, 'Taking egoism seriously,' *Ethical Theory and Moral Practice*, vol. 16 no. 3, 2013, 529–42.

8 G. Enck, 'Pharmaceutical enhancing medical professionals for difficult conversations,' *Journal of Evolution and Technology*, vol. 23 no. 1, December 2013, 45–55.

9 Burgess-Jackson, op. cit.

10 M. Stocker, 'The schizophrenia of modern ethical theories,' *The Journal of Philosophy*, vol. 73 no. 14, August 12, 1976, 453–66; S. Woodcock, 'When will your consequentialist friend abandon you for the greater good?' *Journal of Ethics & Social Philosophy*, vol. 4 no. 2, 2010, 1–23.

11 R. McManus and G. Perruci, *Understanding Leadership: An Arts and Humanities Approach*, New York: Routledge, 2015, p. 15.

12 R. Hershey, 'How the oil glut is changing business,' *The New York Times*, June 21, 1981. Online, http://www.nytimes.com/1981/06/21/business/how-the-oil-glut-is-changing-business.html?pagewanted=all (accessed March 4, 2018).

13 J. Mouawad, 'Oil prices pass record set in 80s, but then recede,' *New York Times*, March 8, 2008. Online, http://www.nytimes.com/2008/03/03/business/worldbusiness/03cnd-oil.html (accessed March 4, 2018).

14 F. Gauss, 'The international politics of the Gulf,' in Louise Fawcett (ed.) *International Relations of the Middle East*, Oxford: Oxford University Press, 2005, pp. 263–74.

15 J. Stork and A.M. Lesch, 'Background to the crisis: Why war?' *Middle East Report*, vol. 167 (November–December), 1990, 11–18.

16 D. Yergin, *The Quest: Energy, Security, and the Remaking of the Modern World*, New York: Penguin Books, 2011, p. 10.

17 United States Department of Defense, *Environmental Exposure Report: Oil Well Fires* (Release No.: 572–98). Washington, DC: U.S. Government Printing Office, 1998.

18 D. Yergin, *The Prize: The Epic Quest for Oil, Money, & Power*, New York: Simon & Schuster, 1991, p. 23.

19 D. Whisenhunt, *Reading the Twentieth Century: Documents in American History*, Lanham: Rowman & Littlefield Publishing Group, 2009, p. 3.

20 Yergin, op. cit., p. 23.

21 Y. Gaidar, *Collapse of an Empire: Lessons for Modern Russia*, Antonia Bouis (trans.), Washington, DC: The Brookings Institution, 2007, p. 102.

22 T. Gustafson, *Wheel of Fortune: The Battle For Oil and Power in Russia*, Cambridge, MA: Harvard University Press, 2012, p. 107.

6

Universal ethics

Stephanie Raible

How can universal standards guide leaders and followers in any context?

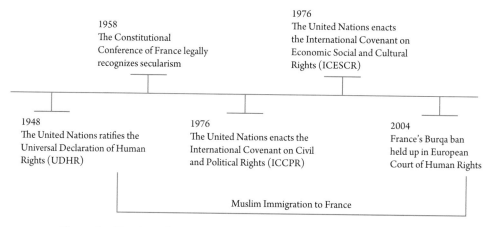

1958
The Constitutional
Conference of France legally
recognizes secularism

1976
The United Nations enacts
the International Covenant on
Economic Social and Cultural
Rights (ICESCR)

1948
The United Nations ratifies the
Universal Declaration of Human
Rights (UDHR)

1976
The United Nations enacts the
International Covenant on Civil
and Political Rights (ICCPR)

2004
France's Burqa ban
held up in European
Court of Human Rights

Muslim Immigration to France

Figure 6.1 Timeline of major works on universal ethics in relation to the case study

Both universal ethics and relativism (Chapter 7) attempt to answer a common problem: finding ethical standards for leadership in any context. However, they conclude differently just how to do that. Universal ethics asserts the need for widespread dialogue and ethical transparency to find a common ground for both well-being and for survival.[1] Whatever source we may appeal to for our ethics, such as faith, tradition, or culture, the appeal of universal ethics spans beyond national boundaries, fields of scholarship, and industry. The hope is that a universal ethic can provide unity and stability in an increasingly interconnected and globalized world. Universal ethics are not just theoretical, because some measure of universal ethical values is already at work today, underpinning our laws, agreements, and behaviors at both individual and collective levels. They help to center our interactions and engagements on the minimal basic consensus of establishing internal peace, economic and legal order, and institutional frameworks.[2] The concept of universal ethical values assumes common 'truths about humanity, regardless of context, community, or culture.'[3] We might think of these truths as a kind of invisible bridge that connects humanity's institutions and collective frameworks to the underlying beliefs and values that hold them together.

The issue of human history brings us to a primary reason for studying and upholding universal ethical values. One argument is that universal values are necessary for sustaining the future world, as there cannot be 'ordering of the world without a world ethic.'[4] To this end, having a common set of universal ethics at an international level allows for a common understanding of perceived values and an ability to distinguish right from wrong.[5] For example, the 1997 UNESCO *Declaration on the Responsibilities of the Present Generations to the Future Generations* says 'that, at this point in history, the very existence of humankind and its environment are threatened.'[6] And therefore 'there is a moral obligation to formulate behavioural guidelines for the present generations within a broad, future-oriented perspective.'[7]

Like our chapter on relativism, this chapter returns to questions rooted in culture. The modern study of universal ethical values has arisen from the perceived need to address challenges raised by the intersection of cultures. So, let us take a moment to reflect on what we mean here by 'culture.' Culture is 'the relatively stable set of inner values and beliefs generally held by groups of people in countries or regions and the noticeable impact those values and beliefs have on the peoples' outward behaviors and environment.'[8] Culture includes both visible and covert elements. Visible facets of culture include behaviors, rituals, cultural products (e.g. music, art, craft, literature), and cultural identifiers (e.g. attire, jewelry, tattoos). Beneath the surface are the covert underpinnings of culture, which include perspectives, philosophies, thought, and values. Our case study will consider how one set of universal values address a cultural conflict: specifically, the desire for Muslim women to wear religiously significant veils within the context of an avowedly secular state.

History

Throughout history, there have been multiple attempts to resolve the question of what universal standards could guide leadership across cultures. This section outlines the history of prescriptive, descriptive, and practical attempts of the philosophers and leaders who have argued for universal ethical values.

Prescriptive attempts

First, let's consider prescriptive attempts, which focus on providing rules for how people ought to conduct themselves. These attempts make authoritative claims in order to establish universal ethics. Several theories in this textbook are underpinned by some attempt to establish a universal ethic. Here, we will briefly consider how virtue ethics, divine command, Kant, and the social contract all attempt to dictate what is 'always right' to do, no matter the context.

Although theories of virtue ethics do not define universal values or action,[9] the earliest records of seeking universal ethics could be attributed to its attempts to define a moral philosophy of virtuous character. As detailed within Chapter 4 on Aristotle and virtue ethics, virtuous people, by nature, do the universally right thing at that moment and within that context. Between the extremes of excess and deficiency, the golden mean is understood to be the middle-ground virtuous behavior given an individual's abilities, available resources, and environmental context. So, the normative prescription here is to always seek the golden mean. Within virtue ethics, it is assumed that a virtuous character is developed through habituation over time. The challenge of this orientation for universal ethics is the presumption that all people would ubiquitously (1) view and judge virtuous action the same way, (2) agree that virtuous behavior would yield eudaimonia (a state of human flourishing), and (3) strive to be virtuous in order to achieve eudaimonia.

Another prescriptive attempt to achieve a universal ethics comes from divine command theory (Chapter 8), which regards religion as the definitive source of morality. Before the twentieth century, much of the Western world expressed confidence in its ability to navigate questions of right and wrong through appealing to ethics rooted in a God-given moral code, as per the divine command theory. The practical dilemma faced by divine command adherents is that there are countless interpretations of the same divine texts, even by those of the same faith. So, while adherents of the divine command theory may be able to agree on the source of their ethical values, they still struggle with specific practical applications. To this end, divine command theory endeavors for establishing universal ethics, but has not shown to be as effective at accomplishing this in practice.

While some other philosophers who called upon religion to establish universal ethics, others appealed to the power of rationalism as a method for reaching ethical conclusions, such as Immanuel Kant's use of reason (Chapter 2). Kant's categorical imperative systematically attempts to rationalize that one should respect humanity, through acting only in accordance with rules that hold for all others. Only those reflections that pass the categorical imperative can be willed to become universal law. For Kant 'only a universal law can provide a rational person with a sufficient reason to act in good faith.'[10]

Social contract theory (Chapter 9) also offers a prescriptive attempt towards a universal value. In its assertion that free and rational people feel that social contracts benefit them, social contracts are cooperatively formed and enforced. Contracts help to create common expectations, securities, rules, and freedoms. When formed among cultures, social contracts are useful in finding common ground and universal points of agreement for conduct. However, there are remaining challenges in practice using social contract theory. It struggles to resolve issues of distrust, repression, coercion, cultural imperialism, threats, and contextually driven difficulties in applying amendments and enforcement. Social contract theory falls short of achieving a fair and sustainable universal ethic, especially when one or more parties feel un- or under-represented.

Descriptive attempts

Beyond the prescriptive attempts towards universalism, there have also been several descriptive attempts to accomplish the same aim. Descriptive attempts chronicle behaviors, patterns, and beliefs. To draw a straightforward distinction between descriptive and prescriptive ethics, we can say that prescriptive ethics focuses on what we 'ought' to do and descriptive ethics focuses on describing what already is being done. For this section, we will review how care ethics and egoism describe universal ethical practices.

When looking to the universal foundations of the ethics of care, its central pillars of care and belonging, as well as a sense of community, kinship, and family (biological or otherwise) are all considered to be universal traits shared across cultures.[11] Think of this as a relational approach to addressing moral obligations. Care ethics builds upon this universal to delineate our moral obligations and actions to our loved ones, as established through the various philosophical lenses offered within the ethics of care. Care encompasses 'everything we do to maintain, contain, and repair our "world" so that we can live in it as well as possible.'[12]

Egoism (Chapter 5) observes only one universal aspect of human nature: individuals are programmed to act in their own interest. Thus, all voluntary acts are motivated by self-interest. Although this may seem to challenge most moral ethical approaches that center on some level of responsibility to others, ethical egoism, a prescriptive side of egoism, settles this through stating that acting in one's best interest is a moral good. In order for an individual to be able to act in their own interest, egoism depends on the individual being free and having free will. When looking to its universal roots, egoism can be seen as sourcing from human nature's interest in survival through balancing one's own needs and interests with other practical realities like the possibility for retribution or conflict.[13]

Policy-based attempts

The catalyst to engage in policy-based attempts towards universal ethics sources from our history because humankind has experienced the pains of operating without a common ground for values. Social and political conflicts, unrest, chaos, power struggles, and the loss of economic opportunity have been regarded as an opportunity for reflection and discussion.[14] The following attempts to establish universals through practical means represent only a small selection of the agencies, declarations, and agreements formed to formalize common, universal values.

The catastrophic devastation of the Second World War was the driving force behind the establishment of the United Nations itself in order to create a forum for global dialogue. In 1945, the United Nations Charter was drafted by 50 countries.[15] Over 70 years since its founding, the United Nations is comprised of 193 Member States, and it serves as the central forum for global discussion. Among the United Nations' greatest achievements were the drafting of two universal human rights declarations: the Universal Declaration of Human Rights (UDHR) and the Convention on the Rights of the Child. The two declarations have served to frame universal understandings of human rights. With only a few but noteworthy exceptions, the two declarations have served as a foundational backbone through which countries have put in place further protections and regulations to support their recommendations.

At the international level, the United Nations Environment Programme serves in a coordinating and advisory role. In addition, many countries have their own agencies that serve to set standards for the protection of the environment. When looking at the national level, the Environmental Protection Agency (U.S.), Environment Agency (U.K.), Ministry of Environmental Protection (China), and Federal Environment Agency (Germany), among many others, operate to lead efforts, promote research, and provide access to information to the public on matters that relate to the environment and the protection of human health from environmental risks. One of the most significant global attempts to find common ground on environmental policy was the Paris Agreement (addressed in Chapter 11), which was ratified by 179 of the 197 Parties to the Convention.[16] The Paris Agreement represents a practical attempt to solidify common standards and expectations to combat climate change and improve environmental conditions worldwide.

Another prominent example of leadership using universal ethical values is within the field of medicine. Beyond the U.N.'s World Health Organization (WHO), voluntary professional organizations also help to set universal ethics of practice. The World Medical Association (WMA) is a voluntary organization of over eight million doctors spanning the globe. The WMA's International Code of Medical Ethics was adopted in 1949, with amendments in 1968, 1983, and 2006.[17] This document helps to set common standards for physicians, including their responsibilities as a practitioner in the field and for their behaviors with patients and their colleagues.

As mentioned previously, relativism (Chapter 7) also attempts to bridge gaps in shared values, laws, and conduct. Relativism positions all cultural practices, moralities, and beliefs as being of equal validity and worth. When looking at one branch of relativism, cultural relativism, morality is contextually bound, culturally defined, and equally privileged. Therefore, what one culture may consider a moral practice, another culture might regard as being dishonorable. Cultural relativism also recognizes multiple circles of culture, which can overlap or conflict. Within a particular context, leaders can be pulled from one cultural circle to another, which can cause confusion and paralysis in decision-making. As a positive, relativism can present a leader with a simple model from which to accept other moral positions and orientations. However, from the universalist perspective, a strong relativistic practice might put leaders into a compromising position, when they could experience instability, uncertainty, and unpredictability.[18] In this respect, universalism helps leaders to move past a point of paralysis and towards clarity, a common foundation, in order to make ethical decisions with confidence.

One primary example stands out when making the argument for universal ethics: Nazi atrocities during the Second World War. After all, if all cultural values are equal, then how could we condemn acts like the Holocaust? During the international dialogue following the devastations of the Second World War, there was a strong impetus to discuss universal ethical values in the form of establishing a common understanding of human rights, or the 'innate, inalienable rights of all human beings in virtue of being human.'[19] Born from the concept of natural rights, human rights are relevant to the discussion of universal ethics because they form a common foundation of human values and ethics.

In response to the war, the Universal Declaration of Human Rights (UDHR) was adopted by the UN General Assembly in December 1948.[20] The UDHR aimed to serve as a universal standard applied to all human beings, across national boundaries and all cultures. The declaration serves as a framework and guide that protects and promotes common respect, rights and freedoms. UDHR established a common set of human rights for all people, as detailed within 30 Articles, with each identifying a different facet of human rights. This framework has been a lasting attempt to structure a set of common understandings for ethical behavior.

Although UDHR is the most recognizable global declaration on universal ethics, there followed other attempts to better represent the unique voices and concerns of other cultures, religions, and nations. These include, but are not limited to, the International Covenant on Civil and Political Rights;[21] International Covenant on Social, Economic and Cultural Rights;[22] Declaration Toward a Global Ethic;[23] Universal Islamic Declaration of Human Rights;[24] Cairo Declaration on Human Rights in Islam;[25] The Bangkok Declaration;[26] and Asian Human Rights Charter: A People's Charter,[27] among others. Readers will find a summary of these in Table 6.1.

Major concepts of universal ethics

The primary assumption of universal ethics is the existence of some common values that are consistent across cultures, and thus 'universal.' These universals identify the core nature and essential characteristics of humanity itself.[28] Scholarship across disciplines has identified the following, among others, to be common threads across all cultures: dualistic thought (existence of binary opposites); religions, belief, or rituals; kinship, community, and family; reciprocity; conflict and war; frameworks of public, government, or social affairs and regulation; law and rules (including a sense of right and wrong); etiquette.[29]

One of the key facets of universal ethics is the attempt to form a common set of moral rules to which we can all appeal. This attempt recognizes a common human need to form a sense of ethics.[30] But of course, rules need application in order to be meaningful. One attempted application of common morals is the United Nations' Universal Declaration of Human Rights. For example, UDHR's Article 15 states the following regarding citizenship rights: (1) Everyone has the right to a nationality; (2) No one shall be arbitrarily

Table 6.1 Summary of human rights documents

Document	Date and Issuing Group	Basic Content
International Covenant on Civil and Political Rights (ICCPR)	Ratified in 1966 by the United Nations	Along with UDHR and ICESCR, serves as foundational text for international human rights. Addresses physical integrity, liberty and security of persons, procedures and rights for the accused, specific individual liberties and political rights.
International Covenant on Economic, Social, and Cultural Rights (ICESCR)	Ratified in 1966 by the United Nations	Along with UDHR and ICCPR, serves as foundational documents for International Bill of Human Rights. Addresses rights for labor, health, education, and adequate standard of living.
Declaration Toward a Global Ethic	Ratified in 1993 by Parliament of World Religions	Interfaith document that calls for commitments to cultures of nonviolence and respect for life, solidarity and just economic order, tolerance and a life of truthfulness, equal rights and partnership between men and women.
Universal Islamic Declaration of Human Rights	Ratified in 1981 by Islamic councils in Paris and London	Based on both the Qur'an and Sunnah, outlines human rights from an Islamic perspective.
Cairo Declaration of Human Rights in Islam	Ratified in 1990 by the Organization of the Islamic Conferences	Guarantees many of the same rights as the UDHR and does this based on Islamic Law (Sharia).
Bangkok Declaration	Ratified in 1993 by Ministers and Representatives of the Asian States	Focuses on commitments of the Asian region to human rights in preparation for the World Conference on Human Rights. Reaffirms commitments to UDHR and adds that terrorism has become a threat to human rights.
Asian Human Rights Charter: A People's Charter	Produced in 1998 by NGOs in South Korea	Endorses UDHR, ICCPR, ICESCR as 'an affirmation of the desire and aspirations of the people of Asia to live in peace and dignity' (Preamble).

deprived of his nationality nor denied the right to change his nationality. Underpinning Article 15 is the common belief that community affiliation is a universal value. Building upon this assumption, the article declares all human beings have the right to national citizenship. Nevertheless, every country has their own laws and regulations as to the rights corresponding to nationality and naturalization processes. To this point, universals are intentionally broad in order to best represent the common ground among cultures, without prescribing specific rules and rights that would be considered inappropriate or unsuitable for any one culture.

Critiques of universal ethics

There are significant criticisms when seeking to frame universal ethics. These critiques align in two overarching categories – (1) ethics cannot be universally established in a fair manner, and (2) universal ethics are not worth establishing.[31] We will now consider these two objections.

Challenges from relativism

One conceptual criticism stems from relativism, which argues that ethical disagreements among cultures are more significant than their areas of agreement.[32] From a relativist point of view, universals should be secondary to showing respect to the values and customs of the other cultures. Because universalism can be viewed as promoting one culture's values over another's, universal values are not viewed as a worthwhile pursuit. For example, the 'universal' concept of individual rights and freedoms has been a contested concept from some Eastern cultures that would favor the more collectivist orientation of obligations and responsibility toward a larger group. Rights are seen as the Western, individualistic complement to freedoms, whereas obligations and responsibility are the Eastern, collective equivalents.[33] From a relativist perspective, promoting the Western versions over the Eastern is not universalism but imperialism.

Ethical imperialism presumes superiority of a specific culture's values, ethics, and perspectives. As a consequence, this ideal culture should serve as the universal standard across contexts and cultures. Historically, ethical imperialism has been a critique against Western societies in their historical colonialism and modern global leadership.[34] Because ethical imperialism typically favors the dominant power's cultural orientation, the established common values lack the voices of underrepresented global powers.[35] Thus, imperialism has favored 'Western' values under the guise of finding universal space. As a consequence, what some view as universal values, others would critique as being oppressively Western. There have been criticisms of the UDHR for this very orientation.[36]

As mentioned earlier, a rule is only as good as its enforcement. So, besides the conceptual critique of universalism, practical criticism is that there is no consistent universal mechanism to hold leaders and followers accountable for their commitment to common values. For example, in spite of declarations like the UDHR, human rights violations can be seen worldwide. Despite the movements to draft and ratify international declarations and agreements, issues such as child labor, sex trafficking, genocide, and discrimination continue to be present and pervasive globally.

Representation of values

One of the greatest challenges of attempting to establish universals is to be representative of all global cultural stakeholders. Thus, another practical critique of universalism questions how representative any established common values can be. With only national level leadership negotiating common ethics, there are populations of people who may feel unrepresented or underrepresented by their leaders. Indigenous and minority populations worldwide can feel that their cultures and voices do not appear within the discussions on universal morals. What makes this event more complicated is that there are so many global cultures. How then do leaders ensure that all voices are accurately and equally represented in the final representation of values?

Five component analysis

Having discussed the features, benefits, and challenges of universal ethics, we next examine how universalism plays out for the five components: the leader, follower, goal, context, and culture.

Under a universal ethical values model, leaders help establish, maintain, and enforce a universal standard of values. Because 'universal' ethics cut across contexts, leaders at international, national, regional, local, organizational, and community levels can all encounter challenges relevant to universal ethics. Leaders must look to the common ground among cultural norms, behaviors, and ethics, in order to find universals among all of their stakeholders. Further, once a common standard of ethical practices and values is established, leaders must share, abide by, and enforce these common moral values. For this to work, leaders must share the common basis of ethical values with their followers. Here, leaders across contexts and fields are charged with safeguarding follower rights and freedoms. In order for leaders

Figure 6.2 The Five Components of Leadership Model applied to universal ethics

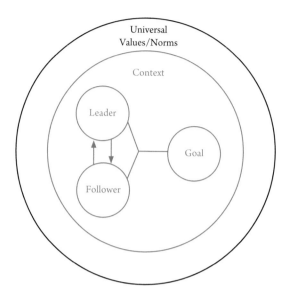

in both the public and private spheres to safeguard and enforce human rights within all areas of their purview, it is critical to have a foundational framework of universal human rights. Beyond establishing, maintaining, and enforcing universal ethical values, leaders also set an example for followers. Because universal ethics are greater than any one person, leaders not upholding universal values can be accountable to their followers and forced to resign, go to trial, or be usurped.

A universal ethical standard is not useful to followers unless they know about it. The perspective of universal ethical values requires followers to be informed on their rights and how the universal values impact their own practices. Followers should be trained on how to conduct themselves within the parameters of the common ethics. This not only includes common values set forth by international declarations, such as the UDHR, but also the established national, regional, industry, and organizational standards. For example, the workers within a community health clinic should be aware of ethical standards set about human rights broadly, as well as established standards set forth by their relevant medical associations, governmental agencies, and medical affiliates or system. In this mode of thought, it is important to ascertain that followers are well informed and trained on how to act in line with these universal values.

As we will see in our followership chapter (Chapter 14), followers also play a critical role in holding their leaders accountable for their practices and enforcement of the universal ethical values. Followers can play a role in promoting universal ethics by having clear expectations for how those universal ethics are drafted, monitored, and enforced by their leaders. Followers are empowered when they are informed for the sake of monitoring and holding leaders' actions to a common, formalized standard. Having an external set of universal ethical values also helps followers to be able to point to common standards to set their expectations and justify any of their concerns.

The goal of universal ethics is to find enough of a common ground in behaviors, social norms, and ethics to be able to peacefully co-exist and to successfully communicate, collaborate, and practice. Küng's basic minimal consensus of internal peace, economic and legal order, and institutional frameworks help to set the essential baseline for why universal ethics are needed at an international and societal level. When paring this down to the organizational level, the goal for universal ethical values is to establish ethical transparency. The intended goal is to have universals in place to guide practice in accordance with a baseline of ethical practices, regardless of the cultural makeup of the organization. One of the central goals of universal ethical values is to help deliver on the promise of a common standard of treatment of other human beings, regardless of cultural orientation. As a consequence, this orientation is meant to protect the rights of both leaders and followers coming from different cultural orientations in practice.

From the perspective of universal ethics and the UDHR, the validity of the leader's actions and legislation should be judged as to the leader's respect of human rights.[37] This rule applies in any context. So, leaders outside of the public sector should also be held accountable for their commitment of the protection of human rights, even though they are not the ones granted power to enforcing cases of human rights violations.[38]

As discussed within the goal portion of the analysis, universal ethical values aim to establish a baseline for common rights. In some contexts, this might be a measure to ensure equality regardless of cultural orientations, but it does not necessarily mean equal treatment of all regardless of culture. This perspective will be unpacked in greater detail within the following case study section, which presents a case where those of minority cultures are asked to adjust their practices, in this case, attire, to align with the expectations established of the majority cultures.

Within the context of universal ethical values, the weight of power centers within the culture component. Where we find agreement in this larger cultural context plays a critical role in determining how leaders and followers relate to each other and what goals are appropriate. Within a globalized world, with those of different cultures interacting with greater frequency, the common standards set and upheld by the United Nations and its agencies, governmental agencies, and industry organizations serve as the foundations for organizational ethical strategy. There have been many challenges to establish common standards for ethical practices and behaviors, but that is to be expected from the intersection of different cultures and their beliefs, attitudes, and convictions.

The presented case introduces the leader (French and European policy makers) and the follower (the Muslim populations in France), along with the goal (protecting French secularism versus religious freedom), context (France and its legal precedents for the bans), and the larger culture (secularism versus the various Muslim norms and values). The stark differences in goals and larger cultures causes tensions between the leader and the follower. The arguments for and against veil bans help to contextualize how these each are manifested. The discussion of UDHR attempts to find if universal ethics can shed some light onto the case.

CASE STUDY

Universal ethics applied to the public wearing of religious attire in France

As a case study, let us consider Muslim women in France, who wish to wear certain religious identifiers. France, along with many other European countries, has been the home to adherents of Islam for centuries. As of mid-2016, Muslims represented roughly five percent of the total population in Europe.[39] With 5.7 million Muslims, France has one of the highest populations within Europe. The proportional percentage of Muslims living across Europe has been increasing, with a significant rate of growth projected to continue for the forthcoming decades. Projections of Muslims residing in Europe in 2050 range from 11.2 percent to 14.0 percent of the total population, with France potentially consisting of a Muslim population of 17.4 percent under medium-level estimates of migration.[40]

The Muslim population in France is diverse in thought, practice, and culture, with a variety of different orientations and reactions to the various French bans on veils in public settings. The diversity of the Muslim population includes all facets of demographics, as they represent a range of ages, professions, educational backgrounds, political affiliations, citizenships, cultural identities, ages, and beliefs. When reporting on the intersection of their French residency and Muslim faith, the majority of French Muslims (72 percent) do not see a challenge between being a French resident and being a devout Muslim, similar

CASE STUDY *(continued)*

to 74 percent of the general French public.[41] In a 2016 survey of 1,029 Muslim people in France aged 15 and older, respondents were classified into three groups based on their responses. Of the respondents, 46 percent were categorized as either secularized or felt alignment between their Muslim culture or faith and contemporary France. In contrast, 26 percent of respondents could be categorized as wanting more ability to express their religious identity, but they accepted secularism, whereas 28 percent of respondents reported with greater opposition to the French secular values and felt disconnected from French society. Some of this group could be classified as seeing their faith as a rebellion to French society, as the group is made up of younger Muslims with less education and training and a higher percentage of unemployment.[42]

France as a secular state

France's regulations on the adornment of religious attire in public environmental contexts have a significant historical legal precedent dating back to the early twentieth century. The French emphasis on *laïcité*, or secularism, grew increasingly important within the French context, in large part as a response to the Catholic Church's historical stronghold on moral issues nationally.[43]

The French legal position on secularism originated with the Law of 9 December 1905. The law cemented the separation between Church and State through six chapters, which detail the principles for the division between Church and State, the 'assignment of property and pensions,' and public religious worship regulations.[44] The law is a crucial and defining legal backbone for French secularism, and its clarifications and interpretations of secularism continue to serve as legal precedent, as seen in subsequent legislation.

The legal protection of secularism advanced decades later, within the Constitution of 1958. One of the most relevant legal defenses of the secular state appears within the 1958 National Constitution's Preamble Article 1, which, along with the Law of 9 December 1905, has been cited as the legal basis for the string of recent, highly contentious regulations relating to Muslim veils and similar body coverings. The Preamble Article 1 of the Constitution of 1958 states:

> France shall be an indivisible, secular, democratic and social Republic. It shall ensure the equality of all citizens before the law, without distinction of origin, race or religion. It shall respect all beliefs. It shall be organised on a decentralised basis.[45]

Despite religion being framed as a personal freedom and a right of all citizens, the Article reaffirms France as a secular nation state first and foremost, which is meant to ensure equality and respect differences in beliefs. In order to uphold its protection as a secular state, French public buildings are regarded as 'neutral ground, where any religious or political symbolism is prohibited.'[46] Article 1 protects France's *laïcité* paradigm and views that religion must not have any place within public affairs. The freedom of religion in

CASE STUDY *(continued)*

France is positioned as a human right, but never in isolation from other universal human rights. France therefore objects to a special status for religious freedom over freedom of conscience.[47]

Secularism continues to play a significant role in all facets of public life in contemporary France. French public schools and offices do not allow students, employees, and visitors to wear religious attire. The public adornment of veils or other religious attire in public schools or buildings is viewed to be in direct conflict with the human right of freedom of conscience, which is defined by the Oxford Dictionary of English as 'the right to follow one's own beliefs in matters of religion and morality,' including the choice not to practice a religion. Therefore, French protections of *laïcité* permit all people to practice religion and adorn religious attire within the appropriate context, such as in private homes and religious buildings. Context is key within the parameters of French laws dealing with secularism, as the separation between religious practices in public and private spheres ensures no conflict with the freedom of conscience, as outlined in the Constitution.

In looking to recent legislation related to *laïcité*, the concept itself was deliberated upon for the first time in the late 2004 Constitutional Convention, on occasion of France's working toward fulfillment of the treaty establishing a constitution for Europe. In its landmark ruling, the Constitutional Council of France conferred legal recognition of the concept of secularism as defined by Article 1 of the 1958 National Constitution.[48] This decision also served to solidify the National Assembly's early 2004 ban on religious symbols and coverings in schools (Law 2004–228).[49] It is upon this basis that subsequent derivative rulings and decrees have been upheld by French courts and governments, as well as the European Court of Human Rights and European Court of Justice in 2011, 2014 and 2017.

Despite France's strong cultural and legal support of secularism, the bans have been met with both domestic and international criticism. The adornment of veils is noted within the Quran on three occasions, but the interpretations of what is meant by these excerpts varies significantly. The modern interpretations of the excerpts on veil adornment carry different interpretations from culture to culture. The modern translation an individual's family or cultural community has on these excerpts can carry a significant influence as to whether a woman chooses to wear a veil or what type of veil she would choose to wear. A woman of Muslim faith chooses to wear – or not to wear – head or face veils based on her comfort and preferences, depending on her cultural background or that of her family.

Those in favor of individual cultural rights view the religious attire bans to be a form of discrimination and a limitation to individual and collective cultural expression and religious freedom. Some purport that regulations are sourced from fears of a minority culture and misunderstandings about the Muslim faith. For those women who wear hijabs, it is not only an expression of religious identity and modesty, but hijabs and other forms of head and face veils represent a sense of comfort and safety.

When looking towards why Muslim women in France report why they or other Muslim women wear veils, there are some common reasons reported. Within a 2016 survey, Muslim women who wear a veil compared to those who do not identified a sense of religious duty

CASE STUDY *(continued)*

as the primary motivation of Muslim women to wear a veil at 76 percent and 66 percent, respectively.[50] Other motivations to wear a veil included a want to display their religious faith (23 percent of veil wearers and 44 percent of non-veil wearers), coercion and imitation (6 percent and 24 percent, respectively), and safety (35 percent across both groups).[51] Other motivations of veil wearing might be related to community and personal identity.[52] Community identity relates to a sense of wanting to show unity, affiliation, and solidarity with other women of the Muslim faith. Individual identity connects to how a woman views herself, how she wants to show herself to the world, and what she finds personally comfortable in her attire.

Within Western countries, the rapid growth of Muslim residents and migrants has been met with cultural misunderstandings and judgments. Beyond the argument of safeguarding the secular state, other prominent arguments for supporting regulation assert that regulations help (1) secure the safety of the women from harm and discrimination, (2) prevent feelings of distance from those who wear veils, and (3) promote the well-being of Muslim women.

The opposition to the public adornment of veils positions that they are not seeking to limit individual rights of religious expression and observance, but they are helping to prevent discrimination and harm. Those advocating for regulation purport that removing religious identifiers prevents discrimination, lessens the chance of poor or hateful treatment of these individuals, and safeguards secularism. For example, French Muslims report higher instances of negative incidents related to their ethnicity or faith (37 percent), compared to those in other countries of Western Europe (Britain 28 percent, Spain 25 percent, and Germany 19 percent).[53] Those supporting regulation assert that this perspective is in the best interest of everyone to prevent discrimination and incidences of violence.

The second prominent argument is that those interacting with women wearing veils struggle to feel connected with the individual adorning the veil. Particularly with regard to the reactions to the wearing of face veils, such as niqabs and hijabs, there is a cultural perception of personal distance created through covering portions of the face. This perspective has been seen internationally in both Muslim-minority countries, like France, and Muslim-majority countries (including in the aforementioned cases in Egyptian universities and university hospitals).

The third argument claims to be founded on a modern, Western perspective of women's rights, stating that some feel as though veils support the oppression of women. Regulating the adornment of hijabs, niqabs, and other veils in public contexts may be seen as an effort to support a Western perception of women's rights or liberation and, thus, the 'well-being' of the women affected by the regulation. To this end, Muslims' treatment of women has especially been an area of concern for non-Muslims. From a 2011 Pew survey, there is a median national average of only 22 percent of non-Muslims within Western Europe, Russia, and the United States who report that Muslims were respectful of women.[54] The results indicate a large distrust of Muslims in how they treat and regard both Muslim and non-Muslim women. Even though this argument can be seen as ethical imperialism, the strength of these sentiments is important to note, as it likely carries some degree of influence on Western societies' view of the practice of wearing face and head coverings.

How UDHR addresses issues of religious belief

What complicates our case is how text from the UDHR can be used to argue for both the pro-secular and pro-religious positions. When reviewing UDHR, leaders (advocates for secularism and regulating some public adornment religious identifiers) might start by citing Article 3, 'Everyone has the right to life, liberty and security of person.'[55] Leaders may argue that aligns with the French Constitution of 1958, in that the Constitution views the liberty and security of persons to be supported by the existence and protection of a secular state. Under this interpretation, residents would have the freedom to their beliefs but with the security of not persecuting, or being persecuted by, others.

Both the leader and the follower would cite Article 18 as the most direct article on this issue. Article 18 of the UDHR states that:

> Everyone has the right to freedom of thought, conscience and religion; this right includes freedom to change his religion or belief, and freedom, either alone or in community with others and in public or private, to manifest his religion or belief in teaching, practice, worship and observance.[56]

Note that Article 18 does not explicitly and directly address the adornment of religious identifiers. So, the preferred interpretation of the leader might focus on the individual freedom to religious choice and to practice and teach religion freely. For the pro-secular view, the French Constitution supports the religious rights stated in Article 18, while balancing Article 3's rights of liberty and security.

Those who advocate for religious freedom of expression would likely present a stricter interpretation of UDHR's Article 18. In its statement that an individual has the right to 'manifest his religion or belief in teaching, practice, worship and observance,' the adornment of religious identifiers (including veils) could be considered part of religious observance. For the follower, religious observance relates to the honor and attainment of moral requirements, which includes the adornment of veils. Because Article 18 explicitly references the right to religious observance in public, religious adherents could claim this would put the legal bans as being in violation of Article 18 of UDHR.

If in agreement with the stricter interpretation of Article 18, there is a further problematic article, Article 7, which, in part, states:

> All are entitled to equal protection against any discrimination in violation of this Declaration and against any incitement to such discrimination.[57]

CASE STUDY *(continued)*

If Article 18 is to be understood as protecting the wearing of religious identifiers, a limitation on the freedom of religious observance would be a violation of Article 18 and would also be eligible for protection against a ban, as a declaration of cultural discrimination, under the protections of Article 7. Arguably under a more liberal interpretation of Article 18, as viewed by the proponents of the bans, French leaders could point to the French Constitution as being in line with Article 7, as the Constitution already 'ensures the equality of all citizens before the law, without distinction of origin, race or religion.'[58]

The two different interpretations of Article 18 by the case's leader and follower are the central issue as to how UDHR is both (1) potentially a problematic representation of universal ethics and (2) falling into some of the greater criticisms of universal ethical values as a practical lens for leadership. To the former point, the follower might raise the criticism of UDHR being representative of Western values, therefore, being a form of cultural imperialism, rather than universal ethics. To the latter point, this disagreement could support the argument that universal values are not worth attempting, as cultural differences are strong and universals among cultures may not even exist.

These different interpretations demonstrate how enforcement of universals are a work in progress and need to be revisited over time. Since the time of the drafting of UDHR, cultural intersections have become much more common within many Western countries. For example, France's Muslim population grew from approximately 0.55 percent of the country's population in 1950/52 to a projected 10 percent in 2020.[59] The commitment to revisit, discuss, and revise existing understandings of universal ethical values is a critical part of the process. Therefore, under a universal ethics approach, it might be appropriate to revisit UDHR again, in order to consider its critiques and to compare its values with those presented within the other existing declarations of universal human rights.

Five component analysis applied to the wearing of religious attire in France

As a final analysis of the case, this section revisits the five components in light of the presented case. Each subsection will review the role, perspective, and challenges of the case's leader, follower, goal, context, and larger culture under a universal ethics lens.

The leader and follower roles can get blurred with universal ethics. In one sense, the 'leader' is actually just following and enforcing the universal ethic, similar to their role in divine command and Kantianism. Within the presented case, the 'leader' generally refers to the policy makers and political leaders at all levels who are responsible for upholding the French Constitution and enforcing French law. This case poses two primary questions for the leader, 'are the enforced universal values truly universal?' and 'how does the leader reconcile cultural differences within a universal ethics approach?'

The notion of followers within a nation-wide example, can also be somewhat unclear. The presented case focuses on the Muslim communities in France, who support some degree of public religious expression through the adornment of head or face veils.

CASE STUDY *(continued)*

Figure 6.3 The Five Components of Leadership Model applied to the wearing of religious attire in the France case study

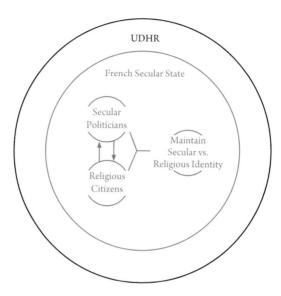

Even within this focused group, there is still significant diversity of opinion. Across the highlighted follower group, the followers had to become advocates for themselves or their peers to make sure their perceived rights of religious observance were respected (for empowered followership, see Chapter 14). When looking beyond the highlighted follower group, those who support strongly French secularism also have basic rights that need to be protected according to the UDHR. In this case, the follower is concerned with questions such as: 'Who enforces universal values?' 'How can the followers' voices best be heard when confronting cultural differences?' and 'How can followers effectively raise concerns and criticisms of existing universal frameworks, such as UDHR?'

The presented case has two goals that are seemingly in conflict with one another. The goal for the French leader is to protect the country's secular identity and its citizens against any form of harm or discrimination. In contrast, the desire of the focal follower group is to maintain their religious identity and observance through wearing veils. While the group's goals are in opposition, they could both appeal to the UDHR. The primary question for the case's goal would center on which interpretation of UDHR's Article 18 is accurate: that of the pro-secular leader or the pro-religious followers.

The context is secular France, which is experiencing increased stress from navigating the increasing cultural difference within the country, including a significant growth in the country's Muslim population. Being within Europe, France has historically both witnessed and experienced some of the world's most devastating religious wars, conflicts, and discrimination, which in turn, ignited and enforced its secular identity and protections. Because of the horrors of the Second World War, the country moved toward relativism as

CASE STUDY *(continued)*

part of its post-war identity, opening its borders to more immigrants from cultures outside of the European continent than it had before in recent history. To this end, the leader and followers should reflect on how this context can embrace what are becoming competing values of secularism and religious liberty.

As mentioned in the context discussion, multiple cultural forces are at work in the larger culture. The competing norms and values existing within the French case include secularism, religious identity, protections of minorities, and the rights guaranteed by UDHR, among others. Both the leader and the followers point to the aforementioned cultural values as informing their goal and their beliefs and actions associated with the goal and its attainment. From a practitioner perspective, it appears that leaders and followers can look to resources in the larger culture like the UDHR for guidelines on how they engage with each other. However, the struggle is that while UDHR may provide some broad guidelines, other cultural and context issues make it difficult to clearly and consistently apply these guidelines. Using UDHR as a starting point rather than a conclusion, the leader and followers should engage in dialogue to find their common universal ethical values and reflect on the challenges of their held norms and values within the French context.

Summary and concluding remarks

Our chapter identifies both challenges and opportunities for its response. First, the criticisms of universal ethical values point out the difficulties of identifying truly universal values, especially because 'universals' can be more representative of groups with greater relative power and privilege (e.g. 'Western'). Another challenge for universal values is enforcement. However, if leaders and followers can work together to find broad common values and have the patience to continually revisit the practical applications of those values – especially when they may appear to be contradictory – then universal ethics can be a model for providing guidance in any context.

Let's return to the opening question of the chapter, 'How could universal standards guide leaders and followers in any context?' The short answer: 'it's tricky.' The guidelines offered must be broad enough that they can be applied in any context, and both leaders and followers will need to continually revisit how those guidelines are being applied. As a check and balance, they will need to make sure a 'universal' value is not just a 'Western' point of view. Also, they will need to find a way for enforcing these values when they are violated.

DISCUSSION QUESTIONS

How might universal ethics influence your personal life, your organization, or your academic institution?

When considering the regulations within your organization, institution, or region, what policies support the individual rights identified within UDHR? What policies might be considered as encroaching on these rights?

What are the ways in which you see bias on all levels (from the individual up to the local cultural context) affecting a leader's ability to uphold universal ethical values in their organization's daily business processes?

Is it the responsibility of leaders to uphold observation of the UDHR within their practice, or are local laws, regulations, and customs more critical to uphold?

When reflecting on the case study, what are the limits to the UDHR? How might the open interpretation of the UDHR's Articles be problematic?

ADDITIONAL RESOURCES

H. Küng, *Global Responsibility: In Search Of A New World Ethic*, New York: Crossroad Publishing Company, 1991.

Küng's work makes the case that a global ethic is necessary for the survival of the human race. He is a significant figure in the discussion of global ethics, and his work has been influential for both the Parliament of the World's religions and the United Nations.

Rushworth M. Kidder, 'Universal Human Values: Finding An Ethical Common Ground,' *Public Management*, vol. 77 no. 6, 1995, 500–8.

Though written in the 1990s, Kidder's article still provides helpful insights through interviewing two dozen 'men and women of conscience' and determining eight common values that can sustain humanity as it moves into the twenty-first century.

UN General Assembly, 'Universal Declaration of Human Rights,' 217 (III) A. Paris, 1948. Online, http://www.un.org/en/udhrbook/pdf/udhr_booklet_en_web.pdf.

For those who wish to better understand the UDHR, the UN provides an easily downloadable PDF copy of the declaration in its entirety. This booklet version is easy to read, and its accompanying illustrations can be helpful for those who wish to explain these concepts to a younger audience.

NOTES

1 H. Küng, *Global Responsibility: In Search of a New World Ethic*, New York: Crossroad, 1991, p. 32.
2 Küng, ibid., p. 28.
3 K. Hutchings, *Global Ethics: An Introduction*, Malden, MA: Polity Press, 2010, p. 231.
4 Küng, op. cit., p. 34.
5 A global imperative and adjoining justification for this are suggested in the 1997 UNESCO Declaration on the Responsibilities of the Present Generations Towards the Future Generations, which asserts 'the necessity for establishing new, equitable and global links of partnership and intragenerational solidarity, and for promoting inter-generational solidarity for the perpetuation of humankind', UNESCO *Declaration on the Responsibilities of the Present Generations to the Future Generations* 1997, (resolution 44), adopted November 12, 1997.
6 Ibid.
7 Op. cit.
8 B. Peterson, *Cultural Intelligence: A Guide to Working with People from Other Cultures*, London: Nicholas Brealey, 2004, p. 17.

9   N. Athanassoulis, 'Virtue ethics,' *Internet Dictionary of Philosophy.* Online, www.iep.utm.edu/virtue/ (accessed March 9, 2018).

10 M.D. Hauser, *Moral Minds: How Nature Designed Our Universal Sense of Right and Wrong,* New York: Ecco, 2006, p. 13.

11 D.E. Brown, *Human Universals,* Philadelphia: Temple University Press, 1991.

12 B. Fisher and J. Tronto, 'Toward a feminist theory of caring,' in E.K. Abel and M.K. Nelson (eds), *Circles of Care: Work and Identity in Women's Lives,* Albany: State University of New York Press, 1990, p. 40.

13 Brown, op. cit.

14 Küng, op. cit.

15 See United Nations, 'History of the United Nations.' Online, http://www.un.org/en/sections/history/ history-united-nations/ (accessed March 9, 2018).

16 See United Nations, 'United Nations climate change.' Online, http://unfccc.int/paris_agreement/ items/9485.php (accessed March 9, 2018).

17 World Medical Association, 'WMA International Code of Medical Ethics.' Online, https://www.wma. net/policies-post/wma-international-code-of-medical-ethics/ (accessed March 9, 2018).

18 C.J. Sanchez-Runde, L. Nardon and R.M. Steers, 'The cultural roots of ethical conflicts in global business,' *Journal of Business Ethics,* vol. 116 no. 4, 2013, 689–701.

19 Hutchings, op. cit.

20 United Nations General Assembly, *Universal Declaration of Human Rights* 1948 (resolution 217 A), adopted December 10, 1948. Online, http://www.ohchr.org/EN/UDHR/Documents/UDHR_Transl ations/eng.pdf (accessed December 17, 2017).

21 Office of the United Nations High Commissioner for Human Rights (OHCHR), *International Covenant on Civil and Political Rights* 1966 (resolution 2200A; XXI), adopted December 16, 1966. Entered into force March 23, 1976. Online, http://www.ohchr.org/EN/ProfessionalInterest/Pages/CCPR.aspx (accessed December 17, 2017).

22 Office of the United Nations High Commissioner for Human Rights (OHCHR), *International Covenant on Economic, Social and Cultural Rights* 1966 (resolution 2200A; XXI), adopted December 16, 1966. Entered into force January 3, 1976. Online, http://www.ohchr.org/EN/ProfessionalInterest/Pages/ CESCR.aspx (accessed December 17, 2017).

23 H. Küng and Council for a Parliament of the World's Religions, *Declaration Toward a Global Ethic 1993,* adopted September 4, 1993. Online, https://parliamentofreligions.org/pwr_resources/_includes/FCK content/File/TowardsAGlobalEthic.pdf (accessed December 17, 2017).

24 Islamic Council of Europe, *Universal Islamic Declaration of Human Rights* 1981, adopted September 19, 1981. Online, http://www.alhewar.com/ISLAMDECL.html (accessed December 17, 2017).

25 Organization of Islamic Cooperation, *Cairo Declaration on Human Rights in Islam 1990,* adopted August 5, 1990. Online, http://hrlibrary.umn.edu/instree/cairodeclaration.html (accessed December 17, 2017).

26 Ministers and representatives of Asian States, *Final Declaration of the Regional Meeting for Asia of the World Conference on Human Rights* 1993, adopted March 29 to April 2, 1993. Online, https:// www.hurights.or.jp/archives/other_documents/section1/1993/04/final-declaration-of-the-regional- meeting-for-asia-of-the-world-conference-on-human-rights.html#_ednref1 (accessed December 17, 2017).

27 Asian Human Rights Commission, *Asian Human Rights Charter: A Peoples' Charter* 1998, adopted May 17, 1998. Online, http://www.refworld.org/pdfid/452678304.pdf (accessed December 17, 2017).

28 W.H. Goodenough, *Description and Comparison in Cultural Anthropology,* Chicago: Aldine, 1970.

29 Brown, op. cit.

30 Küng, op. cit. p. 29.

31 G. Demuijnck, 'Universal values and virtues in management versus cross-cultural moral relativism: An educational strategy to clear the ground for business ethics,' *Journal of Business Ethics,* vol. 128 no. 4, 2015, 817–35.

32 C. Gowans, 'Moral relativism,' in Edward N. Zalta (ed.), *The Stanford Encyclopedia of Philosophy,* Winter

2016 edn. Online, https://plato.stanford.edu/archives/win2016/entries/moral-relativism/ (accessed March 9, 2018).

33 O.A. Sanchez, 'Some contributions to a universal declaration of human obligations,' in T.S. Axworthy (ed.), *Bridging the Divide: Religious Dialogue and Universal Ethics*, Montreal: McGill-Queen's University Press, 2008, pp. 187–95, p. 188.

34 C. Kleist, 'Global ethics,' *Internet Encyclopedia of Philosophy*. Online, http://www.iep.utm.edu/gecapab/#SH4b (accessed March 9, 2018). See N.L. Roth, T. Hunt, M. Stavropoulos and K. Babik, 'Can't we all just get along: Cultural variables in codes of ethics,' *Relations Review*, vol. 22 no. 2, 1996, 151–61.

35 Roth et al., op. cit.

36 Sanchez, op. cit.

37 T. Pogge, *World Poverty and Human Rights: Cosmopolitan Responsibilities and Reforms,* Cambridge: Polity Press, 2002.

38 B. Fasterling and G. Demuijnck, 'Human rights in the void? Due diligence in the UN Guiding Principles on Business and Human Rights', *Journal of Business Ethics*, 116, 2013, 799–814, p. 802.

39 C. Hackett, '5 facts about the Muslim population in Europe,' The Pew Research Center, November 29, 2017. Online, http://www.pewresearch.org/fact-tank/2017/11/29/5-facts-about-the-muslim-population-in-europe/ (accessed December 15, 2017).

40 C. Hackett et al., 'Europe's growing Muslim Population,' Pew Research Center, November 29, 2017. Online, www.pewforum.org/2017/11/29/europes-growing-muslim-population/ (accessed December 15, 2017).

41 J.T. Allen, 'The French-Muslim Connection,' Pew Research Center, August 17, 2006. Online, http://www.pewresearch.org/2006/08/17/the-frenchmuslim-connection/ (accessed December 15, 2017).

42 H. El Karoui, *A French Islam is Possible,* Institut Montaigne, September 2016. Online, http://www.institut-montaigne.org/ressources/pdfs/publications/a-french-islam-is-possible-report.pdf (accessed December 8, 2017).

43 D. Decherf, 'French views of religious freedom,' The Brookings Institution, July 1, 2001. Online, https://www.brookings.edu/articles/french-views-of-religious-freedom/ (accessed December 8, 2017).

44 O. Guerlac, 'The separation of church and state in France,' *Political Science Quarterly*, vol. 23 no. 2, 1908, 259–96.

45 The Constitution of France of 4 October 1958. Online, http://www.conseil-constitutionnel.fr/conseil-constitutionnel/english/constitution/constitution-of-4-october-1958.25742.html (accessed December 8, 2017).

46 Decherf, op. cit.

47 Decherf, op. cit.

48 B. Chelini-Pont and N. Ferchiche, *Religion and the Secular State: French Report, Publicaciones facultad de derecho Universidad Complutense,* 2015. Online, https://hal-amu.archives-ouvertes.fr/hal-01432382/document (accessed December 9, 2017). For the Treaty establishing a Constitution for Europe see: http://www.conseil-constitutionnel.fr/conseil-constitutionnel/root/bank/download/2004505DCen2004_505dc.pdf.

49 Law 2004–228 of March 15, 2004, *Journal Officiel de la République.* Online, https://www.legifrance.gouv.fr/affichTexte.do?cidTexte=JORFTEXT000000417977&dateTexte (accessed December 9, 2017).

50 El Karoui, op. cit.

51 El Karoui, op. cit.

52 T. Perkins, 'Unveiling Muslim women: The constitutionality of hijab restrictions in Turkey, Tunisia and Kosovo,' *Boston University International Law Journal*, vol. 30 no. 529, 2012. Online, http://www.bu.edu/law/journals-archive/international/volume30n2/documents/note_perkins.pdf (accessed December 15, 2017).

53 Allen, op. cit.

54 'Muslim–Western tensions persist,' Pew Research Center, July 21, 2011. Online, http://www.pewglobal.org/2011/07/21/muslim-western-tensions-persist/ (accessed December 9, 2017).

55 UDHR, op. cit.

56 UDHR, op. cit.

57 UDHR, op. cit.
58 The Constitution of France, op. cit.
59 H. Kettani, 'Muslim Population in Europe: 1950–2020,' *International Journal of Environmental Science and Development*, vol. 1 no. 2, 2010, 154–64.

7

Cultural relativism

Stephanie Varnon-Hughes, Stanley J. Ward and Alexandra K. Perry

FRAMING QUESTION

How do culture and context impact leadership?

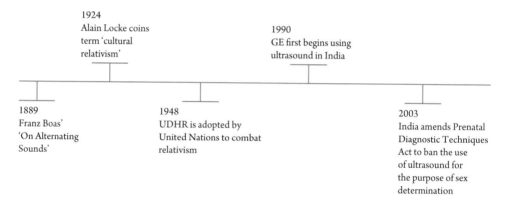

Figure 7.1 Timeline of major works on cultural relativism in relation to the case study

In 2015, U.S. multinational enterprises employed 42.4 million workers.[1] In some of these countries the giving of gifts is simply how business gets done; in other countries, the giving of gifts is viewed as a bribe. When organizations interact with diverse populations – across nations or even within their own national borders – culture and context make a difference. Relativism, based on cultural differences, highlights the impact of culture and context on ethical decisions.

For as long as leaders have engaged with communities outside their own, questions of different values have challenged notions of what it means to lead ethically. Within various cultures, different values dictate different perceptions of what is 'moral,' 'right,' 'good,' and 'just.' Moral/Ethical relativism is a challenge for any leader, regardless of leadership style or a leader's relationship with followers. And yet, despite being a challenge, the critical and creative thinking skills developed by grappling with relativism are also essential for responsive, culturally sensitive leadership.

A variety of factors can contribute to the challenges of relativism in a leadership setting: sometimes issues come from the community of followers; sometimes they come from cultural difference; and sometimes they come from the specific context. Occasionally – and most challenging for leaders – the same goal can be ethically correct in one setting, but unethical in another. For organizations and endeavors that work and collaborate across cultures, a minefield of potential 'improper' ethical decisions exists. However, leaders, by virtue of their very position, must not become mired in relativism. Rather than surrender to 'paralysis by analysis,' leaders must act – even in the midst of differing ethical opinions. Those who choose to express leadership must use their cultural intelligence to make informed decisions and take action. In this chapter, we'll trace the factors that have converged to construct our current understanding of 'ethical relativism,' the key ideas that are essential for leaders to understand and navigate the concept, and the critiques of the model. We will then apply the Five Components of Leadership Model to explore how relativism can be both a challenge and an advantage for any diverse organization. We will then use a contemporary case study to examine relativism's essential themes.

Some criticize higher education because they perceive it as presenting relativism as the only philosophical 'truth.' Our chapter is not making that argument, but rather it is trying to unpack the implications of relativism for leadership. First, let's define what we mean by 'relativism'. It may be helpful to define relativism by way of contrast. Where 'absolutism' tells us that some things are always ethically correct and can be independently verified as such, relativism says that the context must always be taken into account. Relativism is a widely used term in philosophical discussions and can be variously defined as indicated in Table 7.1.[2] To narrow our focus, we will focus on cultural relativism. Thanks to the ubiquity of international media, the Internet, and multinational corporations and organizations, leaders frequently confront challenges related to diverse cultural perspectives.

A favorite way to express the ethics of cultural relativism is to assert, 'When in Rome, do as the Romans.' The struggle here is that the Romans allowed for certain forms of infanticide as well as human slavery. Can leaders from one culture that condemns these practices simply allow for them when in the Roman context? While our Roman illustration may seem dated, it's relevant because when we look at our case study, we will consider how a multinational

Table 7.1 Types of relativism[3]

Type	Major Concepts
Cultural Relativism	Norms and values of right and wrong are based on the conventions of a particular location, group, or culture.
Conceptual Relativism	We determine the categories by which we interpret our experience. There is no pre-determined reality.
Alethic Relativism	Objective truth does not exist. What is true for one person may not be true for another.
Epistemic Relativism	What counts as 'knowledge' is determined by the context which produces it. No one system of knowledge can be proven superior to another.

corporation addressed conflicting cultural views about sex-selective screening for abortions. But first, let's consider the history of relativism as a philosophical concept.

History

Cultural relativism has a long and rich history in ethics literature. As early as the fourth century, Herodotus recognized that when faced with multiple cultural perspectives, humans prefer their own way of doing things rather than trying to find what is 'true.' As a philosophical theory, relativism dates back to the eighteenth-century moral philosopher, Immanuel Kant, who is the subject of Chapter 2. Kant's theory of knowledge was that there are structures that exist a priori, meaning that knowledge of them is independent of any experience. Mathematical facts, the movement of time, or tautologies (such as, 'all men are human') are all examples of a priori truths. Beyond these a priori truths, Kant believed that all knowledge was derived from experience, making it relative to each person so that those with shared experiences would also share more of a knowledge base than those without shared experiences.[4] Though Kant did not use the term 'cultural relativism,' the theory was articulated in his epistemological work.

Cultural anthropologists picked up on the ideas laid out by Kant and his students during the period that spanned both World Wars. With increasing exposure to other places and cultures during the war, academics struggled to make sense of how the different cultures they encountered could have such different and seemingly incommensurate value systems. Cultural relativism was a way of making sense of conflicting values. Linguists, especially, felt that this theory had a lot of explanatory power. Given that language has such a clear impact on the way that we understand our world, it was no wonder that people who spoke different languages might also have different values systems. This idea expanded on an earlier study by Franz Boas, a nineteenth-century anthropologist who studied Native American language and began to notice idiosyncrasies in linguistic convention between groups that he first believed to be meaningless. The longer he studied these groups he began to realize that these idiosyncrasies in pronunciation actually carried great significance.[5] Half-a-century later, during the Second World War, anthropologists began to go back to Boas' work and to use the term 'cultural relativism,' which he had coined.

The challenge with cultural relativism as studied by anthropologists, however, is that it doesn't offer a solution to competing values. Anthropology might describe the radical views of the Nazis as compared to the opposition of the Allied Forces, but when both sides aggressively assert that they are right, how can such a conflict be resolved? According to cultural relativism, there may not be a way to resolve it. The Allied Forces believed they were right based upon their values; so too the Nazis believed that they were right based upon their own cultural ideals. Without moral absolutes, there is no way to determine which group is right.

Cultural relativism hit its peak in the United States during the Vietnam War. The competing 'cultures' in this case were actually based on generation and class. The war was one that many didn't understand and believe in, and it spurred on protests and anti-government movements. Again, academics turned to cultural relativism to describe the vastly different values held by Vietnam opponents and those in favor of the war.[6] While cultural relativism reached its zenith as an ethical construct in the 1970s, most ethical scholars now temper its claims. Now that we have a basic understanding of the definition and history of relativism, we can more closely examine the idea's fundamental assumptions.

Major concepts of cultural relativism

As we try to understand cultural relativism and its impact on leaders, we should first consider five key claims and implications for relativism in a leadership context:

1. Culture and context necessarily dictate our values;
2. As a consequence, values are based on a particular framework;
3. Therefore, no singular viewpoint is prioritized above others;
4. Yet, relativism should not be confused with nihilism;
5. Thus, values become a crucial part of the conversation on relativism.

Readers should note that our discussion of relativism here is not purely theoretical – because that might lead to nihilism – or a rejection of all moral principles – that leaders cannot and should not abide. Instead, our thoughts are guided by a desire to offer a practical form of relativism. Rather than concentrating on individual claims as we have done in previous chapters, we will focus on these critical arguments beginning with our first premise, 'culture and context necessarily dictate our values,' and proceed to relativism's conclusion, 'values become a crucial part of the conversation on relativism.'

If we are raised in a water-rich environment, wasting water is not sinful. If cows are sacred, fast food includes veggie patties and dairy but never meat. Both avowed religious women and mothers are celebrated in the same culture, while the former practice celibacy and the latter do not. So even though values vary widely, we humans are capable of evaluating laws, cultural norms, and individual practices based on factors including human need, issues of scarcity, that which we hold as sacred, and exposure to new technologies or knowledge. That said, even when we are capable of understanding that there are a variety of possible values in a given setting, for the most part, human communities and organizations prefer to operate with one set of values that are predominant.

For example, in the United States, even while vegetarian and vegan menu items options have become more widely available and normalized in restaurants, specific meals (like Thanksgiving dinner) and certain settings (BBQ picnics, parties celebrating football) remain linked to the consumption of meat. The strands of culture that make 'tradition' in the United States – like our Judeo-Christian background, a privileging of Western European values and food practices, and commercial farming and ranching – set up decisions around hospitality and consumption. Once again, although we might understand that there are different values and norms, we still operate within a predominant paradigm, or a particular way of thinking and doing things.

In some countries, a glass of beer or wine at a working lunch is typical. In others, the same glass of beer or wine would be immoral or even illegal. A 'good' team member might need to adapt to both practices within a career at the same company. To succeed in our careers, or to be generous hosts or participants in collaborative endeavors, we often leave the comfort zones of our own preferences and bend a bit to the prevailing values of the cultures and contexts in which we interact.

For example, scholars at academic conferences frequently attend formal receptions and informal gatherings at hotel bars and restaurants. As Islamic studies, inter-religious studies, and Muslim scholars have become more represented in academia, many young, practicing Muslim academics find themselves challenged. Muslims do not believe in consuming alcohol. Personally, they would prefer not to meet in a bar. Professionally, they know it is correct and helpful – they may be left out of critical collaborations and continued joint conversations if they demur.

Here is the point where many of us become paralyzed. This equality of views may seem a logical conclusion from 'values and actions are relative to a particular framework.' Further, in the world of philosophy and ideas, it can be instructive to play with this and investigate this concept. The struggle is that in the actual world, it cannot be an operating framework. At some point, we have to choose if we are going to the bar and having a drink with our colleagues or not. Also, even for relativists, some viewpoints have much more value than others.

For example, most leaders' decisions prioritize the safety, ongoing security, and conditions for individual human lives to flourish above the needs and rights of other living creatures and other possible factors. Economist Amyarta Sen and philosopher Martha Nussbaum call this 'maximum human flourishing' when they evaluate economic systems and how they impact human communities.[7] That is, if a business or government has options that can create opportunities for flourishing (health, autonomy, access to education, economic security and civil liberties) for a greater number of people, they should pursue those options over those choices that either curtail those rights, or only create opportunities for flourishing for a few.

There are still some values we can agree on, such as the value of respecting life, but we struggle to create cross-cultural definitions that work here. If one follows relativism to the false and unhelpful conclusion that because all values are equal, it is impossible to choose how to act responsibly, we come to nihilism – the idea that no possible moral choice exists and so life is meaningless. While many of us wrestle with cynicism and doubt from time to time, part of our identity as leaders includes desiring to bring about change. To foster change, we must believe that current conditions and obstacles can be addressed, and a 'better' outcome can be created and maintained.

Thus, scholars such as Rorty and Nussbaum argue for 'flourishing' as a guiding moral value.[8] Individual humans can flourish; so too can families, cities, businesses, governments, and economies. Questions related to values go beyond the first questions we often ask related to productivity and efficiency: How do we maximize profit? How do we speed up production? How do we beat our competition? How do we cut our losses? Instead, flourishing-related questions should include: How does this decision have a positive impact on the greatest number? Does this policy allow for flexibility and individual choice? Does this budget curtail health care access for those in our community? Do the long-term effects of this decision create environmental or economic harm for this region? Now that we have a better understanding of relativism's fundamental principles let's consider its major critiques.

Critiques of relativism

There are two primary critiques of cultural relativism as an approach to ethical leadership – the first theoretical, and the second practical.

The theoretical critique is of the central tenet of the theory itself: If morality is relative – at least to culture – how is it possible to say that morality exists at all? In other words, if the appraisal of what is right can only be done within the confines of the culture in which an action takes place, is it ever possible to condemn actions that seem to be universally worth condemnation, or to praise those actions that seem inherently good? Cultural relativists are not uncomfortable with this critique. Morality is similar to currency – its value is tied to the culture within which it is circulated, and yes, this causes challenges when cultures collide, but we may find ways to adapt and address these challenges.

It is really in the extreme cases that this critique shows its teeth. While some particular values may be shared across and between cultures, other actions seem impossible to understand through the lens of cultural relativism. How can we condemn mass murder, such as that witnessed in Cambodia under Pol Pot, if we subscribe to a view that moral and immoral action can only be assessed within the confines of particular cultures? The critique asserts that although different viewpoints exist, that does not necessarily entail that they are all right. People can be both sincere and fervent and also simply wrong.

The practical critique is of relativism's utility for leaders. The question it asks is: 'How can leaders make ethical decisions when they lead diverse groups?' Critics claim that relativism makes it difficult or even impossible for leaders to be decisive and take action. This claim, in turn, creates distress amongst followers who look to leaders for clarity and moral guidance. Leaders do not have the luxury of indecisiveness.

Take, for example, a college administrator who is planning for the academic year calendar. The school has a relatively small but present percentage of

Jewish students. This year, the Jewish high holy days all fall on Wednesdays. The administrator considers closing the university on those days to allow students to observe the holidays with their families. However, given how small the Jewish population is, and the number of classes that meet only on Wednesdays, she decides that this would make it impossible for those courses to offer the number of contact hours necessary for the class. She chooses to implement a policy which allows Jewish students to be absent from classes on these days without any penalty to their grade, and without any requirement to make up the work that they missed that day. While this solution is sensitive to the cultural significance of the high holy days, it leaves the university's professors in a bind: Does this mean that the students who observe these holidays are now responsible for less material than the students who do not? Does this mean the material that will be present on cumulative exams cannot be taught on these days? How are faculty to determine which students can 'legitimately' miss these classes, and which students' absences should be deemed unexcused? The truth is, there is no solution to this challenge that is going to satisfy everyone. Relativists would claim that this is acceptable; respecting all cultural beliefs is the right thing to do. Critics look at the practicality of doing so in a society where we welcome diversity and argue that it is not possible for a leader to be decisive enough to embrace cultural relativism truly. This is just one example of the practical implications cultural relativism has upon leaders. However, the ethical theory also has implications for the other aspects of the leadership process.

Five component analysis

We now return to our five components of leadership to clarify how relativism impacts leadership as a phenomenon. Similar to our discussion of the pivotal concepts of relativism, we will strive to provide an analysis that is practical and not purely theoretical. As we can see from Figure 7.2, *cultural values and norms are the keys to understanding the way cultural relativism relates to the Five Components of Leadership Model.*

One implication of cultural relativism is that leaders need a kind of cultural humility as well as to develop skills related to cultural intelligence. As part of that cultural intelligence, they must distinguish between what elements of their ethical system are 'core' to who they are and what parts are flexible, depending on the context.[9] This need for self-knowledge resonates with the authentic leadership model described in Chapter 12, where leaders need to know their core values. One difference here is that authentic leadership does not provide much guidance for how leaders can negotiate the 'flex' needed when dealing with cultural relativism.

Figure 7.2 The Five Components of Leadership Model applied to cultural relativism

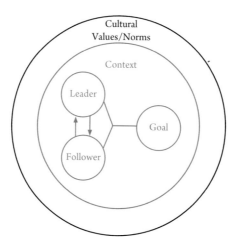

Self-awareness alone will not meet the demands of ethical relativism. Leaders must also be aware of who their followers are and what they hold sacred. This follower-awareness is another example of the humility required by leaders who embrace cultural relativism, and how the ideas of 'core' and 'flex' play an important role. What may make this tricky for leaders is that they must balance the needs of the organization to accomplish certain tasks with the belief-systems of followers who may be limited in their ability to perform certain tasks. Leaders need discernment to recognize what requests from followers are authentic and bear accommodation, which we will consider further in our discussion of 'context.'

On a practical level, even after identifying their own perspectives as well as listening to what followers hold sacred, leaders still have work to do. Leaders trying to address cultural relativism are in a precarious situation because if they place too much emphasis on highlighting the different perspectives in the room, there is a risk of creating even more divisions within the group of followers. One way to address these differences while still encouraging unity is to focus on how the group's different cultural perspectives can contribute to achieving the overall goal.[10]

Relativism also impacts the relationships between various followers. Followers must realize that both peers and leaders may hold beliefs that are contrary to their own, yet their peers and leaders hold those beliefs with equal sincerity. So followers, too, must develop a measure of cultural humility and allow for what is most important to others. Readers should note that once again, awareness of the 'other' and the ability to negotiate critical tasks based on that awareness is a crucial skill set for leaders and followers to accomplish goals within cultural relativism.

A positive consequence of recognizing cultural relativism is that doing so can foster a culture of respect. This culture of respect can be measured to the extent that both leaders and followers are aware of the authentic needs of both each other and the organization, and to the extent that those personal and organizational needs and values are accommodated. In a sense, this accommodation demonstrates an attempt to meet both the task and the relational challenges faced by organizations, where 'task' can be understood as the necessary outputs of an organization and differing personal values are considered part of the 'relationship.'[11]

Determining the validity of a goal and its possible unintended consequences becomes difficult with relativism (as will be seen in our case study). Multiple ethical filters are at play. The possibility for confusion implies a need for leaders and followers to communicate at length about clarifying the goal (like the adage 'measure twice, cut once'). We know that a principal expectation from followers is a desire for clarity, yet ethical clarity can easily be lost here. The good news is that although it is difficult to evaluate a moral stand in settings that experience cultural relativism, once we have negotiated it and found a shared sense of purpose, we can stand there with greater confidence.

Relativism recognizes that even in one specific organization's context, there are still many cultural expectations that make demands on the leader, follower, and goal. As a benefit, relativism draws awareness to what makes people unique even though they share the same immediate context.

Relativism also creates challenges in the context of leadership engagement. One concern is how do we honor another's culture without putting undue stress on the organization? For example, consider a circumstance where a worker's religion demands that he not shave, yet the company requires clean-shaven appearances because of the preferences of the company's clientele. Both the religious adherent and the company are sincere in their desire to uphold their values within a specific context, and both are trying to honor demands placed on them by outside forces (religion or the requirements of a particular client base). Indeed, one solution is to say, 'Well, the religious adherent should simply find employment somewhere else.' But what if the 'clean-shaven' positions provide higher income and more career advancement opportunities than positions that allow for facial hair? Shouldn't leaders also care about implementing a fair and equitable environment?

As we've already discussed, relativism makes it difficult for leaders and followers to achieve ethical clarity, and the temptation then becomes to descend into the abyss of nihilistic cultural values where 'anything goes' or 'might makes right.' That temptation to fall into an unprincipled pragmatism is one more reason that leaders must be intentional in how they choose to engage the cultural values surrounding their context.

More than any other of the ethical models we've considered, relativism advocates for a multitude of cultural spheres that bound leaders, followers, goals, and contexts. Sometimes these spheres integrate neatly, and at other times these spheres conflict with each other harshly. Many human resource programs today struggle with how to navigate diversity in the workplace, precisely because of how these cultural spheres can come into conflict. Other models may project a more monolithic representation of culture. Relativism acknowledges the flurry of interactions going on in the modern world. Let's now turn to a specific instance to illustrate the way cultural relativism may impact the leadership process. For that, we turn to our case study.

CASE STUDY

The use of ultrasound technology in India for sex-selective abortions

In the 1990s, General Electric (GE) brought ultrasound technology to India. Previously, ultrasound machines were bulky and expensive, so traveling doctors could not use them. The potential for doctors, nurses, and medical technicians to go to rural and remote communities and practice preventative medicine was vast, and the potential health benefits were enormous. The process for doing so included partnerships between GE and local doctors. That is, GE knew that local physicians would be best situated to serve as consumers and advocates for the new technology. The corporation invested in ways to help doctors become trained in the latest technology and then serve as part of the salesforce, sharing the capacity for bringing the new tools to broader communities. Instead of going through the government or large hospitals, working with individuals allowed GE to bring their ultrasound technology to areas quickly, and with maximum opportunities for quick sales.[12]

During this time, many people in India viewed female infanticide as an appropriate way to promote the ideal family – where sons were given priority. One Punjabi proverb put it memorably – 'Raising a daughter is like watering your neighbor's garden.'[13] In other words, investing in a daughter was expensive, and another family would receive the benefits of that investment. Sons were the ones who went to work, carried on the family name, were responsible for the care of aging parents, and in the Hindu tradition even lit the funeral pyre of their deceased parent. So tremendous cultural forces and expectations gave priority of

CASE STUDY *(continued)*

place to sons over daughters. This was exacerbated by the tradition of a daughter's family paying a dowry for her marriage. Even though the tradition had been outlawed, it was still practiced.

One unintended consequence of GE's ultrasound technology was that those in the business of providing gender screening were immediately able to purchase the smaller ultrasound machines and set up small businesses providing this service. In many regions in India, there remains a cultural preference for male children, and female infanticide remains a challenge for human rights activists, religious leaders, and policymakers. In some rural areas, there are not enough women for men in the community to marry and start families of their own. While female infanticide is illegal and therefore screening for sex is illegal, many families seek out ultrasounds to either procure an abortion if the fetus is female or to arm themselves with information that would help them decide to dispose of the newborn once it is born. Because of the preference for male children, another kind of market for portable, affordable ultrasound technology existed, and – without meaning to – GE became the perfect deliverer of the tool that would end up exacerbating a complicated national issue with political, ethical, and cultural challenges.

The Indian government and local nationals immediately stepped up education campaigns at both the local and national levels and added legal ramifications, such as requirements for signage, requirements for extra training, and legal consequences for doctors or technicians providing ultrasounds for sex-selective abortions. India's Parliament enacted the Pre-Conception and Pre-Natal Diagnostic Techniques (PCPNDT) Act in 1994 to stop female feticides and work to halt the declining sex ratio in India. The act banned prenatal sex determination.

As a response, GE took their complicity in contributing to the decline of girls' birth and ease of illegal – and to many, immoral – actions seriously. The company was forced to examine cultural values and how some of the needs of the communities served in India, such as access to affordable preventative care, were at odds with other needs in those same communities. They worked to create a culture shift at several levels: first, they reached out to local activists, community health educators, and religious leaders to understand how the problem worked on the ground, especially with poor and rural families who needed male children to help with work and take care of elderly family members. Managers and salespeople within India participated in professional development and training to become familiar with the ethical challenge and with the legal ramifications associated with the technology, as well as to become sensitive to the more systematic issues that made gender selection seem necessary for some families. Sales plans had to take into account that although a purely economic standpoint, increased sales were a boon, ethical planning would call for GE to take a stand on whether or not it wanted to be part of sex-selective abortions, or whether it wanted to use its economic power to provide education and greater access to rights for their Indian consumers.

In the end, GE positioned themselves as economic partners with their Indian clients. Not only did they want to be at the forefront of providing affordable, reliable medical

CASE STUDY *(continued)*

technology, they also wanted to contribute to a society where girls and women have access to rights and education. They wanted to help eliminate the false choice that seemed to require their Indian patients to access illegal technology in a struggle to make sound decisions for their lives and the lives of their families. Indian campaigns on billboards and signs remind viewers that a girl is 'as good as a son' and that all children should have rights to education. Indeed, as economists remind us, literate women propel economies forward. GE also produced cultural studies courses and worked to become partners with health and education providers in Indian states. Of course, this positioning also had a financial advantage – for a multinational corporation with diverse constituents, it would be detrimental to be associated with female feticide and illegal gender selection practices.

Now let's apply the five component analysis to this case. The leader at the start of this case was not an individual leader, but a multinational corporation, General Electric. At the time of this case, GE was in a phenomenal growth period under the leadership of CEO, Jack Welch, but for GE to sell ultrasound products in India in the late 1980s and early 1990s, it needed additional influencers in India.[14]

If we understand GE to be the leader in this case, there are multiple followers. There are the salespeople who delivered and trained on the devices, the medical facilities who purchased them, the doctors who used them, and the patients who received services. All

Figure 7.3 The Five Components of Leadership Model applied to the GE ultrasound and sex-selective abortion in India case study

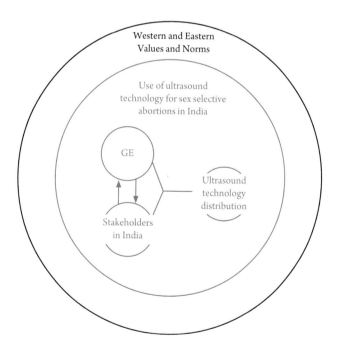

CASE STUDY *(continued)*

of these followers were stakeholders in achieving the overall goal of bringing ultrasound technology to India. As followers implemented that business goal, conflicting cultural values surfaced.

Note that the solution here was not solely administered top-down from the leader. Given the distance between GE's business headquarters in the United States and the Indian continent, a practical solution would require a partnership between the business and the people on site. So, followers also had a role to play in resolving the situation. Not only did GE address the issue, but the Indian government and doctors did as well, and the success of these actions depended on how they were received in the rural communities where sex-selective screening was taking place.

In this case, there was an overall goal at work – bringing ultrasound technology to India. It was the implications of that goal in a particular context that caused the ethical struggle. In that sense, this case is a helpful illustration of 'unintended consequences.' Local business people saw an opportunity to sell sex-selection services that were made even more accessible because of the affordability of ultrasound methods in contrast to the other available options.[15]

So our case not only illustrates different cultural values at work, but it also shows how these values interplay with factors including public health, technological advances, cultural and religious beliefs, and commitments to investors and to economic growth – both internationally and within emerging markets. All of these factors influence how the goal is perceived.

In this case, the context of the leadership engagement was different from the originating context of the leadership organization. The initiative was started in the western hemisphere of the global north and was implemented in the eastern hemisphere of the global south. This contextual difference was part of what led to the unintended consequences. In one context, the sale of ultrasound devices in rural communities could be viewed as providing a beneficial resource that would improve local health as well as economic growth. In another context, these same devices were to provide services that would negatively impact the birthrate of females in India.

The case illustrates multiple cultural forces interacting. Some of those cultural forces include local Indian customs and traditions and preference for male children existing alongside 'Western' values like feminism, individual freedom, the values of Western investors, and the profit motives for both international business leaders and local business outlets.

From the perspective of Western values, Jack Welch had publicly stated that GE was not trying to use ultrasound technology as a way of monetizing India's preference for sons.[16] Additionally, many feminists struggled with the conflicting values of allowing women the freedom to choose an abortion while also trying to value female fetuses.[17] To resolve these cultural differences, neither GE nor the Indian government could simply say that all values were equal. They had to work together, along with other stakeholders to determine a way to move forward. All parties had to understand the different cultural values and norms that were at play to find a way to reach the goal of bringing ultrasound technology to patients in India.

Summary and concluding remarks

To answer the question posed at the beginning of the chapter, 'How do culture and context impact leadership?' we can assert that effective leadership requires 'cultural intelligence' and awareness of the ways cultural values and norms affect the leadership process. Leaders must recognize that no matter what their current context, there are multiple cultural factors at work. Cultural relativism shows that leaders must approach each leadership situation with a certain measure of cultural humility, recognizing that other cultural values may be important for followers and that a leader's particular cultural assumptions may have unintended and negative consequences for these followers. Part of that cultural humility requires leaders to listen to the deeply held values of their followers. Still, it is important for leaders to be decisive. In spite of the fact that there are multiple and often competing cultural contexts at play, leaders must still make decisions. Knowing the difference between a leader's 'core' values and where there might be room to 'flex' can help with this. Decision makers will also benefit from developing trusted relationships with partners who represent various cultural perspectives.

? DISCUSSION QUESTIONS

Share an example where two points of view can be equally 'right' when they are based on a person's cultural values and norms. Follow the outcomes from making a decision from each point of view to their logical end considering consequences, stakeholders, and risks.

Think about your position as a leader paying particular attention to issues of power and privilege. Describe your social context: sex, gender, race, educational attainment, language skills and access, wealth, property ownership, religion, national identity and other aspects of identity. How might your identity affect the way you look at the world?

Have you ever experienced conflict between professional practice and personal belief? How did you deal with this challenge?

When you are participating in a culture unfamiliar to you, how much do you expect that culture to suspend their practices to be welcoming to you as a visitor, and how much are you willing to change to be a gracious visitor? Examples might include: eating or drinking things you normally would not, dancing in public as performance for esteemed teachers or dignitaries, sitting on the floor, removing your shoes, staying up late or rising especially early, avoiding contact with members of the opposite sex, or giving or receiving gifts (even if prohibited by your organization's policies).

In the case of General Electric, what kinds of professional development would you recommend to provide increased awareness of the impact of decisions that are not always just 'business' decisions?

If you were writing a code of conduct for an international organization, from which sources will you draw perspectives and guidance? If there are two opposing perspectives, how will you decide which to adopt?

⊕ ADDITIONAL RESOURCES

P.C. Earley and E. Mosakowski, 'Cultural intelligence,' *Harvard Business Review*, October 2004. This is an often cited article that presents a thoughtful discussion of culture and leadership.

T. Donaldson, 'Values in tension: Ethics away from home,' *Harvard Business Review*, September–October, 1996.
This practical *HBR* article provides guidelines for managers addressing issues related to conflicting economic development and conflicting cultural traditions. As part of his solution, the author suggests the flexible application of an international organization's core values.

H. Miner, 'Body ritual among the Nacirema,' in A. Podolefsky, P. Brown, and S. Lacy (eds), *Applying Anthropology*, 10th edn, New York: McGraw-Hill, 2012, pp. 503–7.
This chapter presents a memorable and creative treatment of culture and cultural studies.

NOTES

1 D. Jenniges, 'Activities of U.S. Multinational Enterprises in 2015,' Bureau of Economic Analysis, December 2017, p. 2. Online, https://www.bea.gov/scb/pdf/2017/12-December/1217-activities-of-us-multinational-enterprises.pdf (accessed February 25, 2018).

2 M. Baghramian and J.A. Carter, 'Relativism,' *Stanford Encyclopedia of Philosophy*, September 11, 2015. Online, https://plato.stanford.edu/entries/relativism/ (accessed February 25, 2018).

3 Our typology is adaptive from the *Stanford Encyclopedia of Philosophy*, ibid. That source lists 'moral relativism' as the fifth type, but also explains that moral relativism, if seen as culturally dependent, can be seen as a sub-type of cultural relativism. That is how we use it here.

4 I. Kant, *Critique of Pure Reason*, M. Weigelt (trans.), New York: Penguin, 1781/2007.

5 F. Boas, *Race, Language, and Culture*, Chicago: University of Chicago Press, 1940.

6 W. Washburn, *Against the Anthropological Grain*, New Brunswick: Transaction Publishers, 1998.

7 A. Sen, *Development as Freedom*, Oxford: Oxford University Press, 1999.

8 R. Rorty, *Consequences of Pragmatism: Essays*, Minneapolis: University of Minnesota Press, 1982.

9 For a helpful TEDx talk on core vs. flex, see J. Middleton, Cultural Intelligence: The Competitive Edge for Leaders. Online, https://youtu.be/izeiRjUMau4 (accessed 13 July 2018).

10 D. Thomas and R.J. Ely, 'Making differences matter: A new paradigm for managing diversity,' in *On Managing Across Cultures*, Boston: Harvard Business Review Press, 2016. Thomas and Ely call this an 'integration' paradigm in contrast to an assimilation or differentiation paradigm.

11 The different perspectives on leaders and followers for the categories of tasks and relationships were part of a classic Ohio State management study in the 1950s. See R.M. Stogdill, O.S. Goode, and D.R. Day, 'New leader behavior description subscales,' *Journal of Psychology*, vol. 54 no. 2, 1962, 259–69.

12 M. Jain, J. Mead, and J. Harris, 'GE healthcare in India: An (ultra)sound strategy?' Darden School of Business, Case No. UVA-E-0337. Online, https://ssrn.com/abstract=1417201 (accessed February 25, 2018).

13 Jain et al., ibid.

14 J. Solomon, 'In India's outsourcing boom, GE played a starring role,' *Wall Street Journal*, March 23, 2005. Online, https://www.wsj.com/articles/SB111151806639186539 (accessed January 4, 2018).

15 F. Arnold, S. Kishor, and T.K. Roy, 'Sex-selective abortions in India,' *Population and Development Review*, vol. 28 no. 4, 2002, 759–85.

16 Jain et al., op. cit.

17 Arnold et al., op. cit.

8

Divine command theory

James N. Thomas

 **FRAMING QUESTION**

What does the divine require from leadership?

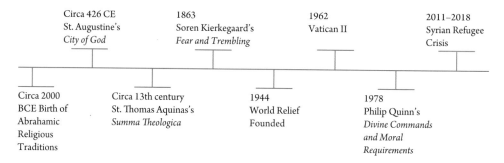

Figure 8.1 Timeline of major works on the divine command in relation to the chapter case study

One of the oldest and perhaps the most controversial concepts in the field of ethics is the divine command theory of moral obligation. This approach advocates the view that ethics depend, at least in part, on God's will and commands.[1] In other words, what makes something morally obligatory is that God commands it. Religious ethicists generally agree that some, or all, moral actions depend on God.[2] Such a theory allows leaders to have an objective ethical framework to guide their leadership practices such as relating to others, daily decision-making, determining motivation, and projecting outcomes and goals. Although this general definition is fairly standard across proponents of the idea, divine command theorists disagree about the specific aspects of the theory and its implications for leaders.

Though the term 'religion' is notoriously broad and covers a number of worldviews, most religions have an ethical base. Some polytheistic religions, such as Hinduism, adhere to a high sense of moral duty. For example, the

Bhagavad Gita teaches that righteous living, or dharma, requires discipline and acting out of a sense of duty to a higher moral law rather than out of merely a concern for the consequences of our actions. Likewise, non-theistic philosophies espouse an ethical base for moral conduct. For instance, Buddhism values the unity and interdependency between persons and, indeed, all living beings. Thus, it teaches that its adherents have a moral responsibility to maintain concern for others and the world in which they live. Confucianism also has prescribed rules of conduct for interactions between people to ensure everyone is treated properly and with due respect.

Religion also plays a part in other areas of human interaction. For example, civil religion is an institutionalized set of beliefs, symbols, and rituals that provide a religious dimension to a nation's collective life.[3] Civil religion claims that morality, at least to some extent, is relative to a particular culture, and religion may even be written into a country's laws. Some examples of this include Sharia law in the Islamic world, derived from the sacred writings of the Quran and Hadith, and the Judeo-Christian influence on United States jurisprudence. Many Muslim majority countries incorporate Sharia law at some level in their legal framework, with many utilizing it as the highest form of law in their constitution.[4] Likewise, American civil religion is often thought of as a blend of Judeo-Christian ideas with nineteenth-century enlightenment thinking.[5]

Though we could examine many different ethical theories grounded in religion, this chapter will focus on the monotheistic traditions of Judaism, Christianity, and Islam. The idea of moral goodness is so closely tied to these religions that ethics are built into their central doctrines. Their religious texts portray God as instructing humans in what they are and are not to do, such as those decrees found in the Ten Commandments.[6] Consequently, divine command theory has dominated the field of religious ethics.

In this chapter, we will examine the concept of divine command theory and how it relates to leadership ethics. We will study the development of divine command theory, its major concepts, and key critiques of the theory. As we have done in previous chapters, we will then look at the critiques of authentic leadership, as well as apply the Five Components of Leadership Model to analyze the theory. We will end our time together with a case study that considers one of the most prominent faith-based relief organizations in the world, World Relief.

Throughout the chapter, we will see how obligation to God's commands compels leaders to hold high ethical standards for their own behavior in the ways they relate to their followers, in the means through which they pursue their goals, and in the way they influence the broader context surrounding them and the organizations in which they lead. In so doing, leaders must be aware of the larger cultural values in play based on God's commands, the intentional and purposeful interaction between leaders and followers to accomplish these commands, and the shared goals of both leader and follower resulting from these commands. The main lesson we can learn from this chapter is that divine command theory is a viable theory of ethics in leadership. This is true as it relates to leadership and its application to the overall context and culture of an organization, in relation to followers, and in the achievement of shared organizational goals.

History

Many Christian thinkers in post-biblical times, including St. Augustine, St. Bernard of Clairvaux, St. Thomas Aquinas, and St. Andrew of Neufchateau claimed that divine commands determined the ethical status of specific actions.[7] For instance, St. Augustine proposed that ethics was the pursuit of the supreme good, which led to human happiness.[8] He argued humans must love objects that are worthy of human love in the correct order. They are to love God first, which allows them to align their other loves, so they might properly foster their happiness and fulfillment. Pre-Reformation Franciscan philosopher and theologian John Duns Scotus was another early voice proposing a divine command approach to ethics.[9] Scotus argued that the only commands God could not take away were to love God and love others. He proposed that some moral truths are necessary truths, and even God can't change those; they would be true no matter what God willed. (We will explore this point a bit more later in this chapter.)

The nineteenth-century Danish philosopher Søren Kierkegaard added another defense of divine command theory in the form of his idea of moral obligation.[10] Kierkegaard contended that God's commands are not arbitrary, but are directed at human flourishing, leading to genuine happiness, even though obedience requires self-denial and a loss of ego.[11] Kierkegaard argued that those whose moral allegiance is grounded in a religious faith might still participate in a pluralistic society without compromising their faith and without elevating a certain religion to any sort of privilege. However, divine command theory is not only found in the area of religion; the concept can also be found in the broader field of ethics, specifically in the work of Immanuel Kant.

Eighteenth-century German philosopher Immanuel Kant, discussed in Chapter 2, was traditionally not known as an advocate for divine command theory. Nevertheless, his ethical system may be interpreted as supporting the validity of a divine command theory of moral obligation. Kant's categorical imperative is an absolute, unconditional requirement that must be obeyed in all circumstances and is justified as an end in itself. Kant's imperative then becomes a universal law that applies to everyone everywhere to follow. Though Kant does not advocate the concept of moral faith as an argument for divine command theory, a contemporary advocate might argue that the concept of a categorical imperative does lean toward this view of morality.[12]

Though divine command theory fell out of fashion during the nineteenth-century enlightenment when more secular ideas of moral obligation arose to the forefront, there has been a remarkable renewal of divine command theory beginning with Philip Quinn's book *Divine Commands and Moral Requirements* (1978). Before Quinn's work, there were various references to divine command theory, but no sustained working out of the approach in a defensible form. Quinn argues that because God is the source of the moral law, people are obligated to obey this law because it is God who commands it.[13] Since Quinn's book, the argument for divine command theory has continued.

One of the most prominent works following in the steps of Quinn's idea of moral obligation is Robert M. Adams' *Finite and Infinite Goods* (1999). Adams contends that the innate goodness of God is the foundation for the obligation to God's commands, which Quinn did not assume.[14] Adams later modified his theory to be accessible to atheists. He does not dismiss the key thesis of his presupposition of God's goodness as the basis for ethical obligation to God's commands, but modifies it by stating that there are necessary moral truths that are independently knowable through experience outside of a belief in God – including the nature of ethical wrongness.[15]

Another prominent voice following Quinn's work is Richard Mouw's *The God Who Commands*. Mouw proposes that everyone 'in the drama of life' is called to build a relationship with God.[16] He contends that divine command theory rests upon the central principles of human sinfulness and humility and trust in a sovereign God. Mouw states, 'The proper human response in the context of this will-to-will confrontation [between God and man] is not so much understanding as surrender.'[17] In other words, people are not to respond in blind obedience to a distant sovereign, but in faithful submission to divine love in the God who commands. The resurgence in the study and advocacy of divine command theory, as well as its historical precedence, merits its consideration as a valid construct for ethical theory.

Major concepts of divine command theory

Since the earliest days of moral reflection, religious philosophy has offered a rich backdrop to answer the fundamental question of ethics – 'What is right and what is wrong?' A central element of religious moral philosophy contends that God exists as the perfect creator of all things. As a result, right and wrong is derived from God and emerges in two distinct ways: (1) Natural Law, which argues that all humans are imbued with the values of life, procreation, knowledge, and sociability and God's will is reflected in the moral reasoning and ethical behavior that result; and (2) Divine Command, which declares something morally good or ethically right based on whether or not it conforms to the will of God as revealed in divine commandments and holy texts. Let's take a closer look at the common themes expressed in these ideas.

Morality comes from God

Divine command theory provides a mediating moral framework in which theistic philosophers and theologians can find a general, ethical common ground. Divine command theory proposes three principles: (1) morality is dependent upon God; (2) therefore, moral obligation consists of obedience to God's commands; and (3) because morality is ultimately based on God's commands and character, the morally right action is the one that God commands or wills.[18] Though aspects of these divine commands differ according to the particular religion, and the specific divine command theorist, all versions hold the claim that morality, rightness and wrongness, and moral obligation ultimately depend on God.

What, then, does it mean for something to be a command from God? God's commands are realized through the general understanding of God speaking, or the 'word' of God. This raises the question of whether God speaks in a literal or metaphorical sense. Varying views exist on this subject, but regardless of a person's opinion on the mode of God's commands – literal or metaphorical – either can sustain support for a robust divine command theory.

How then are God's commands communicated? An assumption might be that God's primary mode of communicating commands to people is through a religion's sacred texts, such as Judaism's Tanakh (Hebrew Bible), Christianity's Bible, and Islam's Quran. Though for most religious traditions, such a vehicle is accepted and even preferred, there are other ways God's moral commands may be communicated, specifically as they relate to moral obligation.[19] For example, some people might defer to natural

law; this is a 'natural' sense of morality given to everyone by God. In fact,
natural law theory is presupposed by divine command theory. If God
exists as a relational person, Creator to creation, then there is a sense in
which God is authoritative. Since God has authority over creation, then
there are 'natural laws' that have been established based on this authority.
As a result, when people act accordingly, they are obeying God's divine
commands. Others might hold that obeying the tenets of religious organization can result in obeying God's commands. Still others might respond
to God's commands through the dictates of their conscience. Divine command theory accepts that God can communicate in any-and-all of these
ways as long as rational human beings understand God's commands. This
brings us to the next major principle in divine command theory – the role
of reason.

Reason

Reason plays a critical role in the access of God's commands within divine
command theory. Theological and philosophical ethics demand that God's
commands, or any ethical position for that matter, be subject to rational
assessment and criticism. Divine command theorists do not advocate a
blind or unreasoning approach to ethics, but rather expect that any moral
obligation associated with God's commands must be measured against God
as the standard of goodness. Of course, God's commands as presented in
religious texts are obviously interpreted through a human lens and are,
therefore, open to misunderstanding. An extreme example of this is the
case of Deanna Laney.[20] In 2004, Laney killed her two oldest sons by hitting them in the head with a rock because she said that God had told
her to do so. She believed that the world was coming to an end and that
God had instructed her to get her house in order. During the investigation,
five mental health experts were called to testify to Laney's actions. All of
them concluded that she suffered from psychotic delusions and could not
tell right from wrong. Laney was eventually found not guilty by reason of
insanity and committed to a state hospital for eight years. Though this is
an extreme example, it illustrates the point that divine command theory
requires some sort of reasonable evaluation to avoid misunderstanding and
misinterpretation.

According to divine command theory, when a command is understood, it
must be evaluated based on the goodness of what is commanded and the
appropriate punishment if the command is not obeyed. The objection of
God's authority and human autonomy will be addressed later in this chapter. For now, it is important to understand that reason might hinder our

understanding of the obligation to God's commands, but not the commands themselves.

A natural question arises: 'What is the moral obligation of the one receiving the commands?' Divine command theory proposes that an action being morally obligatory consists in it being commanded by God. God's commands, by nature of divine goodness, are morally right. Conversely, those things contrary to God's commands are morally wrong, and not morally obligatory. Of course, this assumes that the deity in question is considered the ultimate Good. In other words, the nature of the goodness of the command is critical to our obligation to obey it or not.

In summary, the study of religious ethics helps to answer the questions of 'what is right?' and 'what is wrong?' Divine command theory proposes that morality is dependent upon God and that moral obligation consists of obedience to God's commands based on divine character. The morally right thing to do, then, is to obey God's commands or will. These commands consist of directives given from God through a religion's holy texts, and in a more general sense through an understanding of natural law, religious organizations, or through the dictates of conscience. These commands are not devoid of reason. In fact, reason plays a critical role in discerning what God's command is and what God's command is not. All perceived commands should be measured against the standard of God's goodness and the appropriate punishment of not obeying the command. Therefore, divine command theorists argue that because God is good divine commands are right and should be obeyed.

Critiques of divine command theory

As with any major ethical theory, there are objections to divine command theory's claims. Critics of the theory deride its validity based on several factors. They claim weaknesses in the model for both theists and non-theists and propose that these weaknesses make divine command theory ineffective as a framework for ethical morality. In this section, we will examine two of the basic critiques of divine command theory and rebuttals to those critiques.

The Euthyphro Dilemma

The major critique of divine command theory, and any theistic theory of ethics, comes from a conversation between Socrates and Euthyphro written in Plato's *Euthyphro*.[21] This dialogue is the quintessential objection in philosophical circles of the relationship between God and ethics. Plato, who was a student of Socrates, writes of an encounter between

Socrates and Euthyphro in the king's court. Charges have been brought against Socrates by Miletus, who claims that Socrates has corrupted the youth of that generation by leading them away from a proper belief in the gods. In the course of their discussion, Socrates is surprised to learn that Euthyphro is prosecuting his own father for the murder of a servant. Euthyphro's family is upset with him because of this and believes that what he is doing to his father is wrong. Euthyphro maintains that his family does not see the more significant divine directive in his action. This fosters a conversation between Socrates and Euthyphro on the nature of piety. In the discussion, Socrates asks Euthyphro the now famous question that he, and any theistic philosopher including divine command theorists, must answer: 'Is the pious loved by the gods because it is pious, or is it pious because it is being loved by the gods?'[22] In other words, does God command an action because it is morally right, or is it morally right because God commands it?

This argument, known as the 'Euthyphro Dilemma,' is the standard objection to divine command theory. A divine command theorist believes that if God commands an action, then it is morally right. But the Euthyphro Dilemma suggests that if God commands that we inflict suffering or pain on someone else, then in doing so – based on divine command theory – it would be right. We would be obligated to inflict pain because God commanded it. This is because the reason that inflicting suffering is wrong is simply because God commands us not to do it. The problem that Socrates' question brings up is the arbitrary nature of God's commands, which allows for morally deplorable actions to become morally obligatory, and, thereby, morally justified.

One example dominates the discussion of this issue; Abraham's sacrifice of his son Isaac found in the Torah. (The story is also found in the Quran – although, in the Quran, the son to be sacrificed is Abraham's son Ishmael.) In essence, God speaks to Abraham and commands him to sacrifice his beloved son as an offering to God. Since God commanded it, Abraham begins to obey. Abraham takes his son to the mountain, binds him, seizes a knife, and prepares to take his son's life. At the last minute, an angel speaks and stops Abraham from killing his son saying that his willingness to obey was sufficient to please God. Abraham then finds a ram that had become entangled in the bushes and sacrifices the ram to God in place of his son.[23]

Several questions arise from this account. First, was it right or wrong for Abraham to intend to kill, or actually kill, his son before God commanded it? Was God arbitrary in commanding Abraham to kill his son in light of other biblical commands not to kill or murder? Would Abraham have been wrong in disobeying God in light of the horror of child sacrifice? These questions provide an excellent example of the Euthyphro Dilemma and call into account the viability of divine command theory.

A divine command theorist would counter the argument of the Euthyphro Dilemma in several ways. One possible response is just to accept that if what God commands is to inflict suffering, as in our example here, then it would be morally obligatory given the fundamental premise of divine command theory – no matter how immoral it might seem. Most people find this to be an unacceptable view of moral obligation, on the grounds that any theory of ethics that leaves open the possibility that such actions are morally praiseworthy is fatally flawed.[24]

Another response to the Euthyphro Dilemma is to ask two important questions: (1) Should we love one another because God commands us to do so? and (2) Does God command us to love one another because it is the right thing to do?[25] A divine command theorist can conceive of God's moral goodness as something distinct from conformity to moral obligations, and so as something distinct from conformity to divine commands. But if God commands us to love one another because it is the right thing to do, then moral facts stand over God and divine goodness is subject to them. A way to sidestep this argument is to consider God as the 'supreme standard' of goodness. God does not consult any outside source but acts according to a divine character that defines goodness. In the case of Abraham and his son, God's goodness supersedes the divine command to offer Abraham's son as a sacrifice. Therefore, Abraham has just cause to obey God's command and put his son in harm's way. But doesn't this still breed arbitrariness about God's character? Why should God be the standard and not some other moral character or principle? One could argue that to invoke God as the supreme moral standard is no more arbitrary than to invoke some objective moral principle. Critics contend that the Euthyphro Dilemma is a critical flaw in divine command theory because it forces the divine command theorist to pick and choose which commands to follow. This leads us to the second critique of divine command theory.

What about human free will?

A second major critique of divine command theory deals with the subject of human autonomy, or free will. The idea of autonomy suggests 'a human moral agent is, or should be, a (moral) law unto oneself – that one should find the moral law within oneself.'[26] The idea of autonomy means to be morally mature, deciding freely which moral principles will govern one's life, and by extension that we can make moral decisions for which we should be held accountable. Divine command theory seems to contradict this idea, as it is not our will that governs our lives, but God's will. However, we can counter this argument by stating that divine command theory and moral responsibility are compatible.[27] God commands and humans are responsible for their response to obeying or not obeying those commands, correctly understanding them, and deciding through self-critical evaluation what God has commanded us to do. Therefore, human beings are autonomous because we rely on our independent judgment about God's goodness and what moral laws are consistent with his commands.

There are several traits that might lend to a defense of autonomy as a complementary component of divine command theory.[28] First, is that of responsibility. People who hold themselves responsible for their actions do not abdicate that responsibility simply because of their view of autonomy. They are free agents in the sense that they can choose to submit to God's commands or not. Second, is moral competence. The morally competent person is able to make decisions on their own, including God's commands, based on their prescribed beliefs, understanding, and feelings. Third, is the area of critical thinking. Those who are able to examine ethical ideas in the light of critical scrutiny exercise autonomy over those claims and beliefs, and, therefore, operate autonomously. Fourth, is the ability to care about moral issues. When someone cares about the good in and around their life, they will act autonomously to champion that good in their relationships and responsibilities. God's commands provide the foundation for such good, because of God's goodness, and the motivation to obey or not obey divine commands.

The Euthyphro Dilemma and the question of human autonomy provide two serious critiques of divine command theory. Both should be considered and addressed by theistic ethicists to develop a stronger foundation for a working theory. In doing so, divine command theorists will strengthen the underlying assumptions of the theory and provide a framework for application in all areas of life including, as we will see, within the context of leadership.

Five component analysis

If leadership indeed is a process, as defined in the Five Components of Leadership Model described in Chapter 1, then we can apply a divine command theory of ethics to leadership. If we understand ethics as defined by

Figure 8.2 The Five Components of Leadership Model applied to divine command theory

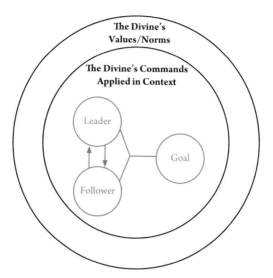

an obligation to God's commands, that God is good, and, therefore, divine commands are for our good and the good of the whole creation, then there is an ethical base from which we can lead. Let's look at each of the five leadership components in light of divine command theory as it is presented in this chapter. These are represented in Figure 8.2 that emphasizes what is important in divine command theory.

In light of the Five Components of Leadership Model, we might compare the largest circle of 'cultural values and norms' to the divine itself and the next larger circle of 'context' to the commands issued by the divine. These outer circles are accessible to both leaders and followers and become the ultimate criteria by which we judge the rightness of a goal. The leader and follower then work together to accomplish the greater goal coming from the larger culture and context.

Since ethical rightness is based on God's commands, and a follower's obligation is simply to obey divine commands, then there is a relationship between leader and follower. Such a relationship corresponds with McManus and Perrucci's argument that the central intellectual focus of leadership is *purposeful interaction*. In their book *Understanding Leadership*, McManus and Perruci argue:

> [T]he central intellectual focus [of the study of leadership] revolves around human beings' *purposeful interaction*. The focus invites debates about ethics and power relations. On the ethical side, purposeful interaction suggests choices to be made – forks in the road to be confronted . . . We can all argue whether the purpose is ethical or not, or who should have the ultimate decision-making authority.

However, *purposeful interaction* is the overarching language that organizes our thinking about leadership.[29]

Ethically, purposeful interaction suggests choices to be made that clarify intent. Leaders and followers bring specific values to the relationship and these values guide their behavior. Intentionality becomes an expression of their values. As they work together in the relationship, such intentionality helps leaders and followers to pursue a common purpose. The follower chooses to accept the leader's commands or directives so that a greater purpose might be attained. As with any ethical theory, the adherence to or refusal of such commands is evaluated by the follower. The result of the follower's response to the leader's directives results in either morally positive or negative consequences.

Such a hierarchical structure could also serve as a critique of this theory, potentially leading to the loss of human autonomy or abuse through co-opting the commands or the interpretation of the commands for the leader's personal benefit. But if the goal of leaders and followers is for some greater purpose, then the leader and follower do not operate out of selfish motives, but together for a greater good. In effect, the leader and follower work symbiotically to see the directives of the leader related to the greater purpose are accomplished. The model becomes transformative, and not merely transactional, in that as the follower obeys the leader's commands, the leader's purposes are accomplished in the follower's life, in the organization, and in the surrounding culture.

So, what happens when leaders and followers disagree about what God has commanded? Several lines of thought prove helpful here. First, if God is good and divine commands are good for people, then both leader and follower need to evaluate the potential positive outcome of obeying God's commands. Second, if they disagree with an interpretation of God's commands, they will need to work together, both making their cases and listening to the other to discern the best road forward. Third, if they reach an impasse, then common ground must be sought in obedience to God's commands so they can continue to work together toward desired goals. Finally, if an agreement or common ground cannot be found, they will need to decide whether or not to continue working together. Now that we have examined the first two components of the Five Components Model, let's look at the next component – the goal.

Obedience to the leader's directives lead to success in accomplishing the stated goal. Though divine command theory is highly structured and hierarchical, the benefits of this theory extend beyond the leader. The goal's validity is measured by its nature of the directives as good for both the follower and organization and, therefore, adherence to these directives results in ethical rightness. A follower's acceptance and adherence to the commands provide legitimacy to the command's moral rightness. Lack of acceptance and adherence to the commands creates disunity, power struggles, organizational inertia, lack of focus on achieving desired goals, and rejection of the leader's vision, ultimately demonstrating moral wrongness. Since the goal is dependent upon the leader's directives, as a result of the transcendent nature of the context and culture of divine command theory, which is demonstrated in the next section, the goal is important, but not as significant as other aspects of the model. We will look at this in a bit more detail in our case study later in this chapter.

The two spheres of context and culture highlighted in the Five Components of Leadership Model are the 'central nervous system' for the divine command theory of moral obligation. As such, when applied in a leadership context, this model should be understood as an ethical leadership model where authority, morality, and ethics transcend both leaders and followers. Of course, a criticism of this theory could be that the leader must interpret God's commands making the leader the most important element of the model. Though this model places a high responsibility on the leader to interpret God's commands correctly, it also, by its transformational nature, allows both leaders and followers to access the two outer circles to understand God's will. The leader is important to the model but becomes subservient to the culture and context and open to input from followers to reach the shared goal. The transcendent nature of the environment of God's commands drives divine command theory-based leadership, because the leader, follower, and goals are all subservient to the demands placed on them by the expectations of the divine. God's commands determine what is right and wrong, and so create a moral environment in which leader, follower, and goal work together. This can only happen as leaders and followers demonstrate an attitude of humility and shared vision, based on the values and norms established by God's commands.

This environment results in established values and norms that guide ethical behavior. Leadership by nature is situational. The values and norms differ by leader and by culture. A strength of a divine command theory-based leadership ethics is that values and norms are established above the leader, follower, and culture. As God establishes moral obligation by divine commands, a moral framework is established to guide leadership practices such as relating to others, daily decision-making, determining motivation, and projecting outcomes and goals across cultural landscapes.

In an ever-changing world, as national borders are blurred, and technology links people across the globe, cross-cultural leadership is the new norm of the twenty-first century. Leaders and followers have to deal with ever-changing contexts and cultural norms to effectively reach desired goals. Understanding the nature of God's commands, as they establish transcendent values and norms, helps the leader and follower to overcome and go beyond contextual and cultural barriers that might have held them back previously. Adherence to the commands to love, serve, care, share, grow, and be accountable, to name a few, demonstrate the cross-cultural nature of divine command theory as a leadership ethic and establish an objective moral framework for leadership in a global context. As such, the circles of context and culture will be the most noticeable in our graphic model. Now that we have seen how divine command theory relates to the Five Components of Leadership Model in the abstract, let's explore how it relates to the model in a specific instance. For that we turn to our case study.

CASE STUDY

A Christian response to the Syrian refugee crisis[30]

As a result of the Arab unrest beginning with the Tunisian Revolution in December 2010, Syrian protesters took to the streets to protest against the torture of students who had participated in anti-government graffiti. The Syrian government responded with force and multiple demonstrations spread all over the country. President Bashar al-Assad, who inherited Syria's dictatorship from his father, Hafez al-Assad, wavered in response between a show of force and the idea of reform. In April 2011, after lifting a decade's-old state of emergency, he responded with force by mobilizing tanks and troops to suppress the protests. In the summer of 2011, escalation of violence against protestors rose, so much so that thousands of soldiers defected and began to launch attacks against the government, bringing the country to the brink of civil war. An opposition government was formed in exile, but because of internal divisions, was not recognized by the United Nations, or Western or Arab powers.

The conflict was made more complicated by Syria's ethnic divide. The Assads and much of the nation's elite, especially the military, belong to the Alawite sect of Islam, a minority in a mostly Sunni Muslim country. Alawites constituted about 12 percent of the 23 million Syrians in the country at that time; while Sunni Muslims, the opposition's backbone, made up about 75 percent of the population.[31] Assad's government had the advantage of firepower and loyal troops, but the insurgents were highly motivated.

In February 2012, the United Nations voted to approve a resolution condemning President Bashar al-Assad. China and Russia, though, as Syria's traditional allies, blocked stronger sanctions against the country. By the summer of 2012, tensions and violence increased dramatically as the country devolved into civil war. By 2013 the United Nations,

CASE STUDY *(continued)*

who stopped collecting statistical data on the conflict in mid-2014, reported over 90,000 people were killed between 2011 and 2013. By 2014, an estimated 250,000 people had died in the dispute. The Syrian Center for Policy Research estimated that at the end of 2015 more than 470,000 people had died in the struggle, representing 11.5 percent of the Syrian population, while the number of wounded was estimated at 1.9 million. A fragile nationwide ceasefire was put into effect in 2016, but, at the time of this writing, the conflict continues.

An unintended result of the Syrian Civil War was the 4.9 million Syrian refugees that fled the violence in their country and the 6.1 million internally displaced people within Syria (at least at the time this chapter went to press). It is essential in understanding this crisis to know the difference between those affected and displaced by conflict and those who are simply migrating to another country. Under both international and U.S. law, a refugee is an individual who has fled his or her country of origin because of a credible fear of persecution on account of their race, religion, political opinion, national origin, or social group. An internally displaced person is one who has fled his or her home but stays within the boundaries of their country.[32] The displacement of over 4.9 million refugees and internally displaced people created one of the greatest humanitarian crises since the Second World War. The United Nations Refugee Agency reported that between 2011 and 2017 there were 50 Syrian families displaced every hour of every day.[33] Three-quarters of these refugees were women and children. They fled to numerous countries including Lebanon, Jordan, Iraq, Turkey, throughout Europe, and even, to a lesser degree, the United States. The need for clean water and sanitation, basic health care, food, shelter, and household and hygiene supplies was extreme, and humanitarian organizations globally mobilized to meet the growing hardship.

Many national, international, and faith-based humanitarian organizations mobilized to meet the needs of these refugees. One of these parties was World Relief, a Christian relief organization based in Baltimore, Maryland with offices in fourteen different states and over a dozen countries. The National Association of Evangelicals established World Relief in 1944 as a response to the humanitarian crisis following the Second World War. They partner with local churches around the world to help provide aid for families and communities in times of tragedy, sickness, conflict, and poverty.[34] Over their 70-year history, World Relief has provided aid and relief through disaster response, health and child development, refugee and immigration services, economic development, and peace building. They desire to 'work holistically with the local church to stand for the sick, the widowed, the orphaned, the alienated, the displaced, the devastated, the marginalized and the disenfranchised.'[35]

World Relief worked in providing help, temporary shelters, hygiene items, and psychosocial counseling to the displaced Syrian families, as well as sponsoring child-friendly spaces for mothers and children. This was done in relationship with local churches, both in the United States and internationally. Over the course of the crisis, World Relief dedicated tens of millions of dollars in aid and provisions to help Syrian refugees.[36]

CASE STUDY *(continued)*

Figure 8.3 Five Components of Leadership Model applied to the World Relief case study

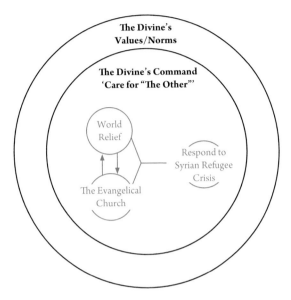

Divine command theory and the Syrian refugee crisis

So, how does World Relief's work demonstrate a leadership expression of divine command theory? Why would this Christian relief organization dedicate effort, time, and money to those who are desperate and in need? Why would a Christian organization be willing to help those of another faith, in this case Muslims, which might appear illogical in light of some of the strictest interpretations of selected divine commands? What are the motivating factors that contribute to their efforts to stand with the most vulnerable people in the world? Why provide resources to someone who can give nothing in return? The divine command theory of moral obligation helps to answer these questions.

World Relief leadership identifies three responses to the Syrian refugee crisis: a compassionate response, a fearful response, and a response of confusion.[37] People can respond compassionately, like when the lifeless body of Aylan Kurdi, a small Syrian refugee boy, washed up on a Turkish beach. The world mourned for this boy and his family as pictures of his lifeless body were broadcast around the world.[38] Another possible response is one of fear. Following multiple terrorist attacks throughout the world at this time, much attention was drawn to the danger of open borders and the threat of terrorists using them as conduits to fulfill their violent agendas. An example of this was seen when then U.S. Presidential candidate Donald J. Trump promised to ban Muslims from entering the United States if elected.[39] A third possible reaction to the Syrian refugee crisis is one of confusion. It is easy

CASE STUDY *(continued)*

to see this crisis as a political issue and not one of compassion and humanity and become confused as to what an appropriate response to this situation would be.

World Relief chose to respond with compassion. Their justification for this response was a belief that God commands them to respond in this way. The Old and New Testaments are rich in imagery regarding refugees. In fact, the Hebrew word *ger*, translated in English as a foreigner, resident alien, stranger, sojourner, or immigrant, appears 92 times in the Old Testament alone.[40] The Old Testament admonishes its readers about their obligations to aliens, widows and orphans no fewer than 36 times.[41] In fact, the most repeated commandment in the Old Testament, other than worshiping the one true God, is to welcome the stranger.[42] Some examples of God's commands include Leviticus 19:33–34:

> Do not take advantage of foreigners who live among you in your land. Treat them like native-born Israelites, and love them as you love yourself. Remember that you were once foreigners living in the land of Egypt. I am the Lord your God.

Deuteronomy 10:18–19 declares:

> [God] ensures that orphans and widows receive justice. [God] shows love to the foreigners living among you and gives them food and clothing. So you, too, must show love to foreigners, for you yourselves were once foreigners in the land of Egypt.

Exodus 23:9 reminds the Israelites that they too were once refugees and they should respond as God responded to them, with mercy and compassion. Moses writes, 'You must not oppress foreigners. You know what it's like to be a foreigner, for you yourselves were once foreigners in the land of Egypt.'[43] Therefore, based on the commands in the Old Testament, those reading the Bible as the word of God are obligated to obey divine commands and demonstrate compassion to the foreigner, alien, and refugee.

The New Testament continues to emphasize this idea. The Gospel writers are quick to remind Jesus of Nazareth's followers that he too was a refugee. Jesus, whom Christians believe to be the Son of God, joins a long line of biblical characters that had to flee their home under persecution including Esau,[44] Moses,[45] King David,[46] and the prophet Elijah.[47] Jesus' story of exile came at his birth with King Herod the Great who ruled Judea from approximately 37 BCE to 4 CE. Herod, who had heard that a new king of the Jews had been born, commissioned troops to murder all boys two years old and younger in the vicinity of the village of Bethlehem in Judea, where Jesus was born. Joseph, whom the New Testament writers refer to as Jesus' earthly father, took Jesus and his mother Mary and fled to Egypt where they lived as foreigners and refugees for several years before returning home.[48]

Jesus also taught his followers how to respond to those around them. His chief command was an extension of the Jewish *Shema*, the central commandment of God in the Old Testament to all faithful Jews. Jesus said, 'You must love the Lord your God with all your

CASE STUDY *(continued)*

heart, all your soul, and all your mind.' This is the first and greatest commandment. A second is equally important: 'Love your neighbor as yourself.'[49] In Luke's Gospel, Jesus goes on to define who our neighbor is in the Parable of the Good Samaritan. In this story, Jesus responds to a question from a lawyer who asked him who his neighbor was. He says that a man was traveling from Jerusalem to Jericho when a group of robbers ambushed him. They stripped the man, beat him, and left him to die. A priest happened by, but because the man was ceremonially unclean, he passed by on the other side of the road. Another man, who assisted the priests in the Temple, saw the traveler and also passed by on the other side of the road. Finally, a Samaritan, who was despised by many for their ethnicity and religious practices, had compassion on the traveler, bound his wounds, took him to a local inn, and paid for his care. Jesus then asks, 'Which of these three, do you think, proved to be a neighbor to the man who was beaten by the robbers?' The lawyer replied, 'The one who showed him mercy.' Jesus said to him, 'You go, and do likewise.' The point of Jesus' story is that everyone is our neighbor, not just the people we like or who happen to look like us.[50]

Therefore, a Christian response to others, especially those in need, is to obey God's command to offer them hospitality and kindness. God's love for humankind, and the Christian's subsequent obligation to love all people, is made clear in Jesus' command, 'You have heard the law that says, "Love your neighbor" and hate your enemy. But I say, love your enemies! Pray for those who persecute you! In that way, you will be acting as true children of your Father in heaven.'[51] He also shares the greatest two of God's commandments, 'You must love the Lord your God with all your heart, all your soul, and all your mind.' This is the first and greatest commandment. A second is equally important: 'Love your neighbor as yourself.'[52] As we can see, those who view the Bible as the word of God, as Christians do, are to obey its commands in response to their neighbors – whomever or wherever they may be.

We see now that World Relief's response to the Syrian refugee crisis centers on obedience to the commands of God as dictated by both the Old and New Testaments. One group of religious scholars apply these commands as a practical and ethical response specifically to the current refugee crisis:

> The application to the present refugee crisis is clear: by Jesus' standard, the Refugee – whether from Syria, Somalia, or Burma, whether living one mile or ten thousand miles from us, whether Christian, Muslim, Buddhist, or an atheist, and whatever else might distinguish them, is our neighbor. The command of Jesus is to love them. That there may be risk or cost involved is not relevant to the mandate to love.[53]

As a result, World Relief, according to the divine command theory of moral obligation, demonstrated an ethically correct response to the needs of millions who suffered as a result of the Syrian Civil War. As this organization lives out the commands and actions of God toward those who are in desperate need, by providing supplies, nutrition and hygiene programs, safe places for children, and psychosocial counseling for victims of violence, they are obeying God's command to love their neighbor as themselves.

CASE STUDY *(continued)*

The Five Components of Leadership Model applied to World Relief and the Syrian refugees

The World Relief case shows the dependence upon the leader–follower relationship to the broader environment and culture for the greater good. Because divine command theory establishes the overarching cultural values and norms as articulated in a religion's holy texts, the leader and follower work to facilitate the goal through obedience to God's commands – even in a hostile environment. Since God has commanded a life of love, compassion, and justice towards others, World Relief works to provide the organizational vision, education, structure, and on-the-ground resources to accomplish this goal. Through partnerships with local churches, empowering local leaders, and providing opportunities for others around the world to help with the refugee crisis, World Relief allows others to join them as they lead out in meeting the needs of those in crisis. Some specific ways they challenge others to join them in this mission of compassion in the United States and abroad is through advocacy, volunteerism, and donations. World Relief provides numerous international touch points where followers and leaders can work together to support the goal, which is based on divine command theory. This transcendence is what makes divine command theory so powerful.

In our case study, the goal is the result of the overarching cultural values and norms and context that led to the symbiotic relationship between the leader and follower. While the goal of meeting the needs of those affected by the Syrian Civil War is the defined mission, it acts as secondary to the cultural values and norms and the context. The goal is the application of a much larger divine command into a particular situation. Though there are other humanitarian agencies – such as Syrian Medical Relief Society, UNICEF, Save the Children, and Doctors Without Borders – that share similar goals for helping refugees, World Relief is different in that the motive for the goal is obedience to a divine command. In doing so, they empower the leaders and followers by encouraging them to be obedient to God's commands to love their neighbor and to provide for those in need.

The context and culture of World Relief are driven by a belief in God and a conviction that divine commands are good for those who obey them. This faith forms the outermost cultural values and norms in which World Relief operates. The context in this instance is the divine command to 'love your neighbor' and extend compassion and hospitality to Syrian refugees. In this context, leaders and followers work together to accomplish desired goals based on God's commands as the higher, overarching values and norms that drive their personal life and the life of the organization.

Divine command theory rests on the presupposition that there is a God, who is good, whose commands are the basis for moral rightness and beneficial for those who follow them. Adherents of this theory have an objective moral framework in which to live ethically moral lives as they obey God's command. Divine command theory, then, provides a model for leaders in fostering moral and ethical conduct in their followers and the organizations in which they lead.

Summary and concluding remarks

Our chapter opened with a question for leaders who wish to live by the divine command theory of ethics: What does the divine require from leadership? To answer this question, leaders in a monotheistic tradition look to authoritative sources for guidance, trusting that these sources reflect both the character of a divine being who is 'good,' and a call to action that is consistent with that divine being's character. Readers must note that leaders following the divine command tradition do not abnegate a responsibility for reasoned consideration of what they perceive to be divine dictates. So, while the commands may be divine in nature, their interpretation and application still require a human element. As an example of that human element at work, our chapter considered the case of how a Christian humanitarian organization, World Relief, chose to respond to a Syrian refugee crisis. Their response was rooted in an interpretation of commands for love of neighbor and the immigrant that are found in both Hebrew and Christian scripture.

 DISCUSSION QUESTIONS

What is your view of God and ethics? How can a theistic framework either help or hinder a better understanding of ethics and leadership?

What are the benefits of a divine command theory of moral obligation as an ethical framework? What are its disadvantages? How might these disadvantages be overcome to sustain a viable ethical theory?

What role does human autonomy play in the development of divine command theory? How does reason factor into the connection between divine command theory and human independence?

What leadership benefits might be obtained from adherence to divine command theory? What leadership challenges might arise from such a theory?

How does the leader–follower dynamic in divine command theory speak to a sustainable ethical framework for leadership? How do context and culture in divine command theory support the leader–follower dynamic in helping them reach their desired goals?

What practical applications does divine command theory present in leadership in a case study such as the Syrian refugee crisis?

 ADDITIONAL RESOURCES

C.S. Evans, *God and Moral Obligation*, Oxford: Oxford University Press, 2014.
This text explores the connection between religion and ethics. Evans specifically sets out to address the objections to divine command theory, and spends a lot of time exploring questions about the role of natural disasters and the problem of evil in understanding divine command theory.

D. Baggett and J. Walls, *Good God: The Theistic Foundations of Morality*, Oxford: Oxford University Press, 2011.
Baggett and Walls provide a thorough overview of divine command theory and aim to reinvigorate debates over theology and ethics in contemporary scholarship.

M. Al-Attar, *Islamic Ethics: Divine Command Theory in Arabo-Islamic Thought*, New York: Routledge, 2010.
Al-Attar looks at divine command theory from an Islamic perspective.

NOTES

1 P.L. Quinn, 'Divine Command Theory of Ethics,' *Encyclopedia of Philosophy*, Detroit, MI: Macmillan Reference, 2005, p. 93.
2 P.L. Quinn, 'Divine Command Theory,' in Hugh LaFollette (ed.), *The Blackwell Guide to Ethical Theory*, West Sussex, UK: Blackwell Publishing, 2000, p. 54.
3 R. Bellah, 'Civil Religion in America,' *Daedalus*, vol. 96 no. 1, winter 1967, 1–21. Online, http://www.robertbellah.com/articles_5.htm (accessed December 4, 2017).
4 Bellah, ibid.
5 J.A. Boss, *Ethics for Life: A Text with Readings*, New York: McGraw Hill, 2011, p. 146.
6 Found in both Exodus 20:1–17 and Deuteronomy 5:6–21.
7 J.M. Idziak, *Divine Command Morality: Historical and Contemporary Readings*, New York: Edwin Mellen Press, 1979.
8 St. Augustine, *The Letters of St. Augustine*, J.G. Cunningham (trans.), North Charlotte, SC: Createspace, 2015. Also see J.M. Idziak, *Divine Command Morality: Historical and Contemporary Readings*, New York: Edwin Mellen Press, 1979.
9 J. Hare, *God's Call: Moral Realism, Divine Commands and Human Autonomy*, Grand Rapids, MI: William B. Eerdmans Publishing Company, 2001, p. 50.
10 S.C. Evans, *Kierkegaard's Ethic of Love: Divine Commands and Moral Obligations*, Oxford: Oxford University Press, 2006, pp. 6–7; and S. Kierkegaard, *Works of Love*, Princeton, NJ, USA: Princeton University Press, 1995, p. 51.
11 Evans, ibid.
12 I. Kant, *Critique of Pure Reason*, P. Guyer and A.W. Wood (eds), Cambridge: Cambridge University Press, 1999; I. Kant, *Critique of Practical Reason*, A.T. Kingmill (trans.), Mineola, NY: Dover Publications, 2004; and I. Kant, *Religion and Rational Theology*, A.W Wood and G. di Giovanni (trans.), Cambridge: Cambridge University Press, 2001. Kant had what was called a 'pre-critical' period and a 'critical' period, and his works in the pre-critical period endorse a view of God that is in line with this description. The latter period doesn't fully address the philosophy of religion and has been interpreted as a departure from a theistic worldview because Kant himself was anti-religion at that point. It is fair to say that Kant endorsed the necessity of a god, or a divine, insofar as he directly addressed religion. He argued that this entity would be a 'regulator', of sorts, but there was no endorsement of any specific religious content. See A. W. Wood, *Kant's Moral Religion*, Ithaca: Cornell University Press, 1970.
13 P. Quinn, *Divine Commands and Moral Requirements*, Oxford: Clarendon Press, 1978.
14 R.M. Adams, *Finite and Infinite Goods: A Framework for Ethics*, Oxford: Oxford University Press, 1999, pp. 42–9.
15 R.M. Adams, 'Divine Command Metaethics Modified Again,' *Journal of Religious Ethics*, vol. 7 no. 1, 1979, 66–79, p. 71.
16 R.J. Mouw, *The God Who Commands: A Study in Divine Command Ethics*, Notre Dame, IN: University of Notre Dame Press, 1990, p. 73.
17 Mouw, ibid, p. 98.
18 Quinn, op. cit.
19 Mouw, op. cit.
20 'Mom who said she killed on God's orders acquitted,' *CNN*, April 6, 2004. Online, http://www.cnn.com/2004/LAW/04/03/children.slain/ (accessed February 22, 2018).
21 Plato, *Five Dialogues: Euthyphro, Apology, Crito, Meno, Phaedo*, J.M. Cooper & G.M.A Grube (trans.), Indianapolis, IN: Hackett Publishing Company, 2002, p. 12.
22 Plato, ibid.
23 See Genesis 22.
24 M.W. Austin, 'Divine Command Theory,' *Internet Encyclopedia of Philosophy: A Peer Reviewed Academic Resource*, 2006. Online, http://www.iep.utm.edu/divine-c/#H3 (accessed July 5, 2017).

25 See W. Alston, 'Some Suggestions for Divine Command Theorists' in Michael D. Beaty (ed.), *Christian Theism and the Problems of Philosophy*, Notre Dame, IN: University of Notre Dame Press, 1990, pp. 303–26.

26 Adams, op. cit., p. 270.

27 Adams, op. cit., p. 272.

28 Adams, op. cit., pp. 272–4.

29 R.M. McManus and G. Perruci, *Understanding Leadership: An Arts and Humanities Perspective*, New York: Routledge, 2015, p. 17.

30 Several key resources are helpful in understanding the Syrian refugee crisis including: S. Bauman, M. Soerens, and I. Smeir, *Seeking Refuge: On The Shores of the Global Refugee Crisis*, Chicago, IL: Moody Publishers, 2016; L. Rodgers, D. Gritten, J. Offer, and P. Assare, *I Am Syria: Conflict Background*, 2015. Online, http://www.iamsyria.org/conflict-background.html (accessed February 20, 2018); United Nations Refugee Agency, 'Internally Displaced Peoples.' Online, http://www.unhcr.org/sy/29-internally-displaced-people.html (accessed February 20, 2018); and World Relief, 'A church leader's toolkit on the Syrian refugee crisis.' Online, https://www.worldrelief.org/church-leaders-toolkit/ (accessed February 20, 2018).

31 Rodgers et al., op. cit.

32 World Relief, op. cit.

33 United Nations Refugee Agency, op. cit.

34 World Relief, op. cit.

35 World Relief, op. cit.

36 World Relief's IRS forms, financial statements, and annual reports can be found at: https://www.worldrelief.org/financial-details.

37 World Relief, op. cit.

38 R. Clarke and C.E. Shoichet, 'Image of 3-year-old who washed ashore underscore's Europe's refugee crisis,' *CNN*, September 3, 2015. Online, http://www.cnn.com/2015/09/02/europe/migration-crisis-boy-washed-ashore-in-turkey/index.html (accessed February 22, 2018).

39 J. Diamond, 'Donald Trump: Ban all Muslim travel to U.S.' *CNN*, December 8, 2015. Online, http://www.cnn.com/2015/12/07/politics/donald-trump-muslim-ban-immigration/index.html (accessed February 22, 2018).

40 Bauman et al., op. cit., p. 30.

41 W.C. Kaiser Jr., 'Leviticus,' *The New Interpreter's Bible: Genesis to Leviticus*, 1, 1994, p. 1135.

42 O.O. Espin, 'Immigration and theology: Reflections by an implicated theologian,' *Perspectivas: Occasional Papers*, Hispanic Theological Initiative, no. 10, fall 2006, 46–7.

43 Not all theologians recognize Moses as the author of the Pentateuch.

44 Genesis 27:10; 27:1.

45 Exodus 2:15.

46 1 Samuel 21:10 and 27:1.

47 1 Kings 19:1–4.

48 Matthew 2:13–23.

49 Matthew 22:37–9.

50 Luke 10:25–37.

51 Matthew 5:43–45.

52 Matthew 22:37–9.

53 Bauman et al., op. cit. p. 35.

9

Social contract theory

Lavina Sequeira

 **FRAMING QUESTION**

What obligations do leaders and followers have to each other?

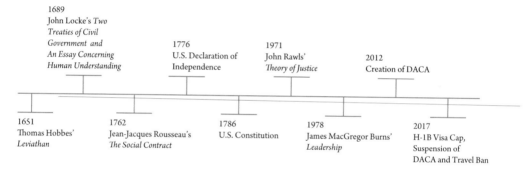

Figure 9.1 Timeline of major works on social contract theory in relation to the case study

John Stuart Mill wrote, 'Though society is not founded on a contract, and though no good purpose is answered by inventing a contract in order to deduce social obligations from it, everyone who receives the protection of society owes a return for the benefit.'[1] Mill's statement beautifully encapsulates the concept of social contract theory. Briefly, social contract theory is a moral and political view asserting the notion of a political society resting on the voluntary agreement between a government and the individuals residing in a particular country. This construct defines the rules and duties of the individuals who are part of that society, as well as the obligations of its government. Individuals implicitly agree to give up some of their freedoms for the mutual benefit of others living in that society and to assure their security in a social structure. This perspective asserts that, due to a shared contract, individuals are morally and politically obligated towards each other and to the society of which they are a part. This perspective provides a philosophical framework for understanding the interactions between a society and its members, and also asks the question, 'What obligations do leaders and followers have to each other?'

In this chapter, we will apply the concept of a social contract to a specific context, place, and time: immigration to the United States in the early twenty-first century. In so doing, we will see how the concept of the social contract has evolved over time and consider the theory's ethical implications. We will also examine the way the theory applies to the Five Components of Leadership Model. But first, let's delve a bit deeper into the concept of a social contract, as well as its primary proponents, ideas, and critiques.

History and major concepts of social contract theory

From a socio-political standpoint, social contract theory asserts that individuals' obligations of morality and participation in political life are dependent on the agreements and contracts adhered to – implicitly, unwritten, unspoken, or otherwise – between the community and themselves, which help aid the governance of society. Historically, the social contract lends itself to nuanced meanings, one being the contract amongst people in setting a society, and second, among people and an authority. While similar ideas can be traced back as far as the Greek sophists, the modern iteration and popularity of the social contract are generally associated with Thomas Hobbes, John Locke, and Jean-Jacques Rousseau. From the lens of morality, the social contract gained momentum in the twentieth century due to Rawls' influential perspectives.[2] Let's take a closer look at each of these perspectives.

In Socrates' time, Athenian society was believed to have established governance. This system is evident in the Platonic dialogues *Euthyphro*, *Crito*, and *Apology*, which mainly focus on a notion of the social contract – a tacit agreement of laws between the government and its citizens. These laws present the citizens' duty towards the state, and the state's duty towards its citizens. In choosing to live in Athens, a citizen was implicitly endorsing the society's laws. But if the laws themselves were unjust, would one be morally obligated to obey them?

Socrates was charged with breaking the laws of Athens by disobeying the Gods of Athens and making up new Gods – consequently corrupting the youth of the community. He was found guilty and sentenced to death by drinking hemlock. While in prison, Crito, his friend, offered to help Socrates escape, but he refused. Socrates said it would be unjust for him to flee since he had every opportunity to leave Athens or disagree with the policy, and the government made no effort to deceive him in any way. Thus, in the Platonic dialogue, *Crito*, Socrates alludes to the social contract in asserting that it is immoral for him to escape prison and punishment – even the death penalty – since he entered into a contract with the state and was obligated to the state for raising him and looking after his children. Speaking in Socrates' voice, Plato writes:

> [He] who has experience of the manner in which we order justice and administer the State, and still remains, has entered into an implied contract that he will do as we command him. And he who disobeys us is, as we maintain, thrice wrong: first, because in disobeying us he is disobeying his parents; secondly, because we are the authors of his education; thirdly, because he has made an agreement with us that he will duly obey our commands.[3]

Here Socrates asserts that the laws must be obeyed; it is a tacit choice to stay in Athens all these years. Therefore, the implicit agreement made between Socrates and the personified laws stands. If broken, then consequences will follow, in this case the death penalty.

In Socrates' view, breaking laws would result in chaos and insecurity and, therefore, lead to injustice. He maintains even if one is victimized unjustly, one must not retaliate in an unjust manner. He asserts, '. . . that neither injury nor retaliation nor warding off evil by evil is ever right.'[4] By escaping, Socrates would be disobeying the law and attempting to challenge the established norms and laws of the state. But Socrates and Plato were not the last to comment upon the social contract. The idea bloomed again during the Renaissance with the thinking of Thomas Hobbes.

Another iteration of the social contract can be found in Hobbes' treatise *Leviathan*. In Hobbes' materialistic conception of the world, human beings are sophisticated mechanical beings with appetites, desires, and aversions. This is the 'natural condition of mankind.' However, the notion of a stateless autonomous condition cannot prevail if a person desires to move beyond a primitive existence. In this condition, human beings will do three things: compete to secure life's necessities, challenge and fight out of fear for personal safety, or for purposes of individual glory and reputation.[5] In this State of Nature, conflict is a realistic possibility where danger, fear, and violent death prevail. Here, 'life of man is solitary, poor, nasty, brutish, and short.'[6]

Therefore, a person's natural desire for security will cause him or her to want self-preservation. Through reason and judgment, people can escape the State of Nature by creating a civil society and live in peace. In *Leviathan*, Hobbes concluded that rationality demands that humans escape their natural condition for self-preservation. To do this, they must be '. . . willing to seek peace and follow it' and 'when others are so to, as far forth as for peace and defense of himself he shall think it necessary, to lay down this right to all things.'[7] Thus, men can be expected to enter a social contract in which they agree to establish a civil society by renouncing the rights they have against one another in the State of Nature. In accepting to live together under shared laws, they submit themselves to the sovereign who is the sole political authority and above accountability.

Hobbes posits that civil society arises out of a voluntary agreement, or a social contract. Because rational people desire peace, they would, by mutual consent, appoint a sovereign – an artificial creature. 'For by art is created the great Leviathan called a Commonwealth or State . . . which is but artificial man; though of greater stature and strength than the natural for whose protection and defense it was intended.'[8] Since the contract is collectively entered into, the Leviathan would act as an enforcer of peace and justice. This absolute sovereign would guarantee an individual's personal security in return for complete obedience. Humanity must allow its natural rights to transition to the state. The transfer of power to the Leviathan is a necessity to ensure peace and to move out of a state of destruction and anarchy. It is necessary to note, in Hobbes' thinking, the sovereign retains total liberty and is not a party to the social contract. Since the power has been transferred, the state remains the absolute authority in making laws, receiving the obedience of the citizens in exchange for social order and public welfare.

The Enlightenment thinker John Locke's views on the matter of the social contract differ from Hobbesian absolutism. His opinion of the State of Nature isn't dark, grim, and miserable as that of Hobbes. Locke's State of Nature is one in which '. . . persons are free to pursue their own interests and plans, free from interference, and, because of the Law of Nature and the restrictions that it imposes upon persons, it is relatively peaceful'; where 'Men [live] together according to reason without a common superior on earth with authority to judge between them.'[9] In this State of Nature, the natural condition of humanity is one of freedom, liberty, and the pursuit of their own interests without interference. The State of Nature does not have a shared authority and is, therefore, pre-political; however, it is certainly not pre-moral. To safeguard this natural condition of freedom in which individuals find themselves, Locke asserts the necessity of individual consent. It is through this consent that political societies are created, and individuals join those societies. One can only become a full member of society by an act of express consent.[10] Locke maintains this is the precondition for the acquisition of private property.

So why is there a necessity for a social contract here? To reiterate, the State of Nature as described by Locke is a state of equality and perfect freedom. Locke asserts in the State of Nature a person acquires private property by mixing his or her physical labor with the materials of nature. But rights need to be relegated if the person wants to enjoy that property. It is for this property that 'man' may decide to leave the State of Nature. Having done this, people are subject to the will of the majority to make 'one body politic under one government.'[11] While there are restrictions on the accumulation and acquisition of private property, to safeguard one's rights to property a person enters into a social contract with others. Locke asserts:

> [T]he enjoyment of property he has in this state is very unsafe, very unsecure. This makes him willing to quit a condition which, however free, is full of fears and continual dangers: and it is not without reason that he seeks out and is willing to join in society with others who are already united, or have a mind to unite for the mutual preservation of their lives, liberties, and estates, which I call by the general name property.[12]

In Locke's view, laws and individual rights can be violated in the State of Nature. Since there is no political governance, the victims can't enforce the Law of Nature in the State of Nature. This sets the condition for the social contract. For the protection of property, men agree to delegate – or transfer – their rights to the government. The government safeguards the rights and property of its citizens. Therefore, the government has limited powers and obligations to its creators due to the nature of the social contract, and can thereby be modified by the citizens at any time.

Another influential Enlightenment philosopher, Jean-Jacques Rousseau, asserted, 'Man was born free; and everywhere he is in chains.'[13] He believed with their very first breath individuals were shackled by invisible chains – from the State of Autonomy of man being free to the modern condition of inequality and dependency. In *The Social Contract*, Rousseau attempted to find a solution to this problem.

According to Rousseau, man by nature is good, free, wise, and benevolent. But as people come together to form social institutions, they develop vices. The accumulation of private property encourages self-interest. Thus, the good State of Nature degenerates due to the acquisition of private property. Since this original state of freedom according to Rousseau is destroyed by inequality due to the corrupting nature of social institutions, it gives rise to the 'right of the strongest.' Rousseau states, 'men reach a point where the obstacles to their preservation in a state of nature prove greater than the strength that each man has to preserve himself in that state.'[14] As uncertainty increases, individuals compare themselves to others leading to public and private values. Since no individual is entitled to have authority over others, it is therefore necessary that individuals give their rights to a community. Thus, 'Each of us puts his person and all his power in common under the supreme direction of the general will, and, in our corporate capacity, we receive each member as an indivisible part of the whole.'[15]

The instability of the state of nature brings people together to form a civil society. Rousseau referred to the agreement among people and the community as the 'Social Contract.' He asserted that the contract must exist between all individual members of the society. A person must agree to surrender his or her individual rights (or will) to be part of a new moral society and to have an equal voice in the making of its laws. Thus, when all members of the state give up their freedoms and liberty, their combined collective individual wills form one 'General Will.' The state and the laws are made by this General Will, as it is the will of the people. This General Will, therefore, acts as the 'absolute power' or the 'public person.' Additionally, it is actively viewed as the 'body politic' or 'sovereign,' and passively the 'state,' ensuring individual rights and complete and free participation in state affairs.[16] It guarantees freedom from alienation and individual autonomy.

This General Will unifies society. It derives its existence from the contract between its individual members. Once the multitude is united, any injury towards an injured member is an injury towards the whole. In this sense, the General Will is always in the right as it is deliberative and resolves differences because it tends to incline itself towards the public good. The General Will demands obedience from every member of its society. As it is a force for good, it is therefore inviolable and infallible. As we will see later in our case study, Rousseau and Locke's thinking had a great deal of influence on the framers of the United States' Declaration of Independence and its constitution. But first we must examine one more view of the social contract proposed by the philosopher you will encounter in Chapter 10, John Rawls.

Rawls holds the view that humans are reasonable, capable of impartiality, and have a capacity for respect and genuine toleration for 'the other.' He claims that from a hypothetical 'Original Position' the principles of justice and equality are chosen behind a 'Veil of Ignorance.' The original position, although a hypothetical agreement, is a result of moral beliefs possessed by

individuals and therefore is obligatory as a real contract after due consideration. In this abstractive view we can discover humans' State of Nature, the
nature of justice – specifically social justice – and the individual requirement
for cooperative living.

Rawls states that the social contract 'implies a level of abstraction,' in that
'the content of the relevant agreement is not to enter a given society or to
adopt a given form of government, but rather to accept certain moral principles.'[17] But why should individuals accept certain moral principles given
that they inevitably hold different worldviews? What makes such principles
'legitimate' in a diverse society? The idea of justice is based on the perspective that society is grounded in cooperation and mutual advantage between
its individual members. While conflicts and shared interests are a part of
society, principles of social justice help 'define the appropriate distribution
of the benefits and burdens of social cooperation.'[18] From this lens, Rawls
asserts 'the principles that free and rational persons concerned to further
their own interests would accept in an initial position of equality as defining
the fundamental terms of their association.'[19] Even though such principles
are based on general considerations, rational individuals would adopt it
without knowing their own personal situation – or what Rawls called the
Veil of Ignorance.

Since the concept of justice in the original position presupposes a conscious
entity – an individual – capable of comprehending its existence and reality, Rawls contends that the most rational choice in the original position is
the acceptance of two main principles of justice. The first principle asserts
equality and liberty of basic rights including the pursuance of the good. The
second principle asserts that individuals be provided equal opportunities to
compete socially and economically as needed to pursue their interests.

In summarizing the above perspectives, it seems clear that Socrates uses the
relationship of a patriarchal unit and society as an argument for the social
contract. The traditional social contract perspective of Hobbes, Locke, and
Rousseau relied heavily on the idea of consent. Hobbes' idea of the social
contract is to succumb to fear and force a sovereign through tacit consent.
Although Locke asserts express and tacit consent, he also seems to suggest that the social contract is one that will bring benefits to the majority
residing in the state. Whereas, for Rawls, making a rational choice on the
basis of ignorance helps in the pursuit of social justice. Now that we have a
better understanding of social contract theory, let's take a look at some of its
critiques.

Critiques of social contract theory

The influence of the social contract through the ages has been enormous. However, it is not without critique. Two main questions to be asked here are: (1) Can a contract be valid if it hasn't been consented to by the individual members? and (2) If the leader – in this case, the government – does not provide proper protections to its members who have entered into the contract, do the followers (the individual members) have the obligation to uphold the contract? Before we answer these questions, let's first consider critiques of the influential theories summarized.

Rousseau asserts that individuals tacitly consent to the social contract by virtue of taking residence in a civilized society. Residence, however, cannot be a guarantee that individuals are fully cognizant of the nuanced nature of the social contract. Socrates, by refusing to leave prison and move to another country articulates a tacit approach to the social contract; here alienation of the will is legitimate. In this perspective, a social contract is an obligation owed to good regimes. For Hobbes, the social contract is an agreement by all persons to abandon their rights to the sovereign who is actually the beneficiary of the social contract. It is a contract made under duress and tacit consent. While consent is the distinguishing factor in Locke's view, he too regards tacit consent in the acceptance of benefits. But does the consent of the majority equate to consent for all its citizens? If primacy is allocated to the majority and consent is left to the majority, it is at the expense of individual rights. In Rousseau's case, the body politic is 'sovereign' and therefore the punishments meted out towards any individual is also to itself. Rousseau completely relies on the tacit consent of the individuals in the state once the political society is instituted.

All these views emphasize individual tacit consent to a certain extent as a way of remaining a member of society. As one author argues, '[Tacit consent] is given by remaining silent and inactive; it is not express or explicit, it is not directly and distinctly expressed by action; rather, it is expressed by the failure to do certain things.'[20] Silence cannot only be interpreted as a form of tacit consent, but also as a form of expressed consent. This raises an ethical concern. If I (an immigrant) as an individual member of a community, like Socrates (a citizen), tacitly agree to follow the rules of the leader (society), and if I reason the leader's rules are unjust, do I still have the obligation to follow society or its rules? Is there a difference in consent between citizens and immigrants? It would seem that the social contract theory is incompatible with this distinction – specifically the natural rights of the individuals. Indeed, Hume in highlighting this flaw in the social contract, emphasizes that the social contract is speculative, fictional, and attempting to justify a preferred form of rule.[21] Similarly, if the contract or agreement is a hypothetical construct then it cannot be said to represent express agreement.[22] These critiques against the social contract use a philosophical lens, but one can also use a pragmatic lens to critique the concept.

For example, the significance of women was largely ignored in earlier philosophical discussions about the social contract, and women were subjugated to subordinate roles in the political arena. One author asserts that the term 'human nature' used in most articulations 'is intended to refer only to male human nature,' which can be problematic as it justifies a male-dominated political view.[23] Likewise, other feminist scholars argue that there has been an implicit contract among men to enforce patriarchy.[24] The ideology of the social contract through the ages may shed light on the patriarchal oppression of women.[25] These perspectives suggest that the social contract can be used as a justification for exploitation of those who are not considered parties to the contract.

Likewise, pluralism asserts social contract theory is problematic due to its theoretical nature and that the contract is between groups, not an individual and the state. If groups have struggles or conflicting interests, then the decisions made by the state will first represent the interests of the group rather than the individual. Accordingly, another scholar, Charles Mills, notes that in the United States, historically whites have had an actual, sometimes explicit but most times implicit, contract to enforce white supremacy that led to domination, subordination, and exploitation of other groups.[26] These are practical concerns that are raised by those critiquing social contract theory, but one may also use a historical lens to critique the theory, specifically in the context of the United States.

From a historical perspective, European settlers to the United States were immigrants when considering the Native Americans who already occupied the land. The clashing of two radically different worldviews lent itself to misconceptions and misgivings, thereby directly contributing to the European–American rationalization of the removal of Native Americans from their own land.[27] Indeed, this was not a social contract in which both parties agreed either tacitly or expressly, but rather a 'contract' based on force and violence.

These are some of the major critiques of social contract theory. Nevertheless, the concept continues to highly influence current thinking about the relationship between a country and those residing in its borders. We turn now to consider how social contract theory relates to the Five Components of Leadership Model.

Five component analysis

In his influential book *Leadership*, James MacGregor Burns identified the key differences between what he referred to as 'transactional' and 'transformational' forms of leadership. For Burns, transactional leadership was a mere exchange between leader and follower – a *quid pro quo* between parties – an honest day's pay for an honest day's work, as it were. Burns argued 'transformational leadership,' contrarily, was a form of leadership in which both the leader and the follower challenged each other to 'higher levels of motivation and morality.'[28] For Burns, transformational leadership was leadership at its best. Both the leader and the follower came away from their interaction better for their time together, and they not only reached their goal, but exceeded it.

Although Burns held an obvious preference for transformational leadership, that is not to say that transactional leadership is not useful. We see regular examples of transactional leadership in Management by Objective (MBO) performance appraisals, as well as in annual bonuses and merit-based pay. Such a form of leadership can be efficacious. On a deeper level, transactional leadership is the foundation of social contract theory. Look at Figure 9.2 – notice the circles around the leader, the followers, and the goal. Those three components of the model are the crux of social contract theory as it relates to leadership. The leader and the followers form a relationship – in this case, for mutual benefit – and in so doing are able to reach a common goal. Notice also the arrows that go both from the leader to the follower and the follower to the leader; it is a mutual process. From the perspective of social contract theory,

Figure 9.2 The Five Components of Leadership Model applied to social contract theory

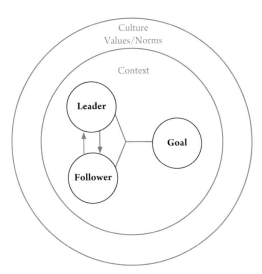

those two arrows are one of the most important parts of the leadership process. We can think of it this way: if one day your boss came to you and said, 'I would really like you to keep working here, but I can't pay you any more,' would you stay? Probably not. That is the essence of the leader–follower relationship through the lens of the social contract theory. I will keep my end of the bargain as long as you keep yours, but if that breaks down, all bets are off.

The goal is the other vital component of leadership according to social contract theory. Remember the first part of the definition of leadership we have been using throughout this book: 'Leaders and followers develop a relationship and work together toward a goal. . ..' We could then ask the question, 'Do the leader and followers need to have a *common* goal?' If we were to apply social contract theory to leadership, the answer might be, 'Not necessarily, but the leader's goal and the follower's goal must be compatible.'

Let's use another employment example. Many people work in jobs that they don't necessarily enjoy. Why? Are they interested in the mission of the organization? Perhaps, but not necessarily. Are they fulfilled by the work they do? Probably not. Then why go to work? It's simple: they do it for the paycheck they receive at the end of the week, of course. The company wants to offer a product or a service to make money, grow the organization, or meet a need, and the employee wants to be able to put bread on his or her table. The goals are not necessarily 'common' in that both the company and the employee are merely a means to each other's ends, but those ends (goals) are compatible. The same is true of the goal for the social contract. As we will see later in our case study, we may all want the same goal, but our reasons for wanting this goal – as well as our means for achieving that goal – may be different, but they must be compatible.

Although the context is still important in social contract theory, as it is in any approach to leadership and ethics, the context is not *as important* as the relationship established between the leader and the follower and the goal. That is not to say the context is completely irrelevant. Although the social contract stipulates that leaders and followers, specifically within the context of a society, are responsible to each other to hold up their end of the bargain, it does not mean that if one party breaks the social contract the other party can behave with impunity.

Consider the Civil Rights protests in the United States in the middle of the twentieth century. The citizens demonstrating were protesting that the State was not fulfilling its end of the bargain – specifically for those of African descent. The scourge of slavery may have been eliminated, but African-Americans still faced discrimination and injustice through the Jim

Crow laws that established the 'separate but equal' context that prohibited them from fully participating in society. Dr. Martin Luther King, Jr. specifically drew the country's attention to the State's failure to honor the social contract in his 'I Have A Dream' speech in 1963 in which he said:

> In a sense we've come to our nation's capital to cash a check. When the architects of our republic wrote the magnificent words of the Constitution and the Declaration of Independence they were signing a promissory note to which every American was to fall heir. This note was a promise that all men, yes, black men as well as white men, would be guaranteed the 'unalienable Rights' of 'Life, Liberty and the pursuit of Happiness.' It is obvious today that America has defaulted on this promissory note, insofar as her citizens of color are concerned. Instead of honoring this sacred obligation, America has given the Negro people a bad check, a check which has come back marked 'insufficient funds.' But we refuse to believe that the bank of justice is bankrupt. We refuse to believe that there are insufficient funds in the great vaults of opportunity of this nation. And so, we've come to cash this check, a check that will give us upon demand the riches of freedom and the security of justice.[29]

Demonstrations against the State's refusal to honor its promise included civil disobedience such as refusing to sit in segregated sections on buses, holding sit-ins at lunch counters that refused to serve people of color, and marching and holding demonstrations in spite of the State's refusal to grant permits for their assemblies. This form of civil disobedience was disproportionally non-violent when compared to the laws denying African-Americans equal rights and the ferocious tactics used to quell protesters, not to mention the beatings and murders of unarmed black people throughout the South. The Civil Rights activists were wise in their careful use of non-violent resistance. Their leaders knew if their followers responded violently, the State would claim that they were not honoring their part of the social contract and they would be struck down with impunity. These peaceful and measured responses to the injustices African-Americans were enduring drew greater attention to the State's breaking of the social contract to serve and protect *all citizens* in exchange for citizens obeying the laws of the State. This illustrates the fact that context matters, even within the confines of the social contract.

But how do cultural values and norms relate to the social contract? For this we need look to various societies around the world and the way each has set up its unique social contract between its citizens and the State. Communist China, for instance, has a very different social contract with its citizens than does capitalist United States, or even the democratic-socialist systems found in Nordic countries. Societies set up various social contracts and their citizens tacitly or expressly enter into these various agreements. Whether these agreements hold or not is reliant upon the parties – the State and its citizens – voluntarily supporting the rules of the agreement. When this breaks down, revolution ensues.

But not every breach of the social contract is met with revolution. Many times, citizens and the State find ways to work around the rules of the social contract, which leads to a breakdown of the contract, but does not completely void it. Consider taxes. Nobody enjoys paying taxes, but those taxes pay for paved roads, clean water, police and fire services, and a wealth of other goods and services on which a civilized society depends. We all enjoy the benefits our collective taxes afford us. Those parties, corporations or individuals, who find ways around paying their fair share of taxes violate the social contract and steal from the State and their fellow citizens. Likewise, those State parties who engage in bribery and graft violate their part of the bargain. But each society has its own values and norms that go into their unique social contract. Swedes may pay a great deal more in taxes in Sweden than do Americans in the United States, but they also receive many more benefits, such as state-sponsored healthcare. It is the particular society's cultural values and norms – that is, what a particular society values – that stipulates the terms of the social contract.

Now that we have a better understanding of the social contract and its relationship to the five components of leadership, let's take a more detailed look at the social contract and its implications found in our case study.

CASE STUDY

Social contract theory applied to immigrants in the United States

The United States has been a nation of immigrants since its inception. She has a long history of welcoming immigrants to her shores. Some immigrants come to the U.S. legally and voluntarily in the hopes of achieving social and economic mobility, while others arrive to avoid persecution and seek asylum, still others enter illegally in the hope of a better life. All of them come full of hopes and dreams of the 'Promised Land.'

A walk through American history notes that the settlers in the early 1600s arrived in search of religious freedom. The next two centuries brought various groups of people to America's shores in search of better lives. However, Africans were brought to America against their will, while some individuals of other nationalities came as indentured servants. The influx of newcomers over the years resulted in anti-immigrant sentiment among certain

CASE STUDY *(continued)*

factions in the United States. The first significant legislation restricting immigration was the 1882 Chinese Exclusion Act.[30] For the next 80 years following the exclusion act, various laws were enacted that excluded groups of people or restricted the number of immigrants from certain parts of the world like Japan, India, and China, while favoring immigrants from European countries. The 1965 Immigration and Naturalization Act ended the quota system that excluded certain groups, and the United States' borders became more welcoming. At this point, the nation began experiencing a shift in immigration policy in favor of diversity.

Today's immigrants come to the U.S. from all parts of the world. They belong to various backgrounds, ethnicities, generations, social economic statuses, and practice a range of religions. In theory, the United States holds the perspective that immigration provides the rich tapestry of diversity that America is known for. It works in the best interests of the State since it permits individuals to better themselves, thereby strengthening the country. The Center for Immigration Studies shares, 'The nation's 42.4 million immigrants (legal and illegal) in 2014 [was] the highest number ever in American history.'[31] 'Immigrants comprised 13.3 percent of the nation's population in 2014 – the highest percentage in 94 years.'[32] The reasons are varied, and include economic, educational, and political reasons; still, others arrived seeking asylum and escaping persecution. While immigration numbers in general are rising, the unauthorized migration of individuals seems to be a major policy concern as 'unauthorized foreigners peaked at 12.2 million in 2007, fell by almost 1 million during the [2008] recession, and may have increased again with economic recovery.'[33]

Current debates to curb unauthorized migration seem polarized at best. Both political parties in the United States – Democrats and Republicans – want some type of immigration reform that could restrain, enforce, or at best discourage entry and employment for those planning to emigrate voluntarily or otherwise. But while the United States' immigration policies in the twentieth century favored diversity, changes in political climate in 2016 once again clouded national perceptions towards immigrants and their descendants causing another round of anti-immigrant hostility. This change was evident in legislation passed around this time, such as the rollback of the Deferred Action for Childhood Arrivals policy (DACA) that allowed people who illegally entered the United States as minors to apply for the ability to legally stay and work in the country; limitations on H-1B work visas that enabled foreign workers to gain employer-sponsored work permits; and a travel ban targeting those who hailed from predominantly Muslim countries. While the 1965 Act opened wide the doors of immigration, the legislation passed in the early twenty-first century seemed to slam them shut. The policies of these eras present two very different views of immigration. This shift in U.S. policy had – and continues to have – ethical ramifications. The rescinding of Deferred Action for Childhood Arrives Act (DACA), the H-1B visa cap, and 'Muslim travel ban' all proposed in 2017 appear discriminatory against certain populations and seem to restrict 'unfavorable' immigration. We shall explore these issues and their ethical implications later in this case study. But first, a brief evaluation of social contract theory in relationship to the United States' Declaration of Independence and the U.S. Constitution is in order.

CASE STUDY *(continued)*

The United States' Declaration of Independence and Constitution

The United States' Declaration of Independence is a restatement of the social contract originally articulated by Locke. The framers of the U.S. Declaration of Independence drew heavily on Locke's view of the Social Contract and his Natural Rights Theory. This historical document outlines the U.S. colonies' grievances against the King of Great Britain and provided a justification for seeking independence. It is based on the Lockean ideas of the natural rights of life, liberty, and property; the property part was substituted with 'pursuit of happiness.' The preamble reads, 'We hold these Truths to be self-evident, that all Men are created equal, that they are endowed by their Creator with certain unalienable Rights that among these are Life, Liberty, and the pursuit of Happiness.'[34]

Further, the framers of the Declaration provided a formal explanation by listing colonial grievances thereby necessitating separation from Great Britain. The introduction of the Declaration reflects this particular idea. It states:

> When in the Course of human events it becomes necessary for one people to dissolve the political bands which have connected them with another and to assume among the powers of the earth, the separate and equal station to which the Laws of Nature and of Nature's God entitle them, a decent respect to the opinions of mankind requires that they should declare the causes which impel them to the separation.[35]

A later document, the U.S. Constitution signed on September 17, 1786, provided the framework for a national government and fundamental laws, one that guaranteed certain basic rights for its citizens. It includes the functioning of a just and fair government that was representative of the people, based on individual rights and the rule of law. It also lists the duties of the government to protect the rights of the individual. The preamble of the Constitution provides a succinct statement about the government. It is an example of the social contract theory in practice. The preamble states:

> We the People of the United States, in Order to form a more perfect Union, establish Justice, insure domestic Tranquility, provide for the common defense, promote the general Welfare, and secure the Blessings of Liberty to ourselves and our Posterity, do ordain and establish this Constitution for the United States of America.[36]

The Constitution highlights a contractual relationship between the three branches of federal government – legislative, executive, and judicial – and its citizens. Built into the contract is a system of checks and balances to ensure no branch of government has too much power. It outlines the government's role and responsibilities to its citizens, as well as the reciprocal rights and duties of the citizens towards the government. If the government fails in its duty to provide the necessary protection, then the people are justified in resisting, even to the point of the dissolution of the government. This iteration of the Social Contract has ramifications for our case study explored here.

CASE STUDY (continued)

Specifically, these documents beg a few questions. If immigrants voluntarily enter the U.S., are they bound by an implicit contract already in place? What about those who enter the U.S. escaping persecution in their homeland? Are they bound by that contract? In what ways does the Social Contract apply to them? Can immigrants choose to reject portions of the contract and yet remain in society? Let's take a closer look at some of these questions.

The Social Contract and immigrants

Let's revisit the Social Contract. In the traditional sense, the Social Contract asserts that government has a duty to protect its citizens from aggression of any kind – aggressions from inside as well as outside the state – from criminals to hostile foreign governments. This suggests that the citizens are provided broad and general protections by the government. The citizens give some of their rights to the government in return for the autonomy and protections it affords. Every citizen of the United States is provided these protections; a lack thereof would be considered an infringement on a citizen's inalienable rights. But what about immigrants who are not yet technically citizens? Do the protections, obligations, and duties that are afforded to the citizens by the government apply to immigrants? And what about illegal immigrants – those who come into the country by primarily breaking the law? Does the government have a moral responsibility to them?

From a purely theoretical lens of the social contract, the state does not seem to have the same obligations to protect immigrants because they are not yet citizens of the state. Neither has the state any moral responsibility to those who enter illegally by breaking the law. If we consider the previous argument that the state has more duty towards citizens as opposed to duties towards non-citizens (the main justification being immigrants are soon-to-be citizens but not yet), the government may have a lower propensity to provide protections towards those who are presently not citizens. So, the obligations that are afforded to its citizens differ from the obligations (or lack thereof) towards non-citizens. In the same vein then, the immigrants or non-citizens are not bound by the existing social contract present. Thus, one might argue that each is not obligated to the other as they are not contractually bound. But in the hopes of gaining citizenship immigrants may express tacit consent. Would tacit consent, in this case, be a sufficient requirement for a social contract?

Additionally, implicit or explicit laws that govern any society may not guarantee that individual members of that society treat each other fairly. While laws are necessary for the functioning of a democratic society, it remains that individuals may access it in nuanced ways. Stereotypes and prejudiced perspectives about the 'other' seem to justify differences in treatment. Perhaps this may be the underlying reason for immigration reform in the form of restrictions placed on those who can enter the State, specifically restrictive reforms based on cultural homogeneity.

Additionally, the lived experiences of immigrants vary based on assimilative and socio-political factors, structural constraints of society, their particular backgrounds, and mainstream perceptions. Most immigrants are drawn to the U.S. for economic reasons

CASE STUDY *(continued)*

and personal freedoms. Some hold the view that immigrants are a financial burden on the United States' economy, while others perceive U.S. workers to be at a disadvantage due to competition from immigrants.[37] The perceptions of immigrants might be at odds with the larger populace. A survey conducted by the Public Agenda Organization in 2003 found 32 percent of immigrants to the United States mentioned lack of civility among its people towards them.[38] That number may be even higher now given the proposed reforms described earlier. If this is the case, perhaps the social contract does not adhere to immigrants in the United States.

It is true that any contract should be explicit signaling consent from both parties, so, if one party fails to hold their part of the contract, then the other party is technically not obligated to honor the agreement. However, the social contract in society depends on the proper ordering of constitutional laws thereby avoiding an excessive concentration of power in the hands of a select few. Therefore, when anyone enters into a country – providing it is with the consent of that country – the individual is implicitly consenting to be bound by the rules of that country's government. If the individual knowingly refuses to respect and abide by the governing rules, then that individual – according to Locke – is at 'war' with that society.

While the social contract may have been notably influential in shaping political thought previously, it has many ethical implications when considering its application in society today. Let's look at three issues that seem to be at odds with the Social Contract – the repeal of DACA, the H-1B visa cap, and the 'Travel Ban of Foreign Nationals.'

Deferred Action for Childhood Arrivals (DACA)

In 2012 the Obama administration created the Deferred Action for Childhood Arrivals program – or DACA for short. The administration announced the directive that certain undocumented youth (under the age of 16) brought into the country illegally by their parents or who came to the United States as young children (under the age of 7) would not be deported. Through executive action, the government granted them temporary permission to stay in the United States – otherwise referred to as 'deferred action.'[39] Additionally, this program allowed those less than 31 years of age as of June 15, 2012, to apply for the DACA program. By 2017, nearly 800,000 immigrants had enrolled or renewed their DACA protected status.[40]

DACA allowed for law-abiding eligible individuals to apply for work authorization and provided relief from the threat of deportation. The Center for American Progress, the National Immigration Law Center, and scholars from the University of California-San Diego fielded a survey that reported DACA improved the lives of undocumented young people.[41] Many of the recipients of DACA contributed positively and in significant ways to the United States. While current numbers are not immediately available, many DACA recipients (also known as 'dreamers') are parents; therefore, their children are citizens of the U.S. by virtue of birth.

CASE STUDY *(continued)*

The U.S. government rescinded DACA in 2017; although, due to federal court orders, the USCIS resumed accepting requests to renew deferred action requests under DACA later that year. Critics of DACA made the case that the policy was a presidential overreach by the previous administration, and many recipients were taking jobs away from legal U.S. citizens and residents. The program's proponents asserted that DACA recipients were making valuable contributions to U.S. society, and ending DACA was punishing children for their parents' decisions.

In the strictest sense of the term, the State is not obligated to protect those who are not citizens or those who have broken the law. Those who are illegal (in the broadest sense of the term) exist outside the jurisdiction of the state. Why would the State provide services and protection to these individuals by taking from those who are citizens and legal aliens of the state? While contextually different, law-abiding DACA individuals provided tacit consent and obeyed the laws of the land even though they were not in a formal agreement. Does this then preclude them from citizenship?

The H-1B visa cap

Let's look at a similar issue. As mentioned earlier, many immigrants come into the country for better economic prospects. Many Silicon Valley Tech companies and other major companies have long depended on highly skilled foreign nationals to meet the needs of particular jobs. Once selected for a position, their H-1B visa is expedited to ensure their immediate arrival. In 2017, the United States announced it would temporarily suspend expedited applications for H-1B visas. Following the announcement, the U.S. Citizenship and Immigration Services (USCIS) suspended 'premium processing' for up to six months.[42] This meant that foreign nationals would have to undergo a longer wait for the visa to be approved. The administration's messages regarding the H-1B status in part read 'The H-1B program is neither high-skilled nor immigration: these are temporary foreign workers, imported from abroad, for the explicit purpose of substituting for American workers at lower pay.'[43] The United States President commented at the time, 'I remain totally committed to eliminating rampant, widespread H-1B abuse.'[44] The United States did later resume premium processing for certain visas later that year.

In critiquing the abuses of the visa program, the directive to 'buy American, hire American' is aimed at – according to some – limiting foreign workers. Others assert that the program allocates positions to foreign nationals at a less expensive cost than that for Americans, thereby restricting opportunities for American nationals. Regardless, changes to this policy impact a workforce that fuels economic growth. While this is a broad generalization, the concern is valid.

While explicitly not concerned with the social contract, the cap on visas does pose an ethical dilemma. The H-1B visa is a non-immigrant visa. Those selected are in the country legally because of the social contract that is in place between the company that hires them and the U.S. government. Let's call this a Social Contract for non-immigrants. From this

---

CASE STUDY *(continued)*

perspective, the protections given to citizens extend to non-immigrants by virtue of work. Setting a cap of visas not only reduces the entry of highly skilled workers into the country, but also reduces the economic capability of U.S. society.

Travel ban of foreign nationals

Finally, we look at yet another issue. In 2017, the White House also released executive order 13769 'Protecting the Nation from Foreign Terrorist Entry into the United States.'[45] The purpose of the order was to target individuals with terrorist ties by denying entry into the U.S. Additionally, the document suspended the entry of individuals from seven countries for 90 days: Iran, Iraq, Libya, Somalia, Sudan, Syria, and Yemen. The travel ban took effect immediately stranding many legal residents and U.S. naturalized citizens visiting their country of birth. A March 6, 2017 document amended and revised the original order with clarifications that the travel ban did not apply to legal permanent residents or current visa holders.

This ban caused concerns for potential students and refugees from these countries. While various aspects of the ban were being heard in the U.S. courts at the time this chapter went to press, the ban in itself is problematic in nature. The countries listed on the travel ban were predominately Muslim. While it is known that many terrorist acts committed around the time of the ban were committed by Islamic extremists, many human rights and religious organizations argued that banning people due to their national and religious background was unethical.

How does the social contract apply here? Security for individuals who are citizens and legal residents are guaranteed protections at home as well as overseas by virtue of the social contract willingly entered into. When the country's laws and protections do not effectively respond to the needs of its citizens the social contract is in danger of collapsing. In the case of the 2017 travel ban, many citizens and legal residents were affected as their birth countries were listed in the document. Additionally, discriminating against people due to their religious and ethnic background is morally reprehensible. The administration defended itself from claims of anti-Muslim bias arguing that the travel-ban orders had nothing to do with Islam. Ironically, by doing this, the administration was tacitly agreeing that restrictions on alien admissions would be unconstitutional, and therefore invalid, if based on religious grounds.

Application of the Five Components of Leadership Model to the U.S. immigrants case study

The model proposed by McManus and Perruci articulate five components of leadership: leaders, followers, the goal, context, and cultural values and norms. For the purposes of analyzing the issue of immigration and social contract, the two components that seem to

CASE STUDY *(continued)*

fit appropriately are leaders (the United States Government and the Courts) and followers (citizens and potential citizens). Let's analyze immigration and social contract through the leadership lens of leaders and followers. Additionally, within the context of U.S. immigration and from the relationship of leader–follower we will extrapolate the goal, one of safety and protection of citizens and immigrants in the context of a post 9/11 world, and holding the cultural value and norms of the American 'Melting Pot' of peoples hailing from nations across the earth.

As McManus and Perruci maintain, leaders provide the energy and vision that guide followers' actions. They assert that the context and culture and the common goal is of utmost importance when evaluating the relationship between the leader and the follower. Consider the United States government and the U.S. courts as the leaders. The three policies discussed here seem to impact immigration negatively. One could assume most U.S. citizens would be in favor of some form of immigration reform. However, examples evaluated here – DACA, the H-1B visa cap, and the travel ban – are decried by many business leaders, religious heads, and human rights advocates. From the lens of the social contract, while the administration may consider itself justified in the strict application of the laws, the government is still based on the will of the people. Only when the will of the people and the government strive for the same ethical ideals can they achieve a good outcome for both parties.

It is a given that leaders exert power in setting an agenda. They have the platform to provide a vision for the future. However, the successful implementation of the vision

Figure 9.3 The Five Components of Leadership Model applied to the U.S. immigration case study

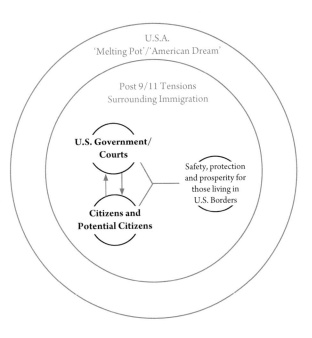

CASE STUDY *(continued)*

ultimately depends on the followers, in this case, U.S. citizens and immigrants. The followers can maximize the vision and further the goals set by the leader. From this perspective, followers shape the legitimacy of the goals through express consent; they can either accept and validate the leader's vision or reject it entirely. A leader, therefore, cannot be successful without the help and cooperation of the followers. Let us consider the immigrants and the administration. The policies proposed by the United States government in 2017 seemed detrimental to the current immigrant situation. Most recipients of DACA were fearful of their future. Obeying the laws and being a model citizen was still not enough to help negotiate a pathway to citizenship. In the case of the travel ban, affected individuals, some of whom were legal residents and had valid reasons for being in the United States, were denied entry into the country. The H-1B visa cap restricted immigration at its conception. In all these cases, the social contract was weakened or broken. For the social contract to be upheld, both parties – leaders and followers – must be ethically and morally responsible and follow the rule of law. If one does not uphold their end of the contract, the other is not expected to uphold theirs. The leader cannot ignore the aspirations of the followers, and the followers must consider the common good rather than their individual good.

Assuming that the social contract is in place, the U.S. government and the courts (the leader) have the legal authority to impartially and uniformly enforce the law in a society for the purpose of providing stability to its citizens and immigrants alike. The law prevails for the purpose of the common good, the leader and follower work together towards the goal of a safe and prosperous society. Since the individuals provide consent (express or tacit), such an environment empowers them to make informed ethical decisions that affect their lives and others in positive ways.

There are some issues with regards to the idealistic perspective articulated above. This view assumes: (1) the law for the common good is not the arbitrary decision of a leader; and (2) followers set aside individualistic and egotistical choices for the maximization of the collective good. With regards to the first assumption, even in democratic societies the possibility of a disconnection between the leader and the follower exists. Additionally, laws for the collective good must not favor political agendas and appease or marginalize specific groups over others, as what appears to be the case with DACA, the H-1B cap, the travel ban. Concerning the second assumption, individuals can be expected to make decisions based on self-interest. (See Chapter 5 Ethical Egoism.) This is not suggesting that individual success is not valued, but success must not come by devaluing others. When one understands that individual success (leader and follower) cannot be to the detriment of the collective good, it sets the ethical framework for a common goal – prosperity and safety, one that is built on mutual trust, benevolence, generosity, and empathy.

Within the perspective of context, immigration according to Martin '. . . is widely considered to be in the national interest, since it permits individuals to better themselves as it strengthens the United States.'[46] In this context, the relationship between the leader and follower is one of interdependence. True leadership takes place only when both the leader and the follower are genuinely invested in each other. When both parties honor the contract

CASE STUDY (continued)

set by working towards a collective good and the leader provides the necessary stability in the pursuit of happiness, a prosperous ethical society is a reality.

There is a real possibility of achieving the American Dream when working together for the collective good. Coined very early by historian James Truslow Adams who asserted 'there has also been the American dream, that dream of a land in which life should become fuller for every man, with opportunity for each according to his ability or achievement.'[47] This can be accomplished with the help and support of the government (leader) that actively protects individuals (follower) in the pursuance of happiness.

Reiterating the assertion of the Declaration of Independence, '. . . all men are created equal, that they are endowed by their Creator with certain unalienable Rights, that among these are Life, Liberty and the pursuit of Happiness,' and 'to secure these rights, Governments are instituted among Men, deriving their just powers from the consent of the governed.'[48] As evidenced by this quote, the Declaration of Independence protects the American Dream. From the nation's inception to modern times, citizens and immigrants both seek opportunities to pursue this dream. While factors of hard work, individual tenacity, education, and supportive networks certainly help towards this individualized achievement, policies such as DACA, the H-1B visa cap, and the travel ban makes this achievement difficult if not impossible. Individuals who are marginalized due to the implementation of these policies may find the American Dream beyond their reach. When the leader and follower work towards the collective goal of a safe and prosperous society, with the leader providing the stability and resources for each individual to maximize their potential and creativity, achievement of the American Dream can become a definite possibility.

Achieving the American Dream is the vision that draws millions of immigrants to U.S. shores. The steady stream of immigrants to U.S. shores has profoundly affected the American character, enriching modern-day life as we know it. However, recent policies put in place by the government is restrictive in setting limitations on immigration. While most maintain that immigration reform is necessary, it shouldn't be devaluing of individuals not meeting a set criteria. Additionally, when the government proposes laws that are not 'by the people, for the people,' it sows seeds of doubt and distrust eroding the social contract between the government and its people. The cleavage between the leader and the followers in this situation weakens their contractual ties. When the contract is broken, one must ask if the other side is ethically required to honor the bargain. Social contract theory would say, 'No, they are not.' This is not to say all is lost; through hardship, valuable lessons can be learned. The U.S. is, after all, 'a nation of immigrants,' and remains, 'By the people, for the people.'

Summary and concluding remarks

What obligations do leaders and followers have toward each other? This question cuts to the heart of leadership – how leaders and followers can work together to achieve a common goal. This case study specifically looked at the social contract and immigration and the interplay of the two. It limits its application to legal immigration. The case study works under the assumption that there is a social contract in place and continues to evolve as new immigrants reach U.S. shores. This necessitates a deeper understanding and validity of the concept of social contract given the changing diverse environment that includes refugees and illegal immigration.

To do this, both leaders and followers must recognize that because of constant external pressures, they must set aside pure self-interest in their commitment to a system where everyone also does the same. Then they must clarify what they will provide for each other as well as what they expect from each other. In this system, both leaders and followers will have to make their expectations clear – what they are providing and what they are giving up in order to reach a mutually beneficial goal.

DISCUSSION QUESTIONS

Are equality and inequality a challenge for leaders who want to use social contract theory as an approach to ethical leadership? Why or why not?

Does immigration constitute a social contract between immigrants and the country that they join? If so, what are the obligations of each?

Should the travel ban be considered a breach of the social contract?

Can the social contract be ethical when one party (e.g. a government) holds substantially more power than the other (e.g. individuals)?

How do refugees factor into considerations of the social contract? Are countries bound by a social contract to help them?

What is the relationship between law and government under the social contract? As politics change, what role should the law play in maintaining the social contract?

ADDITIONAL RESOURCES

J.H. Gittell, *Transforming Relationships for High Performance: The Power of Relational Coordination*, Stanford, CA: Stanford University Press, 2016.

The author uses the social contract as a framework for looking at leveraging relationships in a business context.

J. Douglass, *The Conditions for Admission: Access, Equity, and the Social Contract of Public Universities*, Stanford, CA: Stanford University Press, 2007.

The author explores whether public universities are engaged in a social contract with the public, and what obligations might be an artifact of that contract. It is a practical example of the social contract framework being used to analyze leadership in a contemporary context.

NOTES

1 J.S. Mill, *On Liberty*, Mineola, NY: Dover, 1859/2002, p. 63.

2 T. Reiner, 'Social contract theory,' in M. Bevir (ed.), *Encyclopedia of Political Theory*, Thousand Oaks, CA: Sage, 2010, pp. 1288–93.

3   G. Cronk et al. (eds), *Readings in Philosophy: Eastern & Western Sources*, 2nd edn, Plymouth, MI: Hayden-McNeil, 2004, p. 93.

4   Cronk et al., ibid, p. 91.

5   T. Hobbes, *Leviathan*, C.B. MacPherson (ed.), New York: Penguin 1651/1985, p. 185. Also see S.M. Cahn and P. Markie, *Ethics: History, Theory, and Contemporary Issues*, 5th edn, Oxford: Oxford University Press, 2012.

6   Hobbes, ibid. p. 186.

7   T. Hobbes, *Leviathan*, in R.M. Hutchins (ed.), *Great Books of the Western World*, Vol. 23, Chicago: Encyclopedia Britannica, 1952, p. 87.

8   Hobbes, ibid. p. 47.

9   J. Locke, *Two Treatises of Government and A Letter Concerning Toleration*, G.D.H. Cole (trans.), Stilwell, KS: Digireads.com Publishing, 1689/2005, p. 29.

10   Locke, ibid.

11   Locke, op. cit., p. 101.

12   Locke, op. cit., p. 109.

13   J. Rousseau, *The Social Contract*, New York: Penguin Group-Great Ideas, 1762/2006, p. 2.

14   Rousseau, ibid, p. 14.

15   Rousseau, op. cit.

16   Rousseau, ibid; and R.R. Palmer, J. Colton, and L. Kramer, *A History of the Modern World*, 10th edn, Boston: McGraw Hill, 2007.

17   J. Rawls, *A Theory of Justice*, Cambridge: Harvard University Press, 1971, p. 16.

18   Rawls, ibid, p. 4.

19   Rawls, op. cit., p. 11.

20   J.A. Simmons, 'Tacit consent and political obligation,' *Philosophy and Public Affairs*, vol. 5 no. 3, 1976, 274–91, p. 279.

21   D. Hume, 'Of the original contract,' *Essays: Moral, Political and Literary*, E.F. Miller ed., Indianapolis: Liberty Classics, 1777/1987.

22   R. Dworkin, 'The original position,' in N. Daniels (ed.), *Reading Rawls*, New York: Basic Books, 1975.

23   S.M. Okin, *Women in Western Political Thought*, Princeton: Princeton University Press, 1979, p. 6.

24   C. Pateman, *The Sexual Contract*, Stanford: Stanford University Press, 1989.

25   Pateman, ibid.

26   C.W. Mills, *The Racial Contract*, Ithaca: Cornell University Press, 1997.

27   W.R. Polk, *Neighbors and Strangers*, Chicago: The University of Chicago Press, 1997.

28   J.M. Burns, *Leadership*, New York: Harper & Row, 1978.

29   M.L. King, 'I Have A Dream,' August 28, 1963. Online, https://www.archives.gov/files/press/exhibits/dream-speech.pdf (accessed March 10, 2018).

30   R. Daniels, *Coming to America: A History of Immigration and Ethnicity in American Life*, 2nd edn, New York: Harper Perennial, 2002; D.A. Gerber, *American Immigration: A Very Short Introduction*, Oxford: Oxford University Press, 2011; R. Martin, 'The global challenge of managing migration,' *Population Reference Bureau*, vol. 68 no. 2, 2013. Online, http://www.prb.org/pdf13/global-migration.pdf (accessed March 15, 2018).

31   S. Camarota and K. Zeigler, 'Immigrants in the United States: A profile of the foreign-born using 2014 and 2015 Census Bureau data,' Center for Immigration Studies, October 2016. Online, http://cis.org/sites/cis.org/files/immigrant-profile_0.pdf (accessed March 10, 2018).

32   Camarota and Zeigler, ibid, p. 1.

33   P. Martin, 'The global challenge of managing migration,' *Population Reference Bureau*, vol. 68 no. 2, 2013, p. 6.

34   *The United States' Declaration of Independence*. Online, https://www.archives.gov/founding-docs/declaration-transcript (accessed March 10, 2018).

35   Ibid.

36   *The Constitution of the United States*. Online, https://www.archives.gov/founding-docs/constitution-transcript (accessed March 10, 2018).

37   M. Huemer, 'Is there a right to immigrate?' *Social Theory and Practice*, vol. 36 no. 3, 2010, 429–61.

38   'Now that I'm here: What America's immigrants have to say about life in the U.S. today,' A Report from Public Agenda Prepared for the Carnegie Corporation of New York, Public Agenda, 2003, p. 14. Online, https://www.publicagenda.org/files/now_that_im_here.pdf (accessed March 10, 2018).

39   See the National Immigration Law Center. Online, https://www.nilc.org/ (accessed March 10, 2018).

40   Ibid.

41   T.K. Wong, G. Martinez Rosas, A. Luna, H. Manning, A. Reyna, P. O'Shea, T. Jawetz, and P.E. Wolgin, 'DACA recipients' economic and educational gains continue to grow,' Center For American Progress, August 2017. Online, www.americanprogress.org/issues/immigration/news/2017/08/28/437956/daca-recipients-economic-educational-gains-continue-grow/ (accessed March 12, 2018).

42   U.S. Citizenship and Immigration Services, 'USCIS will temporarily suspend premium processing for all H-1B petitions,' July 24, 2017. Online, https://www.uscis.gov/archive/uscis-will-temporarily-suspend-premium-processing-all-h-1b-petitions (accessed March 12, 2018).

43   M. Green, 'What's the real reason tech companies want to hire foreign workers?' NBC26, February 16, 2017. Online, https://www.nbc26.com/decodedc/whats-the-real-reason-tech-companies-want-to-hire-foreign-workers (accessed March 12, 2018).

44   Green, ibid.

45   'Executive order 13769: Executive Order Protecting the Nation from Foreign Terrorist Entry into the United States,' The White House, January 27, 2017. Online, https://www.whitehouse.gov/presidential-actions/executive-order-protecting-nation-foreign-terrorist-entry-united-states/ (accessed March 10, 2018).

46   Martin, op. cit., p. 5.

47   J.A. Adams, *The Epic of America*, Boston: Little, Brown, and Co, 1931, p. 104.

48   The United States Declaration of Independence, op. cit.

10

Justice as fairness

Alexandra K. Perry

 FRAMING QUESTION

How can leaders and followers work together to create principles that will guide a just society?

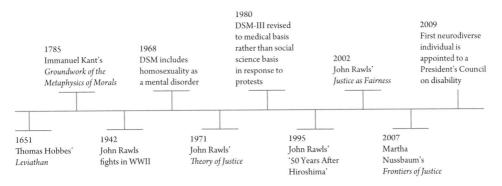

Figure 10.1 Timeline of major works on justice as fairness applied to the chapter case study

Imagine having to establish an entire set of principles and rules to govern a society or organization without any knowledge of its members. What are their strengths and weaknesses? Their habits? Their goals? The catch: You are also a member of this society, but not as you know yourself. All of the factors that you know about yourself might be different. Your race, sex, socio-economic status, age, even your history – there is no way to know what they will be. How would you begin to develop the moral framework for a functioning society without understanding your assigned role within it? You would likely hedge your bets, and create a society where you are most likely to thrive no matter who you end up being. What moral principles would form the underpinning of such a society? This is precisely the question that John Rawls asks us to consider.

This thought experiment is titled The Original Position, and Rawls included it in his most notable work, *A Theory of Justice*, published in 1971.[1] In it, Rawls articulates his theory of distributive justice. The question that Rawls attempts to answer is roughly, 'What would make for a just distribution of the social goods within a society?' He answers this question in one of the longest books in moral philosophy to date, and his answer is – essentially – justice as fairness. For Rawls, a just society is a fair society. In this chapter, we will explore Rawls' thinking specifically in relation to the Five Components of Leadership Model. We will end with a case analysis that examines mental health reform in light of both of these theories of ethics and leadership. But first, a bit more about John Rawls and his ideas.

History

Rawls was a twentieth-century moral and political philosopher who spent much of his career at Harvard. Rawls was a Second World War veteran, and it is often said that his disillusion with war after fighting in the Pacific and seeing the aftermath of Hiroshima strongly influenced his work in moral philosophy.[2] In 1995, Rawls published an article titled, '50 Years After Hiroshima,' in which he lamented the nihilistic mindset that many had toward war. He wrote:

> Undoubtedly war is a kind of hell, but why should that mean that all moral distinctions cease to hold? Also, granted that sometimes all or nearly all may be to some degree guilty, that does not mean that all are equally so. There is never a time when we are free from all moral and political principles and restraints.[3]

This notion that there is always a moral framework and a set of logical, moral principles is a common theme in Rawls' work. It is worth noting given that Rawls' career in philosophy began at the height of the Vietnam War, a time when cultural relativism (discussed in Chapter 7) and moral skepticism were viewed as the prevailing ethical theories. Rawls' work on justice ushered in a new era of moral philosophy that affirmed moral objectivity, and focused on the structure of moral and political systems as a source of justice. While the moral relativists and skeptics focused on concepts like anarchy, Rawls and his predecessors concentrated on the role that these social systems and their leaders played in ensuring the health of a society.

Rawls' best-known work is his *A Theory of Justice*, and it is in this book that he outlines his theory in the most detail while introducing what he defines as the two most important principles of justice: The liberty principle and the equality principle. He would expand on the concept of justice as fairness in two other publications. *Political Liberalism*, published in 1993, focused on the question of whether there could be political legitimacy in a society where there was fundamental and irreconcilable disagreement between citizens over matters of significance, such as morality, law, and religion.[4] *The Law of Peoples*, first published as an article in 1993, and later as a book in 1999, focuses on how peoples ought to live in a society that is just.[5] It fills in some of the details about life inside of Rawls' just society for which *A Theory of Justice* built the framework. Rawls also published a final book posthumously in 2002, titled *Justice as Fairness: A Restatement*, which is a response to thirty years of criticism of *A Theory of Justice*.[6]

Rawls and the social contract

Though Rawls' theory of justice as fairness was a groundbreaking shift from the theories that preceded it, it takes its roots in traditional social contract theory, as well as political liberalism and traditional democratic theory. United States President Bill Clinton famously praised John Rawls for 'helping a whole generation of learned Americans restore their faith in Democracy.'[7] Rawls certainly was influenced by the social contract theories of Hobbes, Locke, and Rousseau, who are each discussed in Chapter 9 in this book. Rawls' work is similar to the work of these contract theorists, but his goal is different. Rather than defend the social contract, Rawls presupposes its worth and sets out to outline the constraints that should be placed upon it. In other words, Rawls asks what limits there are to our ability to enter into a social contract, and what it can morally require of us.

Rawls differs from the other social contract theorists in his view of the power of leaders. While the traditional contract theorists such as Thomas Hobbes and John Locke thought that the social contract primarily served as a mechanism for offering political legitimacy to leaders, Rawls believed that the chief purpose of the social contract was to develop the principles of justice as a group of equal citizens – potential leaders and followers. After these principles were determined, the leader then would be obligated to protect them.[8]

Locke probably influenced Rawls' social contract the most, because he believed that no leadership could be legitimate unless it originated from a state of equal rights, though his idea of equality was very different from Rawls'. In contrast, Hobbes believed that the most logical thing would be for a group to select one individual and offer them ultimate political authority, as long as that individual was selected under fair conditions.

Other social contract theorists, such as Jacques Rousseau, believed that the social contract was a way for leaders and followers to decide upon and implement new rules and policies.[9] This idea also influenced Rawls, though he believed that the power of the social contract was in the constraint, rather than the negotiation of authority. It would be fair to say that while Rousseau thought of the social contract as a tool for development and construction, Rawls thought of it as a tool for evaluation and analysis.

Rawls' theory makes a very sharp implicit distinction between those goods and liberties that one innately has and those goods and liberties that one acquires through social experience and membership in the community that is being governed. His version of the social contract is designed to protect the innate goods while legitimizing the acquisition of those goods and liberties that are not innate to improve the democratic system as a whole. He uses the original position thought experiment to understand where precisely the distinction between innate and acquired liberties falls, and also to determine when the acquisition of liberties and goods is morally permissible.

For leadership, this means that while the traditional social contract theorists outline the contract that the leader and followers might enter into in order to work toward a goal, Rawls' theory of justice tells the leader and followers what *conditions* can be included in that contract, and what *limits* there are to what can be considered requisite of that contract. For example, a social contract theorist might argue that the relationship between a consumer and a company is a contractual one. The company has an obligation to produce a quality product that is advertised accurately. The consumer must pay the agreed upon price and review the product and company fairly. Rawls' theory of justice presupposes this contractual relationship, and instead defines the moral limits of markets – what can be considered a good for sale? It is common for some goods to be restricted from the market, particularly when there is the potential that someone who is less privileged might be exploited by someone who has privilege. For example, organ donation, the adoption of babies, and military enlistment and conscription are all things that push the moral limits of the market and are therefore subject to immense regulation. Rawls relies on his principle of liberty, and principle of equality to make these determinations. Those principles will be outlined later in this chapter.

Rationality as the foundation for justice

Rawls' conception of political liberalism is influenced heavily by Immanuel Kant's work on the human good and rationalism.[10] Both Kant and Rawls define 'the good' as those things that any reasonable person would want, or the way that any reasonable person would act. Rawls defines primary goods as the 'things which a rational man wants, whatever else he wants.'[11] In other words, Rawls defines primary goods as those things that everyone wants, no matter what his or her interests, experience, and lifestyle might be, or those things that humans universally want. This is very similar to Kant's categorical imperative, as discussed in Chapter 2. Kant believed that what made humans unique was their capacity for reason, and therefore reason was the basis for his moral theory. The categorical imperative is the imperative that humans 'act only according to that maxim whereby you can, at the same time, will that it should become a universal law.'[12] This reliance on rationality to determine what is right, or what is good, is ultimately the foundation of justice for both Kant and Rawls.

Rawls also includes rationality in his definition of a citizen. In *Theory of Justice*, he defines citizens as those who are able to participate in a social contract developed in the original position as all humans who are capable of rationality and reasonableness. The original position thought experiment uses rationality as its mechanism for developing the principles of justice that Rawls believes are imperative. Essentially the question Rawls asks is, 'What principles of justice would any *rational* person develop?' If all rational persons would develop the same principles of justice, Rawls takes them to be moral.

Major concepts of Rawls' theory of justice as fairness

Original Position and the Veil of Ignorance

Rawls' theory has several foundational concepts, but perhaps the most vital aspects of his theory are his concepts of 'the Original Position' and his 'Veil of Ignorance.' Rawls used his original position thought experiment as an exercise in what he calls free choice. The thought experiment is purely hypothetical. Rawls is not arguing that this is how leaders and followers ought to design a society or organization, or even that it might be possible to do so. Instead, Rawls is tasking the thought experiment to support his thesis.

This is what Rawls asks of the reader engaged in his thought experiment: Imagine that you are among a group of persons who are entering into a social contract and outlining its terms to provide a moral and political framework to your society or organization. Now, imagine that there is a veil of ignorance in place that makes it impossible for each person to know his or her own position within the society. Each person enters the original position totally blind to his or her own history, personality, characteristics, strengths, or weaknesses.

The veil of ignorance is an essential feature of Rawls' theory because it sets it apart from other social contract theories. To John Locke, for example, the state of nature in which people enter into the social contract is a state in which all persons are 'free and equal,' and a factor of this freedom is complete knowledge of all of the facts about themselves. This is central to Locke's theory because he argues that this knowledge will impact the structure of the social contract. In particular, Locke believes that those with power would willingly distribute social and political goods to maintain that power, and that those who do not have power would limit their ability to gain the power to ensure the continued availability of social and political goods.

In contrast, Rawls thought that the veil of ignorance was critical to the development of fair and just principles. This veil ensures that the contract will not be biased in any way, and that the principles of justice that are developed in the original position will be fair and just. Rawls wrote this mandate in his thought experiment assured 'pure procedural justice at the highest level.'[13] Again, this view sets Rawls' social contract theory apart from others. The common understanding of a contract is that it is fair if and only if all parties have access to all pertinent information. To Rawls, a fair agreement can only be entered into if all parties are restricted access to information, thereby making it equal.

The question Rawls asks after setting up the original position and the veil of ignorance is: 'How would any *rational* person address matters of justice in a society if they did not know their place within it?' The emphasis that Rawls places on rationality in his theory is a nod to the influence of Kant on his thinking. Both Kant and Rawls believe that there is much to be learned through understanding the collective thoughts of those who are rational. If all rational people value X, then X must be valuable. For Kant, this exercise was used to determine the right thing to do, whereas, for Rawls, the exercise is to determine which principles of justice are ultimately valued by all and to make sure they are not biased by self-interest.[14]

Ultimately Rawls believes that there are two primary principles of justice that all rational persons would agree to in the original position. The first principle, often called the greatest equal liberty principle, states, 'First, each person is to have an equal right to the most extensive basic liberty compatible with a similar liberty for others.'[15] This is similar to the test that Robert Greenleaf requires of servant leadership, as discussed in Chapter 13. Leadership must have a positive impact on the least privileged members of society.[16] The second principle, often called the 'difference principle,' states:

Social and economic inequalities are to be arranged so that they are both: (a) to the greatest benefit of the least advantaged, consistent with the just savings principle, and (b) attached to offices and positions open to all under conditions of fair equality of opportunity.[17]

The second part of the difference principle is sometimes called the 'equal opportunity principle.' In the following sections, I will outline these principles in greater detail, and discuss their relevance to leadership.

The greatest equal liberty principle

Rawls believes that any rational person in the original position would insist upon what he calls the 'greatest equal liberty' principle. This principle would assure that every citizen is, at the very minimum, afforded all basic liberties in a way that does not infringe upon the basic liberties of others. These liberties include freedom of conscience, freedom of expression, and due process under the law. This principle, Rawls argues, is rational not only because it provides a safeguard for citizens, but also because of the freedom it allows for a democratic government or organization. If all citizens have access to a fully adequate basic scheme of rights, then democracy can remain neutral to competing moral codes. This means that the leader can allow for productive democratic debate and rational disagreement over morality rather than make judgments about goods and values because all citizens will already have access to a set of liberties that is wholly adequate. This principle also allows citizens the freedom to pursue a life that they define as good, as long as it does not restrict another citizen's ability to do so.

In practical terms, this means that all members of a group, according to Rawls' theory, should be afforded all basic liberties in order to then be self-determining. Factors such as race, sex, and socio-economic status should not determine whether a person gets to vote, marry the person that they love, hold office, be promoted in the office, or advocate for the causes they care most about. Because these are assured, followers can then focus on pursuing their own conception of the good. Additionally, because the leader does not have to make determinations about such things as who can vote, who can marry, whether women receive equal pay, or what values are acceptable, he or she can then focus on doing what they are obligated to do in the social contract.

The leader's role in Rawls' theory of justice as fairness is described in a section of *Theory of Justice* where he describes the non-ideal theory or the problem of states who are noncompliant or only partially compliant with the theory of justice. To Rawls, a leader's role is mostly political, and not moral. The leader should protect democracy, promote the stability of government, work toward international harmony in order to prevent conflict, preserve and improve upon the society for future generations, and ensure that all citizens continue to have access to their adequate set of liberties. Any leader who chooses to ignore the citizens' rights to this set of liberties would be leading a failed state. Followers can also cause a failed state by failing to maintain their end of the social contract.[18]

Rawls argued that the greatest equal liberty principle is the most essential principle, and that it should always take precedence if there is a conflict between principles. However, there is a second principle that he believed would also be a rational outcome of the original position: The difference principle.

The difference and equal opportunity principles

Rawls' difference principle allows for social and economic inequality as long as all citizens already have access to all basic liberties. Rawls argues rational persons in the original position would allow for such inequality if the inequality is to 'the greatest benefit of the least-advantaged members of society.'[19] This is because the factors that lead to the benefit of those who are better off are usually not earned, but rather innate. Straight, white, middle-class males might see an advantage that LGBTQ, minority, lower-class women do not. This advantage is not because they worked to make themselves straight, white, or male, but rather because they were born into this situation. Rawls argues that social stability requires us to benefit those who do not have the same advantage so that they are regarded as equally worthy members of the same society. Removing the veil of ignorance means that the previous state in which all members were equal is now in the past. Allowing for those in privileged positions to, for example, make more money, is fair if it means that those who do not experience the same privilege have more options for employment, or a better world to live in.

The second clause of Rawls' second principle is the principle of equal opportunity. Though this clause comes second in *Theory of Justice*, it is actually conceptually prioritized above the first clause. The equal opportunity principle stipulates that all offices and positions must be open to all citizens through the power of fair equality of opportunity. If there is truly equal opportunity, then and only then are inequalities just.

Critiques of the Rawlsian model

Rawls was praised for his restoration of democratic thought in the realm of political theory at a time when the United States faced a great deal of political upheaval. His theory of justice as fairness provides arguably the most important contribution to political philosophy in the twentieth century. However, his theory has unquestionably been subject to critique, as all theories are. Many unsophisticated criticisms of *Theory of Justice* focus on the hypothetical nature of Rawls' original position. There is concern among some scholars that because the original position is impossible to realize, the principles Rawls claims would naturally be developed by all rational citizens are unverifiable. Critiques of this nature are largely not a concern for Rawls because he acknowledges that the original position is intended as a thought experiment or an exercise in freedom of choice. Nevertheless, there are some critiques of Rawls' theory that are worthy of consideration. In this section, I will discuss the criticism that Rawls relies too heavily on the notion of rationality, and also the critique that capability, rather than equality, needs to be the focus of theories of justice. The latter critique is common in the growing area of care ethics, which has extensively adapted Rawls' theory to respond to the former criticism that his theory is overly reliant on rationality.

Reliance on rationality

There are two ways in which Rawls has been criticized for his theory's reliance on rationality. The first critique focuses on the validity of his thought experiment when its inclusion in the experiment is so restrictive. Rawls sets out to understand the principles of justice that form the foundation of the social contract, '. . . between citizens regarded as free and equal, and as normal and fully cooperating members of society over a complete life.'[20] Rawls' language here has been criticized for being both ambiguous and exclusionary. What exactly would it mean for a citizen to be a 'normal and fully cooperating member of society,' and why would this have to occur over a whole life for their citizenship to be legitimate? Would this clause exclude those who have spent any time at all in prison (and therefore not been fully cooperative)? Would it exclude those who at some time had been irrational, such as elderly persons with Alzheimer's? And how, when Rawls makes it a goal to allow for wide variations in human flourishing, would one define 'normal'?

The second and more significant criticism about Rawls' reliance on rationality is over the implications that this reliance has for the consideration of citizenship. This understanding of the point and currency of equality has implications for who should count as a citizen. Rawls is explicit: All persons in the social contract must have two qualities to be considered citizens, rationality and reasonableness.[21] A reasonable person will recognize their existence in a social sphere and engage in cooperation in order to improve that sphere for both themselves and the others within it. For example, a reasonable person might want a new car, but they will refrain from stealing someone else's car because they would recognize that the car's owner was also a member of the same society and possessed the same rights. In other words, the reasonable person would limit their own pursuit of the good in order to make sure that their pursuit didn't disregard the fact that all other citizens also have the right to pursue the good.

Rationality is the person's ability simply to pursue the good for himself or herself. A rational person can set proper goals and understand how to work toward those goals appropriately. The rational person will have analytic abilities and the desire and capability to utilize the resources available to them in pursuit of the good.

The assertion that rationality is a necessary condition to citizenship in Rawls' social contract is troublesome given the range of human diversity that the principles developed under the social contract would apply. Who would have the authority to determine which goals were proper, how those goals should be sought after, and whether it is necessary for citizens to have a desire to utilize resources? Further, is restricting the voices that contribute to the development of a theory of justice fair when it will apply to those who have been excluded? As Sophia Wong observed:

> We see that the idea of the person is idealized and simplified, and makes no attempt to capture the full scope of human diversity in the population to which the theory of justice will actually apply.[22]

Care ethics: Capability and human dignity

Recently, the field of care ethics has started to focus on this challenge to Rawls' theory of justice by adapting it to be more inclusionary. Theorists like Martha Nussbaum and Eva Feder Kittay modify the question that Rawls asks in his inquiry. Rather than ask what the most equitable way to distribute social goods is, care ethicists ask how the social goods that are distributed can be accessed and utilized by the individuals to whom they are distributed. While Rawls uses rationality as a mechanism for ensuring a fair and equal distribution of social goods, Nussbaum and her colleagues focus on the capability that the recipients have to utilize those goods and the function that each good serves.

Nussbaum uses the concept of human dignity as the milepost by which she measures progress in distributive justice.[23] Are resources being allocated in such a way that all persons are able to live a dignified life? This approach de-emphasizes the role of rationality because it allows for a broader acceptance of human diversity. The idea of 'rational goals,' which is ambiguous in Rawls' theory, can be replaced with a goal that is set based on the particular individual's capabilities. In essence, outcomes of this model will be assessed on a scale that can be adapted to suit the capabilities and notion of the good possessed by each citizen, as long as dignity is the ultimate benchmark for each person's flourishing.

The goal of the care ethics adaptation of justice as fairness is not to change Rawls' thesis, but rather to provide more definition to it in order to better employ it and assess it. Rawls didn't intend for his theory to be exclusionary; rationality was simply intended as a mechanism for determining what is just. The care ethicists adapt Rawls' theory so that it focuses on distribution based on capability rather than an equal starting point. In doing so, the theory increases the number of people who can benefit from the distribution of social goods but also brings into focus the necessary societal adaptions that need to be made to best allow individuals to flourish and live a dignified life. Providing equal access for voting does not benefit those who cannot transport themselves to the polling places or navigate their wheelchair through the door. The care ethics approach calls for a consideration of how society might adapt to the range of capabilities in working toward a goal of promoting human dignity. Maybe polling places are open in a wider range of neighborhoods, and maybe these new polling places include wheelchair ramps. At the very least it would not just be the individuals' utilization of resources that are examined, but the availability of the resources themselves.

Five component analysis

Rawls' theory of justice as fairness results in a very particular approach to leadership, which I will outline here using the Five Components of Leadership Model. The approach draws influence from the traditional social contract theories, limits the role of leadership in a way that is similar to the laissez-faire approach of Ayn Rand, and relies on rationality to construct moral principles in the way that Kant does, yet it is altogether distinct from these theories.

Rawls' theory of justice as fairness results in two moral principles he claims are universally desirable to all rational individuals. The first principle, the principle of greatest equal liberty, asserts all citizens should be afforded an adequate scheme of basic liberties such as the right to engage politically, be free from unlawful arrest, and pursue the good however they define it. The second principle emphasizes that the only just unequal distribution of social goods is an inequality that benefits those who do not receive them. For example, a doctor can justly receive more education than those who are not doctors, because ultimately having doctors in a society will benefit those who do not receive this level of education.

Rawls claims that all citizens who are rational will agree to a social contract based on these principles. However, in contrast to earlier social contract theorists, Rawls does not believe that the social contract affords a leader full and indiscriminate political legitimacy. Instead, to Rawls, the role of the leader is to safeguard the basic liberties for all citizens, but also to afford them the freedom to pursue the good by protecting them from outside risks and ensuring the continued stability of the organization or society. In a way, the outcome looks roughly like a laissez-faire style of leadership similar to that proposed by Ayn Rand; however, Rawls' leader is much more engaged as a citizen than Rand's leader would be.[24]

The leader (or statesman in Rawls' theory) is supposed to promote peace within the society, ensure that the society is ready to protect itself from outside threats or sources, and work to make the society sustainable for future generations. For the leader of an organization this translates roughly to: provide good stewardship for the organization by promoting peace and democratic discussion among followers, insulate the organization from outside challenges such as the economy, competitors, or legislation that may pose a threat to the success of the organization, and aim for sustainability both for the ongoing achievements of the organization, and also for the community that nurtures it.

The goal of leadership under Rawls' theory is to be developed collaboratively by leaders and followers as an artifact of the social contract. Whatever the goal might be, it needs to respect the two principles of justice developed under the original position and must be rationally deliberated. The addendum to this theory provided by care ethicists such as Martha Nussbaum also necessitates that any goal be considerate of the capability of all citizens to utilize the social goods that are distributed.

Rawls' theory of justice as fairness focuses upon the two-way arrows that go between the leader and followers and the process the leader and followers use to determine and reach the common goal (see Figure 10.2). In practical terms, this means that leaders and followers have to engage with one another

Figure 10.2 The Five Components of Leadership Model applied to Rawls' theory of justice as fairness

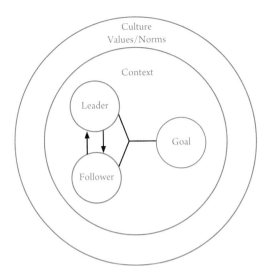

Culture
Values/Norms

Context

Leader

Goal

Follower

not only in pursuit of the goal, but also in order to define the goal. Since no leader is afforded absolute political legitimacy, democratic debate must consistently take place in order to set, evaluate, and re-set goals, and also to evaluate whether the leadership is effective in representing all citizens. Justice as fairness requires a collaborative approach to leadership rather than a hierarchical authority-based model. The board of a nonprofit is a good example to illustrate the role of the goal in a Rawlsian approach to leadership. The goals of nonprofits are typically set through careful deliberation by a board. The president or executive director of a nonprofit is often included on the board but does not have the authority to set goals without the input of the board. Once goals have been set, the leader and follower's efforts at working toward that goal are consistently evaluated, and there is the option for leadership to change if the current leadership is not effective at meeting the goals.

Nonprofit leadership also tends to be distributed, which is very consistent with the way that a Rawlsian would approach working toward goals. There may be a president of the entire nonprofit board, but typically there are a number of subcommittees with their own leadership that is formed to focus on specific goals or specific components of an overall goal. This is consistent with Rawlsian leadership because it allows for the goals to be tailored more individually.

The context and culture of the organization or society are also going to be considerations in a Rawlsian approach to ethical leadership. The context or immediate environment will determine the resources available to the group, which will factor into the determination of goals, and the distribution of resources within the environment. For example, one of the most common challenges facing healthcare organizations today is the opioid crisis, among other drug-related challenges. However, the context that the healthcare organization is in is going to determine which goals are set, and how leaders and followers work toward those goals. For example, a healthcare organization in a metropolitan area might have more local resources to help mitigate the effects of the opioid crisis. Maybe they have access to better drug treatment options for discharging patients who have overdosed, or more social workers within their system. However, one of the challenges in a metropolitan area is that there are often so many different versions of particular drugs that are much more accessible. Therefore, treatment options and approaches have to be constantly reevaluated.

In a more rural area, there are likely far fewer resources available for the healthcare system to utilize. However, there are going to be far fewer outlets for drugs to be trafficked into an area, so the patients that the healthcare system sees are likely to respond to treatment in similar ways. The community is also likely to be culturally more open-minded to grassroots approaches to dealing with the crisis. For example, in rural West Virginia, a group of nurses working in a neonatal intensive care noticed that there was a large number of infants being admitted after being born with drugs in their system. Because the increased number of admissions was causing overcrowding in the NICU, the nurses decided to found a center in a home-like environment where infants could go through the symptoms of withdrawal while receiving round the clock care, and the NICU nurses and physicians could focus on higher risk infants such as those born prematurely or with congenital defects.[25] This sort of approach was highly context- and culture-dependent. While a rural area might respond well to this newly developed resource, a more metropolitan area might make this impossible both because of the high costs associated with beginning such a program, but also because of the tendency for such areas to be very risk-averse and regulation-driven.

In the next section, I outline a Rawlsian approach to leadership by using a case study on mental health reform. After presenting the historical background to the case, I will discuss the challenges that mental health reform presents to leadership, and look at how a Rawlsian might approach this issue using the Five Components Model of leadership to work toward an ethical outcome.

CASE STUDY

Mental health reform

In 1974, the American Psychological Association (APA) began to discuss plans for a revision of the *Diagnostic and Statistical Manual of Mental Disorders* (DSM), a book that serves as the definitive guide for psychologists and psychiatrists in understanding and diagnosing pathology. Mental health professionals were using the second significant revision of the manual, as they had been since its publication in 1968. The push for a third significant revision of the manual came in reaction to a vocal social and political movement that began in the LGBTQ community.

Soon after the revision of the DSM-II in 1968, LGBTQ rights activists began to demonstrate publicly against the APA for the inclusion of homosexuality as a mental disorder. Many in this community viewed this inclusion as simply bigotry, or an attack on deviant 'lifestyles,' fueled by stigma. Activists drew analogies to the civil rights movement of the 1950s and 1960s and claimed that the view of homosexuality as a disorder was an effort toward marginalizing those who were viewed as inferior and stripped them of their liberties.

This movement was called the anti-psychiatry movement, and it was remarkably successful. Without clear boundaries between normal and pathological, and reflecting a mostly psychodynamic, rather than biological, framework of mental health, the APA faced challenges to the legitimacy of mental health diagnoses. Quickly, the APA worked to deflect criticism, and in 1974 the 7th printing of the DSM-II replaced homosexuality as a category of disorder with the title, 'sexual orientation disturbance.'[26] This new category allowed for a more flexible view of homosexuality. If a person's sexual orientation caused a 'disturbance' to his or her well-being, it was treated as a disorder, but the *disturbance* and not the *orientation* was said to be the basis for a diagnosis.

This amendment to the DSM-II was intended by the APA as a short-term remedy to pacify demonstrators, but the APA knew that their manual had to be transformed. Immediately, the APA put together a task force and began to develop the DSM-III. Robert Spitzer, a psychiatrist from Columbia University, was elected chairman of the new DSM task force. Spitzer's goal was clear: bring the DSM in line with the International Classification of Diseases (ICD), the World Health Organization's diagnostic tool for epidemiology and disease.[27]

For Spitzer and his committee, the stakes were high. In addition to the anti-psychiatry protests, the diagnostic methods for mental disorders had come under fire from within. A year earlier, David Rosenhan, a psychologist at Stanford's law school, had published a paper titled 'On Being Sane in Insane Places' in the journal *Science*.[28] Rosenhan had conducted a two-part experiment on the reliability of psychiatric diagnosis. In the first part, Rosenhan and seven 'pseudo-patients' feign psychiatric symptoms in an attempt to gain admission to various psychiatric hospitals. Rosenhan and his pseudo-patients were each admitted to psychiatric hospitals in five different states and diagnosed with mental disorders. Once admitted, they began acting normally again, but were forced to take anti-psychotic drugs

---

CASE STUDY *(continued)*

and remain in the facilities under treatment. The pseudo-patients described the conditions in the facilities as 'dehumanizing' and unethical. After hearing of these initial results, a well-respected psychiatric hospital contacted Rosenhan and asked him to send pseudo-patients to them, claiming that their diagnostic procedure was so fine-tuned that they would be able to detect them. In the months that followed, the facility admitted 193 new patients. Of these, 42 were identified as Rosenhan's pseudo-patients by hospital staff and psychiatrists. In reality, Rosenhan had not sent a single pseudo-patient to the facility. Rosenhan's experiment was, and is, controversial. Some in the social sciences question whether it can rightly be called an experiment, while others claim that it raises important questions about psychiatric diagnosis.

Rosenhan's work and the ongoing scrutiny by LGBTQ rights activists weighed heavily on Spitzer and his colleagues. How could they develop a diagnostic tool that would identify mental illness without bias or subjectivity? The task force's goal was to address this skepticism by bringing psychiatric diagnosis in line with the kinds of clinical diagnostic procedures used by physicians and epidemiologists.

The DSM-III was drafted within a year and was the subject of trials and debates for five additional years before it was published in 1980. Abundant revisions were made to the DSM-II and the new manual, the DSM-III, was barely recognizable. The DSM-II was 134 pages long and listed 182 disorders. It had two main branches: neurosis, which consisted of anxiety and depressive disorders where no break from reality was detected, and psychosis, where hallucinations or delusions were detected. The new DSM-III was 494 pages long and included 265 separate diagnoses.[29]

In an attempt to align psychiatric diagnosis with medical diagnoses, where Spitzer and his task force believed that they rightly belonged, each disorder was placed on an axis with disorders that shared similar characteristics. This new multi-axial system replaced the branches in the DSM-II and was believed to organize disorders in such a way that each disorder was part of an axis that was defined by clinically significant and measurable attributes. Variations within each axis were defined by essential qualities and symptoms as particular disorders.

Mental health reform and justice as fairness

Spitzer's revision revolutionized psychiatry and the process of psychiatric diagnosis. His axial model is still used, and the architecture of the DSM remains the same. A major revision of the manual was published in 1994, fourteen years after the DSM-III, and the newest revision, the DSM-V, was released in 2013.[30] Each of these revisions has been controversial in its own right based on the classification, addition, and deletion of particular disorders. Still, the axial system is widely credited for the medicalization and professionalization of psychiatry.

Though there has been a great deal of progress in psychiatry since Spitzer and his committee drafted the DSM-III, the stigma surrounding mental health, and the scarcity

CASE STUDY *(continued)*

of resources is still one of the most pressing issues in our society. Debates over the medication of pediatric attention deficit disorders, the provision of special education, the accommodation and support of adults with mental illness and cognitive disability, the efficacy of therapeutic practice, and the involuntary admission of individuals into psychiatric facilities are all related to the scope of mental experience: 'What is within the normal range, and what is not?' It is clear that mental experience varies differently from person to person, but it is much less clear how we ought to make sense of this variation. When does a different way of processing, understanding, feeling, or reacting become pathological or disordered? Should all differences be tolerated? In the absence of any harm to another person, is it ethical for variations to be singled out for eradication?

Questions of justice arise in many different contexts when mental health is concerned. For example, most universities now have an office of student or disability services. Educational and mental health professionals in this office often make recommendations as to reasonable adjustments that might be made for students with learning, cognitive, or mental disabilities.

These accommodations often include things that help the student learn, such as note-taking, extra time on tests, or different forms of assessment. It is unclear, however, when these accommodations move from being a reasonable adaptation to an unreasonable advantage because our understanding of mental experience is, to this point, as crude as our understanding of justice.

Five component analysis

Rawls' theory of justice as fairness focuses on two central concerns: equality of resources and consideration of capabilities. Equal access to the resources necessary for citizenship allows for reasonable accommodations to be made in order for individuals to secure employment, participate in the political process, and access public institutions. Wheelchair ramps, minimal federal assistance, free public records, and accessible locations for voting are all artifacts of this view.

While this approach has been relatively successful in consideration of physical disabilities, it falls short in addressing neurodiversity because of its reliance on rationality as an ultimate moral power, as explained earlier in this chapter. Responding to this, care ethicists proposed an alternative approach to understanding human differences based on capability alone, and not the equality of resources. This view has been successful in addressing cognitive disability, but mental illness still poses a challenge, because capabilities might be intact and even intensified, while goal-driven action or the ability to reason are diminished.

Of course, the history of psychiatry and its relationship with contemporary debates over justice and mental health is not without its own controversies, and this further complicates mental health reform. Psychiatry, like all other disciplines, has a history of prevailing theories and naysayers, debates and innovations. Yet it seems as if other areas of medicine have a much less vexed history and a much clearer trajectory of progress.

CASE STUDY (continued)

Edward Shorter, a historian of psychiatry, claims that it is the nature of psychiatry itself that makes it a minefield.[31] Shorter writes:

> To an extent unimaginable for other areas of the history of medicine, zealot-researchers have seized the history of psychiatry to illustrate how their pet bugaboos – be they capitalism, patriarchy, or psychiatry itself – have converted protest into illness, locking into asylums those who otherwise would be challenging the established order. Although these trendy notions have attained great currency among intellectuals, they are incorrect, in that they do not correspond to what actually happened. Psychiatry is, to be sure, the ultimate rule maker of acceptable behavior through its ability to specify what counts as 'crazy.' Yet there is such a thing as mental illness. It has a reality independent of conventions of gender and class, and this reality can be mapped, understood, and treated in a systematic and scientific way.[32]

In other words, humanity is so tangled up with mental activity that it is often hard to distinguish ideas, opinions, and volition from delusion or mood. While historically various political motives, sexual preferences, and philosophical positions have been pathologized, making psychiatry a powerful 'rule maker,' not all mental illness is constructed socially in this way. Shorter's 'zealot-researchers' still exist in debates over autism, Ritalin, gun control, homosexuality, atheism, and in the knotted fragments of almost all other issues over which there is the potential for controversy.

How would a leader apply Rawls' theory of justice as fairness to work toward mental health reform? Rawls' work would say that leaders and followers must work together toward a goal of justice. This does not simply mean the just distribution of goods among the membership of the leader/follower community, but also the addressing of issues of justice within the context of this community. But how does this work in practical terms? Rawls' two principles actually offer some guidance in this. Rawls' principle of equal liberties outlines the basis of the goal for the leader. The goal that the leader and followers work toward is to guarantee a wholly adequate set of basic liberties to all citizens. For mental health reform this means safeguarding those with mental health challenges so that their basic liberties remain intact, but if we accept the modification to justice as fairness as put forward by the care ethicists, it also means developing resources and adaptations to existing social institutions so that dignity is preserved and the social goods being distributed are distributed with an eye toward varying capabilities.

The context of leadership in mental health reform necessitates the acceptance of the care ethicists' emphasis on capability. Leadership in mental health reform must recognize diversity within an organization or society because there have been too many cases in this history of mental health where failing to do so has led to drastic consequences. The pathologizing of those on the LGBTQ spectrum outlined above is one example, but throughout history, there have been numerous examples such as the witch trials, the idea of hysteria, and more. Distributing the same set of social goods to all fails to recognize this diversity and promotes equality in a way that is not sensitive to difference.

CASE STUDY *(continued)*

Figure 10.3 The Five Components of Leadership Model applied to the mental health reform case study

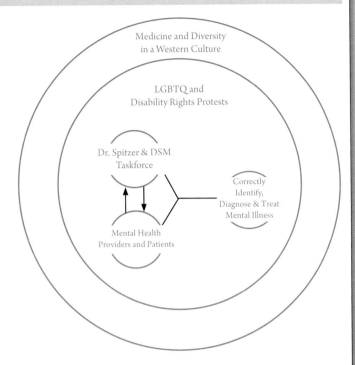

Rawls' second principle of justice, the difference principle, also emphasizes the importance of the leader and followers' recognition of this diversity in their interactions. The second principle that serves to protect the right inequality insofar as it allows citizens to pursue their own conception of the good is based on a foundation of equal opportunity and overall leads to a better life for all, not only those who are privileged.

This means that it is the leader's role to ensure that those with mental illnesses are able to pursue their conception of the good. This defines the leader's responsibility as two-fold: distributing the material and social goods that the community needs, but also providing the social and political protections that are necessary for the flourishing of the group. This is a challenge, as the citizens we are discussing in this chapter often do not, or are not able to, engage politically. Further, because mental health is a spectrum, there is no clear way to represent those who cannot engage politically. They may all have very different experiences and needs. The leader and the follower in Rawls' theory of justice will have to work together to make sure that the perspectives of those who cannot engage politically are considered in the distribution of social goods.

For Rawls, this does not mean that each citizen's experience must be maximized in some way. The goal is not to raise everyone to the level of the privileged, but instead to afford them all basic liberties and equality of opportunity. The care ethics modification of this theory asserts the need to focus on dignity as the benchmark. Are these individuals able to live a dignified life? Political philosopher Elizabeth Anderson says it this way:

CASE STUDY *(continued)*

> Once all citizens enjoy a decent set of freedoms sufficient for functioning as an equal in society, income inequalities beyond that point do not seem so troubling in themselves.[33]

To ensure that all citizens 'enjoy a decent set of freedoms,' the leader and the followers have to work together to make sure institutions and practices are also accessible so as not to restrict citizens of varying capabilities from using them. In *Frontiers of Justice*, Martha Nussbaum wrote 'no matter how much money we give the person in the wheelchair, he will still not have adequate access to public space unless public space itself is redesigned.'[34] For mental health reform, the adaptations that institutions have to make may not be adaptations to physical space but rather adaptations to legislation, policy, and the availability of community resources. The role of the follower, then, is to become a strong and willing advocate, while the role of the leader is to protect basic liberties and to facilitate democratic debate.

Rawls' second principle also emphasizes the right of all citizens to pursue their own version of the good. Moreover, the theory of justice as fairness asserts that it is not the role of democratic institutions to make value judgments about these conceptions of the good, only to protect basic liberties so that citizens have the freedom to pursue the good. For leadership, this means that the leader must remain neutral to the variations of the good that citizens pursue. Again, this reinforces the assertion that the diversity within the environmental context needs to be recognized and protected.

Spitzer and his colleagues did just that with the revision of the DSM in reaction to protests and advocacy from the LGBTQ community. They realized that pathologizing diversity in sexual orientation did not adequately address difference, and fully ignored the capabilities and dignity of individuals. Basing mental health diagnosis and treatment on the experience of the individual and his or her own ability to flourish and live a dignified life in pursuit of the good respected these differences as well as the individual's right to freedom. The revision of the DSM-II was an act of leadership: leaders (Spitzer and his team of mental health professionals) and followers (advocates, allies, and protestors) working together toward a goal (a fair and accurate method for diagnosing mental illness without pathologizing difference) while considering the environmental context, and also the cultural values and norms that influence the institution of psychiatry.

From this evaluation of the case study, there are a few important points to take away. The first is that Rawls' theory of justice as fairness is an appropriate approach to ethical leadership. Rawls does a thorough job of providing guidance to leaders who want to implement his approach, and his two principles make the approach both concrete and realizable. The second is that a contemporary leader working in a diverse society or organization might want to consider also using the care ethics addendum to the theory of justice as fairness. This approach helps to address the challenge and opportunity of diversity by making the theory more inclusive, and also tailoring it to the individual, rather than broadly prescribing a method of distributing social goods. The Five Components Model used to analyze the mental health reform case takes Rawls' theory and translates it into a practical guide that is applicable to contemporary leadership situations.

Summary and concluding remarks

Initially, this chapter set out to explore the question, 'How can leaders and followers work together to create a just society?' Rawls offers the leaders some guidance in addressing this question. First, in understanding justice as fairness, Rawls makes the goal of leadership follower-centric. Using the theory of justice outlined by Rawls as an approach to ethical leadership compels leaders to work collaboratively with followers to ensure that the principles of justice that are developed provide the most comprehensive set of basic liberties to all citizens. Further, the leader's role is to provide the social and political safeguards necessary for citizens to maintain that adequate set of basic liberties. This goal is well-defined throughout Rawls' theory, and this provides guidance to the leader: work with followers toward this goal, within the immediate context that the community falls within, in accordance with the values and norms that shape that community.

So how can leaders and followers work together to create a just society? According to Rawls, leaders and followers must work together to guarantee the basic rights of those who cannot speak up for themselves. They also must have the presence of mind to realize that these rights are needed in order to have a society that makes success an option for all of its members.

DISCUSSION QUESTIONS

What similarities do you see between Rawls' approach to leadership and other social contract theories, as outlined in Chapter 9?

Does the care ethics addendum to Rawls' theory of justice and fairness resolve some of the challenges to the theory? If so, how?

Could a Rawlsian apply the Five Components Model to another culture that is not democratic by nature?

Is Rawls' reliance on rationality too much of a challenge for the theory to overcome?

Do you think that most individuals would agree with the two principles that Rawls claims would be developed in the original position?

What would be some basic liberties that leaders should protect for all citizens?

ADDITIONAL RESOURCES

R. Talisse, *On Rawls: Wadsworth Notes*, Boston: Cengage Learning, 2001.
This resource presents an in-depth basic introduction to John Rawls and his career and works.

M. Nussbaum, 'Nature, Functioning and Capability: Aristotle on Political Distribution,' *Oxford Studies in Ancient Philosophy* (Supplementary Volume), 6, 1988, 145–84.
Nussbaum's article presents the roots of the capabilities approach in ancient Greek philosophy.

R. Dworkin, 'What is Equality? Part 2: Equality of Resources,' *Philosophy and Public Affairs*, 10, 1981, 283–345.

Dworkin's article on the concept of equality provides a good summary of the theory of equality of resources.

NOTES

1 J. Rawls, *A Theory of Justice*, Cambridge, MA: Harvard University Press, 1971.
2 J. Rawls, '50 Years after Hiroshima,' *Dissent*, summer 1995. Online, https://www.dissentmagazine.org/article/50-years-after-hiroshima-2 (accessed March 11, 2018).
3 Rawls, ibid, p. 6.
4 J. Rawls, *Political Liberalism*, expanded edn, New York: Columbia University Press, 1993/2005.
5 J. Rawls, *The Law of Peoples*, revised edn, Cambridge, MA: Harvard University Press, 2001.
6 J. Rawls, *Justice as Fairness: A Restatement*, E. Kelly (ed.), Cambridge, MA: Belknap, 2001.
7 W.J. Clinton, *Remarks on Presenting the Arts and Humanities Awards*, Washington, DC: The Administration of William J. Clinton, 1999. Online, http://www.presidency.ucsb.edu/ws/?pid=56605 (accessed March 11, 2018).
8 T. Hobbes, *Leviathan*, C.B. MacPherson (ed.), New York: Penguin 1651/1985; J. Locke, *An Essay Concerning Human Understanding*, R. Woolhouse (ed.), New York: Penguin, 1689/1997; and J. Rousseau, *On The Social Contract*, D. Silver (ed.), G.D.H. Cole (trans.), 1762/2003.
9 Rousseau, ibid.
10 I. Kant, *Critique of Judgment*, W.S. Pluhar (trans.), Indianapolis: Hackett, 1790/1987.
11 Rawls, 1971, op. cit., p. 92.
12 Kant, op. cit.
13 J. Rawls, *Collected Papers*, S. Freeman (ed.), Cambridge, MA: Harvard University Press, 1999, p. 310.
14 Rawls, 1971, op. cit.; and I. Kant, *Critique of Pure Reason*, M. Weigelt (ed. and trans.), New York: Penguin, 1781/2007.
15 Rawls, 1971, op. cit., p. 266.
16 R. Greenleaf, *The Servant as Leader: Essentials of Servant Leadership*, in L.C. Spears and M. Lawrence (eds), *Focus on Leadership: Servant Leadership for the 21st Century*, New York: John Wiley, 2002.
17 Rawls, 1971, op. cit., p. 266.
18 Rawls, 1971, op. cit., pp. 216–17.
19 Rawls, 1971, op. cit., p. 266.
20 Rawls, 1971, op. cit., p. 12.
21 J. Rawls, 'Kantian constructivism in moral theory,' *Journal of Philosophy*, vol. 77 no. 9, 1980, 515–72, p. 529.
22 S. Wong, 'Duties of Justice to Citizens with Cognitive Disabilities,' *Metaphilosophy*, vol. 40 no. 3–4, 2009, 382–401, p. 386.
23 M. Nussbaum, 'Nature, functioning and capability: Aristotle on political distribution,' *Oxford Studies in Ancient Philosophy* (supplementary volume), 1988, 145–84.
24 A. Rand, *The Objectivist Ethics*, Whitefish, MT: Literary Licensing, 2011.
25 C. Davis, 'Lily's place continuing to care for addicted babies,' Appalachia Health News, West Virginia Public Broadcasting, March 3, 2016. Online, http://wvpublic.org/post/lilys-place-continuing-care-addicted-babies#stream/0 (accessed March 12, 2018). Also see Lily's Place Homepage. Online, http://www.lilysplace.org/ (accessed March 12, 2018).
26 J. Drescher, 'Out of DSM: Depathologizing homosexuality,' C. North and A. Suris (eds), *Behavioral Sciences*, vol. 5 no. 4, 2015. Online, https://www.ncbi.nlm.nih.gov/pmc/articles/PMC4695779/ (accessed March 11, 2018).
27 A. Surís, R. Holliday, and C.S. North, 'The evolution of the classification of psychiatric disorders,' J. Coverdale (ed.), *Behavioral Sciences*, vol. 6 no. 1, 2016. Online, https://www.ncbi.nlm.nih.gov/pmc/articles/PMC4810039/ (accessed March 11, 2018).
28 D.L. Rosenhan, 'The Rosenhan study: On being sane in insane places,' *Science*, vol. 179, January 19, 1973, 250–8.
29 American Psychiatric Association, *Diagnostic and Statistical Manual of Mental Disorders*, 3rd edn, text rev., 1980.
30 American Psychiatric Association, *Diagnostic and Statistical Manual of Mental Disorders*, 4th edn, text rev., 1994.

31 E. Shorter, *A History of Psychiatry: From the Era of the Asylum to the Age of Prozac*, New York: John Wiley & Sons, 1997.

32 Shorter, ibid, p. 18.

33 E.S. Anderson, 'What Is the point of equality?' *Ethics*, vol. 109 no. 2, 1999, 287–337, p. 326.

34 M. Nussbaum, 'The capabilities of people with cognitive disability,' *Metaphilosophy*, vol. 40, 2009, 331–51, p. 337.

11

The common good

Robert M. McManus

 **FRAMING QUESTION**

What does the common good demand of leadership?

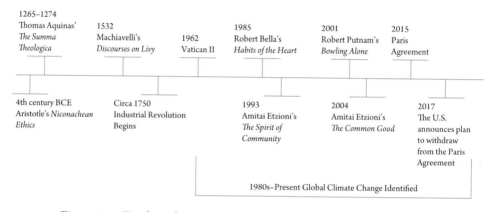

Figure 11.1 Timeline of major works on the common good in relation to the chapter case study

The concept of the common good has a long and expansive history in the study of ethics. Renowned scholars such as Aristotle, Thomas Aquinas, Niccolò Machiavelli, John-Jacques Rousseau, and Adam Smith, as well as contemporary philosophers have all weighed in on the idea of the common good. The concept is most often expressed today through the idea of 'communitarianism' – a philosophy that emphasizes the individual's responsibility to the larger community, and is championed by public intellectuals such as Robert Bellah and Amitai Etzioni.[1]

In spite of its extensive and varied history – or perhaps *because of this* – the concept of the common good is not easily defined and is often contested. As we begin our discussion, it is important to point out that there are several potential meanings for the term 'the common good.' One scholar points out that there are at least four.[2] The first is the corporate good of a social group. A simple illustration of this can be seen whenever a group acts in concert to achieve a common goal, such as when the players on a basketball team work together to win a game. The second use of the word is the sense of the 'public welfare,' such as when a town collects taxes to provide a police force to protect its citizens. The third usage of the term focuses upon the shared interest in securing common conditions in which individuals are equal and free to pursue their own interests.[3] A manifestation of this use of the term can be found in American civil rights legislation, such as the integration of public schools. The fourth sense of the term focuses upon the ways that human beings relate to each other. This use of the term views people as interdependent; as such, they reach their greatest fulfillment in cooperating with others and work towards a goal greater than themselves.[4] For example, we might experience this use of the word when we run a 5K to raise money to find a cure for cancer that we might never see in our lifetime. As we will see, we will touch on aspects of all these uses of the term in our case study at the end of the chapter. However, to begin our discussion, let's start with a general definition of the term 'common good' and fill in the details from there.

For our purposes we will simply define the common good as something that benefits *all of society*, whereas an individual good only benefits a *particular person* or a *certain group* within society. It forces leaders to ask the question, 'What is the best thing to do for all of society?' Given this definition, you do not have to look very far to see examples of the common good. A strong economy, a fair and just legal system, and clean air and water are all tangible manifestations of the concept of the common good.[5]

As we have done in previous chapters, we will trace the intellectual roots of the concept under discussion, as well as consider its major aspects, conclusions, and critique. We will then consider how the idea relates to the Five Components of Leadership Model introduced in Chapter 1. We will conclude this chapter with an application of the common good to the recent Paris Agreement in which more than 150 nations signed an accord to limit their production of greenhouse gas emissions in an effort to keep global warming below 1.5 degrees Celsius above pre-industrial temperatures. We will also address the controversies surrounding the common good and the ways the architects of the Paris Agreement have sought to address them.

History

One of the first philosophers to address the idea of the common good was Plato in his treatise *Republic*.[6] Plato believed 'the good' was an *objective reality* that all people naturally search for as they seek to fulfill their own happiness. Hence, for Plato, the individual good and the common good were closely tied together. As people come together to form communities, they are naturally united in their search for this objective good. However, Plato's student Aristotle more fully developed the concept of the common good and is more often identified as the originator of the idea. In his book *Politics*, Aristotle argued that humans are 'political animals' and as such they can only find happiness by working together in a just community.[7] It is important to keep in mind that, for Aristotle, the common good is more than simply the sum of individual parts: that is, it is something more than just the amalgamation of individuals each seeking his or her own happiness. For Aristotle, happiness is created through community, and a just community logically provides an environment where happiness can most likely be obtained by all of its members. Likewise, Aristotle believed that the common good was *superior* to the individual good. He states this clearly in his *Nicomachean Ethics* where he claims: 'The attainment of the good for one person alone is, to be sure, a source of satisfaction; but to secure it for a nation and for its cities is nobler and more divine.'[8]

Two centuries later, the Roman statesman Marcus Tullius Cicero further developed the concept of the common good in his *De Re Publica*.[9] Like Aristotle before him, Cicero claimed that a community was not simply a collection of individuals, but rather was 'a special assemblage of people in large numbers associated in agreement with respect to justice and a partnership for the common good.'[10] These early Greek and Roman philosophers laid the foundation for continued development of the common good which saw its next incarnation within the early Roman Catholic Church.

One scholar notes 'although the language of the common good is Aristotelian in origin. Its main development in history has been with Christian Theology.'[11] Influential Catholic theologians, such as Augustine of Hippo and Thomas Aquinas, built upon this Greek and Roman foundation of the common good applying it specifically in the context of Christianity. In his book *The City of God*, Augustine argued that the ultimate good is God; thus, if all humanity were to seek God and worship Him and His goodness, it would be united in its quest for and achievement of the common good.[12] (Notice how Augustine seems to hold more of a Platonic view of the common good.) Aquinas built upon Augustine's argument of God as the source of all good, but he echoed more of Aristotle's view that the common good could only be achieved through community.[13] One Catholic scholar summarizes Aquinas' thinking in this regard:

> [For Aquinas] . . . the good of each person is linked with the good shared with others in community, and the highest good common to the life of all is God's own self. For Thomas Aquinas, therefore, the pursuit of the common good carries out the Bible's double commandment to love God with one's heart, mind, and soul, and to love one's neighbor as oneself.[14]

The Catholic teaching of the common good is still at the forefront of Catholic ethics today. The Second Vatican Council in 1962 reaffirmed the importance of the concept of the common good and defined it as 'the sum of those conditions of social life which allow social groups and their individual members relatively thorough and ready access to their own fulfillment.'[15] Likewise, contemporary Catholic teaching regarding social justice invokes the common good when it emphasizes the idea that individuals and people working together can best achieve happiness in a just world; hence, the Church should work to ensure justice for the most disenfranchised and vulnerable members of society.[16]

Although Catholic teachings offer a vibrant theory and practice of the common good, the concept has a long secular tradition as well. The idea surfaced throughout the Renaissance and Enlightenment as the thinking regarding constitutional republics evolved and matured; hence, the idea continues to shape our view of these systems of government even today. For example, Renaissance political philosopher Nicolló Machiavelli in his *Discourses on Livy* argued the primary purpose of government is to secure the *commune benefizio*.[17] Enlightenment thinkers, such as Thomas Hobbes in his *Leviathan* and John Locke in his *Two Treatise on Government* argued that humans are by nature individuals, thus they are vulnerable. So they form communities for their own protection under the guise of the common good.[18] Later philosophers such as Jean-Jacques Rousseau, in his work *The Social Contract*, echo Machiavelli's assertion that the primary purpose of the state is to achieve the common good for its people.[19] Likewise, philosophers such as David Hume in his *A Treatise of Human Nature*, and James Madison in the *Federalist Papers* maintain that the purpose of government is to create a just civil society for the common good.[20] Many of these philosophers and economists noted that defining 'the good' can become troublesome in a pluralistic society. Hobbes and Hume argued that nothing can be considered 'good' or 'bad' in-and-of itself; rather it is how people *react* to something that defines it.[21] This thinking laid the foundation for the division between individualism and collectivism as we will discuss later in this chapter.

In the field of economics, Adam Smith argued in his pivotal work *The Wealth of Nations* that the common good *is an amalgamation of the individual good*.[22]

This represents a very different way of thinking about the idea of the common good in comparison to the early philosophers and religious thinkers who developed the concept. Smith argued that the common good is driven by the invisible hand of the market to insure a maximum creation of wealth, which is the ultimate common good.

These intellectuals deeply influenced Western thinking about the common good and the way the concept was institutionalized through forms of government and economic systems throughout the world. However, these understandings of the common good present a more liberal pluralistic – or individualist – take on the concept of the common good in that they all emphasize the person's rights to pursue his or her own happiness, as opposed to the individual's responsibilities to his or her community. For that, we turn to a more recent understanding of the common good – that proposed by communitarians.

The communitarian approach to the idea of the common good rose to its zenith in the 1980s with the work of public intellectuals such as Robert Bellah (*Habits of the Heart*), Robert Putnam (*Bowling Alone*), and Amitai Etzioni (*The Spirit of Community*); although other prominent scholars such as Charles Taylor, Alasdair MacIntyre, Michael Sandal, and Michael Walzer have made significant contributions to communitarian philosophy.[23] Communitarians argue '*a person must be understood in the context of his or her community.*'[24] Etzioni argues, 'if we consider society as composed of families, communities, national bonds of affection, identity, and shared values, we realize the importance of society in general, especially for the formulation of informal promotion of the good.'[25] As such, communitarians argue that 'the good' must be conceived of as social rather than purely individual.[26]

This is not to say that communitarians do not acknowledge individual rights, but they do point out that excessively individualistic societies, particularly in the West, 'have lost their equilibrium, and are heavily burdened with antisocial consequences of *excessive* liberty.'[27] Pollution, gun proliferation, and hate speech are just a few of the anti-social excesses of liberty. This is not to say that communitarians are hostile to the idea of individual freedom and autonomy. Indeed, many point out that some governments, particularly in the East, suffer from totalitarianism and authoritarianism in which individuals are forced to set aside their autonomy for the good of the group. Communitarians argue that these societies have gone too far in the other direction.[28] Rather, communitarians contend that there must be a balance between extreme individualism on one side on the spectrum and extreme universalism on the other. They call for a righting of the lack of balance on both sides of this continuum. They argue that a new golden rule should read: 'Respect and uphold society's moral order as you would have society respect and uphold your autonomy.'[29]

But how does one define 'community' or 'society' in the age of globalism? These terms take on an additional dynamic when one realizes that our individual and communal bonds now cross international boarders by means of ecology, technology, politics, and trade. Communitarians argue that we must expand our idea of 'community' to take into consideration our present cosmopolitan reality. Amitai Etzioni notes:

> There is a strong human tendency to include only the members of one's community, be it defined as family, village, or nation. However, justice may compel us to treat all human beings equally. Can particularistic obligations be justified in the face of such universal claims . . . One tends to forget that nation-states are a relatively recent social construction, neither natural or divine. Indeed, a strong case can be made that, in this day and age, the more we separate community from state, the more peaceful the world may become.[30]

Other scholars further articulate this need by adapting Aristotle's original admonition to a global context: 'To secure the good for an interdependent world is nobler and more divine than to do so for a single neighborhood, city, or nation-state.'[31] A healthy natural environment, a reduction in the spread of communicable diseases, and the elimination of weapons of mass destruction are 'goods' that affect us all. As such, communitarians call for us to broaden our understanding of what constitutes one's community.[32]

Major concepts of the ethic of the common good

Now that we have an understanding of the history of the thinking about the common good, we can move on to some of the major themes, applications, and criticisms of the concept.

The primacy of the individual versus the primacy of the community

Which should we consider as more important – the individual or the community? Philosophers have debated this question for millennia. The truth is, the West – and in particular the United States – has always held these seemingly competing values in tension with one another. We can trace this tension back to democracy's birthplace in ancient Greece, and specifically to Plato and Aristotle's competing approaches to leadership. For example, in his *Republic*, Plato argues that leaders are special; that is, they have a natural disposition to discern 'the Good, True, and Beautiful' better than the rest of us. These natural born leaders are inherently better and wiser than their counterparts. Plato prescribes that societies identify these individuals when they are children and then set them apart to be trained for positions of leadership when they become adults. These Philosopher-Kings, as Plato labeled them, sit at the top of the hierarchy and rule those beneath them – such as the guardians (warriors) and producers (the rest of society) – in wisdom and benevolence.[33] Again, to Plato leaders are special; since they know the Good, they should define the common good for others.

In contrast, Aristotle thought that leaders were like almost everyone else. He thought that followers who had the chance to live and work under various types of leaders throughout their youth would know how to better lead when they were in such a position later in life. Since they would have learned what it was like to be a follower, they could act with empathy and justice when they became leaders. Aristotle refers to this as the 'life-cycle of leadership.'[34] This is obviously a more communitarian approach to leadership. However, Aristotle took this one step further as it related to the common good. Remember, as we learned earlier, Aristotle believed that happiness can only be created through people working together in community. One scholar summarizes it this way: 'Plato and Aristotle present a vision of the common good that cannot simply be reduced to the sum of all private interests, but whose promotion is nonetheless conducive to those interests – virtuous, fulfilled citizens and harmonious communities are both consequences of the pursuit of the good life.'[35]

We have started with Plato and Aristotle because they represent two sides of a continuum representing the primacy of the individual and a command-and-control view of leadership, versus the primacy of the group and a connect-and-collaborate side of leadership as seen throughout the study of philosophy and ethics. This continuum manifests itself through the years as scholars have sought to understand the common good. The implications for leadership can best be stated as a fundamental question: 'Should the common good be determined and shaped *by the leaders for their followers*, or should the common good be determined and shaped *by the community of followers for each other*?'[36]

The question of the primacy of the individual or the primacy of the group is not just a philosophical exercise; the answer has real life implications. Voices on the political left and political right often share similar concerns as to the way the question is answered. Should the rights of the individual be impinged upon for the sake of the common good? Societies throughout the world, and particularly in the West, have often grappled with this question and have *usually* settled on the primacy of the rights of the individual – or what is referred to as individualism or pluralistic liberalism. On the other hand, if there is a compelling threat to the larger community, societies create mitigating laws that permit a reasonable infringement upon these individual rights. This represents a more communitarian view. For example, many Western societies value individual freedom of speech, but it is still illegal to shout 'Fire!' in a crowded theater when no such fire exists. Or consider the last time you went to the airport. Chances are you were searched or scanned before boarding the plane.[37] Most Western societies prohibit an *unreasonable* search, or a search that is not motivated by evidence of any wrongdoing. Conversely, in the case where there is a potential danger to others, as in our airport example, the common good may outweigh individual rights. This is a difficult decision to balance and adjustments are constantly required to insure proper respect for both individual rights and the common good.

The costs and benefits of the common good

It is important to point out that the ethic of the common good is *not* a matter of simple utilitarian ethics – that is, the greatest good for the greatest number of people. The grandfather of utilitarianism, Jeremy Bentham, argued, the very notion of society as distinct from an aggregate of individuals was a fiction.[38] Likewise, John Stuart Mill maintained that societal pressure to make individuals conform to a communal idea of a 'good' was nothing short of coercion.[39] The purpose of the common good is to benefit *all of the community*, not just the majority. The minority must also benefit from the common good. That is why the Catholic tradition of social justice and the common good pay special attention to the least advantaged in society. Justice *must* be the basis for defining the common good, otherwise the concept could quickly devolve into what some of its detractors fear the most – that it be used simply as a rhetorical trope for the tyranny of the majority. The common good requires cooperation from all of those members of the community who will *share the costs and the benefits* of the common good.

And there are costs associated with achieving the common good; and, indeed, some people may shoulder more of these costs than others, but all will reap the benefits. As we will see later in our case study, the core idea of the common good is that what affects one of us affects all of us. We all rely on fresh air, fresh water, and a healthy natural world to meet our most basic needs. This is true for the farmer, the stockbroker, and the coal miner. It is also true that each of these people may have to somewhat limit their personal happiness to achieve the greater good for themselves, as well as for the larger community. The farmer may have to limit the use of pesticides on her crops, which may mean a decreased harvest. The stockbroker may have to invest in companies that have lower profit margins because of regulations designed to protect the environment. And the coal miner may have to learn a new trade in order to feed his family. Nevertheless, each of these individuals also benefits from the fresh air, clean water, and healthy natural world that these sacrifices protect. It is also incumbent upon the rest of the community to help care for those who may pay a higher price to help achieve the common good. Farmers who face decreased yields may need to receive government subsidies to remain solvent. Companies investing in technology to help ensure a cleaner environment may need tax breaks to support their bottom line. And coal miners who can no longer mine for coal because of the move to cleaner alternative sources of energy may need to receive subsidized training in other professions and trades to help them transition into new jobs. This comes as a cost to all of society as well. The common good is not free.

The common good is increasingly used to call for cooperation on some of the world's most pressing problems. This is the crux of the matter as it relates to leadership: leaders must learn to take responsibility for the common good and more fully consider the larger implications of their actions when making decisions for their followers and organizations and consider both current impacts as well as that on future generations. They must learn to ask not what is best for just themselves, their followers, and their organizations, but rather what is best for *everyone*. When faced with the question 'Are you your brother's keeper?' they must learn to respond, 'Yes, I am.'

Critiques of the common good

Now that we have a better understanding of the common good, it is important to also consider its potential liabilities. For that, we will look at two major critiques of the idea: the belief that the common good is a fiction, and the free rider problem.

There is no such thing as the common good

It should be noted that there are many who eschew the very notion of a 'common good.' They argue individuals can only determine the 'good' for themselves. Both libertarians and pluralistic liberals may fear that the idea of the common good may lead to governmental restrictions on individual liberties. Likewise, many libertarians and laissez-faire conservatives argue that societies prosper only when individuals are 'granted as much autonomy as possible.'[40] Ayn Rand was a twentieth-century intellectual who left an indelible mark on many people's thinking about the common good. Rand agreed with Bentham that the *very idea* of a common good was nothing more than a fiction. Her basic argument was that a society is simply an *amalgamation of individuals* – nothing more. There is no such thing as 'society' or 'the tribe,' as she calls it. As such, the concept of good or bad can only pertain to an *individual*. You cannot separate the good from those who will benefit from it. Rand writes:

> Only on the basis of individual rights can any good – private or public – be defined and achieved. Only when each man is free to exist for his own sake – neither sacrificing others to himself nor being sacrificed to others – only then is every man free to work for the greatest good he can achieve for himself by his own choice and by his own effort. And the sum total of such individual efforts is the only kind of general, social good possible.[41]

Rand believed that the term 'the common good' was merely a rhetorical tool used to force one person's idea of the good, or a particular group's idea of the good, on to others. This leads to a power struggle to define what is good. The winners in this struggle inevitably impose their own idea of good onto the losers, which become, in her words, sacrificial animals. In fact, Rand maintains that the concept of the common good is the basis for all totalitarian regimes and dictatorships.[42] Many people still find Rand's objection to the common good compelling and her criticism remains a major argument for many opposing the idea of the common good today, especially among those who hold to a capitalistic conservative worldview and those with libertarian political views. In response to this criticism, some contemporary communitarians argue that these groups 'take an important truth, that freedom is essential to human dignity, and stretch it until it becomes a falsehood.'[43] On the other hand, communitarians also acknowledge that this criticism is, indeed, sometimes warranted.[44]

The tragedy of the common good: The free rider problem

Another concept relevant to our discussion here, and of particular interest to our case study later in this chapter, is how one defines the term '*common*.' The term '*the commons*' refers to the idea that some assets are communal, in that they don't belong to any one person, but are available to everyone. Examples of the commons in the natural world include things such as the air we breathe, the rivers and oceans, and the wide variety of wildlife and ecosystems throughout our planet; whereas, examples of commons that can be found in our social world include things such as city parks, libraries, and scientific research. The problem arises, however, when someone takes more than their fair share of these commons.

The ecologist and philosopher Garrett Hardin is often associated with this idea. In his article 'The Tragedy of the Commons' Hardin provides his readers with an example of what happens when someone takes more than their fair share of a commons.[45] He draws a picture of a pasture that is available to a group of ten ranchers. The pasture has enough grass to feed ten cows comfortably. So, each rancher can keep one cow on the land. But what happens if one rancher says, 'I'm going to keep two cows on the pasture'? Over time, the other cows are going to have about 10 percent less food to eat, so they will weigh about 10 percent less and be about 10 percent less productive. On the other hand, the rancher with two cows on the land receives almost twice the benefit he had with only one cow. When the other ranchers realize what is happening, they will say 'Why shouldn't I benefit from having two cows on the land, too!' and they each add an extra cow to the pasture. If too many ranchers do this, the common pasture will be useless in no time and will cease to feed any cows. This is the tragedy of the commons. Hardin argues:

> Each man is locked into a system that compels him to increase his herd without limit – in a world that is limited. Ruin is the destination toward which all men rush, each pursuing his own best interest in a society that believes in the freedom of the commons. Freedom in a commons brings ruin to all.[46]

Economists refer to this as the 'free rider problem.' Thus, Hardin believes that the commons must be regulated by society to reduce individual freedom in an effort to promote the common good.

Five component analysis

As we have done in previous chapters, we now turn to the Five Component Analysis to better understand how the common good relates to the leadership process.

One could argue that the primary thesis of the book you hold in your hands is that it is not only important that leaders and followers work to reach a goal, *but how leaders and followers reach that goal is equally important.* The same is true when working for the common good. *The common good affects all aspects of the five components of leadership.* It can be conceived as a 'superlayer' enveloping the other parts of the Five Components of Leadership Model as shown in Figure 11.2.

Leaders and followers must work together to determine the common good and how the goal of the common good should be achieved. If leaders simply

Figure 11.2 The Five Components of Leadership Model applied to the ethic of the common good

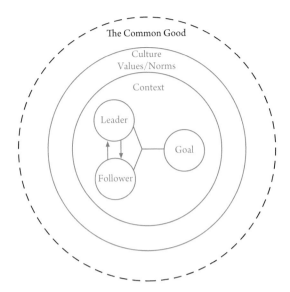

impose their personal interpretation of the common good upon their followers, then the critics of the common good may indeed be right to call such an act dictatorial, and perhaps even tyrannical. On the other hand, if followers only seek their individual self-interests without concern for their fellow followers, leaders, and the communities they create, there is little hope of achieving a just environment to foster happiness – for the individual *or* for the community. Rather, leaders and followers must work *together* to determine the common goal and best means of achieving it.

Notice the two arrows between leaders and followers that represent a mutual relationship between the two parties. In our case, these arrows represent the negotiation and reciprocal influence that must take place when defining the common good. This is needed to prevent the abuse of power between leaders and followers and one party exerting a coercive influence over the other. Also notice the lines connecting the leader and the followers to the goal. After leaders and followers have identified the common goal, they must also both pursue the best means to achieve it. Again, this prevents one party's particular will from overpowering the other and ensures an equal commitment from both the leader and followers to achieving the agreed-upon common goal.

The common good forces leaders and followers to take a grander view of the goal, which is the creation of the common good. This is graphically represented here with the addition of a dotted-circle encompassing the entire model. The common good takes into consideration all aspects of the five components of leadership – the leaders, the followers, the goal, the environmental context, and the cultural values and norms. True, leaders and followers still work toward smaller goals, but these are better thought of as the means to achieve the larger goal, which is the common good.

The common good also affects the context because it is the situational factors found therein that dictate the specific common good that is to be achieved. The common good may be driven by contingencies in the context that call for leaders and followers to come together to address a pressing exigency. There is an example within the realm of business that illustrates the way in which the common good interacts with the environment; that is, the advent of corporate social responsibility. The famed management professor Peter Drucker said, 'In the complex of organizations in which we live, the organizations – and that means the professionals that manage them – must surely take responsibility for the common weal.'[47] Most business professionals today realize that they cannot simply concentrate upon creating wealth for their shareholders, but must consider all of the stakeholders in a situation – employees, customers, communities, and the environment as well as shareholders. This is the kind of thinking that is needed to promote the common good, and is becoming more of a standard in business, sometimes expressed in the phrase 'the triple bottom line – people, planet, and profit.' Likewise, those working in the public and non-profit sectors increasingly understand the intersections of globalization and the importance of looking outside of one's own tribe in an effort to create the common good in a globalized world. This has particular relevance as we look to create the common good in an environment of competing cultural values and norms.

The common good requires us to embrace the widest reaches of community in an effort to meet its needs. This presents perhaps the biggest challenge in achieving the common good. How does one achieve the common good in a pluralistic multicultural world? Some would argue that such a goal is nothing more than wishful thinking. Others take a much more optimistic view. Arguing for the faith in the common good, one ethicist maintains that such a conviction '. . . is a matter of believing that the good of different persons in not so irreconcilably competitive as to make it incoherent to have the good of *all* persons as an end.'[48] It is with this hope that we turn to our case study.

CASE STUDY

The Paris Agreement and the common good[49]

History

The planet is warming.[50] The last time the earth's temperature was cooler than the historical worldwide average was 1985.[51] This information is not new. Scientists as early as 1859 predicted our current global warming trend in light of the increased use of fossil fuels in the Industrial Revolution. In fact, modern-day scientists still base their models for climate change on a model first developed in 1896.[52] Scientific data reveals that the earth has always gone through periods of warming and cooling caused by changes in the tilt of the earth's axis and the shape of its orbit around the sun.[53] However, never has the earth experienced such a dramatic rise in temperature in such a short amount of time as we have seen in the last 30 years.[54] Actually, long-term historical data and our current planetary orbit indicate that the earth should be entering a global cooling period; however, the opposite is happening.[55] Scientists overwhelmingly agree with studies that support the theory that the earth is warming because of a dramatic increase in fossil fuel consumption creating an overabundance of greenhouse gasses, specifically carbon dioxide – CO_2.[56] These gasses trap the earth's heat and lead to the phenomenon that we now refer to as global warming. This trend has myriad consequences such as a rise in sea levels, coastal flooding, violent storms, droughts, wildfires, species loss, mass emigration, and disruptions in agricultural production.[57] Recognizing these threats, various groups around the world have sought to work in collaboration to combat climate change and mitigate its effects.

In 1992 the United Nations Framework Convention on Climate Change (UNFCCC) was formed with the goal of 'preventing dangerous human interference with the climate system' by stabilizing greenhouse gas concentrations.[58] However, because the current rate of climate change is already having negative effects on ecosystems around the planet, the UNFCCC's more pressing goal is to attempt to *limit* the amount of global warming to a manageable level and work toward mitigating its effects. The Paris Agreement (*Accord de Paris*) established in 2015 is the UNFCCC's most recent attempt to achieve this goal.[59]

The Paris Agreement is an arrangement between 197 countries to combat global warming. At the time this chapter went to press, 179 countries had signed on to the accord. The agreement outlines a plan for participating countries to limit their greenhouse gas emissions in an attempt to keep global warming to less than 2 degrees Celsius (3.6 degrees Fahrenheit) above pre-industrial averages – the more specific aim is to limit global warming to 1.5 degrees Celsius (2.7 degrees Fahrenheit). Although it does not designate a specific date to achieve this goal, the Agreement says that participating countries should seek to meet the goal 'as soon as possible' and reach net-zero emissions by the second half of the twenty-first century.[60]

In sum, the Paris Agreement provides a structured process for governments to address climate change in a way that encourages transparency and flexibility, while still being facilitative rather than punitive in nature. It provides us with an excellent application of

CASE STUDY *(continued)*

the ethic of the common good. We will examine the way the Paris Agreement fits the definition of the common good and seeks to reconcile the tension between the primacy of the individual and the primacy of the community. We will apply the concept of the common good to the outcomes of the Paris Agreement and discuss the costs and benefits of its implementation. We will also address the controversies surrounding the common good, and how the leaders and regulators of the Paris Accord have sought to address them. Finally, we will apply the Five Components of Leadership Model to the Paris Agreement to see how its authors addressed each component of the model.

The Paris Agreement and the common good

Let's begin with the fourth sense of the term 'the common good' that we discussed at the beginning of this chapter. As you will recall, this definition focuses upon the ways that human beings relate to each other. It views people as interdependent; as such, they reach their greatest fulfillment in cooperating with others and work towards a goal greater than themselves.[61] Global climate change has the potential to jeopardize the world's food and water supply, increase coastal flooding, destroy natural habitats, spread insect borne illnesses, produce more violent storms, and lead to emigration crises worldwide.[62] In the truest sense of the word, it is to everyone's advantage to address global climate change and address the effects of global warming.

We can also apply the third use of the term to our case study – that which focuses upon the shared interest in securing common conditions in which individuals are equal and free to pursue their own interests. The Paris Agreement acknowledges this through its formation under the auspices of the United Nations and in its authors' efforts to obtain consent for its specifics and implementation from governments throughout the world. The Agreement itself is an attempt to create a set of equal rights and equal liabilities for all those involved. The Agreement provides a common legal framework that requires all parties to contribute to mitigating climate change and communicate their Nationally Determined Contributions to the Secretariat of the Convention. Unlike previous agreement of its kind, the Paris Agreement is bound by international law. It provides a legal structure for countries to track and report their progress on meeting their Nationally Determined Contribution, which will be reviewed by UN climate experts as well as a global audience. This enhanced transparency provides a mechanism to 'name and shame' those countries that are not making tangible efforts to achieve the agreed upon goal.

As we discussed earlier, the common good often comes at a price to individual good. How much any one person or group should pay for the common good is always a matter of contention. The current call issued by the Paris Agreement for countries to limit their greenhouse gas emissions seems reasonable to those industrialized countries whose economies have already benefited from cheap oil and the widespread prosperity and progress that it seemed to bring. However, less developed countries might call foul as they are prevented from using these types of resources in building their own prosperity and progress.

CASE STUDY (continued)

Likewise, there are some countries who disproportionately contribute to the glut of greenhouse gasses or who have historically used far more than their fair share of the earth's energy stores. The four countries that are currently the worst emitters of carbon include: China, the United States, the European Union, and India.[63] The United States alone uses about 20 percent of the world's energy resources, despite hosting only about 5 percent of the world's population.[64] China's use of energy and carbon emissions has skyrocketed in recent years as it has become the 'factory for the world.'[65] Other Western countries, such as members of the European Union, also use more of the earth's sources and emit more than their fair share of greenhouse gasses. Shouldn't these countries have to more drastically limit the production of these pollutants since they have created a larger portion of the problem? Additionally, it is predicted that poorer countries – such as those in Africa, South America, and Southeast Asia – will ultimately be much more adversely affected by global warming than will wealthy industrialized countries.[66] Shouldn't wealthier countries that have caused this problem by their vast consumption of energy and release of greenhouse gasses have to assist in relieving the havoc they have wrought on these poorer countries? If justice is foundational to building the common good, shouldn't countries such as this be required to pay a larger portion of the burden in creating the common good for the planet? According to the ethic of the common good, the answer is 'yes,' and the Paris Agreement allows for this.

The Paris Agreement recognizes that developed and developing countries have their own unique circumstances and resources that affect their relationship with the natural world and their ability to address the larger goal while sustaining their economies; thus, more developed counties are expected to take the lead in addressing climate change and assisting lesser developed countries in meeting the overall goal. The Agreement also establishes a collective goal of providing USD 100 billion per year to 2025 and annually thereafter to fund efforts to combat climate change. This amount may increase over time, but it cannot decrease. Developing countries are urged to provide *voluntary* financial support, while more developed counties are required to report twice a year on their financial contributions to this collective goal.

This cost discrepancy leads us to the primary theme that runs throughout conversations about the common good: how does one balance the rights of the individual with the rights of the group? The authors of the Paris Agreement have sought to address this by giving participating parties a variety of options to accomplish the group's goal. Ratifying countries can decide how to best limit their own emissions and set their own goals, but all of the participating countries must report on their efforts to reduce their emissions to the Secretariat of the Convention every five years beginning in 2023. The participating countries must submit their efforts to a third-party expert panel, but the review is designed to be 'facilitative, non-intrusive, non-punitive . . . and respectful of national sovereignty.'[67] The Agreement also offers a process to help countries to ramp up their efforts, regulations, and plans to meet the goals of the Agreement before it goes into force in 2023. The Agreement also offers guidance on how countries can devise their own Nationally Determined Contributions.

CASE STUDY *(continued)*

Participating countries are expected to drastically limit their output of greenhouse gasses, as well as to develop and implement technologies designed to capture and sequester carbon gas emissions. This can be achieved through myriad ways, such as developing and protecting forests, which help to eliminate CO_2 from the atmosphere.[68] Developed countries could also offer financial incentives to developing countries to reduce emissions through deforestation and forest degradation (REDD+). Importantly for developing countries, the Agreement notes that countries should seek to achieve the goal 'in a manner that does not threaten food production,' although it does expect the agricultural sector to take the lead in helping achieve the overall goal of the Agreement.[69] The agreement also allows public and private entities to work together to meet the parties' Nationally Determined Contribution. Developed and developing countries can also work in tandem by transferring mitigation outcomes internationally, such as emissions trading. Developed countries are expected to provide information, technology, and capacity building support to developing countries, and developing countries are expected to supply information on support needed and how the support they receive will be utilized. Thus, the Agreement allows for a variety of means for participating countries to meet their own goal and contribute to the overall goal of the Agreement. As you can see, the Paris Agreement tries to balance the rights and sovereignty of individual countries with the common good of the planet.

The Paris Agreement is the most comprehensive piece of international legislation of its kind. It is a call for governments around the world to cooperate to address one of the most pressing problems of the twenty-first century. It forces leaders and followers to take collective responsibility for the common good and more fully consider the environmental impact of their actions now and for future generations.

Criticisms of the Paris Agreement

However, the Paris Agreement is not without its detractors. Some suggest that the Agreement is potentially bad for economies that have traditionally benefited from less expensive forms of energy, such as coal. As Ayn Rand would say, there is no common good – good and bad can only be determined by the individual. In this case, governments such as the United States and China, which rely on coal and other fossil fuels and are the two biggest emitters of greenhouse gasses, will have to make significant changes in their infrastructure and preferred sources of energy, costing tax payers a great deal if they are to meet the goal set forth by the Agreement. Oil companies and governments in the Middle East that depend upon the sale of oil are also in jeopardy of decreased profits. Employees ranging from petroleum engineers to coal miners will have to find other work. Governments will have to adopt new standards and regulations. In short, economies and people all over the world will have to adapt to the changes proposed in the Agreement. Hence, there are many who would argue – at least in this case – the common good is not so good for them personally. Yes, there will be large costs associated with the Paris Agreement – at least USD 100 billion a year, and this does not include the hidden costs associated with the private

CASE STUDY *(continued)*

sector such as those employees who earn a living in the carbon-based energy industry who may lose their jobs. However, it is to *everybody's* benefit to address global climate change, and those who incur the most costs also stand to reap the benefits.

Another criticism of the Paris Agreement relates to the free rider problem we discussed earlier. The parties signing on to the accord are able to set their own Nationally Determined Contributions. However, the agreement is specifically designed to be 'facilitative, non-intrusive, non-punitive . . . and respectful of national sovereignty'.[70] In short, there is no formal mechanism to regulate and punish countries who are not holding to the Agreement. Rather, it only offers assistance to governments to help them set their own regulations and guidance on how to set these Nationally Determined Contributions. The United States has even threatened to pull out of the Paris Agreement, although it is one of the biggest emitters of greenhouse gasses.[71] The punishment for such action would be more diplomatic and political rather than financially costly.[72] Likewise, although the Agreement is bound by the Warsaw International Mechanism for Loss and Damage, smaller countries adversely affected by climate change could claim foul, but they would have no recourse for justice or compensation from larger governments who have caused so much of the problem. Finally, the Agreement does not present a definite timetable for participating governments to meet the goal of limiting global warming to 1.5 degrees Celsius above pre-industrial levels, but rather simply says that the goal should be met 'as soon as possible'; nor does it require any of the signers to specifically 'pledge' or 'commit' to doing so. One critic notes, 'So averse is the agreement to anything that may be seen as too binding that its announcement was delayed at the very last minute as the United States insisted on replacing the word "shall" with "should" in relation to the responsibility of industrialized countries to mitigate the effects of climate change'.[73] Hence, the Agreement does open itself up to criticism of the tragedy of the commons and the free rider problem so often levied against those who seek the common good. In this case, one of the biggest emitters of CO_2 – the United States – could potentially benefit from the sacrifices made by other countries. If the United States were to pull out of the Paris Agreement, it would be considered unethical when judged by the standard of the common good.

Five component analysis

Finally, we now turn our attention to the way McManus and Perruci's five components of leadership relate to the Paris Agreement.

The Paris Agreement requires the governments of the world to take a grander view of the goal, which is mitigating global warming. This is graphically represented here with the addition of a dotted-circle encompassing the entire model and is labeled as the natural world. A healthy natural world is vital for leadership; it is the most basic context for all human interactions.[74] In the case of the Paris Agreement, the signing parties still work toward their specific goals of their Nationally Determined Contributions, as well as develop

CASE STUDY *(continued)*

Figure 11.3 The Five Components of Leadership Model applied to the Paris Climate Agreement and the common good case study

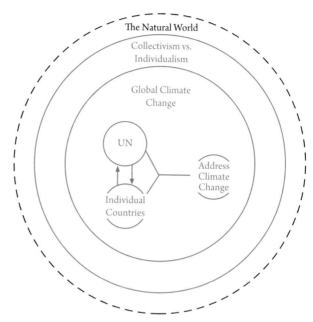

technology and secure financial support to help them meet these goals, but these are simply a means to an end to achieve the larger goal of mitigating climate change.

As we stated earlier, *how leaders and followers reach the common good is as important as the goal itself.* In the case of the Paris Agreement, the United Nations Framework Convention on Climate Change (UNFCCC) worked with a broad coalition of world governments to determine the goal of mitigating climate change and how that goal should be achieved. If the United Nations simply imposed a goal upon these governments, it is unlikely that government would comply and the United Nations itself might be labeled as dictatorial.

Again, we refer to the arrows between leaders and followers that represent a mutual relationship between the two parties. In our case study, these arrows represent the negotiation and reciprocal influence that must take place when agreeing to the goal and the means to achieve it – in this case the UN is the leader and the various world governments are the followers. Likewise, the intersecting lines connecting the leaders and the followers to the goal represents the importance of the UN and these various governments working together to achieve the goal once they have determined the goal to be met. The Paris Agreement models leaders and followers working together to best determine the common goal and best means of achieving it.

The context for the Paris Agreement is the rise in global temperatures due to anthropomorphic climate change through the release of greenhouse gasses. This is the pressing exigency that called for the United Nations and governments worldwide to

CASE STUDY *(continued)*

come together to create a common goal. In so doing, the parties to the Paris Agreement acknowledged that they can no longer focus exclusively upon their own countries. They recognized that these various bodies are interconnected through the natural world, and to care for the whole they are also caring for themselves. It was this unique environmental context that makes the ethic of the common good so compelling in this instance.

The Paris Agreement is special in that, through its sponsorship through the United Nations, it wholly acknowledges the cultural values and norms that encompass the leadership process. In 1992, key players such as the United States refused to sign another international treaty sponsored by the United Nations Framework Convention on Climate Change, the Kyoto Protocol. More recently, a new climate change initiative hosted in 2009 by the UNFCCC in Copenhagen also failed to achieve global agreement. The framers of the Paris Agreement learned from these failures and took a 'bottom-up' approach that allowed each government to devise its own strategy to reduce greenhouse gas emissions.[75] There were dozens of meetings leading up to the meeting that produced a week-and-a-half of talks and negotiations between countries and required compromises on all sides. By listening to the concerns of all parties, the hosts of the Paris Agreement were able to address the values held by the wide array of nations represented. Key players who had resisted efforts from the UNFCCC in the past, such as China, the United States, and India, approved the final document.[76] By acknowledging the competing values and norms from all the countries represented at the convention, the framers of the Paris Agreement were able to successfully develop a treaty and advance the common good. Countries can determine their own contributions and take into consideration their unique systems and resources as they contribute to the goal of mitigating climate change and honoring the agreement.

Summary and concluding remarks

So, 'What does the common good demand of leadership?' According to the common good, leaders and followers must push themselves to consider more than what is merely beneficial for themselves and their organizations. They must also consider the impact of their actions on everyone who is touched by their organization. Rather than simply ask 'How will this benefit *us*?' leaders and followers must ask 'How will this benefit *us and them*?' To make this switch, leaders and followers must start expanding their view of 'stakeholders' and start thinking about how their organization impacts the world at large. The common good perspective can help leaders and followers see this bigger picture as being in their best interest.

Contributors to the Paris Agreement would be wise to listen to the words of Amitai Etzioni when he says, 'No society can flourish without some shared formulation of the common good.'[77] If countries only seek their individual self-interests without concern for the other parties to the Agreement, then there is little hope of reducing climate change, and these countries, future generations, and the Earth itself will suffer the consequences.

DISCUSSION QUESTIONS

What are some other specific instances of the common good that you believe leaders would be wise to consider?

How compelling do you find the 'free rider' problem to be to the idea of common good? What might be a way or ways for leaders and followers to ensure all parties care for the commons?

How should a leader respond if their followers have competing ideas of what constitutes 'the good'?

If the United States does withdraw from the Paris Accord, should individual U.S. citizens have any personal responsibility to help mitigate global climate change? Why or why not?

The common good is considered to be one of the most controversial ethical positions. Can you think when the idea of the common good may have been abused? When and where?

Is the ethic of the common good even worth pursuing if the idea can potentially be misused? Justify your answer.

ADDITIONAL RESOURCES

R. Bellah, R. Madsen, W.M. Sullivan, A. Swidler, S.M. Tipton, *Habits of the Heart: Individualism and Commitment in American Life*, 3rd edn, Berkeley, CA: University of California Press, 1985/2017.
This book is often cited in the field of leadership studies and articulates the idea of communitarianism in a succinct and accessible manner.

R.D. Putnam, *Bowling Alone: The Collapse and Revival of American Community*, New York: Simon and Schuster, 2000.
Putnam details the breakdown of social capital in American society and warns readers of its consequences.

A. Etzioni, *The Common Good*, Cambridge: Polity, 2004.
This is scholarly work from a leading intellectual on the idea of the common good in which he presents the idea and addresses its detractors and its critiques.

NOTES

1   These great minds in the fields of philosophy, religion, government, economics, and ethics each have their unique interpretation and approach to the idea. Likewise, Asian traditions have their own distinctive approach to the concept of the common good that emphasize harmony; whereas, Western approaches tend to focus upon the political and social implications of the concept. For example see, D. Solomon and P.C. Lo (eds), *The Common Good: Chinese and American Perspectives*, Dordrecht, Netherlands: Springer, 2014. For the sake of simplicity and to focus our discussion, this chapter will focus upon a Western conceptualization of the concept.

2   P. Riordan, *A Grammar of the Common Good: Speaking of Globalization*, London: Continuum, 2008, pp. 59–60. Riordan notes, 'If the only possible use of common good talk were in the rhetoric of totalitarianism, then there would be little to be said in its favour. However, this exploration of the grammar of the common good shows that there are several possible and legitimate uses of the language' (Riordan, 2008, p. 69).

3 Some may refer to this as an 'individualist-instrumentalist' use of the term. See L. Honohan, *Civic Republicanism*, London: Routledge, 2002, p. 152.

4 Riordan, op. cit.

5 M. Velasquez, C. Andre, T. Shanks, and M.J. Meyer, 'The Common Good,' The Markkula Center for Applied Ethics, Santa Clara University. Online, https://www.scu.edu/ethics/ethics-resources/ethical-decision-making/the-common-good/ (accessed December 2, 2017).

6 Plato, *Republic*, 2nd edn, G.M.A. Grube (trans.), revised by C.D.C. Reeve, Indianapolis: Hackett Publishing Company, 1992.

7 Aristotle, *Politics*, B. Jowett (trans.), Miniola, NY: Dover Publications, 1885/2000.

8 Aristotle, *Nicomachean Ethics*, 1094b, in *Complete Works* (ed. J. Barnes), Cambridge: Cambridge University Press, 1984, vol. II. p. 1728. Aristotle's use of the word 'common' translates to something close to 'unified.'

9 Cicero, *De Re Publica*, C.W. Keyes (trans), Cambridge: Loeb Classical Library, 1943.

10 Cicero, ibid. Book 1 Chapter XXV.

11 Riordan, op. cit., p. 7.

12 Augustine, *City of God*, Henry Bettenson (trans.), London: Penguin Books, 1972/2003.

13 T. Aquinas, *The Summa Theologica*, The Fathers of the English Dominican Province (trans.), New York: Benzinger Brothers, 1948/Reprint, Notre Dame, IN: Christian Classics, 1981.

14 D. Hollenbach, *The Common Good and Christian Ethics*, Cambridge: Cambridge University Press, p. 4.

15 *Pastoral Constitution on the Church in the Modern World, Gaudium et Spes, Promulgated by His Holiness, Pope Paul VI, on December 7, 1965*. Online, http://www.vatican.va/archive/hist_councils/ii_vatican_council/documents/vat-ii_const_19651207_gaudium-et-spes_en.html (accessed December 3, 2017).

16 See Pontifical Council for Justice and Peace, Compendium of the Social Doctrine of the Church. Online, http://www.vatican.va/roman_curia/pontifical_councils/justpeace/documents/rc_pc_justpeace_doc_20060526_compendio-dott-soc_en.html (assessed December 3, 2017).

17 N. Machiavelli, *Discourses on Livy*, trans. H.C. Mansfield and N. Tarcov, Chicago: The University of Chicago Press, 1996; also see H. Waldemar, 'The Common Good in Machiavelli,' *History of Political Thought*, vol. 31 no. 1, 57–85.

18 T. Hobbes, *Leviathan*, Mineola, New York: Dover Publications, 2006; and J. Lock, *Two Treatise on Government*, Translated by Lewis F. Abbott, Manchester: Industrial Systems Research, 2009.

19 J. Rousseau, *The Social Contract*, trans. Maurice Cranston, New York: Penguin Putnam Inc, 1968.

20 D. Hume, *A Treatis of Human Nature*, Mineola, New York: Dover Publications, 2003; and A. Hamilton, J. Jay, and J. Madison, *The Federalist Papers*, London, England: Penguin Books Limited, 1987.

21 Riordan, op. cit., p. 17.

22 A. Smith, *The Wealth of Nations*, New York: Random House, 1776/1994.

23 R. Bellah, R. Madsen, W.M. Sullivan, A. Swidler, and S.M. Tipton, *Habits of the Heart: Individualism and Commitment in American Life*, 3rd edn, Berkeley, CA: University of California Press, 1985/2017; R. D. Putnam, *Bowling Alone: The Collapse and Revival of American Community*, New York: Simon and Schuster, 2000; and A. Etzioni, *The Spirit of Community: Rights Responsibilities and the Communitarian Agenda*, New York: Crown Publishers, 1993.

24 M.J. Sandal, *Liberalism and the Limits of Justice*, Cambridge: Cambridge University Press, 1982, p. 179.

25 A. Etizioni, *The Common Good*, Cambridge: Polity, 2004, p. 5.

26 C. Taylor, *Sources of the Self: The Makings of Modern Identity*, Cambridge, MA: Harvard University Press, 1989, p. 170.

27 A. Etzioni, *The New Golden Rule, Community and Morality in a New Democratic Society*, New York: Basic Books, 1996, p. xvii.

28 Etzioni, ibid.

29 Etzioni, 1996, op. cit., xviii.

30 Etzioni, 1996, op. cit., pp. 4–5.

31 Hollenbach, op. cit., p. 220.

32 Hollenbach, op. cit., pp. 215–216.

33 Plato, op. cit.

34 Aristotle, op. cit.

35 A. Etzioni, 'The Common Good,' in M.T. Gibbons (ed.), *The Encyclopedia of Political Thought*, ed.,

Hoboken, NJ: John Wiley and Sons, 2015. Online, https://pdfs.semanticscholar.org/f321/69cf59dc0533 8ac8673d26a5367df5601b6e.pdf (accessed December 3, 2017).

36 For further discussion regarding the way leadership holds a tension between the primacy of the individual and the primacy of the community, see R. McManus and G. Perruci, *Understanding Leadership: An Arts and Humanities Perspective,* New York: Routledge, 2015.

37 Riordan, op cit., uses examples such as these in his explanation of the common good.

38 Quoted in Etzioni, 2004, op. cit., p. 7.

39 J.S. Mill, *On Liberty,* D. Spitz (ed.), Norton Critical Edition, New York: W.W. Norton, 1975, p. 71.

40 Etzioni, 1996, op. cit., pp. 3–4.

41 A. Rand, *The Ayn Rand Column,* 2nd edn, Irvine, CA: Ayn Rand Institute Press, 1998, p. 91.

42 A. Rand, *Capitalism, The Unknown Ideal,* Centennial Edition, New York: Signet, 1986, p. 12.

43 Etzioni, 1996, op. cit., p. 11. Etzioni is quoting R.P. George who is quoting P. Strobin, 'Right, Fight', *National Journal,* vol. 27 no. 49, 1995, 3022.

44 Etzioni, 1996, op. cit.; and Riordan, op. cit.

45 G. Hardin, 'Tragedy of the commons,' *Science,* vol. 162 no. 3859, 1968, 1243–48. Online, http://science. sciencemag.org/content/sci/162/3859/1243.full.pdf (accessed March 14, 2018).

46 Hardin, ibid, p. 162.

47 P.F. Drucker, *Adventures of a Bystander,* New Brunswick, NJ: Transaction, 1997, p. 293.

48 R.M. Adams, *Finite and Infinite Goods: A Framework for Ethics,* Oxford: Oxford University Press, 1999, p. 378.

49 I extend my gratitude to Dr. David J. Brown, Professor of Biology and Environmental Science at Marietta College, for his assistance in helping me research and write this case study.

50 L. Dahlman, 'Climate change: Global temperature,' September 11, 2017, NOAA Climate.gov. Online, https://www.climate.gov/news-features/understanding-climate/climate-change-global-temperature (accessed March 14, 2018); and R.J.H. Dunn, D.F. Hurst, N. Gobron, and K.M. Willett (eds), '2017: Global climate,' in *State of the Climate 2016,* Bulletin of the American Meteorological Society, vol. 98 no. 8, 2017, S5–S62. Online, http://www.ametsoc.net/sotc2016/Ch02_GlobalClimate.pdf (accessed March 14, 2018).

51 NOAA National Centers for Environmental Protection, State of the Climate: Global Climate Report for January 2018. Online, https://www.ncdc.noaa.gov/sotc/global/201801 (accessed March 14, 2018).

52 S. Arrhenius, 'On the influence of carbonic acid in the air upon the temperature of the ground,' *Philosophical Magazine and Journal of Science,* vol. 5 no. 4, April 1896, 237–76; and NOAA National Centers for Environmental Protection, 'State of the Climate: Global Climate Report for January 2018.' Online, https://www.ncdc.noaa.gov/sotc/global/201801 (accessed March 14, 2018); Also see: https://earthobservatory.nasa.gov/Features/Milankovitch/ (accessed March 14, 2018) for an accessible explanation of the Milankovitch cycles.

53 M. Milankovitch, 'Theorie mathematique klimalehre des phenomene thermique produits par la radiation solaire,' *Academie Yougoslave des Science et des Arts de Zagreb,* Gauthier-Villars, 1920. (This is the original article in which Milankovitch proposed the idea.); Also see W.A. Broecker and J. van Donk, 'Insolation changes, ice volumes, and the O18 record in deep-sea cores,' *Reviews of Geophysics,* vol. 8, 1970, 169–97; and J.D. Hays, J. Imbrie, and N.J. Shackleton, 'Variations in the earth's orbit: pacemaker of the ice ages,' *Science,* vol. 194, 1976, 1121–32. These two articles feature studies that tested Milankovitch's hypothesis and demonstrated the accuracy of his prediction.

54 Dahlman, op. cit. Dahlman states the rate of temperature increase since 1980 has been faster than in the last 100 years.

55 The idea that the planet should be cooling was first proposed by Milankovitch. See Milankovitch, op. cit. Also see https://earthobservatory.nasa.gov/Features/GISSTemperature/giss_temperature2.php (accessed March 14, 2018). This resource provides an explanation for observing cooling from 1940 to 1970, and the popular press articles about 'global cooling.' An often-cited 1980 orbital model by Imbrie predicted 'the long-term cooling trend that began some 6,000 years ago will continue for the next 23,000 years.' See J.Z. Imbrie, 'Modeling the climatic response to orbital variations,' *Science,* vol. 207 no. 4434, 1980, 943–53. More recent work suggests that orbital variations should gradually increase 65 N summer insolation over the next 25,000 years. Earth's orbit will become less eccentric for about the next 100,000 years, so changes in this insolation will be dominated by changes in obliquity, and should not decline enough to cause an ice age in the next 50,000 years. See A. Berger and M.F. Loutre, 'Climate:

An exceptionally long interglacial ahead?' *Science*, vol. 297 no. 5585, 2002, 1287–8; and A. Ganopolski, R. Winkelmann and H.J. Schellnhuber, 'Critical insolation–CO_2 relation for diagnosing past and future glacial inception,' *Nature*, vol. 529, 2016, 200–3.

56   This is referred to as the 'Keeling curve' based upon CO_2 measurements at the Mauna Loa Observatory since 1958. See https://scripps.ucsd.edu/programs/keelingcurve/ (accessed March 14, 2018). Also see C.D. Keeling, S.C. Piter, T.P. Whorf, and R.F. Keeling, 'Evolution of natural and anthropogenic fluxes of atmospheric CO_2 from 1957 to 2003,' *Tellus B*, vol. 63 no. 1, February 2011, 1–22.

57   Intergovernmental Panel on Climate Change, 'Summary for policy makers,' in T.F. Stocker, D. Qin, G.K. Plattner, M. Tignor, S.K. Allen, J. Boschung, A. Nauels, Y. Xia, V. Bex and P.M. Midgley (eds), *Climate Change 2013: The Physical Science Basis. Contribution of Working Group 1 to the 5th Assessment Report of the Intergovernmental Panel on Climate Change*, Cambridge: Cambridge University Press, 2013. Online, http://www.ipcc.ch/pdf/assessment-report/ar5/wg1/WG1AR5_SPM_FINAL.pdf (accessed March 14, 2018).

58   'First steps to a safer future: Introducing The United Nations Framework Convention on Climate Change,' United Nations. Online, http://unfccc.int/essential_background/convention/items/6036.php (accessed March 14, 2018).

59   'Paris Agreement,' United Nations, December 2015. Online, http://unfccc.int/files/essential_background/convention/application/pdf/english_paris_agreement.pdf (accessed March 14, 2018).

60   'Paris Agreement,' ibid, p. 4.

61   Riordan, op. cit. pp. 59–60.

62   Intergovernmental Panel on Climate Change, op. cit.

63   Carbon Dioxide Information Analysis Center, Environmental Sciences Division, Oak Ridge National Laboratory, Tennessee, United States, The World Bank. Online, https://data.worldbank.org/indicator/EN.ATM.CO2E.KT?name_desc=false (accessed March 14, 2018).

64   World Population Balance, 'Population and energy consumption.' Online, http://www.worldpopulationbalance.org/population_energy (accessed March 14, 2018). Population data source: Population Reference Bureau; 2012 World Population Data Sheet. Energy data source: U.S. Energy Information Administration 2012. This website suggests a little less than 5% for U.S. population as percent of world population and about 18% of energy consumption. This data was from 2012.

65   See Carbon Dioxide Information Analysis Center, op. cit.

66   United Nations Framework Convention on Climate Change (UNFCCC), 'Climate change: Impacts, vulnerabilities and adaptation in developing countries.' Online, https://unfccc.int/resource/docs/publications/impacts.pdf (accessed March 15, 2018).

67   'Paris Agreement,' op. cit., p. 16.

68   'Paris Agreement,' op. cit.; and see U.S. Forest Service, Climate Change Resource Center, Forests and Carbon Storage, USDA. Online, https://www.fs.usda.gov/ccrc/topics/forests-carbon (accessed March 14, 2018).

69   'Paris Agreement,' op. cit., p. 3.

70   'Paris Agreement,' op. cit., p. 16.

71   M.D. Shear, 'Trump will withdraw U.S. from the Paris Climate Agreement,' *New York Times*, June 1, 2017. Online, https://www.nytimes.com/2017/06/01/climate/trump-paris-climate-agreement.html (accessed March 14, 2018).

72   B. Plumer, 'Q&A: The Paris Climate Accord,' *New York Times*, May 31, 2017. Online, https://www.nytimes.com/2017/05/31/climate/qa-the-paris-climate-accord.html (accessed March 14, 2018).

73   H. Selin and A. Najam, 'Paris Agreement on climate change: The good, the bad, and the ugly,' *The Conversation*, December 14, 2015. Online, http://theconversation.com/paris-agreement-on-climate-change-the-good-the-bad-and-the-ugly-52242 (accessed March 14, 2018).

74   R.M. McManus, 'Toward an understanding of the relationship between the study of leadership and the natural world,' in B.W. Redekop, D Rigling Gallagher, and R. Satterwhite (eds), *Innovation in Environmental Leadership: Critical Perspectives*, New York: Routledge, 2018, pp. 97–115.

75   J. Worland, 'What to know about the historic "Paris Agreement" on climate change,' *Time*, December 12, 2015. Online, http://time.com/4146764/paris-agreement-climate-cop-21/ (accessed March 14, 2018).

76   Worland, ibid. The Agreement was even drafted in such a way that allowed the President of the United States to sign the agreement rather than having to submit the agreement to Congress, which could have resulted in yet another failed attempt to address worldwide climate change.

77   Etzioni, 2004, op. cit., p. 2.

Section II

In Section II, we now move on to specific leadership models that seem to lend themselves well to discussions of ethics and leadership. While the common good ethical model demonstrated itself to be equally concerned with all five components of leadership, our next chapter will start with a consideration of authentic leadership – a model that is decidedly focused on the individual leader over the other four components.

Our chapters in this section will address authentic leadership, servant leadership, followership, transformational leadership, and adaptive leadership. As we progress through this material, readers will note an expanding circle of concern – moving from a focus on the individual leader and that leader's core values, to broader concerns about followers, goals, context, and larger cultural values and norms. All the leadership models here have implications for the five components, but as editors, we asked ourselves, 'What seems to receive the most attention if we use this leadership model as a lens for a particular ethical leadership situation?' As we engage in case studies, readers will have the opportunity to reflect on examples from both business and political engagement in multiple locations – particularly the United States, Liberia, and South Africa.

12

Authentic leadership

Phyllis Huckabee Sarkaria

? FRAMING QUESTION

How can I lead with integrity?

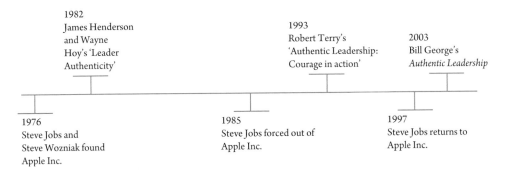

Figure 12.1 Timeline of major works on authentic leadership in relation to the chapter case study

Though relatively new compared to many other theories of leadership, the concept of authentic leadership has its origins in ancient Greece. Authenticity played a significant role in the teachings of early philosophers.[1] Shakespeare reflected their views in his play *Hamlet* when he penned the well-known words for Polonius, 'To thine own self be true.' This statement highlights the importance of demonstrating one's ethics when leading and relating to others, yet it reflects only part of the concept of authentic leadership. The ensuing centuries slowly refined the idea of authentic leadership as a model for guiding and directing leaders.

In this chapter, we will examine the concept of authentic leadership. We will study the development of various theories and models relating to the idea, and focus on key concepts running throughout the literature on the topic, while introducing several of the scholars who have been pioneering the study of this approach to leadership. As we have done in previous chapters, we will then look at the critiques of authentic leadership, as well as apply the Five Components of Leadership Model to analyze the theory. We will end our time together with a case study that considers one of the most well-recognized inventors and leaders of the twenty-first century – former Apple Inc. Chief Executive Officer, Steve Jobs.

Throughout the chapter, we will see how authentic leadership compels leaders to hold high ethical standards for their own behavior, in the ways they relate to their followers, the means through which they pursue their goals, and the ways they influence the broader context surrounding them and the organizations in which they lead. In so doing, authentic leaders must be self-aware, practice balanced processing, maintain a personalized moral perspective, and seek to be transparent in their relationships with others. Perhaps the primary lesson we will learn in this chapter is that to *truly* practice authentic leadership is challenging, but is a worthy aspiration for leaders who want to set a high ethical bar for themselves and others.

History

The contemporary study of authentic leadership can be traced back to 1982 when two researchers, James Henderson and Wayne Hoy, published findings on leadership authenticity recognizing that social scientists had formerly focused more on the impact of *inauthentic* behavior on organizations. They presented a perspective that authentic leaders accept responsibility for defining the way leadership manifests itself because of *who* they are rather than allowing their title or position to determine how they lead.[2] Being guided by one's ethical core more than external forces is a fundamental premise of authentic leadership. The authors went on to develop a measure of authenticity based on statements that addressed, among other things, a leader's tendency to be more relational versus operating 'by the book,' a willingness to admit mistakes and acknowledge not having complete information, and acting in ways that were perceived as cooperative rather than manipulative. These common themes have subsequently continued to influence the literature on authentic leadership.[3]

A significant body of knowledge on authentic leadership was not explicitly developed for some time after Henderson and Hoy's work. Scholars Bruce Avolio, Fred Walumbwa, and Todd Weber recall early years of study of authentic leadership flowing from discussions of transformational leadership behaviors that were not necessarily genuine.[4] Other early researchers studying authentic leadership focused more on positive psychology and servant leadership, both of which share common elements with authentic leadership.[5] Transformational and servant leadership, discussed in more detail in Chapters 15 and 13, share some attributes with authentic leadership but have developed as specific and separate areas of leadership studies. The focus of past research concentrates more on the challenges of inauthentic behavior and benefits of positivity rather than measuring the impact of authenticity, a subtle but important difference.

As a newer way of thinking about leadership, theories and models of authentic leadership are still being formed and defined. In 1993, Robert Terry described authenticity as 'action that is both *true* and *real* in *ourselves* and in the *world*.'[6] Terry underscored that action is at the heart of all leadership theories. For leadership to be authentic, he observed that self-knowledge, as well as the context of the greater world in which the leader and the organization operate, should factor into decisions on the appropriateness of specific actions. In his view, the intent is not sufficient to be authentic; a successful action is necessary. While these thoughts provided students of authentic leadership some parameters to ponder, it also highlighted the challenges of defining authentic leadership because there are many subtleties and nuances to consider. In some ways, authentic leadership might be akin to how Supreme Court Justice Potter Stewart described pornography in his landmark 1964 opinion when he said, 'I know it when I see it.'[7] Indeed, authenticity can be as much about the followers' perception of the leader as it is about the internal motivations that drive the leader's behavior.

Another decade passed before retired Medtronic CEO and Harvard Business School professor Bill George published a book titled *Authentic Leadership* that described characteristics of authentic leaders.[8] George was concerned with an ethical gap he observed in corporate leadership after the failures of Enron, Arthur Anderson, WorldCom and other large corporations and felt it was necessary to highlight the organizational benefits of authentic leadership. More practical than theoretical, George's book brought the subject of authentic leadership out of the domain of academia and into the realm of popular thought. His ideas garnered widespread attention, leading to interest in authentic leadership development programs and further research into the impact of authentic leaders on their organizations and teams. Both academic and practitioner efforts, however, remained focused primarily on the ways authentic leaders influence their followers.

In 2005, *Leadership Quarterly* published a special issue that focused exclusively on authentic leadership.[9] Similar to Bill George's book, the *Leadership Quarterly* edition was published, at least in part, in response to concerns about corporate scandals that derived from poor leadership and destructive business practices that ended up devastating employees, retirees, and investors.[10] It was around this time that scholars began to define authentic leadership as requiring advanced moral development.[11] Building on transformational leadership and other leadership theories and models that emphasize ethics at their core, the definition of authentic leadership evolved to incorporate a distinctly ethical dimension.

Now that we have a basic understanding of the history of authentic leadership, let's look more closely at the foundational concepts of authentic leadership and how it is conceived today.

Major concepts of authentic leadership

Like other models of leadership, authentic leadership seeks to identify the behaviors and traits that make leaders more effective. Authentic leadership shares some ideas with leader-centric models, because self-awareness, understanding of one's values, and congruent behavior are all critical aspects of the concept. Similar to transformational leadership, authentic leadership considers the traits and behaviors of leaders as they relate to and impact followers. The leader, follower, and context in which they interact are all inextricably intertwined.

With additional research and practical application of the concepts of authentic leadership, four primary attributes have come to define authentic leadership: awareness of self and others' perceptions of the leader; actively seeking information and alternative points of view before making decisions; consciously behaving in a way that is consistent with one's positive personal values; and acting transparently so that others see the congruence between the leader's actions and personal values.[12] These characteristics are closely related and interwoven. No single aspect is more important than another. Each influences an overall perception of authenticity and congruence between words and actions, contributing to the leader's credibility and trust.

Self-awareness

Authentic leaders take time for reflection and seek to understand themselves and their motivations. Through heightened self-awareness, leaders are better able to regulate their actions and reactions, reducing impulsive, unpredictable behavior and increasing trust and engagement within their work environment.[13] A number of graduate schools of business, including Harvard, Stanford, Dartmouth and the University of Chicago, have identified self-awareness as a critical leadership capability that predicts effectiveness in managing others and success as a leader.[14] In fact, self-awareness has been suggested by some to be more critical to leadership success than technical ability or intellect.[15] Leaders who are self-aware have a strong sense of identity and direction, whereas low self-awareness not only limits leaders but can 'impede organizational performance'[16] by making worse decisions, engaging in less coordination and showing less ability to manage conflict.[17] Nevertheless, self-awareness, while a crucial aspect of authentic leadership development, is not adequate on its own. Many skills and behaviors contribute to actual and perceived authenticity.[18] Knowing more about one's self is useful. How we behave in interactions with others ultimately demonstrates authenticity or lack thereof.

Balanced processing

By engaging in what the authentic leadership literature calls 'balanced processing,' leaders demonstrate an openness to consider all relevant information objectively.[19] This behavior demonstrates an unbiased interest in new ideas as the leader seeks out alternative views and opinions before making decisions. The idea is to consciously reflect on information that the leader may be lacking, recognizing that others may have vital insights from their perspective that the leader does not see. Balanced processing does not mean the authentic leader seeks to be proven wrong, but it does imply an openness to new ideas and information and a willingness to accept that the leader may not always be the one with all the answers. This humility leads us to consider authentic leadership's third common theme – the leader's values.

Internalized moral perspective

Authentic leaders have a clear understanding of their values. They engage in introspection and actively seek to demonstrate these ideals to others. Authentic leaders draw upon a clear sense of purpose and 'inner system of belief.'[20] This begs the question, can a leader have clear, but evil, intent and still be considered authentic? Arguably by being clear as to what they stand for and transparent in their actions, it would be possible to be what one might call 'authentically evil.' However, the model that has evolved to define authentic leadership requires *positive* core values. Indeed, many scholars of authentic leadership believe an 'advanced level of moral development' is necessary for a leader to be truly authentic.[21] By understanding their values and communicating their values to others, authentic leaders can develop relational transparency with their followers.

Relational transparency

Authentic leaders are accountable for their actions, striving to be transparent in how their decisions and actions are consistent with their values. However, it is through the relationship with others that leaders can be perceived to be more or less authentic. Though leader-centric, the authentic leadership model highlights the interaction between the leader and followers as a measure of authenticity. Leaders who are self-aware and have clear motivations create greater transparency. The give-and-take in their relationships enhances this transparency, just as their openness to feedback influences their followers' perceptions of them and allows them to lead more authentically. Leaders cannot simply declare themselves authentic; instead, they must act in a way that others perceive as personifying their beliefs. Authentic leaders 'own' their successes *and* their mistakes, and they encourage followers to do the same. As Bill George has explained, 'Being authentic as a leader is hard work and takes years of experience in leadership roles. No one can be authentic without fail; everyone behaves inauthentically at times, saying and doing things they will come to regret. The key is to have the self-awareness to recognize these moments and listen to close colleagues who point them out.'[22] Engaging in these behaviors allows leaders to grow in wisdom and authenticity. This openness to feedback from followers also encourages more open communication because authentic leaders show through their actions that they value courageous followers that are willing to 'speak truth to power,'[23] strengthening the bonds of trust and improving communication within their relationships. In this way, the authentic leadership model pairs well with the followership model discussed in Chapter 14.

Authentic leadership has been studied from different perspectives that all consider variations of these four core ideas, as summarized in Table 12.1. For example, Robert W. Terry identified 'seven C's of authenticity' which include: consistency, concealment, correspondence, comprehensiveness, coherence, convergence, and conveyance.[24] Under Terry's model, leaders move from good intention to 'the embodiment of intention in the world,'[25] acting in a way that matches words with actions and looks beyond a single action to consider how that decision will ripple through the organization. He cautions that authentic leaders must be mindful of the consequences of their actions and beware of rationalization, engaging in dialogue with followers to understand and gain greater insight, particularly when divergent opinions exist. Through openness to other perspectives, the leader can encourage the development of authenticity in followers by modeling appropriate behaviors and being receptive to the contributions of others. In such a way, authenticity is both given and received.

Bill George also framed authentic leadership in terms intended to be readily applicable by leaders. George identifies five dimensions of authenticity: purpose, values, relationships, self-discipline, and heart.[26] These dimensions are reflective of the four primary attributes mentioned above. George emphasizes that developing and applying these characteristics could result in a positive organizational culture, inferring that healthy cultures produce better outcomes than do toxic cultures. Through this application of authenticity, leaders can connect with followers in a way that increases follower engagement and loyalty to the common goal and organization. Even leaders who are hard on their followers can, through the very manner in which they challenge those individuals, convey that they are interested in the followers' success.[27]

More scholarly assessments have also echoed these four primary attributes.[28] One set of researchers determined that there was more to authentic leadership than 'being true to oneself' and sought to develop a tool for measuring behaviors and attitudes in the workplace.[29] The result of their research, the Authentic Leadership Questionnaire (ALQ), provided a validated measure for those seeking to be more authentic, classifying the characteristics under self-awareness, balanced processing, internalized moral perspective, and relational transparency. In many ways, these four measures have become the gold standard for assessing authentic leadership and providing a path for leadership development.

Authentic leadership has been defined in numerous ways. As research on the subject has matured, the definition of authentic leadership has emerged to reflect measures of self-awareness, balanced processing, internalized moral perspective, and relational transparency. Leaders who aspire to be more authentic in their work with others and those who seek to encourage new leaders to be more authentic can look to these measures to determine where

Table 12.1 Approaches to authentic leadership

Seven C's of Authenticity (Terry, 1993)	Five Dimensions of Authenticity (George, 2003)	Authentic Leadership Questionnaire (Walumbwa et al., 2008)
• Consistency • Concealment • Correspondence • Comprehensiveness • Coherence • Convergence • Conveyance	• Purpose • Values • Relationships • Self-discipline • Heart	• Self-awareness • Balanced processing • Internalized moral perspective • Relational transparency

growth opportunities exist. However, a higher level of scrutiny of authentic leadership brings to light the paradoxical nature of this model when moving from theory to application.

Critiques of authentic leadership

There are a number of intervention-based training programs available in the marketplace purporting to help companies develop authentic leaders and assist individual leaders who wish to 'find' their authenticity.[30] Yet, as one scholar notes, 'there is little evidence-based research on whether these prescriptions or how-to strategies [are effective].'[31] Readings in the popular business press suggest that the term 'authentic leadership' is widely used but not necessarily well understood in the business world. Stanford professor of management Jeff Pfeffer has called authenticity 'misunderstood and overrated.'[32] Experience with leaders who excuse poor behavior through an 'excessive need to be me'[33] may turn individuals and organizations away from learning more about authentic leadership as a model for leadership. Further, the focus on authenticity has been mocked as damage control by corporations concerned about revelations of inappropriate leadership.[34] Comments like this tend to ignore the positive moral and ethical content that defines the character of authentic leadership.

Let us not confuse authenticity with authentic leadership. A leader might be true to himself and still not be an authentic leader. Boas Shamir and Galit Eilam tell the story of a junior military officer who had tried to influence a higher-ranking officer during wartime.[35] He failed, and the resulting action cost many in his unit their lives. Based on this experience, the commander went on to justify unyielding and aggressive behavior. He believed that had he been more forceful with his superior – more himself – a different outcome might have occurred. The lessons he took from the experience convinced him that he had been right and should not compromise or accept alternative points of view. His inability to consider the situational nature of leadership caused him to be 'himself' in ways that were destructive to his relationships. The misperception that authenticity is about being oneself without regard to moral values or self-control creates a challenge for those seeking to apply the authentic leadership model to their work as leaders. This tension to articulate what makes a leader 'real' could cause some to dismiss authentic leadership as non-substantive because of a lack of understanding.

Research over the past decade or more suggests that there is a clear moral component to authentic leadership.[36] Still, the connections have not been thoroughly studied to understand which values enhance authenticity. There could even be debate as to what constitutes a 'positive' purpose or value of a leader, and there is some disagreement that pro-social behaviors are a requirement of authentic leadership. While the measures contained in the Authentic Leadership Questionnaire (ALQ)[37] include high standards of ethical conduct, one might assert that an individual with nefarious goals who acts consistently with evil intent and inspires others to do the same is an authentic leader because of congruence between values and action. Such an argument, however, misses the insight into authentic leadership that the four primary attributes provide, which point to the need for a strong ethical core to engage in introspection and reflection to understand self and others. Even that perspective leaves open for discussion the question of whether authenticity is only evident in leaders with awareness, self-control and accountability for living positive values.[38]

A potential dilemma is apparent in determining that positive values are a prerequisite of authentic leadership; however, the goal of the authentic leader is to be effective in relationships and interactions while still expressing the unique style and character that define his leadership.[39] Another way to think about this is that it is not simply a particular act that matters, but rather the behaviors surrounding that act and the results from that act within the larger context.[40]

Leaders who strive to be more authentic consistently scan the landscape of their relationships and results, learn from their experiences and adjust as they move forward to increase alignment between values and outcomes. As these leaders gain insight into themselves, humility typically begins to play a more significant role in their interactions with others, further reflecting growth as a leader. While a desire for authenticity in relationships – work-related or otherwise – might be reason enough to focus on these areas for self-development, there are also specific ethical implications for the practice of authentic leadership. We now turn to consider the ethical implications of this theory more closely.

Ethical implications of authentic leadership

The emphasis authentic leadership places on personal integrity and self-awareness carries an ethical implication for leaders as their followers look to them for guidance and direction. When leaders behave authentically, they are perceived as being more ethical, as possessing more integrity, and as being more trustworthy.[41] Researchers have identified some desirable outcomes when authentic leadership behaviors are demonstrated, including increased trust as well as overall improved organizational performance.[42] This point is reinforced by scholars who have found a direct positive correlation between demonstrated self-awareness – an essential attribute of authentic leadership – and increased trust within organizations.[43] Transparent, authentic leaders can further increase trust when they seek others' input, disclose relevant information for decision-making, and reveal personal motives and thoughts that help others understand the positive moral and ethical development behind their words and actions.[44]

The perception of a leader as authentic creates a safe and trusting environment for followers to, in turn, be their authentic selves; thus creating a positive context for leaders and followers to work together.[45] Just as the presence of trust facilitates a positive culture, a lack of trust can cause followers to focus on self-protection instead of engaging with the leader to reach a common goal.[46] This self-protection may cause followers to justify poor behavior or act unethically out of fear. Hence, authentic leadership may help create an ethical environment for leaders *and* followers where the 'right thing to do' is valued by all in the organization.

This brings us to the overall quality of relationships between all members of an organization. Thinking about these relationships provides more insight into how leaders can influence followers to reach their common goals.[47] Development of healthy, positive relationships through the demonstration of authentic behaviors that reflect ethical congruence might point to ways that followers can support and influence one another when working together. While many underlying arguments of those studying authentic leadership are that authenticity leads to better performance,[48] the focus of authentic leadership has remained mostly on positive impacts on individual followers, not necessarily on group dynamics; though many of these influences may be extrapolated to broader results. As Bill George has noted, leaders who are open about their beliefs and willing to share their vulnerabilities empower their followers to ask for help and share their uncertainties in turn.[49] The openness and trust that flows from better knowledge of self and others that is congruent with a positive moral foundation can create a greater connection, leading to more ethical cultures and behavior, which in turn strengthens team performance.[50]

Increased trust, improved cooperation, and positive organizational culture would seem to suggest authentic leadership as an answer to many challenges that any organization may face. By applying the principles of authentic leadership to interactions with colleagues and within teams, one might assume similar positive organizational influences. This could be particularly impactful when the members of a leadership team demonstrate authenticity with one another.

Five component analysis

Greater clarity around what it means to be an authentic leader may be possible by stepping back to look beyond the leader-centric focus and consider the broader view within which leaders perform. Let's now examine authentic leadership using the Five Components of Leadership Model introduced in Chapter 1. We will specifically concentrate on the first four elements of the model.

Authentic leadership begins with the individual leader who possesses a strong moral core and self-awareness and extends to what that leader brings to the followers, goals, context, and culture. This is reflected in how the leader's sense of self manifests through transparency and openness with followers. Because the authentic leader knows who she is and what she stands for, she is comfortable considering different points of view and is concerned with doing what is right for the people she leads.

Being authentic is not about perfection. Authentic leaders are fallible human beings. There is potential for any leader to disappoint followers or err in pursuit of a goal. Authentic leaders genuinely desire to be better leaders, to connect with their followers, and to inspire positive outcomes. They recognize that no one is perfect, perhaps particularly themselves, and seek to improve themselves on an ongoing basis because of their sincere desire to live their values.

Figure 12.2 The Five Components of Leadership Model applied to authentic leadership

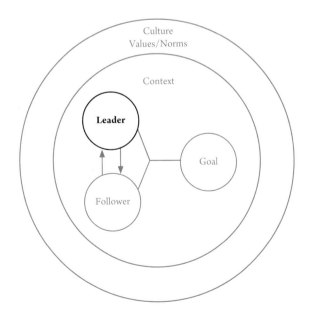

Like servant and transformational leadership, there are explicitly ethical aspects of authentic leadership that exercise intrinsic influence on the leader and the leader's relationship with followers. Authenticity is not about following a formula for success but rather having a strong ethical core, aligning personal values with those of the organization, and being able to share with followers how one's values are reflected in thought and action.

Such alignment is typically demonstrated externally through transparency and openness to new ideas. This behavior allows leaders to work with followers in a unique partnership such that both leader and followers learn and grow. By modeling the attributes of authentic behavior for followers, authentic leaders support the development of followers to become authentic in their interactions. Trust develops between leaders and followers to the benefit of the individuals and the organization as a whole, as authentic leaders foster the development of positive work environments that reflect their firm moral standards, transparency, and integrity.

From time to time, followers in any organization may feel pressure to 'do whatever it takes' to achieve a goal. Authentic leaders in such situations draw on knowledge of their values and awareness of their strengths and weaknesses to inspire others to deliver their best while still behaving ethically. This leads us to the way authentic leaders go about achieving goals.

There are challenges of 'knowing, showing, and remaining true to one's real self'[51] given pressures to conform and reach goals that, at times, seem unobtainable. Similarly, organizational culture and environment can influence the ways these goals are achieved. Because authentic leader behavior impacts organizational climate, authentic leaders are also often able to affect goals, either directly or indirectly. The openness and transparency that exist between authentic leaders and their followers as they work toward goals worthy of their commitment are aspects of authentic leadership that can lead to stronger performance and better results.

Researchers have explored the impact of authenticity on team effectiveness and productivity, measuring a 59 percent improvement in performance of teams where leaders exhibit authentic behaviors.[52] Further, a study comparing the effect of authentic leadership and transformational leadership suggests that authentic leadership behaviors correlated with stronger group and organizational performance, showing greater influence over results relative to transformational leadership.[53] Yes, authentic leadership emphasizes a leader's values and ethics, and it also results in leaders and followers effectively achieving their goals.

A fundamental aspect of authentic leadership is the leader's ability and willingness to share feelings and information openly and appropriately. The authentic leader's actions and followers' perception of the leader's authenticity serve as a stimulus to the organizational climate and cultural norms. Situations faced by the leader and how the leader responds reflect the values and norms of leadership, with actions sending a strong signal to followers as to what is, and is not, acceptable behavior in the organization.

All organizations evolve to a certain extent. Within the organizational evolution, leaders may exercise positive influence to guide the culture. Authentic leaders help craft meaningful goals that support the aspirational culture and environment that develops as the organization's purpose is identified and pursued. Over time, transparency and trust demonstrated by the authentic leader can become the norm, and a healthy climate for accomplishing great things can evolve within the organization. As authentic leaders influence and are influenced by followers in definition and pursuit of goals, they provide an example that can impact the immediate context and organizational culture in positive ways.

Authentic leadership reflects the process through which leadership occurs and recognizes that leaders are continually developing and seeking to improve. As a result, the perception of authenticity may vary depending on the context or follower. A leader is not viewed as 'authentic' simply because she determines to be so. The interconnected nature of leadership embodies how the environmental aspects of context exercise influence on – and are influenced by – the authenticity of the leader.

Challenges to the authentic leadership model and discussion of the five components of leadership as it pertains to authentic leadership exemplify the influence that leaders can have beyond those they directly lead, particularly when they are highly visible, public figures. How leaders handle themselves in stressful situations can demonstrate integrity to moral principles and increase trust and credibility with constituents, or the leader's actions can come across as selfish and a poor model of leadership. Leaders may be considered either unifying or polarizing, depending on a particular follower's relationship with the leader. This raises the question of how leaders might be seen by some as authentic while others view them negatively.

Considering the five components of leadership in a specific context is one way to test the defined boundaries of the authentic leadership model.

Turning now to our case study, we will examine one such individual who is known for his fame and associated visibility. Through his words, actions, and the lore that surrounded his success and his failures, this leader set an example, but did he represent the self-aware and balanced authentic leader or was he authentic to more selfish ends in his pursuit of success?

CASE STUDY

Steve Jobs and authentic leadership

Steve Jobs is one of the iconic business leaders of our time. He has been both praised and vilified for his leadership style. In Apple, he created an amazingly successful company, and at the same time Jobs' life was a series of failures. He dropped out of college. He was removed from the company he founded. His subsequent ventures struggled. Yet Jobs' perseverance in seeking perfection and dedication to doing work that he loved served as his guiding light. Even when being difficult, it was clear to followers what mattered to him. This became part of the ethos and story around Apple. Bill George speaks of leaders who use their stories to convey the difference they want to make 'and inspire others to join with them in pursuing common goals.'[54] Jobs understood the value of the story and used it to form Apple's company culture and to launch products that changed the face of technology.

Jobs' evolution and learning as a leader eventually brought him full circle. It is difficult to argue with the results he achieved in bringing Apple back from the brink of bankruptcy in the late 1990s. He returned to the organization that he founded, wiser from the lessons of failure that contributed to his earlier departure and kinder, according to those who worked most closely with him.[55] Drawing on those missteps, which he readily conceded, he began to build Apple into an innovation powerhouse.

Jobs co-founded Apple Computers in his parents' garage in 1976 with limited technology skills and no engineering background but a vision for what personal computing could become. As the company grew, he struggled to implement that vision in a rapidly evolving environment. After bringing in more experienced business leaders, he was sidelined by the board of directors in 1985 and decided to leave the organization. For the next decade, he pursued other opportunities, founding NeXT – a computer and software company – and purchasing a computer animation studio from George Lucas that became the dynamic and wildly successful Pixar Studios. NeXT sold only 50,000 computers and ultimately narrowed its focus to software. Jobs was struggling but happy in his continued pursuit of innovation and excellence.

It seemed that Jobs had moved on in his life, but when Apple purchased NeXT in 1996, he connected once again with the organization he founded. As Apple faced financial and leadership challenges, he was enticed to resume the role of CEO in 1997. From that point on, Jobs built Apple into one of the world's most powerful brands and a highly-valued

CASE STUDY *(continued)*

company over the decade that followed. He did this through a clear and intuitive understanding of what was important – to him, to customers, and to the company – and by staying true to principles of simplicity and focus in living out his values around passion, innovation, and perfection. He was consistent in his expectations that his followers demonstrate the same kind of curiosity, dedication, and rabid enthusiasm. Jobs was not afraid of failure in business as long as he learned from mistakes, and he spoke frankly at industry forums about blunders and lessons learned, not just successes. While Jobs cared deeply about the success of the organization, his behavior and communication suggest less concern about accumulating the trappings of wealth for himself than making a difference in the world.

Jobs could be brutal to those whose ideas he viewed as inferior and at the same time, he knew that the secret to differentiation for Apple was to gather ideas from many creative minds to change the world of technology by competing through innovation in design, not merely increased functionality. When he returned to Apple, his vision and direction helped the company reinvent itself and become an incredibly successful brand with revolutions in design and functionality in the personal device space, introducing the iMac, iPod, iPhone, and iPad, among other products.

Jobs continually innovated and was viewed as disruptive in many industries, whether it was finding a way to put one-thousand songs in customers' pockets (the iPod) or creating a platform for external applications developers to produce infinite functionality in a single device (the iPhone). Apple set a new standard for the retail shopping experience when the company began to open Apple stores. Instead of focusing on increased sales volume, associates in Apple stores were responsible for helping customers find solutions.[56] Jobs addressed Apple's retail strategy in much the same way that he thought about product development. Design was important, innovation was crucial, and the user experience was at the forefront. Steve Jobs continued in his role as Apple CEO until he stepped down in 2011, just before he passed away from cancer at the age of 56.

Five component analysis

Examined using the Five Components Model of leadership, a conclusion as to Steve Jobs' authenticity as a leader appears to be highly situational. Regardless of whether or not he was an authentic leader – which we'll take up further in a moment – he had a strong influence on followers, the goals of his organization, the context in which work was performed, and the culture of the company whose success was deeply intertwined with his own. Steve Jobs, the leader, was a presence that overshadowed all else.

Authenticity touches each of the five components. In Jobs' case, whether or not he was viewed as an authentic leader appears to depend on the situation. As already noted, introspection is required of authentic leaders to understand themselves. Interactions between leaders and followers impact their relationships. The authentic leader

CASE STUDY *(continued)*

Figure 12.3 The Five Components of Leadership Model applied to the Steve Jobs case study

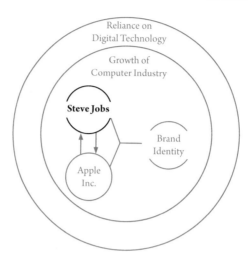

exercises influence on goals, the environment, and the overall organizational culture. Ultimately, the authentic leader is accountable for the kind of culture under his direction. Let's examine Jobs a bit deeper in light of authentic leadership and the Five Components Model.

Steve Jobs has been called 'authentic' because of his willingness to call things as he saw them, but is that really what authentic leadership is all about? Though certainly leader-centric, the authentic leadership model also reflects leadership characteristics that recognize the interactive nature of the leader within the organizational culture as he relates with followers. Clarity of purpose and sufficient self-awareness to transparently work with and enable others to reach great heights reflect the leader's authenticity. Authentic leaders continually seek to do 'what's right for their constituency,'[57] developing relationships that encourage others to be similarly ethically congruent, transparent, and balanced in decision-making and interactions.

Steve Jobs was known for being curious, passionate, impatient, dedicated, spiteful, and persistent. He was said to be rough, rude, and often abusive, but possessed the ability to inspire. He was profoundly private and kept his personal life out of the spotlight as much as possible, though he lived a very public life in other ways. Family was a high priority for Jobs, and that meant his wife and children but also his Apple 'family.' Though Jobs had not embraced the responsibilities of fatherhood when he was younger, he came to be a devoted husband and father as he grew and evolved as a person and a leader. By accepting his failures, both personal and professional, and learning from them, Steve Jobs applied the same focus and pursuit of excellence to his own life that he had to his many corporate ventures. In this way, he was authentic as a leader.

In his 2005 Commencement address at Stanford University,[58] Steve Jobs reflected on the things that mattered to him personally. Authentic leaders typically seek to understand their

CASE STUDY (continued)

motivations to reduce unpredictable behavior and appropriately share this self-knowledge with their followers. Knowing themselves and their inspiration allows these leaders to be more 'real' with followers. Before the graduation speech, Jobs was articulate about the things that mattered to him professionally: innovating to solve customer problems, deliver beautifully designed products, and conceive solutions before customers knew they needed them. However, his public persona up to that point in his career did not suggest that he was particularly introspective.

Jobs spoke to the audience at Stanford University about the importance of loving the work you do, focusing on the things that matter, and trusting in something that guides your life.[59] He observed that often the design of one's life only becomes apparent over time and looking back with the accumulated wisdom of years. His speech was reflective and transparent in expressing his firmly held belief that one should not settle. Though more open than his public persona had been to that point, the speech reflected values that Jobs had held dear for some time.

While Jobs' early years as a founder and leader may not have involved much introspection, by the time he returned to the helm at Apple in the late 1990s, Jobs knew himself and was clear to the point of being relentless about his values. He actively demonstrated his passion and dedication to innovation through his work. Jobs' adherence to the practice of Zen Buddhism might have suggested a kinder, calmer countenance, and in this manner, Jobs reflects the fallibility of humankind. He sought to do what he loved and be more accepting of the results, yet he continually struggled to accept the failings of himself and others. Jobs trusted his intuition and was committed to excellence. He expected no less of himself than he did of others, but his typical reaction to ideas or people who frustrated him suggests that he wrestled with being authentically aligned to his moral core.

As Apple's leader, Steve Jobs was viewed by some as inspiring and others as demeaning. He had a passion for distilling products to their simplest essence, almost a purity of design and thinking, and could excite followers about the possibilities of their work with his vision. He acknowledged that he could be both demanding and selfish and yet many of those who worked most closely with Jobs tended to revere him for his leadership. Others have described him as a manipulative bully who ruled through fear. Perhaps he was aware of this reputation and felt it served his purpose to achieve results. Perhaps he had good intentions but was unaware of how his behavior affected followers. Walter Isaacson – whose biography of Jobs is often quoted as providing support that Job was a jerk – is quick to defend the CEO's reputation, suggesting that 'genius worship' has led to multiple interpretations of an incredibly complex individual.[60]

Because, or perhaps in spite of, Jobs' visionary abilities, it could be difficult for him to pursue an unbiased interest in others' ideas and opinions before making decisions; however, he was always looking for new ideas and ways to improve products. Jobs' form of empathy was about intuition, not intellect, and while he could be a formidable sparring partner, he respected those who were willing to push back when they had a better solution and could make a case for their ideas.

CASE STUDY *(continued)*

When followers did not understand his vision or were less confident that they could meet what they saw as unrealistic and unrealizable goals in a short period of time, he could be unrelenting in his abuse. He could be unyielding as he pushed for better, smarter, more creative technology. At the same time, his drive to challenge Apple employees to be the best they could be inspired many to accomplish what they initially thought was impossible. In spite of clear deficits as a leader, those who knew him best and worked most closely with him were long-term, loyal followers.[61]

Many of Jobs' followers speak of his consistent commitment to shared values and vision to accomplish great things together.[62] This seems inconsistent with stories of poor behavior. Did he lack self-insight or was he purposefully a jerk? Did he suffer from a major character flaw or was he clueless as to how he impacted others? In a 2011 *Forbes* article titled 'Steve Jobs was a jerk, you shouldn't be,'[63] David Coursey suggests that Jobs was just being himself and that a lack of empathy was at the core of his poor behavior. If true, Jobs would not be considered an authentic leader. Yet the comments of those closest to him suggest that public perceptions of the 'known' Steve Jobs is perhaps more a creation of collective conscience and the myth of greatness than an accurate reflection of who he really was. Though Jobs combined his abuse with the ability to deliver on an incredible imagination, one might wonder if he could have accomplished the things that he did without being able to connect to the talented people who would help him achieve these feats of innovation. Either way, from the perspective of the authentic leader, *how* one leads is as important as *what* one accomplishes.

But can you be an authentic leader without consideration for the means in which a goal is achieved? Authentic leadership as a model emphasizes an ethical posture and moral approach to leadership. Yet ethically, Jobs seemed to straddle a vast chasm. In addition to Jobs' behavior toward followers, he led an organization that faced issues with its overseas suppliers because of unsafe, sweatshop-like working conditions.[64] In many of these instances, workers were treated poorly, and some even died. (Apple's poor manufacturing environment is detailed in the case study presented in Chapter 2.) At no point did Jobs appear to express concern about the manufacturing situation overseas or seem willing to provide leadership in applying Apple's standards for worker welfare to the employees in those factories. Although, after repeated reports of unsafe working conditions, Apple did later respond to this situation. Still, an unwillingness to address issues around the poor working conditions at Apple's overseas manufacturing sites would not have been considered 'authentic leadership' by anyone paying attention. Was this failure of leadership an oversight, misplaced trust in those who were responsible for that aspect of the business, or a disregard for persons with less power, status, and influence? This seeming disregard for the workers' lives he impacted through his corporate and personal success raises questions about whether or not Steve Jobs could be considered an authentic leader.

When Jobs came back to Apple in 1997, the company was in poor financial shape and working on a wide array of products – what Jobs described to a MacWorld audience as not the 'right' products. Instead of being afraid of further failure associated with Apple, Steve

CASE STUDY *(continued)*

Jobs brought determination and enthusiasm for the company's potential to his position as leader. This helped him focus his followers on the need to develop products that would change the world and to continue to do so in an exceptional way. He was unrelenting in his approach and authentic in his desire to achieve positive outcomes. Followers who worked most closely with him in his 'second act' at Apple understood that, even when he behaved badly, it came from a place of caring and wanting to make a difference through innovation. In turn, these followers said they gave their best to Apple with extraordinary results.[65]

Jobs' decisions were consistent with his values, and he was accountable for his actions, readily admitting failure and pushing others to do more than they thought they were capable of because he believed in their potential. As he stated upon his return to Apple in 1997, 'I have the scars to show for my mistakes.'[66] He then went on to praise the employees working on highly challenging issues and changes that were necessary to save the company. Jobs acknowledged that mistakes would be made along the way, and promised 'when we find the mistakes, we'll fix them.' This mindset did not pretend to have the 'right' answers but instead to continue to pursue the answers that would have the most positive long-term result for the company, adjusting and learning along the way. This is, indeed, in keeping with the balanced processing and relational transparency that are hallmarks of authentic leadership.

In many respects, it appears that Jobs' ability to inspire and engage as an authentic leader was inconsistent. At his worst, he inspired some to lead in an abusive way and manipulated others to achieve success. At his best, he demonstrated the importance of growing and evolving as a leader to achieve greater authenticity in interactions with followers. Leaders may declare themselves authentic, but it is the experience of those working with them that ultimately determines how they are viewed. The business results that Steve Jobs achieved as a leader are indisputable; whether he did so as an authentic leader is subject to debate.

Consider the full scope of Jobs' career and how he grew in his authenticity as he came to terms with his personal challenges and story. His continual evolution as a leader speaks to his willingness to apply the same rigor and expectations to himself that he did to his companies, their products, and the people who made them. Jobs recognized his failings, including the very public humiliation of being removed from the company he created. He learned from his mistakes and came back to demonstrate the value of those lessons.

Some have observed[67] that to emulate Jobs' 'jerk-like' behaviors in hopes of achieving similar results is to miss the essence that led to his brilliance as a leader. Jobs was not simply critical of others; he was self-critical and always seeking to improve the customer experience. His ability to generate loyalty was key to his success. Though stories of Jobs' bullying and abusive behavior are legendary, those who worked most closely with him praised him for his leadership. Said one, 'I consider myself the absolute luckiest person in the world to have worked with him.'[68] They saw that his actions were congruent with his values and recognized the genius and caring for his passion. Jobs' closest followers came to trust him implicitly, knowing he had the customers' and company's best interests at heart when he drove relentlessly for perfection.

Summary and concluding remarks

This chapter on authentic leadership began with the query: 'How can I lead with integrity?' Answering this question is a first step in the journey of becoming an authentic leader. As a first step, authentic leaders engage in self-examination and clarify those core values. By then taking action in a way that is consistent with those values, they show integrity as a leader. Socrates taught that the unexamined life is not worth living. The authentic leader embraces examination of self and understanding of her authenticity; however, being 'real' is not sufficient on its own. Authentic leaders are not pursuing status or 'image' or focused on creating a specific persona. Rather, developing self-awareness grounded in a clear understanding of the moral fiber of one's self enables the leader to consciously act in ways that demonstrate the values that she holds dear.

Authentic leadership goes beyond the leader's good intentions and requires combining intention and action to match the values of the organization where the leader works. For this to happen, leaders must engage in self-reflection and be open to other points of view, inviting followers to speak up when they believe the leader is not acting according to publicly stated values. Ultimately, the true test of authentic leadership comes when a leader is under significant pressure. Such stress can help leaders clarify core values as well as test their faithfulness to those values, promoting the practice of authentic leadership.

? DISCUSSION QUESTIONS

How do we recognize 'authentic' leaders? Likewise, how do we respond to 'authentic' leaders who embrace values with which we disagree?

Why might some followers see a leader as 'authentic' while others do not?

How might Steve Jobs have accomplished the same results in a 'kinder and gentler' environment? Could he have been faithful to his values without pushing followers so hard? If so, would it have been as effective?

Considering all aspects of authentic leadership, is an ethical component necessary to be an authentic leader? In other words, do you think it is possible to act congruently with a corrupt value system and still be considered an authentic leader? Why or why not?

Take a few minutes to reflect on your values. What value most clearly defines who you are and how you behave?

Steve Jobs used the power of story to relate to others. What is the most significant issue – positive or negative – you have experienced as a leader? How did it shape the leader you have become?

Leaders often find themselves in circumstances where they are confident they know the answer, but others may not agree. What actions would an authentic leader be likely to take in such a situation? What are the risks of such action? The rewards?

Much of the research into authentic leadership addresses the influence of authenticity on positive organizational outcomes, yet it is possible for a leader to be authentic and still not achieve the 'right' results. How might an authentic leader respond when faced with adverse outcomes that are attributable to his or her actions?

What accomplishment are you most proud of? Where have you 'blown it'? As you think about these two questions, consider how often you reflect on your actions and how frequently you ask others for feedback. How might engaging in greater self-reflection and increased pursuit of feedback improve your leadership?

 ADDITIONAL RESOURCES

E.C. Dierdorff and R.S. Rubin, 'Research: We're not very self-aware, especially at work,' *Harvard Business Review*, March 12, 2015.
This resource provides a succinct analysis of authenticity in the workplace.

W.L. Gardner, B.J. Avolio and F.O. Walumbwa (eds), *Authentic Leadership Theory and Practice: Origins, Effects and Development*, Bingley, UK: Emerald Group Publishing, 2005.
This is a rich resource regarding the study of authentic leadership written for a scholarly audience.

M. Heffernan, *Beyond Measure: The Big Impact of Small Changes*, Simon & Schuster/ TED Books, 2015.
While not explicitly about authentic leadership, this book is a wealth of ideas and exercises for leaders who seek to increase their self-awareness, effectiveness, and connection with followers.

NOTES

1 For a history of the concept of authenticity, see S. Harter, 'Authenticity,' in C.R. Snyder and S. Lopez (eds), *Handbook of Positive Psychology*, Oxford: Oxford University Press, 2002, pp. 382–94. Greek and Roman influences on authenticity are also mentioned in R. Riggio, 'What is authentic leadership? Do you have it?' *Psychology Today*, January 22, 2014. Online, https://www.psychologytoday.com/blog/cutting-edge-leadership/201401/what-is-authentic-leadership-do-you-have-it (accessed September 17, 2017).

2 J.E. Henderson and W.K. Hoy, 'Leader authenticity: The development and test of an operational measure,' Paper presented at the annual meeting of the American Educational Research Association, New York, March 19–23, 1982. Online, http://files.eric.ed.gov/fulltext/ED219408.pdf (accessed February 27, 2017).

3 This influence occurred in spite of Henderson and Hoy's authenticity assessment not being validated to confirm that it measured what it purported to measure.

4 B.J. Avolio, F.O. Walumbwa, and T.J. Weber, 'Leadership: Current theories, research, and future directions,' *Annual Review of Psychology*, vol. 60, 2009, 421–49.

5 For more information, see P.A. Duignan, and N. Bhindi, 'Authenticity in leadership: An emerging perspective,' *Journal of Educational Administration*, vol. 35 no. 3, 1997, 195–209; and F. Luthans and B.J. Avolio, 'Authentic leadership: A positive developmental approach,' in K.S. Cameron, J.E. Dutton and R.E. Quinn (eds), *Positive Organizational Scholarship: Foundations of a New Discipline*, San Francisco, CA: Berrett-Koehler, 2003, pp. 241–58.

6 R. Terry, *Authentic Leadership: Courage in Action*, San Francisco, CA: Jossey-Bass, 1993, pp. 111–12. Emphasis on original.

7 378 U.S. at 197 (Stewart, J., concurring).

8 See also George's *True North* (2007), which expands on the concepts in *Authentic Leadership* (2003) with a focus on developing a personal leadership plan to be more authentic.

9 This special edition of *Leadership Quarterly* included B.J. Avolio and W.L. Gardner, 'Authentic leadership development: Getting to the root of positive forms of leadership,' *The Leadership Quarterly*, vol. 16 no. 3, 2005, 315–494.

10 See D. Ackman, 'Worldcom, Tyco, Enron – R.I.P. Forbes.' *Forbes*, July 1, 2002. Online, https://www.forbes.com/2002/07/01/0701topnews.html (accessed June 6, 2017).

11 See W. Gardner, B. Avolio, and F. Walumbwa, 'Authentic leadership development: Emergent trends and future directions,' in W.L. Gardner, B.J. Avolio, and F.O. Walumbwa (eds), *Authentic Leadership Theory and Practice: Origins, Effects and Development*, Oxford: Elsevier Science, 2005, pp. 387–406. The authors pointed out that leaders need a strong ethical core to engage in the introspection and reflection necessary to truly understand themselves and others.

12 See F.O. Walumbwa, B.J. Avolio, W.L. Gardner, T.S. Wernsing, and S.J. Peterson, 'Authentic leadership: Development and validation of a theory-based measure', *Journal of Management*, vol. 34, 2008, 89–126. While included by numerous early scholars of authentic leadership in one form or another, the four primary attributes of authentic leadership are drawn primarily from the research and conclusions of Walumbwa et al. that resulted in the creation of a validated assessment of authentic leadership.

13 The following sources highlight the importance of self-awareness not for the sole purpose of being one's self, but to promote alignment between the leader's values, feelings, and thoughts and behaviors. See M. Bamford, C.A. Wong, and H. Laschinger, 'The influence of authentic leadership and areas of worklife on work engagement of registered nurses,' *Journal of Nursing Management*, vol. 21 no. 3, 2012, 529–40. C.D. Cooper, T. Scandura, and C.A. Schriesheim, 'Looking forward but learning from our past: Potential challenges to developing authentic leadership theory and authentic leaders,' *The Leadership Quarterly*, vol. 16 no. 3, 2005, 475–93; Gardner et al., 2005, op. cit.; W. Gardner, C. Cogliser, K. Davis, and M. Dickens, 'Authentic leadership: A review of the literature and research agenda,' *The Leadership Quarterly*, vol. 22 no. 6, December 2011, 1120–45; and B. Tate, 'A longitudinal study of the relationships among self-monitoring, authentic leadership, and perceptions of leadership,' *Journal of Leadership & Organizational Studies*, vol. 15 no. 1, 2008, 16–29.

14 See M. Showry and K.V.L. Manasa, 'Self-awareness – key to effective leadership,' *IUP Journal of Soft Skills*, vol. 8 no. 1, March 2014, 15–26.

15 Showry and Manasa, ibid.

16 Showry and Manasa, op. cit., p. 23.

17 E.C. Dierdorff and R.S. Rubin, 'Research: We're not very self-aware, especially at work,' *Harvard Business Review*, March 12, 2015.

18 C. Peus, J.S. Wesche, B. Streicher, S. Braun, and D. Frey, 'Authentic leadership: An empirical test of its antecedents, consequences, and mediating mechanisms,' *Journal of Business Ethics*, vol. 107 no. 3, 2012, 334–48. The authors address the complex connection between self-awareness and other skills and behaviors in achieving authentic leadership.

19 For more information on balanced processing see: B. Avolio, W. Gardner, F. Walumbwa, F. Luthans, and D. May, 'Unlocking the mask: A look at the process by which authentic leaders impact follower attitudes and behaviors,' *The Leadership Quarterly*, vol. 15 no. 6, 2004, 801–23; B.J. Avolio, F.O. Walumbwa, and C Zimmerman, 'Authentic leadership theory, research and practice: Steps taken and steps that remain,' in D. Day (ed.), *Oxford Handbook of Leadership and Organizations*, Oxford: Oxford University Press, 2014, pp. 331–56; Gardner et al., op. cit., 2005; and Gardner et al., 2011, op. cit.

20 T. Pearce, *Leading Out Loud: Inspiring Change Through Authentic Communication*, San Francisco, CA: Jossey-Bass, 2003, p. 10.

21 Walumbwa et al., 2008, op. cit., p. 93.

22 B. George, 'The truth about authentic leaders,' *Harvard Business School: Working Knowledge*, July 2016 [Web Log]. Online, http://hbswk.hbs.edu/item/the-truth-about-authentic-leaders (accessed February 27, 2017).

23 For more information on the value of courageous followers to leaders see I. Chaleff, *The Courageous Follower: Standing Up To and For Our Leaders*, San Francisco: Berrett-Koehler, 2009.

24 See Terry, op. cit.

25 Terry, op. cit., p. 224.

26 B. George, *Authentic Leadership: Rediscovering the Secrets to Creating Lasting Value*, San Francisco, CA: Jossey-Bass, 2003.

27 B. George, 'Leadership styles: Becoming an authentic leader,' August 28, 2015 [Web Log]. Online, http://www.billgeorge.org/page/leadership-styles-becoming-an-authentic-leader (accessed February 27, 2017).

28 For a more detailed examination of authentic leadership scholarship, see Avolio et al., 2004, op. cit.; B. Avolio and W. Gardner, 'Authentic leadership development: Getting to the root of positive forms of leadership,' *The Leadership Quarterly*, vol. 16 no. 3, 2005, 315–38; Cooper et al., 2005, op. cit.; Gardner et al., 2005, op. cit.; and Avolio et al., 2014, op. cit.

29 F.O. Walumbwa, B.J. Avolio, W.L Gardner, T.S. Wernsing, and S.J. Peterson, 'Authentic leadership: Development and validation of a theory-based measure,' *Journal of Management*, vol. 34 no. 1, 2008, 89–126.

30 Course offerings range widely from training presented by organizations like The Authentic Leadership Institute to Harvard University. See www.authleadership.com; and www.exed.hbs.edu/programs/ald/.

31 P.G. Northouse, *Leadership: Theory and Practice*, 7th edn, Los Angeles: Sage, 2016, p. 208.

32 J. Pfeffer, *Leadership BS: Fixing Workplaces and Careers one Truth at a Time*, New York: Harper Collins, 2015, p. 85.

33 For an excellent discussion of things leaders should stop doing to improve their leadership see M. Goldsmith, *What Got You Here Won't Get You There*, New York: Hyperion, 2007, pp. 96–8.

34 E. Guthey and B. Jackson, 'CEO portraits and the authenticity paradox,' *Journal of Management Studies*, vol. 42 no. 5, 2005, 1057–82.

35 B. Shamir and G. Eilam, 'What's your story?: A life-stories approach to authentic leadership development,' *The Leadership Quarterly*, vol. 16 no. 3, 2005, 395–417.

36 See especially Gardner et al., 2005, op. cit.; and Walumbwa et al., 2008, op. cit.

37 Walumbwa et al., 2008, op. cit.

38 While positive moral development has become a recognized measure of authentic leadership, Shamir and Eilam exclude morality, alternately defining authentic leaders as having a high level of integrity between belief and action. However, without a moral component, it is possible that perceptions of authenticity could be manipulated by unethical leaders or those with nefarious goals. See Shamir and Eilam, op. cit.

39 Gardner et al., 2011, op. cit.

40 Terry, who put action at the heart of all leadership theories, explores the alignment of values and outcomes for authentic leaders in more detail. See Terry, op. cit.

41 For more detail see K.H. Mhatre, *Rational Persuasion and Attitude Change: The Impact of Perceived Leader Authenticity and Perceived Leader Ability on Target Outcomes*, Doctoral dissertation, 2009, Available from ABI/INFORM Global (Order No. 3355629).

42 For more on trust and team performance see: S. Ozham and A. Ceylan, 'Collective efficacy as a mediator of the relationship between authentic leadership and well-being at work,' *International Business Research*, vol. 9 no. 6, March 2016, 17–30; B. Avolio, W. Gardner, F. Walumbwa, F. Luthans, and D. May, 'Unlocking the mask: A look at the process by which authentic leaders impact follower attitudes and behaviors,' *The Leadership Quarterly*, vol. 15 no. 6, 2004, 801–23; W. Zhu, D.R. May, and B.J. Avolio, 'The impact of ethical leadership behavior on employee outcomes: The roles of psychological empowerment and authenticity,' *Journal of Leadership and Organizational Studies*, vol. 11 no. 1, 2004, 16–26; M. Higgs and D. Rowland, 'Emperors with clothes on: The role of self-awareness in developing effective change leadership,' *Journal of Change Management*, vol. 10 no. 4, December 2010, 369–85; S.M. Norman, B.J. Avolio and F. Luthans, 'The impact of positivity and transparency on trust in leaders and their perceived effectiveness,' *Leadership Quarterly*, vol. 21 no. 3, 2010, 350–64; and S. Simsarian Webber, 'Leadership and trust facilitating cross-functional team success,' *Journal of Management Development*, vol. 21 no. 3, 2002, pp. 201–14.

43 See Norman et al., 2010, op. cit.; and F. Erdem, J. Ozen and A. Nuray, 'Relationship between trust and team performance,' *Work Study*, vol. 52 no. 6/7, 2003, 337–40.

44 Norman et al. (2010) built on the theoretical work of Gardner et al. (2005) linking authentic leadership behaviors and transparent communication with increased trust.

45 For a description of this result in more detail see: S. Ozham and A. Ceylan, 'Collective efficacy as a mediator of the relationship between authentic leadership and well-being at work,' *International Business Research*, vol. 9 no. 6, March 2016, 17–30. Others have addressed different aspects of safety and trust leading to higher productivity and better outcomes for organizations. For examples see: A. Emuwa, 'Authentic leadership: Commitment to supervisor, follower empowerment, and procedural justice climate,' *Emerging Leadership Journeys*, vol. 6 no. 1, 2013, 45–65; S. Sinek, 'Why good leaders make you feel safe' *TED*, March 2014. Online, http://www.ted.com/talks/simon_sinek_why_good_leaders_ make_you_feel_safe (accessed February 27, 2017); Henderson and Hoy, op. cit.; and Tate, op. cit.

46   See Erdem et al., op. cit.; and R.C Mayer and M.B. Gavin, 'Trust in management and performance: Who minds the shop while the employees watch the boss?' *Academy of Management Journal*, vol. 48 no. 5, 2005, 874–88.

47   For more detail on the positive impacts on performance from authentic leadership see: H. Wang, Y. Sui, F. Luthans, D. Wang and Y. Wu, 'Impact of authentic leadership on performance: Role of followers' positive psychological capital and relational processes', *Journal of Organizational Behavior*, vol. 35 no. 1, January 2014, 5–21.

48   See B. George, 2003, op. cit.; Avolio et al., 2004, op. cit.; Gardner et al., 2005 and 2011, op. cit.; and Avolio et al., op. cit.

49   B. George, *True North: Discover your Authentic Leadership*. San Francisco, CA: Jossey-Bass, 2007, p. 176.

50   Studies have suggested knowing one's self and acting consistently with that insight led to better team effectiveness. See C. Peus et al., op. cit.

51   Gardner et al., 2005, op. cit.

52   J. Politis, 'The relationship between team performance, authentic and servant leadership', *Proceedings of the European Conference on Management, Leadership & Governance*, 2013, 237–44. For more on greater team effectiveness resulting from authentic leadership behaviors see: Avolio et al., 2009, op. cit.; and Peus et al., op. cit.

53   Banks, McCauley, Gardner, and Guler consider authentic leadership, building on the work of Boies, Fiset and Gill who found that transformational leadership behaviors influence team outcomes by supporting trust in, and communication with, team members. G.C. Banks, K. Davis-McCauley, W.L. Gardner, and C.E. Guler, 'A meta-analytic review of authentic and transformational leadership: A test for redundancy,' *The Leadership Quarterly*, vol. 27 no. 4, August 2016, 634–52; and K. Boies, J. Fiset, and H. Gill, 'Communication and trust are key: Unlocking the relationship between leadership and team performance and creativity,' *Leadership Quarterly*, vol. 26 no. 6, 2015, 1080–94.

54   B. George, 2007, op. cit., p. 8.

55   A. Grant, 'To Be a disrupter, you don't have to be an asshole,' June 28, 2017 [Web Log]. Online, https:// www.linkedin.com/pulse/disrupter-you-dont-have-asshole-adam-grant (accessed July 1, 2017).

56   Y. Kane and I. Sherr, 'Secrets from Apple's genius bar, full loyalty, no negativity', *Wall Street Journal*, June 15, 2011. Online, https://www.wsj.com/articles/SB10001424052702304563104576364071955678908 #ixzz1PWIoz79K (accessed March 15, 2018).

57   F. Luthans and B.J. Avolio, 'Authentic leadership: A positive developmental approach' in K.S. Cameron, J.E. Dutton, and R.E. Quinn (eds), *Positive Organizational Scholarship: Foundations of a New Discipline*, San Francisco: Berrett-Koehler, 2003, p. 248.

58   B. Schlender and R. Tetzeli, *Becoming Steve Jobs: The Evolution of a Reckless Upstart Into a Visionary Leader*, New York: Crown Publishing, 2015.

59   Schlender and Tetzeli, ibid.

60   See B. Austin, 'The story of Steve Jobs: An inspiration or a cautionary tale?' *Wired*, July 23, 2012. Online, https://www.wired.com/2012/07/ff_stevejobs/ (accessed January 7, 2018).

61   W. Isaacson, *Steve Jobs*. New York: Simon & Schuster, 2011; and 'The real leadership lessons of Steve Jobs,' *Harvard Business Review*, April 2012. Online, https://hbr.org/2012/04/the-real-leadership-lessons-of- steve-jobs (accessed January 7, 2018).

62   Isaacson, 2011, ibid.

63   See D. Coursey, 'Steve Jobs was a jerk, you shouldn't be,' *Forbes*, October 12, 2011. Online https:// www.forbes.com/sites/davidcoursey/2011/10/12/steve-jobs-was-a-jerk-you-shouldnt-be/   (accessed February 24, 2017).

64   See case study in Chapter 2 on Kantian Ethics.

65   Isaacson, 2011, op. cit.

66   Two articles that explore this particular presentation are J. Bariso, '20 years ago, Steve Jobs demonstrated the perfect way to respond to an insult,' *Inc.*, July 26, 2017. Online, https://www.inc.com/justin-bariso/20- years-ago-steve-jobs-demonstrated-the-perfect-w.html (accessed August 1, 2017); and C. Guglielmo, 'A Steve Jobs moment that mattered: Macworld, August 1997,' *Forbes*, October 7, 2012. Online, https://

www.forbes.com/sites/connieguglielmo/2012/10/07/a-steve-jobs-moment-that-mattered-macworld-august-1997/#5efaae93edd5 (accessed February 24, 2017).

67 See both Isaacson, op. cit.; and Coursey, op. cit.
68 Isaacson, op. cit., p. 100.

13

Servant leadership

Maribeth Saleem-Tanner

 **FRAMING QUESTION**

How can leaders serve their followers and organizations?

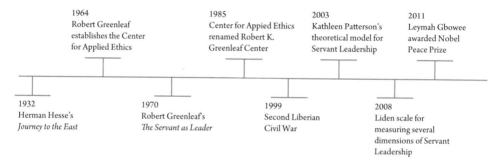

Figure 13.1 Timeline of major works on servant leadership in relation to the chapter case study

In an era where global interconnectedness, collaborative work teams, corporate social responsibility and employee wellness are increasingly the norm in corporate culture, it can be difficult to appreciate just how much of a paradigm shift Robert K. Greenleaf's seminal essay, 'The Servant as Leader' seemed to many at the time of its publication in 1970. It was a time, Greenleaf explains in the opening pages of his now iconic work, when 'A fresh, critical look is being taken at the issues of power and authority, and people are beginning to learn, however haltingly, to relate to one another in less coercive and more creatively supporting ways.'[1] To those reading Greenleaf's essay for the first time during the Nixon administration, in a country reeling from the Vietnam War, continuing racial tensions, and women campaigning for equal rights, the suggestion that the future of American corporate and institutional culture should move from hierarchy and authority toward inclusiveness and service was not an obvious or widely accepted conclusion.

In this chapter we will begin by exploring the notion of servant leadership as developed by Greenleaf, including historical and cultural examples that informed the model, as well as current academic research being done in the field. After discussing the evolution and key concepts for the model, our focus will turn to critiques and limitations of servant leadership in both theory and practice. Like the other chapters in this book, we will also consider how the Five Components of Leadership Model can be applied to servant leadership and then conduct a case study. The case will examine the role of servant leadership in the Liberian women's peace movement in 2003, and in the subsequent political involvement of female leaders. Finally, we will offer additional resources for study and discussion questions. As the chapter progresses, readers will engage in a thoughtful analysis of how servant leadership, itself values-based, can be understood and applied in terms of both an individual and institutional ethical framework with the power to reshape relationships and power structures on all levels of society and engage both leaders and followers in active, ongoing work toward more caring, just and participatory institutions and communities.

History

Servant leadership as a formal concept in leadership studies traces its roots directly to a single twentieth-century author, Robert K. Greenleaf. However, the idea of the leader as servant has roots that spread deeply and widely throughout history and cultures, including in a variety of religious traditions. The writings of the ancient Chinese philosopher Confucius have a strong focus on the importance of relationships, and the reciprocal care between elders/leaders and the youngers/followers, as well as on the need for humility, care, altruism and practice of reciprocity between leaders and followers within family and social structures.[2] In 'The Servant as Leader,' Greenleaf cites his own interpretation of Confucian teachings, wherein the responsibility for the behavior of followers rests heavily on the leader; a king is responsible for the well-being of his subjects, and has a duty to create an environment in which those subjects can thrive and behave ethically. Confucian philosophy also places high value on development of character, duty and honor in leaders. This worldview is similar to servant leadership in its emphasis on the importance of the individual leader as a force that shapes societies, and the belief that the quality of a society directly reflects the essential quality of its leaders, not simply skills or capabilities of leaders, but personal attributes such as humility, care for followers and knowledge.

Western audiences may be more familiar with the servant leadership of Jesus of Nazareth, who eschewed traditional hierarchy and political structures in favor of personal connection with his followers, serving as a friend and teacher rather than a lord and master. Ken Blanchard, who describes his Situational Leadership Model as 'a servant leadership model' in his Forward to *Focus on Leadership: Servant Leadership for the Twenty-First Century*, believes 'Jesus exemplified the fully committed and effective servant-leader,'[3] citing Jesus' words to his disciples in Matthew 20:27, 'Instead, whoever wants to be great among you must be your servant.' This along with other examples in the Christian Bible, such as stories of Jesus healing social outcasts, interacting respectfully with children, and washing his disciples' feet, all speak to an inversion of traditional leader–follower relationships, as does Jesus' climatic action of self-sacrifice for the redemption of humanity.

With this connection to ancient religious and philosophical traditions in mind, it is not surprising that the thesis of Greenleaf's 'The Servant as Leader' essay – that great leadership emerges only through a deep, authentic desire to serve – is framed with the dramatic language of prophecy, and supported by references to literature rather than social science research. Specifically, Greenleaf frames his definition of the servant leader with Hermann Hesse's short novel, *Journey to the East*, and French philosopher Albert Camus' exhortation to *Create Dangerously*. Greenleaf directly credits Hesse's novel, first published in Germany in 1932, as the inspiration for his idea of the servant as leader. The story describes a group of men on a journey who become unable to complete their quest after the departure of their servant, Leo, from the group. The end of the novel reveals that Leo was, in fact, the revered leader of the Order that had sponsored the group's journey, and a man of great spiritual as well as positional power, who chose to present himself to the group in the role of servant. This ideal of the leader as one who empowers, supports and enables the work of a group through selfless service to followers is the essence of servant leadership. From Camus, Greenleaf draws a belief in the power of individual action, and the primacy of motive and character in determining impact. What Camus calls 'hope,' Greenleaf reinterprets as leadership: 'millions of solitary individuals whose deeds and works every day negate frontiers and the crudest implications of history. As a result . . . each and every man, on the foundations of his own sufferings and joys, builds for them all.'[4]

While the tenets of servant leadership have strong philosophical and spiritual dimensions, the concept as defined by Greenleaf is solidly grounded in organizational leadership, and has been widely applied in business and institutional settings. Greenleaf's personal and professional experiences shaped his interest in and insights on leadership, service, and ethics. As a person who spent his professional life in large institutions, Greenleaf based his writings, and his thinking, on a framework wherein the organization is the primary unit of analysis. His upbringing in Indiana, influenced by the industrial economy and labor tensions around him, likely played a large part in his complex emotional and intellectual relationship with institutions and industry, which he saw firsthand could become either forces for community development or for human exploitation, depending on the quality of leadership. Greenleaf's belief in the power of the individual to influence collective well-being, and in the importance of working for the common good, grew also out of his life experiences, including his father's participation in community life and the Quaker religious tradition.

These early influences set Greenleaf's moral compass, and influenced the mindset in which he began his career with AT&T in the 1920s. Throughout his 40-year tenure working in management research, training and development for the massive telephone company, Greenleaf observed firsthand the turbulent organizational and societal dynamics surrounding the Great Depression, the rise of labor unions, the war and post-war industrial era, and the social upheaval of the 1960s. In the 1960s and 1970s, after retiring from AT&T, Greenleaf built a thriving second career in organizational consulting and teaching, working with a variety of corporate and academic institutions. Greenleaf was keenly interested in what he perceived to be a loss of trust in institutions, which was a guiding theme in his writings and lectures throughout the 1960s and 1970s. In 1964, upon his retirement from AT&T, he brought together his interest in philosophy and business through establishment of the nonprofit Center for Applied Ethics in Indianapolis, Indiana; in 1985, it was renamed the Robert K. Greenleaf Center and still maintains headquarters in Indianapolis and an office in Atlanta, Georgia.

Several well-known authors, both popular and academic, have integrated Greenleaf's servant leadership concepts in their work in the last 40 years, among them Ken Blanchard and M. Scott Peck in the 1970s and 1980s, as well as Stephen Covey, Peter Senge, Margaret Wheatley, Larry Spears, and Kent Keith in the 1990s and 2000s.[5] The variety of thinkers influenced by this concept illustrates the flexibility of the servant leadership model, which can be applied to individual and institutional behaviors in a variety of contexts.

Since the early 2000s, there has been a move by some scholars to further formalize Greenleaf's concepts. Dirk van Dierendonck's extensive review and synthesis of servant leadership literature in 2010 attempted to generalize six core servant leadership behaviors that are practiced in any number of settings and reflected in a variety of literature on servant leadership: 'Servant-leaders empower and develop people; they show humility, are authentic, accept people for who they are, provide direction, and are stewards who work for the good of the whole.'[6] Over the past decade, the development of measurement tools has also sparked increased interest among organizational psychologists and other social scientists in defining and understanding the development, process, and outcomes of servant leadership as distinct from other leadership approaches through quantitative research.

Major concepts of servant leadership

In 'The Servant as Leader,' Robert K. Greenleaf clearly and eloquently poses the defining question for servant leadership in terms of both the motivations that should propel one toward servant leadership, and also the outcomes that should be experienced by followers of the true servant leader: 'The servant leader is servant first. It begins with the natural feeling that one wants to serve. Then conscious choice brings one to aspire to lead. The best test is: Do those served grow as persons; do they, while being served, become healthier, wiser, freer, more autonomous, more likely themselves to become servants?' Through unpacking this short, dense passage we can begin to explore the shape and contours of modern servant leadership, as defined by Greenleaf.

Integration of service and leadership

Much has been written on the semantic implications of the term 'servant leader.' As many have pointed out, it is largely in the union of two terms that have traditionally been seen as opposites that the power and meaning of this model resides. When servant and leader are brought together as a whole, we are forced to rethink our assumptions about the purview of each of these roles, as well as their status. At the same time, while 'servant leadership' holds both service and leading in a cohesive whole, Greenleaf highlights the primacy of service in the dynamic relationship between actions traditionally thought of as leading, and those seen as serving. Peter Vaill's foreword to *The Power of Servant Leadership* describes it well when he explains 'I think Greenleaf is saying that leadership is a special case of service; he is not saying that service is a special case of leadership.'[7]

The primacy of service, and the goal of the leader to be of service to others, distinctly sets servant leadership apart from James MacGregor Burns' transformational leadership. While both models include a focus on the personal characteristics of the leader, engagement of followers in creating a vision, and nurturing the leadership potential in others, the transformational leader achieves this largely through the mechanism of inspiring, goal-setting and role-modeling – a very different role than serving. Certainly, servant leadership can be understood as a kind of transformational leadership, and has some shared outcomes with other types of transformational approaches. Both mechanisms of leadership may create change in people, in organizations, and in values; however, the motivation behind and focus of each is distinct. A transformational leader aims to leverage followers' growth to optimize performance, while the servant leader, guided by altruism and humility, makes follower growth itself her or his main concern.[8]

In this frame, we can see servant leadership as inherently anti-hierarchical, both in execution and in philosophy. There is no designation of specific duties, powers, or prestige that belong to the leader, rather than the servant. The servant leader does not receive or seek to receive adulation, glory or credit for success, even as a means to inspire others. Rather, the servant leader seeks a position of leadership only insofar as that position offers the most effective vantage point from which to support and nurture others. In business leadership, this reorganization or rejection of hierarchy is sometimes articulated as an inverted pyramid, whereby customers, and the front-line staff who interact with them, become positioned at the 'top' of the organizational structure, and management and policy-makers are positioned at the bottom. Ken Blanchard articulates the impact of servant leadership in business in these terms:

> When you turn a pyramid upside down philosophically, who works for whom when it comes to implementation? You work for your people . . . [t]he difference is between who is responsible and who is responsive. With the traditional pyramid, the boss is always responsible, and the staff are supposed to be responsive to the boss. When you turn the pyramid upside down those roles get reversed. Your people become responsible and the job of management is to be responsive to their people . . . [the manager's] job is to help them win.[9]

Choosing servant leadership

The 'conscious choice' described by Greenleaf is, therefore, a choice to take a position of leadership with the explicit aim of empowering followers to succeed. The desire to take on responsibility for the success of the group is what, in one sense, distinguishes servant leadership from other forms of service. While Dr. Martin Luther King Jr. famously opined 'Everybody can be great, because everybody can serve,'[10] not everyone who serves takes on a leadership role. Leadership for servant leaders consists of accepting an obligation to do everything in one's power to ensure the good of followers. To reference back to the inspirational character from Hesse's *Journey to the East*, the great spiritual leader of the order Leo chooses to accompany the part of travelers in the role of a servant. In this role, Leo tends to the travelers' needs, provides encouragement and entertainment, and makes sure they are able to continue; though by all rights, Leo could have easily – and perhaps effectively – taken the role of a guide or formal leader, simply telling the party where they needed to go and how. This example illustrates how the conscious choice to take on the role of servant leader is both a personal and a strategic decision. Servant leadership posits that authority, hierarchy and coercive power – leading by force and position – may get things done in the short term, but it is collaboration, nurturing, caring and investing in the growth of others – leading through service – that ultimately results in better long-term outcomes for individuals, institutions and society alike.

Outcomes for followers

The long-term outcomes of servant leadership are the subject of Greenleaf's 'best test.' He describes the goal of this leadership approach as growth, well-being, and a perpetuation of leadership. In later writings, Greenleaf explained 'I believe that caring for persons, the more able and the less able serving each other, is what makes a good society.'[11] Again, the complication of the leader–follower relationship, and a disruption of hierarchy, is key here; servant leadership is not simply the leader serving the follower indefinitely, but the creation of a reciprocal relationship, in which parties on both sides of the dynamic – whether it be leader–follower, privileged – oppressed, or any other traditional dyad with a distinct power differential – fully participate in service, and so grow together toward a shared vision in which all can feel equal ownership and satisfaction.

This value of mutuality also supports the servant leadership approach's social justice goals – in the way that 'a rising tide lifts all boats,' the more caring and inclusive leaders and their resulting institutions become, the better off will be all of those who are affected by these leaders and institutions, including the traditionally disenfranchised or disempowered. If servant leadership is truly integrated into the culture of a group or institution, there can be no tolerance for the idea of winners and losers, those who benefit and those who are left out. The enterprise of any institution, in this model, is only successful insofar as all of those involved with the enterprise are considered essential to, and able to benefit from, the results. To put it another way, there is no question of whether the ends justify the means in servant leadership; in Greenleaf's words, 'means determine ends.'[12]

At some level, then, the means and ends of servant leadership are one and the same: to create a process by which all of those involved grow and benefit, and work together toward a shared vision. From this follows Greenleaf's rule that all effective motivation in servant leadership is achieved through persuasion. The effective servant leader engages followers in creation of a shared mission and vision, and creates an environment in which all are motivated to work toward this mission because they have a personal, authentic commitment both to the mission and vision itself, and also to their personal well-being. As Greenleaf describes it, when workers are taken care of, nurtured, and actively engaged by their workplace, they develop a sense of purpose and vocation – their motivation to help the company succeed, therefore, rests largely in their desire to continue being able to work there and be a part of the institution. The servant leader can, therefore, hold her or his followers accountable to high standards and excellence through a shared commitment to purpose and sense of mutual accountability, rather than through coercion or fear.

The notion of motivation in the servant leadership model goes beyond a desire of followers for perks, or a pleasant workplace, or professional development opportunities, grounded as it is in the ethic of service, rather than self-interest. Greenleaf believes that internal motivation and sense of calling, which he compares to the Buddhist concept of right livelihood in the noble Eightfold Path,[13] is produced when the business itself becomes 'a serving institution – serving both producers [workers] and users [consumers]' through providing meaningful work and services or goods to these constituencies, respectively.[14] Within the institution, this is described as a 'people-building' versus 'people-using' approach.[15] A people-building institution may provide perks and incentives, but this is as an added dimension of care for its people, not as an ameliorative measure to keep people working in an unfulfilling or transactional people-using environment. This idea of the business as a servant institution has connections to current trends in both employee wellness and diversity initiatives and also, more deeply, in companies developing mission statements, decentralized decision-making structures, and social responsibility initiatives.

Servant leaders as shapers of culture

Servant leadership posits that as leaders are able to cultivate and practice servant behaviors consistently and intentionally, they will inspire and empower others to do the same. If servant leaders are successful, both they and their followers will make ethical choices, perpetuating a culture of service, care and responsibility throughout their organizations. To put it in terms of reference to another model described in this book, followership, effective servant leaders create good followers, or in some articulations of followership dynamics, effective partners.

One way to visualize the mechanism by which servant leadership operates to create this culture is described by Kathleen Patterson in terms of a progression through seven virtuous constructs. In Patterson's model, these virtues are characteristics of the servant leader, which are operationalized through the process of servant leadership. The root of this process is *agapao* love – the virtue through which leaders see their followers as whole, valuable people, and prioritize their needs. From this stems a sense of humility – valuing others rather than over-valuing the self – and altruism, or concern for the good of others. From this foundation, servant leaders are able to have faith in the future of people and organizations, which forms the basis for a guiding vision. Servant leaders also demonstrate trust in the abilities and potential of their followers, and earn reciprocal trust by being transparent and behaving with integrity in all situations. All of these beliefs and resulting behaviors form the basis for true empowerment of followers, and a dedication to serving those followers, which sets the culture of service within effective servant leaders' organizations.

Critiques of servant leadership

Theoretical concern: Varying understandings of servant leadership

Robert Greenleaf was a prolific writer, addressing, re-addressing, and developing a variety of themes and applications of servant leadership throughout his essays and lectures. However, he never created a definitive list, model, or typology of servant leadership. In the decades since his death, many scholars have worked to distill his ideas to lists or themes.

Larry Spears compiled a list of 'Ten Characteristics of the Servant-Leader,' drawn from Greenleaf's writings. His list includes: listening, empathy, healing and a desire for wholeness, awareness of both self and others, reliance on persuasion rather than authority, conceptualization and ability to dream, foresight, stewardship, commitment to the growth of people, and focus on building community.[16] Looking at this list in terms of themes, one finds items related to interpersonal interactions, including a desire to learn from followers (listening), a capacity to understand and appreciate followers as people (empathy), and an intense compassion (healing and desire for wholeness). One also sees a set of characteristics that are about how the servant leader interacts with the environment. The servant leader commits to an honest assessment of reality, including thoughtful consideration of ethics and a willingness to own up to difficult or uncomfortable situations (awareness). She or he also eschews commanding in favor of consensus-building (persuasion), cultivates an ability to think long term and develop a vision (conceptualization), and possesses an ability to intuitively predict likely outcomes in various situations (foresight). Finally, the list includes a set of characteristics that define how the servant leader interacts with the institution in which she or he works, with a focus on sustainability and social good (stewardship), developing the potential of followers rather than simply maximizing outputs (commitment to the growth of people), and creating an ethos of care and interdependence among followers (building community).

Anne Fraker focuses more specifically on Greenleaf's discussions of the role of servant leadership in business ethics, communicated through his management trainings. She points out that Greenleaf seldom used the term 'ethics,' believing that ethical behavior was a result of individual courage, rather than a formal code or belief system. However, Fraker points out that Greenleaf does distill some themes in his work that are connected to ethical behavior and ethically sound institutions. Ethical business practices result from leaders with a commitment to service, including strength to make right choices, openness to knowledge, ability to understand past and present circumstances well enough to anticipate future issues (foresight), ability to sustain enthusiasm and inspiration (*entheos*), sense of purpose and an ability to laugh.[17]

More recently, social science research by Liden et al focused on seven specific servant leader behaviors that contribute demonstrably to positive outcomes for followers, such as increased engagement, increased organizational commitment, and increased organizational and community citizenship behaviors. These servant leader behaviors include: conceptual skills, emotional healing, putting followers first, helping followers grow and succeed, behaving ethically, empowerment of followers, and creating value for the community.[18]

These three examples illustrate one of the challenges of this model, which is the fact that, as Van Dierendonck explains in his extensive 2010 review of servant leadership literature, 'However, despite its introduction four decades ago and empirical studies that started more than 10 years ago, there is still no consensus about a definition and theoretical framework of servant leadership.'[19] Without a clear, agreed upon structure to understand this model, it becomes both difficult to study and also easy to dismiss as simply a restatement of transformational leadership theory with religious overtones. Those who would try to build a coherent, comprehensive model of servant leadership based on Greenleaf's writings will find the task daunting.

G. James Lemoine Jr's 2015 prize-winning dissertation work on servant leadership acknowledges this challenge, and addresses this lack of a consistent conceptual model through suggesting an updated definition of servant leadership:

> [As] influential behaviors, manifested humbly and ethically within relationships, oriented towards follower development, empowerment, and continuous and meaningful improvement for all stakeholders (including but not limited to those being led, communities, customers, and the leader, team, and organization themselves).[20]

This gives a useful, and specific framework that may well help focus both understanding and social science research going forward.

Still, the scope of the concept itself is far-reaching, and touches on personal and spiritual development, organizational culture, business structures and more. This has led, and will likely continue to lead, to a huge number of variations in scope and interpretation among those who claim to all be practicing or defining servant leadership.

Practical concern number one: Effectiveness

Beyond the limitations of the model's nonlinear historical development and broad scope, there are reasonable concerns about its effectiveness and practicality. Despite a growing body of research that demonstrates effective positive outcomes, common criticism of servant leadership is that it is ineffectual, or weak, and that servant leaders will not be able to successfully navigate situations with followers that require structure and direction. The model has some answers to this critique, as effective servant leaders are required to possess foresight as well as an ability to direct followers through persuasion (rather than coercion). However, this can be a delicate balancing act in practice between accountability and empowerment, and the method of leadership through persuasion can, in some cases, begin to either genuinely become, or at least begin to feel to followers like, manipulation. At the point where the servant leader is perceived as manipulative, she or he loses critical bonds of trust, and perceptions of authenticity, undermining the ability to lead effectively.

Also of concern is the conflict that can arise when individuals try to practice servant leadership within an institutional context that is grounded in hierarchical models of power. While the idea of servant leadership focuses on creating success for followers, an individual who practices it in an environment where it is not accepted or valued may be setting both her or himself, and the followers who rely on that leader's support, up for failure. Similarly, some express concern that the leader in the role of servant may create not empowerment, but dependency among followers. It is of note here that the original inspiration for Greenleaf's servant leader, the character of Leo in Hesse's *Journey to the East*, at some point abandoned his party, who consequently were not able to complete their journey successfully without him.

Practical concern number two: Time

One other significant challenge of this model, acknowledged by Greenleaf himself, is the time required to implement it successfully. Particularly in institutional or social contexts that have been dominated by command and control leadership models, the transformation of both followers as individuals and also institutional structures must be a long-term process. In a situation where an institution or group must respond to an immediate crisis or opportunity, the time required to build bonds of trust or actively create relationships and solicit input may simply not be feasible. In cases such as these, the utility of servant leadership is limited.

Practical concern number three: The role of the individual

While we can speak about building servant institutions and shifting cultural values, the mechanism for these changes rests mainly on building specific kinds of relationships between individuals over time. Even Peter Drucker, who worked closely with Robert Greenleaf over many years, struggled with the focus of servant leadership on long-term personal transformation rather than on immediate effective action. As Drucker describes it, 'Bob [Greenleaf] was always out to change the individual, to make him or her into a different person. I was interested in making people *do* the right things, in their actions and behavior.'[21] One ethical dilemma that might arise from this situation is how to address a situation in which a follower has behaved contrary to institutional policy or norms, or has put self-interest above institutional or societal goals. If one believes that the development of the follower as an individual is the responsibility of the servant leader, it might be considered best for the leader to spend time and energy trying to educate or persuade the follower to behave differently, or to develop a different value system. However, it may be more beneficial for the good of the institution, the goal, or even the other followers for the leader to take corrective action or administer consequences, even if that corrective action does not contribute to the growth and development of the individual who violated the policy or norm. In this case and others, in working toward the ideal to serve all followers well, the servant leader may well find her or himself in conflict between competing interests and needs.

Practical concern number four: Spoilers

A final consideration when looking to implement a servant leadership approach is the danger of what in peace negotiations are called 'spoilers' – those who have a personal interest in disrupting or preventing a successful outcome. Servant leadership rests on an assumption that all followers are valuable people, capable of contributing to the common good. There is little clear guidance in the servant leadership model for how to deal with those who might be actively working to undermine the goals of the institution, sabotage the outcome, or hurt fellow followers. A dramatic example of this phenomenon is the 1995 assassination of Israeli Prime Minister Yitzhak Rabin by a militant Israeli nationalist who opposed peace negotiations with the Palestinians. Less significant examples happen every day in organizations, such as when a manager who is asked to implement a new policy makes her or his disdain of the policy known to subordinates, or implements it haphazardly with the goal of having it deemed a failure and repealed. Servant leadership rests on the consent and active engagement of followers, and so is effective only to the degree of the desire and willingness of followers to participate in the process, to behave ethically, and to allow themselves to be served.

Five component analysis and ethical implications of servant leadership

With all of that in mind, we will now turn our analysis, as in previous chapters, to the application of the Five Components Model to servant leadership.

Years ago, I was invited to lead a workshop on supervision strategies at a statewide conference for nonprofits. We talked mostly about structures and strategies – how to monitor and manage staff and volunteers, how to communicate expectations and give effective feedback, how to balance the time required to supervise people effectively with the time needed to get one's own work done. During the Q&A portion of the session, one of the attendees brought up a situation in which she was struggling to motivate an employee to improve her performance. In the course of addressing her question, I suggested creating regular times to meet with the employee to get updates on her work and offer feedback, and included the specific suggestion that some of that weekly meeting be dedicated to learning more about the employee's goals, interests and life outside of the office in order to establish a more supportive relationship. The workshop participant paused in taking notes, seeming to have a moment of insight.

Figure 13.2 The Five Components of Leadership Model applied to servant leadership

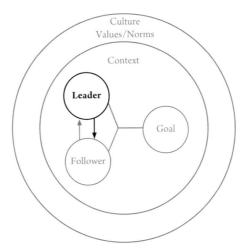

'Right!' she exclaimed. 'I usually jump right into talking about tasks and keep the meeting focused on her performance. But you're saying I have to spend that time on small talk to make her feel like I care about her as a person.'

I thought about this for a moment, and then responded: 'Well, the key is that you actually *do* have to care about her as a person.' This exchange captures the essence of what sets servant leadership apart from other types of leadership, namely the authentic focus on the follower as the object of primary concern. Therefore, all of the components of the Five Components Model can be understood in servant leadership primarily in the context of how they affect the follower. This is represented in Figure 13.2 by the emphasis placed on the leader and the downward arrow pointing towards the follower.

While the leader and follower are represented as separate on the Five Components diagram, it is most appropriate in servant leadership to view them as two parts of the same whole, since the leader–follower relationship is the crux of servant leadership. In the context of servant leadership, the arrows which represent the interaction between leader and follower on the Five Components Model take on a deep, personal dimension, representing not only cooperation and exchange, but an ongoing relationship of mutuality, shared power and genuine concern. The two-way arrow also represents the goal in servant leadership to have those served become servants themselves. Through relationship with the servant leader, followers are both served and given opportunities to serve. This relationship has the power to impact institutions on a large scale, but it is enacted through an ongoing series of individual leader–follower interactions.

In understanding how the goal functions in servant leadership, one can return to Greenleaf's assertion that means determine ends. In this formulation of servant leadership, goal accomplishment is an organic result of the practice of servant leadership, because the leader uses the goal as a mechanism through which to facilitate the growth of followers. This runs counter to many common assumptions about the relationship between leadership and goals, but it is consistent with Greenleaf's assertion that servant leaders begin with an impulse to serve, and then make a conscious choice to lead as a means of serving. To use another example from Greenleaf's writing, 'the work exists for the person as much as the person exists for the work.'[22] Put another way, 'the business exists as much to provide meaningful work to the person as it exists to provide a product or service to the customer.' In practice, then, goal setting in servant-led organizations functions always as a collaborative process, whereby the leader actively listens to the needs of followers, and then sets goals based on her or his understanding of these needs. In practice, this could take the form of the servant leader facilitating a visioning process, and then working actively to support followers in reaching it. This is in contrast to the theory of adaptive leadership, introduced in Chapter 16, where the goal is to give the work back to the people.

One question we may ask here is whether there might sometimes be worthwhile, noble, important goals that do not inherently result in the growth of followers? Servant leadership would posit that a successful servant leader can use almost any goal as a means to facilitate the growth of those being served, as long as that goal is achieved through a process that is caring and nurturing to all followers. This flexibility has perhaps contributed to the popularity of servant leadership among business managers, who see the potential in this leadership practice to create mutually beneficial outcomes for workers and the organization to which those workers contribute. This aspect of mutually beneficial outcome is at the core of Greenleaf's vision of servant institutions, whereby the practice of servant leadership within the institution implements a mandate of ethical, caring behavior toward employees and stakeholders at all levels.

Because servant leadership deals so much in abstracts, values, principles and relationships, context has a different kind of importance here than in some other modes of leadership. In servant leadership, it is the responsibility of the leader to understand and navigate the elements of the environment that may impact the follower. The ability of the leader to skillfully navigate the environmental context, anticipating and navigating challenges in order to support followers in reaching the goal is articulated in servant leadership terms as 'foresight.'

Servant leaders act upon, rather than within, the cultural circle in this model. If we accept Greenleaf's formulation that the ultimate goal of servant leadership is to create more servant leaders, it is clear that in this dynamic the leader doesn't respond to the current values and norms of the culture, but instead works actively to create a culture of service and community through promotion and practice of servant leadership. Greenleaf's vision of a world of 'servant institutions' is an example of what this leader-driven cultural change might look like. The case study of the women's peace movement in Liberia, which follows, is another good example of the power of the servant leader to actively shape or re-shape the cultural context in which leadership takes place.

CASE STUDY

Leymah Gbowee and the Liberian women's peace movement

Robert Greenleaf describes his desire for a 'more serving society . . . the climate that favors service, and supports servants,' and believes 'the basics [of solving social problems] are the incremental thrusts of individuals who have the ability to serve and lead.'[23] If we believe Greenleaf's vision, a more serving society – one comprised of both servant leaders and servant institutions – has ethical behavior embedded in its structures. If one's primary concern is for the well-being of people, then the choices that flow from that concern will necessarily be ethical choices, within the limitations of the practical concerns noted above. Accepting that this serving society is a worthwhile goal, how on a practical level can servant leadership most effectively be utilized to work toward a more service-oriented, and so more ethical, society? This is the question that we take up through the lens of the women's peace movement of Liberia and the ongoing legacy of its leader, Leymah Gbowee.

Historical context: Gbowee as servant leader

In 2011, Liberian peace activist Leymah Roberta Gbowee was awarded a Nobel Peace Prize, along with Africa's first democratically elected female president Ellen Johnson Sirleaf, and Yemeni human rights advocate Tawakkul Karman. The prize that year highlighted the contribution of women around the world to the struggle for peace, stability, and gender equality. Of the 2011 awardees, Gbowee was the only one of the three with no formal political association or position.

Gbowee, a trained social worker who addressed trauma recovery in ex-child soldiers, rose to international prominence as the head of Women of Liberia Mass Action for Peace. This non-violent movement brought Muslim and Christian women together to pressure Liberian leaders to bring an end to their 14-year civil war through the signing of a peace agreement in 2003. In her Nobel lecture, articulated almost entirely in terms of collective work and

CASE STUDY *(continued)*

accomplishments, Gbowee describes how the women of Liberia 'used our pains, broken bodies and scarred emotions to confront the injustices and terror of our nation.'[24]

Gbowee describes the moment that catalyzed her movement-building work in a 2012 TED Talk:

> Several years ago, there was one African girl. This girl had a son who wished for a piece of doughnut because he was extremely hungry. Angry, frustrated, really upset about the state of her society and the state of her children, this young girl started a movement, a movement of ordinary women banding together to build peace.[25]

This story clearly demonstrates that the desire for leadership grew for Gbowee from a desire to serve, a passion to fulfill a need for her child, and so for the children of others as well. In the pursuit of a peace agreement, Gbowee quite literally put her life and her body on the line in her work: leading groups of women in daily protests to pressure political leaders in the administration of dictator Charles Taylor into negotiations, organizing a sex strike among wives to pressure their husbands to get rebel leaders from the LURD opposition group to the table with Taylor to broker a cease-fire, and threatening to publicly disrobe in order to shame both of the warring parties back into participation during stalled peace talks. The act of engaging her entire self – including her physical body – into advocacy for the women and children of Liberia demonstrates the depth of her commitment to her followers, her community, and their shared goal of peace. Her ability to navigate complex political and social dynamics in service of long-range objectives (foresight), build effective coalitions based on deep relationship (empathy and healing), leverage cultural norms in service to her cause (awareness and conceptualization), and speak boldly and compellingly to both her peers and to global leaders (persuasion) demonstrate the power of her leadership. The combination of these factors defines Gbowee as a servant leader.

Legacy and current challenges

After her Nobel Peace Prize, Gbowee has gone on to prominence as a speaker, author, member of international advisory groups and founder of the Gbowee Peace Foundation. While she has continued to work in a servant leadership role, she has also addressed some of the inherent challenges of this mode of leadership. In a 2010 interview for the *United Nations Africa Renewal* magazine, she describes 'serious competition amongst women' in the post-war Liberia, wherein 'the collective way we embraced peace building is disintegrating because everyone is seeing herself as the next big thing.'[26] Adding to the complexity, Mariam Persson writing in 2012, describes the persistence of 'chains of command and rebel structures of war, which officially have been demobilized, at the same time within the informal sphere, for different reasons [such as a need for security], are maintained and mobilized.'[27] In other words, the security situation in Liberia is still uncertain, and as a result, some of the wartime networks of power have been maintained and are still at

CASE STUDY *(continued)*

play in the country's politics. And while the Liberian civil war has ended, the country still struggles with the fallout of decades of exploitation, militarization and ethnic tension, and experiences relatively high levels of insecurity and violence, including violence toward women. While the scope and power of Gbowee and her fellow Liberian women's accomplishments should not be downplayed, the continuing struggle to build sustainable, compassionate, service-oriented political and cultural structures in Liberia offers an opportunity to push the boundaries of the servant leadership framework in order to bring to light new aspects of its ethical implications.

It is worth noting as we explore this case that servant leadership developed from, and is most often applied to, organizations, not nations. However, while the socio-political arena on a national level is undoubtedly more complex than even the largest multinational organizations or corporations, the differentiation between leadership aimed at consolidation of wealth and power versus leadership aimed at securing the well-being and empowerment of all followers is salient in both contexts.[28] There is a clear contrast between unethical leadership wherein people are seen as resources to be used in pursuit of profit and power, as exemplified by the dictatorship of Charles Taylor in Liberia, and ethical servant leadership, wherein people are seen as potential leaders to be nurtured and developed for the common good, as exemplified by Leymah Gbowee's leadership of Women of Liberia Mass Action for Peace.

That being the case, the legacy of Gbowee's work begs two questions. How can servant leaders balance the goal to develop and empower their followers with the goal of maintaining a spirit of service and collective benefit in their sphere of work? And, can servant leadership by an individual or subgroup within a larger context effectively contribute to positive outcomes and ethical behavior on a large scale? In both of these questions, conclusions drawn from the example of the Liberian peace movement can be applied to organizational and community contexts as well.

We'll begin with the second question, whether servant leadership at the individual or small group level can effectively influence larger culture. Greenleaf clearly believes so, and makes the point throughout his writing that institutions, and societies, are made up of individuals and so can be pushed toward change primarily – maybe only – through changes in the hearts and minds of individuals. This is why the end goal of servant leadership is to move followers into the role of servant leaders themselves, and why servant leaders must be constantly, consciously engaged in developing relationships with followers and actively building a service-oriented culture. In an undated writing, 'Ethics of Business,' Greenleaf states, 'Even if the tradition of high ethical practice is long established in a business, unless individuals continue to inject new life into it and adapt it to new conditions, it is likely to deteriorate.'[29] To return to the five component analysis, the leader, and the dyad of the leader and follower in relationship, must constantly be active in shaping and reshaping the environment and context. Servant leadership posits that the norms, codes and values of an organization, or a society, are not static, but responsive to the influence of the environment as well as to the actions and beliefs of the individuals within that organization or society.

CASE STUDY *(continued)*

Without active work to develop a culture of service, it is not surprising that the dynamics of an organization or culture tend to return to the default or previous state. In the case of Liberia, this is a particularly difficult problem. Writing about Ellen Johnson Sirleaf's 2005 rise to the Liberian presidency, journalist and Liberian native Helene Cooper explains in the lead up to the 2003 Accra peace talks, 'Liberia was dubbed one of the world's worst places,'[30] with literally hundreds of civilian casualties piling up each week from the civil war. The 14-year civil war 'left a quarter of a million dead, displaced five times that number and saw a generation of children drugged and turned into killers themselves. An estimated 70% of women were raped.'[31] Immediately after the signing of the peace agreement and the departure of Charles Taylor, Cooper describes the jockeying for position and influence that engulfed the remaining political players as they came to terms with the 'post-apocalyptic' humanitarian and political landscape of the recovering nation. In the wake of war came a political culture rife with corruption, bribery and grudges, along with a gutted economy and a torn social fabric. It is in this context that, although war formally ended in 2003, there has been a tendency for power structures and loyalties to default to those networks of influence established during the war. This tendency to recreate wartime networks of power comes often out of necessity as citizens seek protection, resources and a means of economic livelihood that are not being provided by the current government leadership at the community level.[32]

During the war, the culture of greed and violence was confronted through a powerful demonstration of servant leadership by the women of Liberia. It would stand to reason that a culture of service should again be effective in confronting ongoing challenges. After all, the election of the country's first female head of state in 2005 was largely the result of a campaign by now President Sirleaf to engage women and civilians throughout the country in dialogue about the future and how to rebuild the nation, a listening and follower-centered approach clearly based in a servant leadership framework. However, in practice, the ability of individual servant leaders to perpetuate a culture shift is limited, in this case by several factors, the most important of which may be the inner circle of the context in the Five Components Model. Even President Sirleaf, a standard bearer for women's rights and peace, is a deeply complicated figure who openly acknowledges political and moral compromises that she has made and continues to make in order to try to maintain peace and create economic and political stability. In her role as a political veteran and global negotiator 'steeped in the politics of African power,'[33] Sirleaf has been able to secure resources that are desperately needed by her people, but often in ways that are objectively unethical, such as bribery. In this sense, Liberian politics in the post-war, female-led world has a decidedly utilitarian ethical bent that sits uncomfortably beside the moral, spiritual doctrine of relationship, empathy and individual authenticity that forms the foundation of ethics in servant leadership.

In this situation, we see what is perhaps one of the most difficult aspects of Greenleaf's model – the characterization of the context as a landscape that the leader navigates with and on behalf of the followers. In this formulation, the context seems to be posited as ethically

CASE STUDY *(continued)*

neutral; it is a space that a servant leader can engage, wherein the individual who is leading works to eliminate obstacles for followers, but always through means that are consistent with her or his personal ethical code. A political leader, such as President Sirleaf, then, breaks from servant leadership when she chooses to give money to a corrupt official in order to secure a political advantage which she believes will be good for the country, or makes a policy that gives primacy to political feasibility rather than protection of marginalized followers. This indicates that there is a limit to the scale on which servant leadership can effectively be practiced within an environment that has serious material and security limitations.

One way to understand this limitation is to return to the basis of servant leadership as defined by Greenleaf, which is that the servant leader is servant *first*, and leader only by virtue of a desire to serve. In an environmental context larger than an organization – particularly one where scarcity or insecurity exists – leaders are often compelled to act in ways that privilege the leader identity over the servant identity, because these leaders cannot effectively be in direct relationship with followers in the dynamic, ongoing way that true servant leadership requires.

Accepting this challenge, what is the role of servant leadership in shaping ethical cultures within challenging environmental contexts? To engage this question, we shift focus from President Sirleaf's political leadership to Leymah Gbowee's community-based leadership. If it is not practically effective to practice servant leadership in a political context that is not already service-oriented, it stands to reason that the ultimate goal of servant leadership is to work long term to create more and better servant leaders within this context. If servant leadership can become widespread, the shift in the outer circle (values) of the Five Components Model will be able to overcome obstacles to ethical behavior within the inner circle (context) that are otherwise an impediment to individuals acting ethically in deep, consistent ways on an individual basis. This is a dynamic process, but servant leadership posits that it is possible to strengthen the power of the leader–follower influence to the point where it shapes the culture in which the leaders and followers operate.

Currently in Liberia, in Gbowee's view, younger women who were not actively engaged in the peace movement, and mentored by servant leaders, seem to be recreating a hierarchical, individualistic leadership structure, leading to the disintegration of the movement that had been based in a culture of service. So in the case of current female political leadership in Liberia, the restrictions of the context and cultural values are defining the leader–follower relationship, and not the other way around. This returns us to the question first posed: How can leaders balance the goal to develop and empower their followers with the goal of maintaining a spirit of service and collective benefit in their sphere of work? One answer, then, is to deal with the limits of the current context through a utilitarian perspective shaped by a servant leadership ethos, while working to shift the culture through active cultivation of servant leadership.

Key to this in practice is the process of mentoring and working with emerging leaders, so that the coming generation of political, community, and institutional leadership is immersed

CASE STUDY *(continued)*

in a servant leadership culture. Those who have been nurtured as servant leaders, and built the corresponding individual moral compass and ethical commitment, will then work within their spheres of influence to move groups and institutions toward a more service-oriented culture. This model is already at work through the efforts of Gbowee to nurture young women as leaders in West Africa.

At her TED Talk in 2012, Gbowee expressed the goal of her work as engaging others to help girls fulfill their dreams and potential. In her own words:

> Will you journey with me to help that girl, be it an African girl or an American girl or a Japanese girl, fulfill her wish, fulfill her dream, achieve that dream? Because all of these great innovators and inventors . . . are also sitting in tiny corners in different parts of the world, and all they're asking us to do is create that space to unlock the intelligence, unlock the passion, unlock all of the great things that they hold within themselves. Let's journey together.[34]

In the interview that follows, Gbowee frames her work in terms of generational change, saying she wants to look back in 20 years and see another female African leader carrying on the work she has begun. She also alludes to the power of servant leadership to shape the political sphere in a story describing working with a group of young women in Liberia to engage them in a local election. The girls asked candidates how they planned to help young women in the community – in other words, how they planned to be a servant leader, supporting the most vulnerable and marginalized. The candidate who did not engage the girls positively was voted out of office as a result of their efforts.

While this is just a single example in one village, the long-term goal is clearly to reshape the political sphere such that an attitude of servant leadership, and a dedication to ethical leadership that is based in an ethos of care for followers, become the expected norm. It is the same long-term goal that Robert K. Greenleaf worked toward when he shifted his focus to teaching, and made a point to focus much of his personal work on college campuses in his effort to transform American culture and leadership to a more service-focused orientation.

Five component analysis of Leymah Gbowee and the Liberian women's peace movement

Reviewing the case in terms of the Five Components Model shows us how each element of servant leadership has been enacted in the Liberian women's peace movement.

The leader–follower dyad in this example has Gbowee as the leader acting in dialogue and cooperation with followers to create change. Gbowee came to her position as a leader through engaging fellow women in conversation about what they wanted and needed, and then in organizing them through collective action to achieve those shared goals. The relationship between leader and follower in this example is also dynamic, since Gbowee as a servant leader works to empower those around her to step up into a leadership role themselves.

CASE STUDY (continued)

Figure 13.3 Five Components of Leadership Model applied to Leymah Gbowee and the Liberian Women's Peace Movement case study

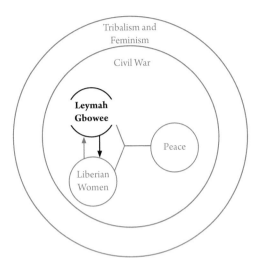

The goal, in this case, is the establishment of a peaceful society wherein all the needs of citizens are met through just, cooperative, non-coercive processes. In keeping with the servant leadership model of 'the means are the ends,' the goal in this case, broadly stated, is to free the country from the violent grip of dictatorship and civil war and establish a functional civil society. The empowerment of the people of Liberia to participate in collaborative, non-violent, organized political and social engagement is the means by which this end is accomplished. Simply stated, empowering followers to reach the goal is synonymous with the accomplishment of the goal.

The constantly changing context of war and peace, security and insecurity, prosperity and poverty, forms the backdrop of this case. In this context, one is struck by the impressive ability of Gbowee and others in the peace movement to change tactics – from prayers to marches, from marches to sex strikes, from public campaigns to quiet political negotiations, and more – as the situation evolved. Moreover, the servant leader quality of foresight is clearly at play in Gbowee's ability to intuitively understand this shifting context and to apply effective pressure at the exact right points to, for example, move the peace talks forward, or promote disarmament. The ability of Gbowee to step up and successfully direct the leader–follower actions within this changing context is the hallmark of an effective servant leader.

Gbowee based her actions as a leader during the war clearly on a deep understanding of the culture values, and norms of Liberian society. During the civil war in Liberia, women could not, and did not, want to engage in conflict on the male-dominated military or political stage. Instead, Gbowee's work as a leader drew on the culturally relevant role of women as mothers, wives and caretakers, and leveraged the power of those roles and the associated social values in order to achieve the goal of empowering women and ending the

CASE STUDY *(continued)*

war. What could not be achieved by political power and brute force, the women's movement successfully achieved through wielding the power of cultural norms to create hope, empathy, or even shame among political and military forces. For example, Gbowee organized daily marches of women to pressure Charles Taylor to engage in peace talks. Rather than mount an intimidating or armed campaign, which could have easily drawn a violent repressive response, women attended these protests dressed all in white, barefoot and singing.

The male military and political leaders were compelled by cultural values and norms to acknowledge and engage with the women when they presented themselves in this manner. Beyond the ending of the war, the work of Gbowee to mentor and empower young women in and beyond Liberia continues to draw on the cultural values and norms in which these followers are embedded – promoting cooperation, connection, respect and a sense of family. At the same time, she simultaneously actively works to build the power of service-oriented and ethical norms among followers to influence political and social structures toward justice and inclusion.

Summary and concluding remarks

We began this chapter by asking: 'How can leaders best serve their followers and organizations?' The answer, according to servant leadership, is at the same time simple and significant: by taking care of them and helping create an environment in which those followers can grow into leaders. A better world will emerge when there is a shift in culture, away from exploitation of followers and valuing of profits, and toward a nurturing environment that values people. This culture shift, whether in a corporation or a country, must involve a concerted effort by current servant leaders to strengthen the power of the leader–follower dyads in enough structures and institutions so that there can be a concerted effort across sectors to overcome challenges in the environmental context and reshape cultural norms. This is a lofty goal, but we have seen in both academic literature and the case study that there are practical ways to work toward this long-term vision. Leaders must develop their ability to listen, empathize, and value their followers, respecting them not only as co-creators of success, but also as human beings with inherent worth.

As a matter of personal practice, practitioners might consider developing their own capacity as servant leaders through activities and education that build their skills in listening, dialog, consensus-building, facilitation, mentoring and teaching. Time invested in reflection about one's own values, and investment in spiritual and emotional development should also prove valuable in developing the skills required for servant leadership.

? DISCUSSION QUESTIONS

Which of the ethical models described in the first part of this book most closely align with the values of the servant leadership model?

Do you believe this type of leadership is realistic, and practical? Can a leader truly possess all of the traits and characteristics Greenleaf identifies?

Is there any situation you can think of in which acting as a servant leader might not be ethical?

Are there any situations in which a leader might reasonably, and ethically, prioritize accomplishing a goal over the development of followers?

In an unstable or unsafe situation, how is it possible to truly practice servant leadership?

Can politicians be servant leaders and be successful? Should we expect our politicians to truly be 'public servants'? If so, how would that look different than what we currently see?

The outcomes of servant leadership are largely holistic and long-term. How might a servant leader measure and judge success in their day-to-day work?

The very term 'servant leadership' can seem like a paradox or oxymoron. In what other ways does ethical leadership require leaders to challenge preconceived notions of 'leadership' as a phenomenon?

In what situations might a servant leadership model actually be a hindrance to achieving organizational goals? How could you resolve this as a leader?

How can leaders know when they have moved beyond 'persuasion' into 'manipulation'?

ADDITIONAL RESOURCES

K.M. Keith, *The Case for Servant Leadership*, Indianapolis: The Greenleaf Center, 2015.
This book serves as an accessible overview of the concept of servant leadership, including an appendix comparing it to other models of leadership as well as many examples.

R.C. Linden, A. Panaccio, J.D. Mueser, J. Hu, and S.J. Wyane, 'Servant leadership: Antecedents, processes, and outcomes,' in D.V. Day (ed.), *The Oxford Handbook of Leadership and Organizations*, Oxford: Oxford University Press, 2014, pp. 357–79.
This source presents an overview of the development of servant leadership as a research area, and a theoretical model.

The Greenleaf Center for Servant Leadership (www.greenleaf.org) offers workshops and resources, as well as an annual conference. The Center has also published a series of books with collections of essays, adapted chapters, and excerpted writings from a variety of contemporary thinkers.

Readers interested in further exploring the case study on the Liberian Peace movement should watch Abigail Disney's excellent 2008 documentary *Pray the Devil Back to Hell*.

NOTES

1 R. Greenleaf, 'The Servant as Leader: Essentials of Servant Leadership,' *Focus on Leadership: Servant Leadership for the 21st Century*, L.C. Spears and M. Lawrence (eds), New York: John Wiley, 2002, p. 21.

2 J. Riegel, 'Confucius,' in E.N. Zalta (ed.), *The Stanford Encyclopedia of Philosophy*, summer 2013 edn. Online, https://plato.stanford.edu/archives/sum2013/entries/confucius/ (accessed February 23, 2018).

3 K. Blanchard, 'Foreword,' Spears and Lawrence, op. cit. p. xi.

4 Camus quoted in Greenleaf, 2002, op. cit., p. 23.

5 Robert E. Greenleaf Center for Servant Leadership, 'What is servant leadership?' Online, https://www. greenleaf.org/what-is-servant-leadership/ (accessed February 23, 2018).

6 D. van Dierendonck, 'Servant leadership: A review and synthesis,' *Journal of Management*, vol. 37 no. 4, 2011, 1228–61, p. 1228. Originally published online, September 2, 2010.

7 P. Vaill, 'Foreword,' R. Greenleaf, *The Power of Servant Leadership*, L.C. Spears (ed.), San Francisco: Berrett-Koehler, 1998, p. xii.

8 K. Patterson, 'Servant leadership: A theoretical model,' unpublished manuscript, Servant Leadership Research Roundtable, Regent University School of Leadership Studies, August 2003. Online, https:// www.regent.edu/acad/global/publications/sl_proceedings/2003/patterson_servant_leadership.pdf (accessed February 23, 2018).

9 K. Blanchard, 'Servant-leadership revisited,' *Insights on Leadership: Service, Stewardship, Spirit, and Servant-Leadership*, L.C. Spears ed., New York: John Wiley, 1997, p. 25.

10 M.L. King, 'The drum major instinct,' *A Knock At Midnight: Inspiration from the Great Sermons of Reverend Martin Luther King, Jr.*, P. Holloran and C. Carson (eds), New York: Time Warner, 1998, p. 182.

11 Greenleaf, 2002, op. cit., p. 17.

12 R. Greenleaf, 'Coercion, Manipulation, and Persuasion,' in D. Frick and L. Spears (eds), *On Becoming a Servant Leader*, New York: John Wiley, 1996, p. 128.

13 R. Greenleaf, 'Business, ethics, and manipulation,' in D. Frick and L. Spears (eds), *On Becoming a Servant Leader*, New York: John Wiley, 1996, p. 118.

14 Greenleaf, ibid., 1996, p. 117.

15 R. Greenleaf, *Servant Leadership: A Journey into the Nature of Legitimate Power and Greatness*, 25th anniversary edn, Mahwah, NJ: Paulist Press, 2002, pp. 53–4.

16 L. Spears, 'Tracing the past, present, and future of servant leadership,' Spears and Lawrence, op. cit., pp. 4–8.

17 A.T. Fraker, 'Robert K. Greenleaf and business ethics: There is no code,' in L. Spears (ed.), *Reflections on Leadership: How Robert K. Greenleaf's Theory of Servant Leadership Influenced Today's Top Management Thinkers*, New York: John Wiley, 1995, pp. 42–5.

18 R.C. Liden, A. Panaccio, J.D. Meuser, J. Hu, and S.J. Wayne, 'Servant leadership: Antecedents, processes, and outcomes,' in D.V. Day (ed.), *The Oxford Handbook of Leadership and Organizations*, Oxford: Oxford University Press, 2014, pp. 357–79.

19 van Dierendonck, op. cit., p. 1229.

20 G.J. Lemoine, 'Closing the leadership circle: Building and testing a contingent theory of servant leadership,' Georgia Institute of Technology, unpublished dissertation, 2015, p. 3. Online, https://smartech. gatech.edu/handle/1853/53862 (accessed February 23, 2018).

21 P. Drucker, 'Forward,' in D. Frick and L.C. Spears (eds), *On Becoming a Servant Leader*, pp. xi–xii.

22 R. Greenleaf, *Servant Leadership*, Mahwah, NJ: Paulist Press, 1977, p. 142.

23 Greenleaf, 2002, op. cit., p. 5.

24 L. Gbowee, Nobel Lecture, *Nobelprize.org*, December 10, 2011. Online, https://www.nobelprize.org/ nobel_prizes/peace/laureates/2011/gbowee-lecture_en.html (accessed February 24, 2018).

25 L. Gbowee, 'Unlock the intelligence, passion, and greatness of girls,' TED2012. Online, https://www.ted. com/talks/leymah_gbowee_unlock_the_intelligence_passion_greatness_of_girls/transcript (accessed February 23, 2018).

26 M. Fleshman, 'Even with peace, Liberia's women struggle,' *AfricanRenewal*, April 2010. Online, http:// www.un.org/africarenewal/magazine/april-2010/even-peace-liberia%E2%80%99s-women-struggle (accessed February 24, 2018).

27 M. Persson, 'Demobilized or remobilized? Lingering rebel structures in post-war Liberia,' in M. Utas (ed.), *African Conflicts and Informal Power: Big Men and Networks*, London: Zed Books, 2012, p. 102.

28 K.M. Keith, *The Ethical Advantage of Servant Leadership: Guiding Principles for Organization Success*, Atlanta: Greenleaf Centre for Servant Leadership (Asia), 2013.

29 Fraker, op. cit., p. 37.

30 H. Cooper, *Madame President The Extraordinary Journey of Ellen Johnson Sirleaf*, New York: Simon & Schuster, 2017, p. 135.

31 A. Hirsch, 'Can President Ellen Johnson Sirleaf save Liberia,' *The Guardian*, July 22, 2017. Online, https://www.theguardian.com/global-development/2017/jul/23/can-president-ellen-johnson-sirleaf-save-liberia (accessed February 23, 2018).

32 Persson, op. cit.

33 Hirsch, op. cit.

34 Gbowee, op. cit.

14
Followership

Stanley J. Ward

How can followers partner with their leaders to do the right thing?

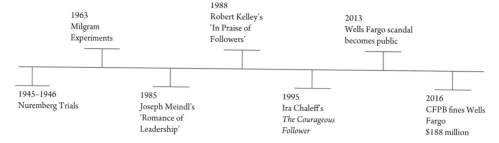

Figure 14.1 Timeline of major works on followership in relation to the chapter case study

For centuries, leaders have pondered what to do with followers, including how to relate to them. For example, in his advice to a young prince, Machiavelli infamously addressed whether it is better to be feared or loved by followers – while love is good, fear is more effective. The conclusion of those thoughts by Machiavelli and others often emphasized followers should be dominated or used as cannon-fodder.[1]

Though followers were certainly considered, the primary concern was still leader-centric. As leadership studies continued to develop, this leader-centric perspective was shared by the 'great man' leadership model expressed in the nineteenth century.[2] In the twentieth century, leadership and organization thinkers began to better appreciate the role – and power – of followers, which eventually led to 'followership' as a small but growing body of knowledge in the early twenty-first century. The Followership concept contributes to a more robust understanding of leadership by challenging leader-centric models, empowering the role of followers. Empowered followers are a critical component for ethical leadership, though a role that includes risks for leaders and followers alike. All of this adds up to a renewed appreciation for the vital role of followers in an organization.

In our chapter, we will start by considering the development of followership in the twentieth century and its ongoing growth. After discussing key concepts and important contributors for the model, we will then consider critiques against 'followership' as a term for leadership studies. Like the other chapters in this book, we will also consider how the Five Components of Leadership Model analyzes followership and then conduct a case study. The case will consider the recent Wells Fargo scandal, first made public by the *Los Angeles Times* in 2013, and what the scandal can teach us about followership.

As the chapter progresses, readers will see how followership serves as an ethics-oriented leadership model for a variety of reasons. Among these reasons, and perhaps most important among them, is how followers can *remind* leaders of the core ethical principles of an organization, and how followers can *refuse* to follow leaders who blatantly disregard ethical leadership practices. This capacity to both remind and refuse transforms followers from passive 'yes-people' to active partners in an organization's success.

History

Previous to 1950, Mary Parker Follett's work demonstrates an early appreciation for the influence of followers. Read by business leaders in the 1920s and 1930s she emphasized that both management and labor shared certain common concerns, and these concerns could serve as a focus point for the management–labor relationship. When businesses like Walmart or JCPenny call their employees 'associates,' we see her impact still today. Her power model for leaders was *co-active* and not *coercive*.[3] Like the common good discussed in Chapter 11, the shared concerns of management and labor will become an important ethical foundation as the followership model develops.

In the aftermath of the Second World War, the Western world realized the importance of assertive followers. The Nuremberg Trials (1945–1946) judged influential actors from the Nazi regime who carried out the Holocaust or other war crimes. Some defendants claimed they could not be held responsible for their actions because they were merely following orders as faithful members of the Nazi party. (For instance, the common please was that these followers were not the ones who initiated the orders, and therefore they were not responsible for their actions.) The tribunal rejected such claims, finding those who carried out the orders to be morally culpable. To clarify the moral obligations of followers, Nuremberg Principle IV states that, 'The fact that a person acted pursuant to an order of his Government or a superior does not relieve him from responsibility under international law, provided a moral choice was in fact possible to him.'[4]

During the second half of the twentieth century, issues of followership received increasing attention. In 1963, a psychologist from Yale University, Stanley Milgram, wanted to better understand the Nuremberg defense of the Nazi followers. Just how much harm would a person be willing to do to another person in the name of obedience to authority? To answer his question, he created a famous series of 'education' experiments where participants were asked by a 'researcher' to administer an electrical shock to a 'learner' every time the learner got an answer wrong. For each wrong answer, the shock increased – until it reached possibly deadly levels. The 'learner' was actually an actor, who merely pretended to experience increasing levels of shock, and would sometimes even beg the research participant to stop.[5]

During the 1980s and 1990s, additional appreciation for the power of followers can be seen in James R. Meindl's work. Meindl viewed leadership not as something independent from followers, but actually a construction of followers.[6] He posited a 'romance of leadership' where followers made a 'fundamental attribution error' and attributed organizational results to individual leaders. Going even further, he later posited a 'social contagion' theory where the group prescribes what leadership is, so the individual leader could actually be taken out of the equation.[7] So with Meindl, we see the root of power more in the hands of the followers than in the hands of the leader.

Then, in 1988, Robert Kelley published a *Harvard Business Review* article that became an often-cited resource for followership: 'In Praise of Followers.' Kelley later followed the popular HBR article with a book, *The Power of Followership*. Recognizing the power of engaged followers, he explained that followers who were highly committed to the mission of the organization would be powerful contributors. Similarly, engaged followers motivated by concerns contrary to the mission of the organization could be highly destructive. He recognized that courageous followers were necessary to keep organizations ethical – an idea that would be further developed by Ira Chaleff's work in the twenty-first century. Likewise, his article suggested ways that organizations could train for more effective followership as well as more effective leadership. Further, organizations needed to change how they defined 'leadership' and 'followership,' because these were temporary 'roles' in an organization and not a state of being.

Early in the twenty-first century, this new appreciation for the role of followers can be seen to coincide with growing complexities for leaders, such as globalization and the Internet. Another indication of a growing appreciation for leadership's complex and non-linear nature can be seen in books such as Wheatley's *Leadership and the New Sciences* and Heifetz's concept of 'adaptive leadership,' well expressed in the title of his book, *Leadership Without Easy Answers* (adaptive leadership is addressed in Chapter 16).[8] Multiple factors had to be considered for effective leadership in complex situations. Might followers have a crucial role to play in solving the 'wicked problems' confronting humanity?[9]

Two writers contributed substantially to the discussion of followership in the early twenty-first century: Ira Chaleff and Barbara Kellerman. Chaleff continued the discussion on courageous followers and added to it with a discussion on 'intelligent disobedience,' which also reflected on the previously mentioned Nuremberg trials and the Milgram experiments.[10] Kellerman also developed a typology for followers and continued to challenge the primary emphasis on leaders themselves as a central force for 'leadership.' Recently, Kellerman has described a 'followership paradox,' that while followers may be acting more, they often act alone or in uncoordinated efforts, and not always effectively.[11] As a result: 'Emboldened followers make it hard for leaders to lead. Ineffectual followers make it easy to see why leaders usually remain in place, no matter how evidently inadequate. No wonder collective problems remain impervious to collective solutions.'[12]

For our purposes, we will consider followership as *a partnership between leaders and followers where both hold each other accountable for the success of the organization.*

Major concepts of followership

After reviewing the growing work around 'followership,' this chapter will next consider the dynamics of leader–follower relationships, typologies of followers, and what happens when the leader–follower relationship breaks down: the whistleblower and responding to toxic leadership. The hallmark concept for followership is a dynamic view of leader–follower relationships and understanding followers as partners in leadership interactions, instead of seeing them simply those who implement the leader's wishes. With that overview in mind, let's consider the dynamics of the leader–follower relationship.

Dynamics of the leader–follower relationship

Followers aren't so different from leaders

Robert Kelley memorably points out that the idea of followers as contributors is contrary to how many perceive followers. Followers are not simply 'sled dogs whose destiny is always to look at the rear end of the dog in front of them, but never to see the wider horizon or make the decisions of the lead dog.'[13] Instead, followership is an active mode of being, in which followers can make decisions that have real consequence for both the organization and themselves. Especially in a knowledge-based economy, followers must be able to move into self-directed leadership.[14] Interestingly, the traits that make for great leaders are also associated with the traits that make for great followers.[15] Followership models point out that the status of 'leader' and 'follower' are actually mutable roles. In fact, the same person may play both roles, though in different work relationships. The mid-level manager would be a classic example – this manager is seen as a 'leader' by his direct reports, and likewise is viewed as a 'follower' by his direct supervisor. As a consequence, the chasm between 'leader' and 'follower' is not as great as one might suppose. In reality, the followership model is about developing 'leadership' skills in followers and recognizing that leader and follower titles are really roles instead of permanent conditions. With this in mind, some scholars call for followership that is about learning to think like a leader.[16]

So, in order to fully appreciate how followership and leadership are not so different, we need to try different terms. Perhaps a better term for empowered followers would be 'ownership.' Followers must own their personal responsibility for shaping the direction of a community or organization. For example, Avolio discusses psychological ownership as an important part of followership, arguing that more owners are needed as the external and internal demands on organizations increase and as even remote workers can make decisions and take actions that have significant impact on the organization. Benefits of psychological ownership include a sense of place, a sense of self, and a sense of efficacy.[17] This sense of place, self, and efficacy can provide the strong presence necessary for followers to challenge toxic leaders.

Empowered followership, or ownership, can be expressed through courageous behaviors. In Chaleff's discussion of courageous followership, he lists several examples of how followers must be courageous. His list of behaviors could just as easily be described as the behaviors of a 'leader' as much as of a courageous follower: assuming responsibility, serving, challenging, participating in transformation, taking moral action, and speaking to hierarchy.

And by no means does the courage of a follower abnegate courage for a leader. In fact, when followers take these courageous actions, leaders need similar courage in order to listen to their followers.[18] When we consider our case study of the Wells Fargo scandal, a breakdown in the listening behaviors of leaders will be one noted contributing factor in the scandal.

Active followers are empowered followers

When one considers the various typologies suggested for followers, one can see the traditional notion of followers as 'passive' and a status not accorded with praise. (For example, at this time, I know of no universities offering majors in 'followership' or proudly listing the 'followership' accomplishments of their students.) Yet, when we consider follower typologies, followers are not merely passive recipients of the action. Consider Table 14.1, Follower typologies. The organizing factors for these typologies often relate, at least in part, to the activity level of the follower. Readers will note that as the level of organizing factors increases, the followers' descriptive title also shows increased presence on the part of the follower and the increasing presence of terms that are considered as positive.

Table 14.1 Followership typologies

Source	Organizing Factors	Types (ordered by increasing presence of organizing factors)
Abraham Zaleznik's (1965)	Dual axes of dominance–submission and activity–passivity	Impulsive Subordinates; Compulsive Subordinates; Masochistic Subordinates; Withdrawn Subordinates
Robert Kelley (1988)	Follower independence of thought; Extent of follower activity	Sheep; Yes People; Alienated; Effective Followers; Survivors
Ira Chaleff (1995)	Support or challenge for leaders	Implementers; Partners; Individualists; and Resources
Barbara Kellerman (2008)	Involvement/Engagement	Isolates; Bystanders; Participants; Activists; Die Hards
Rosenbach, Bitmann, and Potter (2012)	X/Y axis of relationship initiative and performance initiative	Subordinates; Contributors; Politicians; Partners

Sources: A. Zaleznik, The Dynamics of Subordinancy. Boston: Harvard Business Review, 1965; R. Kelley, "In praise of followers," Harvard Business Review, November 1988. Online, https://hbr.org/1988/11/in-praise-of-followers (accessed 17 July 2018); I Chaleff, The Courageous Follower, Oakland: Berrett-Koehler 1995; B. Kellerman, Followership. Boston: Harvard Business Review Press, 2008; W. E. Rosenbach, T. S. Pittman, and E. H. Potter, "What makes a good follower," in W. E. Rosenbach, W.E., R. L. Taylor, R.L. & M. A. Youndt eds. Contemporary Issues In Leadership, 7th edn., Boulder, Westview Press, 2012.

Perhaps the simplest typology we can offer here is 'good' versus 'bad' followers. Kellerman demonstrates an emphasis on activity in her discussion of 'good' versus 'bad' followers: (1) Followers who do something are almost always preferred to those who do nothing. (2) Good followers actively support good leadership (which Kellerman describes as effective and ethical leadership) and actively resist bad leadership (that which is ineffective or unethical).[19] With an increasing appreciation for followers as actors whose decisions have consequences for both their leaders and their organizations, followers can be understood to have an increasing importance as moral actors in their various settings. As a thought experiment, simply imagine how 'courageous followership' might have impacted the moral atrocities addressed in the Nuremberg trials. More engaged followers who possessed a strong moral compass and were willing to endure great personal risk could have mitigated some of the Holocaust's horrors. By reviewing the typologies listed here, readers will note that as followers become more active, they are also described in more positive terms.

Why this growing emphasis on the empowerment of active followers? Part of it may come from a growing distrust for leaders. Kellerman points out that the balance of power has shifted away from a leadership monopoly to more influence for followers, and some of that shift is because of a growing contempt for leaders.[20] So a healthy followership might just be the cure for a failing leadership. A study of followership forces leadership practitioners to spend time considering the wealth of follower types and their influence in the organization. The variety of followership typologies demonstrate that followers cannot be lumped into one homogeneous and passive bundle, and their variety goes beyond sorting into only 'good' and 'bad' types.

Followers are moral agents

Followership is critical because it allows those in a non-authoritative role to still have agency in their settings. Given Principle IV from the Nuremberg Trials, empowered followership skills are necessary because followers are morally culpable for their actions, even when following orders. Ethical followers do not have the luxury of being passive. Bass explains that the opposite of leader is not 'follower' but rather the completely disengaged or apathetic, because both leaders and followers can be transformational when they are fully engaged and following something larger than themselves.[21] Chaleff's *Courageous Follower* provides another emphasis on how followership is not a passive activity and illustrates the power of a leader–follower relationship that is based on mutual accountability to a higher purpose. In this case, the core of the leader–follower relationship focuses on the purpose of the organization. It is this shared commitment to a common purpose that then empowers followers to take moral action when needed. In sum, leaders hold followers accountable to the organization's purpose, and followers are empowered to likewise hold leaders accountable for following that same purpose.

Even more powerful than a shared sense of mission, a commitment to core values allows the follower to serve as a force for moral accountability. Values are a resource that followers can use when they query and appeal unclear or ill-advised directives from their leader.[22] In his discussion of the Milgram experiments, Chaleff notes that a distinguishing quality for those who disobeyed an order from an authority figure was a stronger sense of obedience to something else, something higher.[23] When we view followers as active moral agents, then the result of the Nuremberg trials makes more sense. While 'loyal Nazis' may have just been following orders, there are other values to be considered than simple 'obedience.' More to the point, obedience is a misappropriated value when the obedience is following orders to carry out genocide.

In his work specific to followership, Chaleff also suggests that followers should develop a variety of communication skills in order to best serve as a trusted voice for the leader. In his work on intelligent disobedience, Chaleff later says that followers who disobey must clarify *why* they do so and do so clearly, with a strong voice that does not use 'mitigating language.' His basic formula for the follower is to (1) understand the mission, (2) clarify the order as needed, (3) make a conscious choice, and (4) assume personal accountability for your choice.[24] Intelligent disobedience is not the same as 'civil disobedience.' Civil disobedience is intentionally disruptive and violates laws. Intelligent disobedience '[does] not flagrantly violate existing laws.'[25]

One of the ways that followers can be active moral agents is by serving as a 'whistleblower.' Admittedly, the status of 'whistleblower' represents a breakdown of trust in the organization, and it could require the follower to break with the value of 'loyalty' or 'obedience' in order to take action on a higher value. In *Courageous Followers*, Chaleff points out being a whistleblower is not the same as courageous followership. One can take the corrective actions of a courageous follower without disavowing the leader. Likewise, one can be a whistleblower who is motivated by something other than the best interests of the organization.

The decision to become a whistleblower is not an easy one, because the action can have great cost for both the organization and the whistleblower. For example, Fred Alford uses the imagery of a 'scapegoat' and explains that the Greek word for such, *pharmakos*, can be translated as both 'poison' and 'cure.' And, the scapegoat/whistleblower serves as both in an organization.

The cure is that it puts our sins at a distance, but the whistleblower can also be seen as a poison to their industry. Between one-half to two-thirds of whistleblowers lose their jobs, and many are not able to find employment again in their industries.[26]

Active followers can respond to toxic leaders

Perhaps one of the most positive outcomes of the model is an ability to recognize and respond appropriately to toxic leadership. Jean Lipman-Blumen defines toxic leadership at its most basic level as those leaders who leave us worse than when they found us, or those who intentionally enhance themselves at the expense of others.[27] Why do we support such leaders? Lipman-Blumen explains that they give followers a sense of meaning, safety, and stability. When we review our discussion of followership so far, we can see a number of ways that active followers can serve as a check and balance against toxic leadership. Fundamentally, engaged followers are not just passive yes-people. Likewise, engaged followers do not simply disengage when they see leaders who are a threat to the organization or who disregard core values. When they perceive a threat, followers can use their communication skills to speak up, remind leaders of the mission, and provide alternative decisions. When necessary, followers can practice intelligent disobedience. As a final step, active followers can serve as whistleblowers – though often at great cost.

In conclusion of this section, if one forced me to identify a single outcome of the followership model, especially from an ethical perspective, I would say the greatest outcome is that it demonstrates that 'good followers' are not simply those who take orders. Followership is not passive. From a consideration of 'ethical leadership,' healthy followership is essential in an organization for two reasons: (1) its potential to empower good leaders and (2) its potential to resist bad leaders.

Much of this chapter has considered how followers can respond to bad leaders and why followers should do so. However, we would be remiss not to pause for a moment and remind ourselves of the power of followership for supporting good leaders. In the same way that followers can be a check and balance for bad leadership, they are also a powerful dynamo for good leadership. Passive followers have a negative effect on an organization – they do not resist bad leadership and they do not support good leadership. Passive followership represents a threat to our organizations. Therefore, while leadership training is still important for organizations, they would also do well to invest some of those resources in developing active followers and training leaders how to respond to such followers. Likewise, organizations must invest in creating a culture that welcomes and empowers good followership. Kellerman puts it this way: 'we can't reduce the number of bad leaders unless we reduce the number of bad followers.'[28]

Critiques of followership

Followership is a powerful concept for organizations who wish to reinforce consistent ethical practices. Yet, it also has drawbacks as a concept. These drawbacks include theoretical concerns and practical concerns. Let's start our discussion of followership's challenges with a discussion of two theoretical challenges and then discuss practical concerns.

Theoretical challenge number one: The limits of language

From a theoretical standpoint, the very term 'follower' may be one of the biggest obstacles for the followership model. To be a 'follower' can easily become equated with being a passive recipient of the actions or commands of the leader. If one starts with the 'great man' model of leadership as an assumed, then the follower's role is minimized. Because of this, Joseph Rost suggests using the term 'collaborator' instead, in an effort to recognize the active role that followers can play in organizations.[29] He suggests that the term 'follower' only reinforces the great-man leadership model. Similarly, in *Hard Times*, Kellerman notes that while follower seems to be the only obvious antonym for leader, people still use a variety of terms to express the idea: 'stakeholder, constituents, participants, subordinates, employees, group members, or team members.'[30] So, to really discuss followership as an ethical resource in organizations, we need to rely on terms inspired by Follett's work, like 'associate,' and 'partner,' or at minimum, terms like 'engaged follower.' By either redefining followership with more active and engaged language or finding new terms altogether, we can view the follower role in an entirely new light. We must come to understand the follower as a partner who works with the leader, sometimes even holding the leader accountable, for the sake of the organization's missional success.

Theoretical challenge number two: The hierarchical nature of organizations

Intuitively, not everyone can be a leader – so how do we understand organizational charts for 'empowered followers'? One suggestion from Gene Dixon in *Art of Followership* is to change the chart from a top down leader/follower relationship to viewing all members of the organization as leader–followers who exhibit different qualities in different contexts, with the hope that such a sense of organizational structure would call leader–followers to be more self-aware of how their work impacts both those to whom they report and those whom they manage. Such a construct would also recognize that titles like 'leader' and 'follower' are not permanent character traits, but rather flexible roles.[31] For example, even CEOs often have a board that holds the chief executive accountable for certain results.

Practical concern number one: Risks for followers

Theoretical concerns are not the only possible shortcomings of the followership model. There are practical risks for both followers and leaders. An imminent concern for followership is related to the hierarchical nature of organizations mentioned above. In this case, we consider the power difference between leaders and followers. Leaders have access to resources that followers lack. Because of the power difference between leaders and followers, followers are dependent upon the functioning of things like ethics hotlines. They need reinforcement from external resources if they are to take the difficult stand sometimes required.

Also, in an employment setting, followers are generally dependent on the income and other benefits that go with their job. How can they risk the repercussions of speaking up if to do so is to risk their livelihood? To go further, to speak up as a 'whistleblower' can have dire consequences not just at that current place of employment, but for a worker's future in an entire industry. Another struggle for followership is that correcting bad leadership is sometimes not in the best interest of individual followers.[32] For example, if the employee benefits financially or in other ways because of poor leadership, what then would inspire the follower to speak up?

Practical concern number two: Risks for leaders

Leaders may also fear the idea of empowering followers because it can risk creating an antagonistic relationship between leaders and followers. For organizations that depend on order, efficiency, or the authority of leaders, the followership model might be perceived as a threat. For followers to be truly empowered, leaders must relinquish a certain degree of control and be more open to critical feedback from subordinates. Leaders may thus be required to change their self-concepts about the nature of their power and status. So, for followership to work, both leaders and followers will have to take risks.

Ethical implications of followership

The real ethical power source for followership has two dimensions. First, it elevates how leaders view followers. No longer are followers seen as cannon fodder. Now they are partners for the success of the leader, and even more importantly for the success of the organization and its mission. Next, the power source for the follower himself is rooted in ethical concerns – either common concerns (where leader and follower have a shared set of values) or in contrary concerns. With that in mind, here are some observations on followership as an ethical leadership model:

- Followership supercharges any leader–follower relationship where leader and follower share common ethical concerns. In this case, the follower is a partner who can empower the leader to pursue those ethical concerns. When leaders seem to lose sight of those shared concerns, the followers can remind leaders to reevaluate their actions.
- Followership gets tricky when leader and follower are operating under different ethical concerns. For example, a leader might be fully 'authentic' in his drive for success and pursuing an implied social contract with investors (who expect the leader to report quarterly profits). At the same time, the follower may see these actions as actually taking advantage of those who can't speak up for themselves (like in our Wells Fargo case, where non-English speakers seemed to have been targeted for services they did not request).
- What this means for followership is that it can be a leadership model to reinforce any of the ethical models we discussed in section two of our text. However, *how* followers show support for that ethical model will vary. For example, the concerns of an engaged follower who supports the common good might look different from an engaged follower who supports a social contract that rejects the notion of a 'common good.'
- Thus, those who wish to be fully empowered followers and partners for their leaders would do well to have an ethical vocabulary. Empowered followers must also practice their communication skills to reinforce core values in the organization, redirect the leader when needed, and in the most extreme cases, resist the leader entirely.

Five component analysis

As with the other chapters, we now turn to a consideration of how the Five Components Model can help us understand the focus of our chapter on followership. Let's start our analysis with a riddle that comes from one of my favorite comic books – *Usagi Yojimbo*. In a discussion with a fellow Samurai Warrior, Usagi considers a Bushido riddle that asks him to choose between two different examples. The first example is that of a warrior who loyally follows a good leader. The second example is about a warrior who faithfully serves an evil leader. The riddle asks which is the better example of Bushido. Usagi responds that the warrior who faithfully serves the evil leader is the better example, because loyalty is the foundation of Bushido.[33]

In the riddle's model of followership, we see two primary sources of authority:

- Culture, as expressed through the tenets of the Bushido riddle.
- The leader himself, no matter what his moral intent.

The Bushido riddle exemplifies the 'diehard' follower type mentioned by Kellerman. In this case, the Samurai follows the orders of his master – even if those orders are wicked and require the Samurai to sacrifice his own life. If we understand followership in purely passive terms, then this would also be our view of followership in the Western world. However, when we discuss terms like 'courageous followers,' 'intelligent disobedience,' and 'good followers,' we enter into a new understanding – one that promotes an ethical leadership model. Let's take a look at how each of the five leadership components is addressed by the followership described in the current chapter.

Shamir described followers as 'constructors' of leadership.[34] With his description we see an emphasis on the relationship between leaders and followers,

Figure 14.2 The Five Components of Leadership Model applied to followership

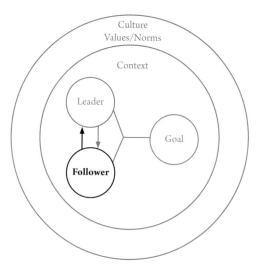

instead of leaders over followers. So, we are moving away from a purely linear view of leadership. Additionally, although the model's title may feature the term 'follower', in reality, followership considers much more, such as the relationship between leader and followers, the goals, the organizational context, and the larger values that guide the organization. In this sense, the followership model provides a robust understanding of leadership (ironically, given the label 'followership'). Regarding the leader–follower relationship, the one key component seems to be that the follower has a responsibility to assess the leader and the goal, all within a larger context – that of an organization's purpose, values, and vision. Additionally, titles like 'leader' and 'follower' are not permanent states of being, but fluid and interchangeable roles, depending on the situation.

This is where the conversation about toxic leadership can come to play. Given that the follower is not seen as passive, the follower can be morally culpable for 'just following orders'. The moral dilemma of 'just following orders' was highlighted in the Nuremberg trials, when Nazi soldiers who helped carry out the Holocaust claimed they were not morally responsible for their actions, precisely because they were following orders. One consequence of the Nuremberg trials was that moral, and by extension, legal, culpability extended beyond obedience to authority. So, a strong followership model that views followers as individually responsible agents can serve as a corrective force for toxic leadership.

To apply this back to the Five Components Model, both the leader's 'circle' and that of the follower are important. The follower partners with the leader for success. Both are accountable to something other than themselves – the purpose of the organization, or a higher ethical principle. This accountability was illustrated in the Milgram experiments (discussed earlier in the chapter) where participants refused to follow the orders of a so-called expert, because the participant appealed to a higher moral code.

So what then are the practical interactions between follower and leader? Followership rightly reminds us that followers can decide whether to resist the leader or to support the leader, and that those choices themselves are not simply either/or. We might consider the extreme range of responses for followers to be outright disobedience at one end of the spectrum and unquestioning obedience at the other end. In most circumstances, healthy followership avoids these extremes.

For example, if the follower believes the leader is about to make a bad decision, the follower can provide support to the leader by questioning the current decision. Yes, it might look like resistance in the short term, but the overall motivation for questioning the leader's decision is to help the leader be successful in the long term. While the 'whistleblower' option may seem to represent a complete breakdown between leader and follower, even then the follower is motivated by a larger concern for the success or survival of the organization. In this case, the follower is bringing to light practices that hurt the organization's integrity.

The goal is still important, but simply accomplishing the goal is not the final measure for success. There is another concern that determines the goal's validity – namely the values of the organization or the larger values of the culture. The goal should be consistent with this larger purpose. So, the circle representing the goal, while still important, should attract less of our notice.

From the perspective of the leader, good followers may be those who simply crank out product – accomplishing goals. But if we choose to see followership as a skillset for ethical leadership in an organization, then the responsibility of the follower for simply achieving the goal becomes much more nuanced. Followers must ask themselves if the goal itself is moral as well as evaluate how the goal is being achieved. Our Wells Fargo case study will further illustrate this point.

The context is also a powerful factor in the leader–follower dynamic, because it is in this sphere that we can often find pressures that challenge healthy leader–follower relationships and may cause leaders to make unethical requests of their followers. These pressures can include the need to make sales quotas, industry trends, or regulations that threaten the organization's ability to achieve its goals and prosper. Likewise, the environment also includes resources that can help a follower respond to unhealthy pressure from a leader. If there is a high demand for the skills of a follower, he can choose to work elsewhere. If the organization has an ethics hotline or HR process for addressing concerns, the follower can use those resources. There may even be legal precedents to which a follower can appeal.

If we choose to see the sphere of culture as the locus for things like 'values,' 'purpose,' and 'mission,' then we quickly see the importance of culture for engaged followership. The real power source for followership is the ability of the follower to know those core values, to communicate them, and to act on them – even if it means refusing the directives of the leader. When the follower looks to the cultural circle instead of an organizational chart, suddenly the follower's role does not seem so fixed. Leaders and followers are both in service to the purpose of the organization at minimum, and to even higher values based in larger cultural concerns like ethics and morality. The cultural spheres of concern provide the moral compass for the followership model, and because of this, the model should be understood as an ethical leadership model – that is, a model where authority rests in something transcending the leader himself.

So, to return to our riddle of the wicked master, according to the typology suggested by Barbara Kellerman, the Samurai would be a 'diehard' follower, but he would not be a 'good' follower. Kellerman says good followers resist bad leaders. Thus, the courageous follower would need to start with express- ing concern to his master, possibly practicing intelligent disobedience. If that does not work, then the follower would want to actively resist his master. Depending on the organization, this resistance could go as far as whistle- blowing. For the Samurai to claim he was 'just following orders' from his wicked master would not remove him from moral culpability.

CASE STUDY

Followership and Wells Fargo bank

After considering followership as a concept, we now move into an analysis of followership in a particular context. Our Bushido illustration above provides a helpful reference for the case we are about to consider, where some followers were asked by managers to do things that the followers were not comfortable with. The case we will discuss begs us to consider what the appropriate response is of a follower when he is asked to do something that makes him uncomfortable. When managers ask direct reports to be a 'team player' by doing something that bends the rules (if not breaks them entirely) in order to achieve a business goal, how should direct reports respond? What does engaged followership look like in these circumstances? More to the point, what resources are available to followers when they are put in such a circumstance?

History

As one of the largest banks in the United States, Wells Fargo had been described as one of the best banks in the world. It was lauded for its customer-savvy and trustworthy reputation, especially after the financial crisis of 2008. For example, in 2012, *Forbes* described Wells Fargo as 'The Bank that Works.'[35] The brand tried to contrast itself to how much main-street America viewed Wall Street with suspicion. Instead of New York City, the bank's headquarters was in San Francisco, where Wells Fargo began in 1852. Wells Fargo was such a trusted financial institution that billionaire investor Warren Buffet was one of the bank's largest shareholders in 2013. Then-CEO John Stumpf was described as a down-to-earth dispenser of aphorisms like 'people don't care how much you know until they know how much you care.'[36] To reinforce the company's culture, Wells Fargo had produced a 'vision

CASE STUDY (continued)

and values' booklet[37] in the 1990s, and that booklet continues to be part of the company's culture today. It emphasizes building relationships with customers, putting their needs first, and engaging in ethical behavior.

That stellar reputation was publicly challenged in December 2013, when the *Los Angeles Times* released a report about a 'pressure cooker sales culture' at Wells Fargo.[38] At the time, Wells Fargo was the nation's leader in selling add-on services to its already-existing customers. The *Times* article described high pressure sales tactics such as employees being forced to stay after work and work during weekends if they did not meet sales quotas, threats of being fired if they went for two months without meeting their sales goals, being chastised and embarrassed in front of other managers, being coached to open unwanted accounts through forging client signatures or begging family members to open accounts, and even being told to falsify the phone numbers of angry customers so they could not be reached for customer satisfaction surveys.[39]

A helpful summary for some ethical failings is that when external pressures exceed internal resources, destructive behaviors result. In these specific leader–follower interactions, the external pressures were a continual push to sell products. For these managers, the pressure to 'cross sell' became greater than the company's publicly stated values on customer service – values that could provide an internal ethical compass for managers and staff. Cross selling was the core of Wells Fargo's growth strategy. Along with finding new customers, bankers were to sell additional financial products to current customers. Employees were told to strive for the 'Great 8,' by selling an average of eight financial products per customer.

As investigators began to dig into the case, they discovered that complaints about fraud accounts dated back to 2005 – the year John Stumpf became president of Wells Fargo. Stumpf himself repeated the mantra that 'eight is great.' Later analysis revealed that thousands of employees created as many as two million unauthorized accounts for customers,[40] and that the sales of accounts were incentivized.[41] Fines for these false accounts totaled over 185 million dollars. As the details of the Wells Fargo scandal began to emerge, two factors were particularly disturbing: (1) who was disproportionally affected, and (2) how workers who spoke up were treated.

As one looks for trends among who was targeted by these sales practices, three groups emerge: (1) friends and families of the workers, (2) non-English speakers, and (3) the elderly. Regarding how friends and family of Wells Fargo employees became targeted, some bought cheap policies for friends and family, paid the premiums themselves and then canceled after the first month. In a 3 October 2016 lawsuit, one worker described being wrongfully fired after following her manager's directions to open accounts in the names of family members.[42] Another employee said he was criticized for 'not being a team player' when he refused to open accounts for friends and family with or without their permission.[43]

CASE STUDY *(continued)*

Hispanic populations seemed to have been particularly affected or targeted by these sales practices. For example, Arizona, which has a high Hispanic population, was disproportionately affected by sales practices.[44] Also, as more information came to light about these sales practices, products sold by Wells Fargo on behalf of Prudential were also identified as part of the problem. Wells Fargo sold unauthorized Prudential Insurance accounts, in some cases withdrawing premiums from their customers' accounts. Bankers who helped make these sales happen got credit toward their sales quotas. Even more disturbing, many of the customers who complained to the Prudential customer service line did not speak English and needed a Spanish interpreter.[45] The lawsuit says that the majority of these accounts were sold to Hispanic sounding names in southern California, south Texas, south Arizona, and south Florida.[46] One worker claimed that bankers also opened accounts for elderly people who they thought would not notice.[47]

With pressure for sales goals leading to unethical actions, what responses could followers take? Some quit or retired early, in spite of the financial consequences. Others refused to accommodate their managers' directives and called the hotline. At least one employee used social media to satirize the bank and its management practices. Some even tried to contact the CEO directly.[48]

Results of the scandal include career derailment, congressional hearings, and declining account numbers. After the 2013 *Los Angeles Times* article,[49] Wells Fargo fired approximately 5,300 employees, mostly low level. At the time, the bank employed nearly 270,000. CEO Stumpf eventually resigned. But career derailment was not just for the wrong doers. Particularly disturbing was the negative impact on those who spoke up – some were blackballed by the financial industry.[50] Besides the cost of fines for fraudulent accounts, the bank also experienced declines in business. In January 2017, the bank reported 200,000 fewer checking and 200,000 fewer credit card accounts opened than one year previous (a 31 percent drop for checking and a 47 percent drop for credit card applications).[51]

Five component analysis

The instances mentioned in the public descriptions of the Wells Fargo case illustrate a case where followers were forced to serve as 'yes-people' or 'implementers' instead of partners who could speak to leadership about questionable ethical practices. In a healthy leader–follower relationship, the organization's core values stand at the center of the relationship. These values allow both leader and follower to hold each other accountable to certain standards. In the leader–follower interactions described here, the publicly stated customer-centered values of Wells Fargo were ignored for the sake of a different goal. Followers were ostracized if they could not achieve the goal or if they questioned the way the goal was being obtained – even when their concerns were rooted in a fear that the organization was being 'unethical.'

CASE STUDY *(continued)*

Figure 14.3 The Five Components of Leadership Model applied to the Wells Fargo case

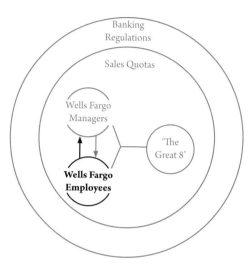

So what possible responses could followers give? Chaleff's commentary on the Milgram experiments seems helpful here – 'If you are uncomfortable with what you are told to do, speak up early and do not let your discomfort be dissipated by answers that are technical rather than moral.'[52] Chaleff also points out that the options for followers are not simply to obey or to disobey. There is a spectrum of possible responses. Followers can ask for clarifications from managers and state their concerns that the directives given by a manager violate other ethical guidelines. Similarly, followers can follow directives as much as possible, but only to the extent that a direct action does not violate an ethical principle. Only once these examples are exhausted should the follower then consider outright refusal to follow directives, possibly bringing other resources to bear in order to counteract these directives or quitting their position. For example, a nurse who disagreed with the prescribed meds from a doctor hooked up the IV as the doctor ordered, but then told the doctor he would have to open the valve himself. In this case, the nurse followed directives as far as possible, and then left the consequential actions to the doctor himself. By forcing the doctor to be immediately responsible for what happened to the patient, the nurse helped the doctor reassess the situation.[53]

To return to the Wells Fargo case, it was achieving the goal that really defined the leader–follower relationship. The goal had been set by the highest levels of management in the company and described as 'The Great Eight.' While the positive financial impact of the goal for the organization had been considered, the negative consequences related to how that goal was pursued were not considered. As a result, the organization also suffered financial loss in the form of penalties/sanctions. Sometimes organization goals may appear to be in conflict. In this case, 'customer service' was a stated goal while in reality profit at the expense of customers became the practice. One way to recognize what is truly valued in an

CASE STUDY *(continued)*

organization is by examining what the organization is willing to 'pay' (sacrifice, suffer) for the value. In the instances described in this case study, hitting monthly sales goals prevailed over other concerns.

One commentator on the Wells Fargo scandal pithily observed 'you get what you measure.'[54] If the sales goal is the only thing measured, then Wells Fargo's relationships and the stated values of the organization will inevitably come in second. Without some form of reporting, those stated values are not kept in front of the leaders or followers, and the progress on those values is not assessed in any meaningful manner.

Part of the tragedy here is also that the organization was previously known for its ethical business culture as expressed in both in-house and public documents. Given the previous observation that you get what you measure, I encourage readers to consider what tools needed to be in place to assess the consistent implementation of those publicly stated values. Such systems are especially important for empowered followers. Followers must have a higher value that they can appeal to in order to contradict ethically dubious directives from leaders. And, because of the power imbalance between leaders and followers, these values need to be reaffirmed in as many ways as possible – through both public proclamation and internal assessment.

Another breakdown here was in one of the tools that helps adjust an organization's culture. The ethics hotline is a way for followers to speak up and point out ethical failures in an organization's culture. Yet the hotline here did not receive the follow up needed in order for it to be an effective moderator of organization culture. The public also became outraged when former CEO Stumpf said 'we have a few bad apples,' blaming employees instead of the high-pressure culture at the bank.[55]

One may point to a competitive environment that demands continual increase in revenue as a root of the problem. Others have noted the problems inherent with a continual push for business growth that focuses on the short-term gains of investors. In this case, it seems that a similar pressure for continual short-term returns led to internal ethical failures and long-term consequences.

Besides the failure of the ethics hotline within Wells Fargo's corporate culture, two other resources seem to have failed in their intended purpose of providing protection from toxic situations like the one at Wells Fargo. While the culture of Wells Fargo may have pushed for more sales, there were supposed to be protections in place to keep these kinds of things from happening in the banking industry. For example, the Sarbanes–Oxley Act (SOX) protects employees of certain companies from retaliation for reporting alleged mail, wire, bank or securities fraud; violations of the SEC rules and regulations; or violations of federal laws related to fraud against shareholders.[56] The Act covers employees of publicly traded companies and subsidiaries, along with their contractors, subcontractors and agents.[57]

A second resource is the Consumer Financial Protection Act.[58] This Act protects employees performing tasks related to consumer financial products or services from retaliation for reporting reasonably perceived violations subject to the jurisdiction of the

> **CASE STUDY** *(continued)*
>
> Bureau of Consumer Financial Protection.[59] These preventative failures are significant for our discussion of followership because they highlight how followers need effective resources throughout the five components of a leadership system in order to do the difficult work of being a true partner with their leaders.

Summary and concluding remarks

So how then can followers partner with leaders to do the right thing? I suggest four fundamental responses to the question. First, ethical followers strive to be partners for good leaders and to re-direct or resist bad leaders. Second, ethical followers access external resources such as higher values and the organization's mission – and they are able to reinforce these values by developing feedback loops that report when these values are being ignored or outright violated. Third, ethical followers realize that they have access to a range of responses when they believe a leader is operating outside of what is appropriate – these followers have the savvy to take responses that go beyond simple 'obedience' or 'disobedience.' Finally, ethical followers remember that they are morally culpable for their own actions, even if it means direct disobedience to their leader's commands.

For organizations to empower this kind of followership, leaders will need to see corrective feedback from followers as an asset to the organization as well as their own leadership success. And followers will need additional training in order to understand and apply the full range of responses they can engage when they believe their leader has abandoned the organization's core values. In the Wells Fargo case, we saw an example of where a better partnership between managers and employees could have made a significant difference for both the company and its customers, and we considered what made the situation so difficult as well as what was needed for effective followership.

? DISCUSSION QUESTIONS

When organizational values conflict with personal values, how can followers respond?

How does describing followers as 'owners' or 'partners' change your view of followers?

What are the advantages and disadvantages of removing the emphasis from individual leaders to looking at leader–follower interactions or group processes in order to understand leadership?

Which of the ethical models described in the first part of this text speak to the behaviors initiated in the Wells Fargo scandal? How might leaders invoke these ethical models in a way that would be received in a for-profit organization?

Imagine that you made a call to the ethics hotline and there was no response. How could you follow up?

How can the Wells Fargo case be used to strengthen the position of followers in an organization?

Imagine you were a Wells Fargo employee, what followership strategies could you have used in that situation?

For effective followership to take place in an organization, what should be measured and how?

 ### ADDITIONAL RESOURCES

Barbara Kellerman, *Followership*, Boston: Harvard Business Press, 2008.

Kellerman has much to say that challenges traditional, 'leader-centric' thinking. Her followership book is a good place to start in following her work and should be read alongside the work by Ira Chaleff, already discussed in this chapter.

G.J. Sorenson and G.R. Hickman, *The Power of Invisible Leadership: How a Compelling Common Purpose Inspires Exceptional Leadership*, Los Angeles: Sage, 2014.

Readers who want to better understand the power of purpose and values in guiding an organization should consult the literature on invisible leadership. Sorenson and Hickman are a good place to start.

Jean Lipman-Blumen, *The Allure of Toxic Leaders*, Oxford: Oxford University Press, 2005.

To fully appreciate the importance of empowered followers, readers should also consult the literature on toxic leadership. Doing so will help followers recognize leadership that must be resisted and how to avoid following into its traps.

NOTES

1 There are certain 'classic' texts that 'well read' leaders should get to know. Among those books are Machiavelli's *The Prince*, and Sun Tzu's *The Art of War*. I wouldn't recommend these texts as guides to 'ethics,' but they are helpful reminders that leadership is a practical skill and not just a thought exercise. Likewise, those texts might give readers insight into how the person 'across the table' is viewing them.

2 See Thomas Carlyle's *On Heroes, Hero Worship and the Heroic in History*. It's another one of those 'classics.'

3 As described by D.A. Wren and R.G. Greenwood, *Management Innovators: The People and Ideas that Have Shaped Modern Business*, New York: Oxford University Press, 1998. They also point out that Warren Bennis views Follett's work as foundational for modern leadership writing.

4 I. Chaleff, *Intelligent Disobedience: Doing Right When What You're Told to Do is Wrong*, Oakland, CA: Berrett-Koehler Publishers, 2015a, p. 65.

5 For a full discussion, see S. Milgram, *Obedience to Authority: An Experimental View*, New York: Harper Collins, 2009.

6 J.R. Meindl, S.B. Ehrlich, and J.M. Dukerich, 'The romance of leadership,' *Administration Science Quarterly*, vol. 30 no. 1, March 1985, 78–102.

7 J.R. Meindl, 'On leadership: An alternative to the conventional wisdom,' in B.M. Straw and L.L. Cummings (eds), *Research in Organizational Behavior*, Greenwich, CT: JAI Press, 1990, pp. 59–203.

8 See R. Heifetz, *Leadership Without Easy Answers*, Cambridge, MA: Harvard University Press, 1998; and R. Heifetz, *The Practice of Adaptive Leadership: Tools and Tactics for Changing Your Organization and The World*, Boston: Harvard Business Press, 2009.

9 Wicked problems are those problems that lack a clear, technical solution. For a discussion of wicked problems and leadership, see K. Grint, *Leadership: A Very Short Introduction*, Oxford: Oxford University Press, 2010.

10 I. Chaleff, *The Courageous Follower: Standing Up To and For Our Leaders*, 3rd edn, San Francisco, CA: Berrett-Koehler Publishers, 2015b; Chaleff, 2015a, op. cit., p. 65.

11 B. Kellerman, *Hard Times: Leadership in America*, Stanford, CA: Stanford Business Books, 2015.

12 Kellerman, ibid, p. 282.

13 R.E. Kelly, 'Rethinking followership,' in R. Riggio, I. Chaleff, and J. Lipman-Blumen (eds), *Art of Followership*, San Francisco: Jossey-Bass, 2008, p. 6.

14 R.G. Lord, 'Followers' cognitive and affective structures and leadership processes,' Riggio, Chaleff, and Lipman-Blumen, op. cit., pp. 255–66.

15 For example, a 1955 study by Hollander and Webb indicated the same peers nominated as most desired leaders were also nominated as most desired followers. See B.M. Bass and R. Bass, *The Bass Handbook of Leadership: Theory, Research, and Managerial Applications*, 4th edn, New York: Free Press, 2008.

16 J. Maroosis, 'Leadership: A partnership in reciprocal following,' Riggio, Chaleff, and Lipman-Blumen, op. cit., pp. 17–26.

17 B.J. Avolio and R.J. Reichard, 'The rise of authentic followership,' Riggio, Chaleff, and Lipman-Blumen, op. cit., pp. 325–37.

18 Chaleff, 2015b, op. cit.

19 B. Kellerman, 'What every leader needs to know about followers,' Harvard Business Review, December 2007. Online, https://hbr.org/2007/12/what-every-leader-needs-to-know-about-followers (accessed 17 July 2018).

20 Kellerman, 2015, op. cit.

21 B.M. Bass and R. Bass, op. cit.

22 Chaleff, 2015b, op. cit.

23 Chaleff, 2015b, op. cit.

24 Chaleff, 2015b, op. cit., pp. 38, 43, and 2.

25 Chaleff, 2015b, op. cit.; Chaleff, 2015a, op. cit., p. 19.

26 Avolio and Reichard, op. cit.

27 J. Lipman-Blumen, 'Following toxic leaders: In search of posthumous praise,' Riggio, Chaleff, and Lipman-Bluman, op. cit., p. 182.

28 B. Kellerman, *Bad Leadership: What It Is, How It Happens, Why It Matters*, Boston: Harvard Business Review Press, 2004, p. 21.

29 J. Rost, 'Followership: An outmoded concept,' Riggio, Chaleff, and Lipman-Bluman, op. cit., pp. 53–65.

30 Kellerman, 2015, op. cit., p. 270.

31 G. Dixon, 'Getting together,' Riggio, Chaleff, and Lipman-Bluman, op. cit., pp. 155–76.

32 Kellerman, 2004, op. cit.

33 S. Sakai and U. Yojimbo, *The Dragon Below Conspiracy*, 4th edn, Seattle, WA: Fantagraphics Books, 2005, p. 66.

34 B. Shamir, P. Rajnandini, M.C. Bligh, and M. Uhl-Bien (eds), *Follower-Centered Perspectives on Leadership*, Charlotte, NC: Information Age Publishing, 2007.

35 H. Touryalai, 'Wells Fargo: The bank that works,' *Forbes*, January 25, 2012. Online, https://www.forbes.com/sites/halahtouryalai/2012/01/25/wells-fargo-the-bank-that-works/#5c9fbf60718e (accessed October 25, 2017).

36 J.G. Stumph, 'How Wells Fargo CEO built the team at the world's most valuable bank,' *Fortune*, July 23, 2015. Online, http://fortune.com/2015/07/23/john-stumpf-culture/ (accessed October 25, 2017).

37 For a recent example of Wells Fargo's vision and values booklet, see *Our Code of Ethics and Business Conduct: Living Our Visions, Values, and Goals*. Online, https://www08.wellsfargomedia.com/assets/pdf/about/corporate/code-of-ethics.pdf (accessed March 14, 2018).

38 E.S. Reckard, 'Wells Fargo's pressure-cooker sales culture comes at a cost,' *Los Angeles Times*, December 21, 2013. Online, http://www.latimes.com/business/la-fi-wells-fargo-sale-pressure-20131222-story.html (accessed October 25, 2017).

39 Reckard, ibid.

40 Reckard, op. cit.

41 Reckard, op. cit. Spokesperson for WF said that bankers typically derive 15–20% of total earnings from sales incentives.

42 Reckard, op. cit.

43 S. Cowley, 'Wells Fargo workers claim retaliation for playing by the rules,' *New York Times*, September 26, 2016. Online, https://www.nytimes.com/2016/09/27/business/dealbook/wells-fargo-workers-claim-retaliation-for-playing-by-the-rules.html (accessed October 25, 2018).

44 J.F. Peltz, 'Wells Fargo fires former L.A. regional president, 3 other managers after scandal,' *Los Angeles Times*, February 21, 2017. Online, http://www.latimes.com/business/la-fi-wells-fargo-20170221-story.html (accessed October 25, 2017).

45 S. Cowley and M. Goldstein, 'Accusations of fraud at Wells Fargo spread to sham insurance policies,' *The New York Times*, December 9, 2016. Online, https://www.nytimes.com/2016/12/09/business/deal-book/wells-fargo-accusations-sham-insurance-policies.html (accessed October 25, 2017).

46 Cowley and Goldstein, ibid. The three whistleblowers at Prudential who brought this information forward were fired and later filed a wrongful termination suit.

47 Cowley, September 26, 2016, op. cit.

48 These examples are taken from numerous sources, including Reckard, op. cit.; Cowley, September 26, 2016, op. cit.; Cowley and Goldstein, December 9, 2016, op. cit.; S. Cowley, 'At Wells Fargo, complaints about fraudulent accounts since 2005', *New York Times*, October 11, 2016. Online, https://www.nytimes.com/2016/10/12/business/dealbook/at-wells-fargo-complaints-about-fraudulent-accounts-since-2005.html (accessed October 25, 2017); and C. Arnold, 'Former Wells Fargo employees describe toxic sales culture, even at HQ,' NPR.org. Online, http://www.npr.org/2016/10/04/496508361/for-mer-wells-fargo-employees-describe-toxic-sales-culture-even-at-hq (accessed January 14, 2017).

49 Reckard, op. cit.

50 See Arnold, op. cit.

51 Peltz, op. cit.

52 Chaleff, 2015a, op. cit., p. 94.

53 Chaleff, 2015a, op. cit, p. 94.

54 M. Levine, 'Wells Fargo opened a couple million fake accounts,' *Bloomberg*, September 9, 2016. Online, https://www.bloomberg.com/view/articles/2016-09-09/wells-fargo-opened-a-couple-million-fake-accounts (accessed January 14, 2017).

55 L. Shen, 'Former Wells Fargo employees to CEO John Stumpf: It's not our fault,' *Fortune*, September 19, 2016. Online, http://fortune.com/2016/09/19/former-wells-fargo-employees-to-ceo-john-stumpf-its-not-our-vfault/ (accessed January 14, 2017).

56 See 18 U.S.C. § 1514A Civil Action to Protect Against Retaliation in Fraud Cases. Online, https://www.gpo.gov/fdsys/granule/USCODE-2010-title18/USCODE-2010-title18-partI-chap73-sec1514A (accessed March 14, 2018).

57 See 29 CFR 1980. Online, www.whistleblowers.gov (accessed March 14, 2018).

58 See 12 U.S.C. § 5567 Consumer Financial Protection Act. Online, https://www.gpo.gov/fdsys/granule/USCODE-2014-title12/USCODE-2014-title12-chap53-subchapV-partE-sec5567 (accessed March 14, 2018).

59 See www.whistleblowers.gov, op. cit.

15

Transformational leadership

Benjamin P. Dean

FRAMING QUESTION

How can leaders create positive change for themselves, their followers, and their organizations?

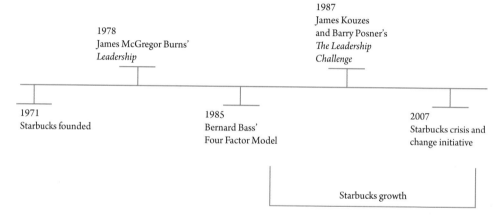

Figure 15.1 Timeline of major works on transformational leadership in relation to the chapter case study

Nelson Mandela stands as a historic example of how a transformational leader's behaviors can positively impact people, and even transform them as a nation. In 1995, the people of South Africa had dismantled apartheid and recently had elected Mandela as its first black president. But the country still faced daunting challenges of poverty, crime, and racial conflict. That year, Mandela recognized that the upcoming Rugby World Cup's Final Match in Johannesburg presented a unique opportunity to change people's perspectives about race and move them toward a more unified future.[1]

The events are portrayed in the film *Invictus*.[2] As South Africa's Springboks rugby team was still training for the match, Mandela met for tea with the team's captain, François Pienaar. Mandela emphasized the importance of transforming the Springboks team from being perceived as part of the old order dominated by whites, to a team that could represent the future and hopes for all South Africans. In their meeting, Pienaar genuinely felt encouraged and inspired by Mandela, a leader who had been imprisoned for nearly thirty years yet was willing to forgive and to reconcile. As the match approached, a close bond formed between Mandela and Pienaar.[3] Together they demonstrated a firm belief that South Africans could rise above racial divisions and that the Springboks team could inspire unity as a nation. Indeed, the Springboks team won the Final Match. At the end, to South Africans' cheers in a full stadium Mandela entered wearing a Springboks team jersey and presented the Cup to Pienaar and South Africa's winning team. From the spirit of that sports victory, the people of South Africa could envision what had before seemed impossible – a far greater unity among the people and achievement for their future as a nation.

In this now-iconic sports event, we can see the potential for transformational leaders to influence people toward positive outcomes that represent significant and lasting change. Transformational leadership represents one of the most well-known and widely embraced approaches to leadership today. The fact that the transformational approach to leadership has been adopted in so many contexts and so many places suggests that leaders find it works and followers tend to embrace leaders who use it. Broadly speaking, transformational leadership tends to produce positive outcomes for leaders and for followers. Leaders who demonstrate transformational leadership behaviors generally prove effective in influencing, motivating and enabling others to achieve goals.[4] Indeed, research studies show that these factors constitute an effective overall approach to leadership in organizations.[5] In addition to the effectiveness of transformational leadership, much of the approach's popularity derives from its positive association with ethical behaviors, which positions transformational leadership within the broadly defined group of ethical or values-based leadership models.

This chapter begins by examining the different sources from which the transformational leadership approach emerged and shows how several different streams essentially have converged. Focusing on the essential aspects of leadership that characterize the transformational approach, we will consider certain crucial ethical implications. This chapter will compare transformational leadership with several other major leadership approaches and will show the elements of transformational leadership that either overlap or contrast with the elements of those other approaches. The chapter will also address some of the limitations and challenges of transformational leadership. And as in previous chapters, we will also analyze this theory of leadership by applying the Five Components of Leadership Model.

This chapter shows the core components that define transformational leadership and place it well within the broad category regarded as ethical or values-based leadership. The transformational leadership approach becomes most apparent through leadership behaviors directed toward changing organizations and developing people in ways that achieve positive results. As a way of looking at transformational leadership dynamically applied in an organizational context, we will look at the transformational approach of Howard Schultz, CEO and Chairman of Starbucks Corporation, an organizational leader who has been highly regarded as innovative and effective. As we will see in an actual crisis faced by Schultz at Starbucks, one of the most serious ethical dilemmas that a transformational leader may face arises from circumstances where the needs and goals of an organization seem to conflict with the needs and welfare of its people.

History

The modern concept of transformational leadership rests on the writing of James McGregor Burns.[6] Burns articulated a concept of 'transforming' leadership, which he described as a process of social influence by which leaders and followers engage in the process of mutual change and development, raising each other to higher levels of morality and motivation.

The transformational approach, rather than reflecting one distinct theory, represents a collection of several theoretical models and overlapping sets of behaviors that describe 'transformational leadership.' Several means thus exist to articulate the transformational leadership approach. The work by Warren Bennis and Burt Nanus reflects one of these models.[7] Bennis and Nanus described a transformative approach to leadership as consisting of four behaviors of leaders seeking to transform organizations: presenting a clear vision of the future, shaping the understanding of followers into shared meanings, generating the followers' trust in a leader, and developing the followers' competence. Developing followers' awareness of their own competence involves leveraging their learning and creativity. Through those kinds of transformative behaviors, a leader genuinely focuses on followers and engages closely with them to inspire and develop them.[8]

Another well-known formulation of transformational leadership emerged from James Kouzes and Barry Posner.[9] They identified five leadership practices: modeling the way, inspiring a shared vision, challenging the process to achieve change, enabling others to act, and encouraging the heart through recognition and celebration. The components of Kouzes and Posner's description of transformational leadership overlap with some of Bennis and Nanus' elements, but Kouzes and Posner included a more explicit emphasis on change and the processes required to achieve change.

Similarly, Philip Podsakoff and his colleagues described transformational leadership as six distinct dimensions: articulating a vision, providing an appropriate (role) model, fostering acceptance of group goals, expecting high performance, giving individualized support, and generating intellectual stimulation. Leaders using these kinds of transformational behaviors enhance their engagement with followers and help both leaders and followers to reach their goals.[10] They also help leaders to build trusting relationships with followers, which is an essential dynamic in the leader–follower relationship.[11]

The best-known formulation of transformational leadership, however, comes from a model derived by Bernard Bass.[12] Bass and his colleagues identified four key elements: idealized influence (also referred to as charisma), inspirational motivation, intellectual stimulation, and individualized consideration. Research shows that these factors constitute an effective approach to leadership in organizations.[13] Each of these elements will be individually addressed in the next section, which looks at the common themes reflected among the several ways of viewing the transformational leadership approach.

Table 15.1 provides a summary of these five main formulations or typologies that comprise the primary literature about transformational leadership.

Major concepts of transformational leadership

Even though these theoretical models of transformational leadership vary in their elements, the collections of behaviors that define the elements of these various constructs remain consistent enough that transformational leadership stands as a distinct approach to leadership that can be powerful and effective. Each of the various ways of conceiving this leadership approach shows that transformational leadership's defining behaviors are useful and practical in leading people and organizations. Although in a later section of this chapter we will examine some critiques of transformational leadership, we will also see that studies on the behaviors characterizing the transformational approach fairly consistently produce positive outcomes in a variety of settings.

As Bass' model comprises the most commonly recognized set of dimensions describing transformational leadership, we can apply the four main

Table 15.1 Major typologies of transformational leadership

Models and Sources:	Behaviors/Components:
'Transforming' Leadership by Burns (1978)	• A process of mutual change and development by which leaders and followers raise each other to higher levels of motivation and morality
Transformational Leadership by Bass (1985, 1997); Bass & Steidlmeier (1999); Bass & Riggio (2006)	• *Idealized Influence* – Functionally equates to charisma • *Inspirational Motivation* – Manifests a leader's high expectations to instill in others a desire to exert greater efforts aimed at higher moral standards • *Intellectual Stimulation* – Engages others in ways that challenges them and encourages more creativity and innovation, and • *Individualized Consideration* – Reflects a leader's supportive actions toward a follower
'Transformative' Leadership by Bennis and Nanus (1985)	• Presenting a clear vision of the future • Shaping the understanding of followers into shared meanings • Generating the followers' trust in a leader, and • Developing the followers' competence
Transformational Leadership by Kouzes and Posner (1987, 2002)	• Modeling the way • Inspiring a shared vision • Challenging the process to achieve change • Enabling others to act, and • Encouraging the heart through recognition and celebration
Transformational Leadership by Podsakoff, et al. (1990)	• Articulating a vision • Providing an appropriate (role) model • Fostering acceptance of group goals • Expecting high performance • Giving individualized support, and • Generating intellectual stimulation

components of that model. By this framework we can also trace the themes and behaviors common among the various formulations or typologies of transformational leadership.[14]

Idealized influence

Transformational leaders seek to inspire followers and encourage them to achieve goals reflecting higher purposes. Idealized influence thus constitutes a crucial component in Bass' model for analyzing transformational leadership and centers on leaders serving as role models for followers.[15] The set of elements presented by Kouzes and Posner include a leader modeling the way. Likewise, the transformational leadership elements derived by Podsakoff et al. expressly describe leaders as providing appropriate role models to followers. This same element corresponds to a dynamic Bennis and Nanus identified by which leaders build trust so others will follow them.

The effectiveness of transformational leadership depends on a leader's behaviors and the extent to which people allow themselves to be influenced by the leader and are willing to embrace the leader as a model to follow. In this regard, the effectiveness of transformational leadership depends both on the leader's behaviors and on how followers view and understand those behaviors. The followers' perceptions of the leader's behaviors also prove to be crucial. Such follower perceptions determine how much impact these behaviors will have. Followers look to transformational leaders as exemplary role models.[16] This idealized influence represents a transformational leadership factor sometimes referred to as 'charisma,' which will be discussed later in more detail when we compare transformational leadership and charismatic leadership.

Inspirational motivation

Transformational leaders endeavor to engage followers in a process that seeks meaningful goals and positive change. Transformational leaders also communicate expectations and seek to motivate followers' performance toward achieving goals and accomplishing change. For Podsakoff et al. and for Kouzes and Posner, this element emerges as articulating and inspiring a shared vision. This overlaps with what Bennis and Nanus described as presenting a clear vision of the future. The leader leverages this focus on the shared vision, according to Podsakoff et al., to inspire and motivate followers, while expressing high standards of performance by followers.

According to Bass, transformational leaders generate inspirational motivation by expressing high expectations of followers, instilling in others a desire to exert greater efforts, and giving meaning to work that seeks higher goals or standards.[17] From the perspective of Burns' early description of the transformational approach, such efforts may aim toward raising followers' moral standards.[18] This element of inspirational motivation in combination with the element of idealized influence magnifies a leader's impact on followers even further because these two elements of transformational leadership tend to merge into one compelling dynamic.[19] The studies of transformational leadership provide considerable evidence that this approach ties closely and positively with moral reasoning processes and with leadership integrity. Studies such as these also provide evidence that transformational leaders hold greater capacity for moral reasoning and tend to display more leadership integrity.

Intellectual stimulation

Intellectual stimulation engages others mentally in ways that challenge them and may also enhance creativity and innovation.[20] Kouzes and Posner describe transformational leadership as challenging an existing process to achieve change. Such leaders, according to Bennis and Nanus, shape the mental understanding of followers to form shared meanings. According to Podsakoff et al., a leader leverages intellectual stimulation to foster group acceptance of goals.

Individualized consideration

Individualized consideration reflects a leader's supportive actions toward a follower, such as by attending to followers' needs through two-way communication.[21] Interrelated with the dimensions of intellectual stimulation and individualized consideration, Burns saw this leadership approach as involving a process of mutual change in which leaders and followers develop each other and raise each other to higher levels of motivation and morality.[22] Podsakoff et al. identifies the element as giving individualized support to followers. Bennis and Nanus observed these as leaders who develop followers' competence. Kouzes and Posner described transformational leaders as those who enable others to act and who recognize and celebrate followers in ways that encourage the heart.

Transformational leadership distinguished from other major leadership approaches

Transformational leadership shares important features with other major approaches to leadership that are found in this book. Even so, in the key aspects that will be identified in this section, transformational leadership remains sufficiently distinct to be recognizable from these other approaches. The present section will compare and contrast transformational leadership with the following approaches available to a leader: charismatic leadership, transactional leadership, servant leadership, visionary leadership, and authentic leadership.

Charismatic leadership

Transformational leadership shares many behaviors with charismatic leadership. How then can one distinguish the two approaches? According to one well-known set of elements defining the charismatic leadership model, a charismatic leader likely fits the following characteristics or behaviors: dominance, a strong desire to influence others, self-confidence, and a strong sense of moral values.[23] The last of those elements – a sense of moral values – fundamentally brings charismatic leadership into the broad group of ethical models, at least to the extent such leadership is others-directed. How ethical is the leadership of a given charismatic leader will depend on that leader's underlying motivations and values.[24] But this means that the influence exercised both by charismatic leaders and transformational leaders connects with followers through moral values, consequently permitting both approaches a claim to the broadly defined category of ethical leadership.

The other elements of charismatic leadership – the strong desire to influence others and dominant, self-confident behaviors – differ from the features defining transformational leadership, even if a given transformational leader displays some of those charismatic personality traits. By this analysis, one person could meet both the essential elements defining a transformational leader and a charismatic leader. The particular 'socialized' form of charisma, similar to what one should see in authentic transformational leadership, represents a more ethical form of charisma because in this case a leader is genuinely seeking to use influence and power on behalf of the group to serve the followers' and organizational needs rather than a 'personalized' form of charisma, which seeks simply to serve the leader.[25]

Transactional leadership

In contrast to transformational leadership, transactional leadership involves much less emphasis on inspiration or vision. Indeed, one may view transactional leadership not as an ethical leadership model, but rather as a values-neutral approach to leadership.[26] The transactional leader engages followers in a more tangible, fairly direct exchange of mutual benefits. A leader and a follower join in a kind of quid pro quo transaction by which the leader gains the loyalty or services of a follower by explicitly or implicitly promising to deliver benefits to the follower in return. A clear example of a transactional leadership approach arises in political campaigns in which a politician promises certain legislative outcomes and perhaps even patronage benefits for political followers who support the leader's campaign and vote for that leader. Once elected to office, the political leader is expected to 'make good' on those campaign promises.

Transactional leadership depends mainly on motivating others by essentially appealing to a cost–benefit calculation and self-interest analysis. In that regard, the leader–follower relationship relies much more heavily on an economic rationale than an ethical basis. Because of the economic foundation of transactional leadership, transactional leaders – in contrast to transformational leaders – tend to engage in much less personal interaction with followers once the parameters of the mutual exchange are established and set into motion. The leader awards followers so long as they perform; and followers perform so long as the leader fulfills his or her end of the bargain. When the flow of mutual benefits stops, the leader–follower relationship begins to break down. Indeed, transactional leaders may be threatened by followers if they actively engage the kinds of followership behaviors described in Chapter 14. Conversely, the developmental nature and aims of transformational leadership suggest that a transformational leader would likely welcome active followership.

As we saw earlier, transformational leaders make a stronger positive impact on people and organizations and therefore tend to be more effective than transactional leaders. Motivation inspired by transformational leaders also rouses more effort by followers in organizations than does the contingent rewards approach – the 'carrot or the stick' method – exercised by transactional leaders.[27] While transactional leadership and transformational leadership are comprised of distinct elements, they can be conceived as a 'full range' of leadership behaviors that places transactional leadership and transformational leadership at opposing ends of a single continuum.[28]

Servant leadership

Transformational leadership's emphasis on followers resembles a similar focus in another influential ethical leadership approach – servant leadership, which is discussed in detail in Chapter 13. Both transformational leadership and servant leadership leverage ethical means and ends to influence others in positive ways. And both transformational and servant leadership seek to develop people individually and collectively, thus enhancing followers' organizational commitment and engagement.[29] Yet the two leadership approaches still differ overall. While servant leaders exert influence mainly through satisfying followers' needs, transformational leaders exert influence mainly through satisfying their followers' perception of leaders' effectiveness.[30] Transformational leaders tend to be more directed toward the goal,[31] whereas servant leaders appear more focused on the follower's needs.[32] Whereas most theories of leadership, including transformational leadership, consider influence their primary focus, servant leadership shifts the attention to service, emphasizing the needs of followers.[33] A servant leader's loyalty may lie more with the individual than with the organization, whereas the opposite applies to a transformational leader.[34] As we will see later when we discuss developing people, a transformational leader in an organization may have to confront an ethical choice when faced with a decision about whether to improve the capabilities of followers as individuals or of followers collectively.

Visionary leadership

The critical element of transformational leadership that seeks to motivate followers by inspiring them essentially involves encouraging followers to see and focus on a clear vision. In this critical aspect, transformational leadership shares an essential dimension with a model of leadership known as visionary leadership. While future research may better define and provide more support for this model, the best-known model is the one by Kouzes and Posner.[35] Tying visionary leadership with their concept of transformative leader behaviors (as those described above), Kouzes and Posner observed that for a leader to be able to help people and organizations change, that leader must be viewed as credible enough that people can embrace the vision the leader presents and hopes to achieve. A potential criticism of visionary leadership is one that affects transformational and charismatic leadership, which is that the three may be conflated because they substantially overlap with the dynamics of idealized influence.

From the perspective of transformational leadership, however necessary may be the leader's credibility and trustworthiness in offering a vision, this aspect constitutes only one element among several on which the effectiveness of a transformational leader will depend. For this reason, the visionary leadership approach may offer less to followers and organizations, as compared with what transformational leadership and its multiple dimensions deliver to followers and organizations. Accordingly, we will move to another leadership approach, one which could be considered qualitatively distinct from transformational leadership.

Authentic leadership

One of the most recent developments in understanding leadership relates to authentic leadership. As its label suggests, authentic leadership focuses on the extent to which a leader is genuine and is real with followers. (Authentic leadership is discussed in detail in Chapter 12.)

Authentic leaders relate to others through behaviors that reflect a thorough understanding of one's values, specifically regarding their sense of who they are, where they want to go, and what are the right things to do.[36] For example, a manager in a supervisory position over a team may have serious concerns about whether the organization will provide sufficient resources to achieve production targets imposed on the team. In the dilemma of whether to be transparent about the resource problem ahead, we suppose that an authentic leader might choose to be more transparent with team members and more forthcoming with relevant information (both negative and positive) to preserve interpersonal trust and to strengthen bonds in the leader–follower relationship.

Work on authentic leadership as a theory began partly due to a perceived need to go beyond the aspect of transformational leadership research. Taking at face value transformational leadership's defining elements, one would assume that a transformational leader's motivations toward the welfare of followers must be genuine and authentic. However, a leader could outwardly manifest transformational behaviors while hiding actual intentions and motivations that focused more on the leader's self-interest. Theories of transformational leadership thus began to emphasize an 'authentic' transformational leadership versus an inauthentic, 'pseudo-transformational' leadership.[37] So, a primary means of comparing authentic leaders with transformational leaders relates to how well transformational leadership serves as a standard of a leader's real intentions toward followers.[38] Bass, through his refinement of an 'authentic' form of transformational leadership, seems to have provided a glimpse into the importance of this additional ethical dimension insofar as a transformational leader must present himself or herself to followers in a relationship that is genuine and real. In any event, transformational leadership and authentic leadership appear to be complementary and thus a leader may benefit by drawing on the key behaviors of both approaches.

Having compared and contrasted transformational leadership with several other important approaches to leadership, we now need to address certain critiques of transformational leadership based on what some reviewers consider to be limitations of this approach.

Critiques of transformational leadership

Even though transformational leadership has emerged as a well-established and–broadly–accepted approach to leadership, critics of the approach continue to raise challenges. We will focus in particular on three of the major critiques here.

Overlap and confusion between transformational and other approaches to leadership

Despite years of study, there is no single clearly established, uniformly accepted construct of transformational leadership. Even under Bass' theoretical development of transformational leadership – essentially the most well-established and best-known conceptualization – some controversy exists as to whether studies bear out its four dimensions as sufficiently distinct and verifiable. For example, the components of idealized influence and inspirational motivation tend to merge when practiced. Similarly, those same elements – idealized influence and inspirational motivation – may hold the weakest support from research studies on transformational leadership. As mentioned earlier, the full-range of leadership that places both transformational and transactional leadership on one continuum also reflects some amount of overlap between those two forms of leadership.[39] To some degree, a leader using either approach can be engaging in transactional exchanges for mutual benefit. The further practical problem is that while a leader may display transformational behaviors, one cannot be sure what the leader's hidden intentions or motives may be.

Another notable limitation of the transformational leadership model arises from its overlap and confusion with charismatic leadership. The transformational leadership and charismatic models hold in common a high level of interpersonal engagement with followers. This is illustrated by the strong ties of trust that followers form with a leader and that can be leveraged into leadership influence. In both models, leaders are communicating expectations, inspiring followers, and motivating them toward higher performance goals or standards. Although this accurately states a problem insofar as charismatic leadership and transformational leadership can be conflated or confused, the two are not coextensive. One still can meaningfully distinguish transformational leadership from charismatic leadership. Indeed, aside from idealized influence and inspirational motivation, the other four components of transformational leadership appear to extend beyond the defining characteristics of charismatic leadership.

Calling followers to a higher ethical level

As noted earlier, a debate revolves around whether one can accurately characterize transformational leadership as consistently calling followers to a 'higher level of motivation and morality.'[40] And as seen in the studies cited earlier, transformational leadership does bear a close connection with moral reasoning and with leadership integrity. Those studies further suggest that leaders whom followers identify as engaging in transformational leadership tend to be leaders whom followers also identify as being ethical. Taking into account those other studies that focus on the leader–follower dynamics that describe the idealized influence component of transformational leadership, followers are likely to affirm and adopt those behaviors of leaders with whom the followers personally identify. By logical extension, followers similarly would be likely to affirm and emulate ethical behaviors manifested by those leaders whom followers describe as transformational. In this regard, one may rightly view transformational leadership as fundamentally applying an ethical approach to leading people and organizations. And when the leadership behaviors depart from a positive approach to people, those behaviors begin to define a fundamentally different – possibly pseudo-transformational or unethical – way of leading people.

Also, as noted earlier, a potential problem arises to the extent that leaders who appear transformational may hide intentions or motivations that actually are rooted in self-interest. This was the key reason why, as noted above, some researchers began to distinguish authentic transformational leadership from a less authentic, pseudo-transformational leadership.[41] The main difference between authentic transformational leaders and pseudo-transformational leaders is the intention or the moral/ethical values of the leader, apart from the behaviors displayed outwardly.[42] This possibility of a leader deceiving followers about his or her real intentions or motives suggests the need to consider the possibility of less ethical results from what may appear on the surface to be transformational leadership behaviors.

Transformational leadership's potential 'dark side'

So far during this discussion of transformational leadership, we have purposefully examined transformational leadership as an ethical model of leadership. From this perspective, as we have already pointed out, transformational leadership maintains a significant connection with leader integrity and with moral reasoning ability. Even so, as perhaps implied by a pseudo-transformational view of leadership, the strong bonds that a transformational leader (or a charismatic leader) forms with followers could be abused.

The transformational leader's core capacities for creating a vision and inspiring the members of an organization may also carry the potential for achieving unethical purposes.[43] This dynamic by no means limits itself to transformational leadership; indeed, one can observe the same problem occurring in negative forms of charismatic leadership. But leaders who exercise influence over followers through unhealthy interpersonal relationships and negative actions can become manipulative and destructive. In the most severe manifestations, such leaders descend beyond values-neutral, amoral leadership into unethical forms of leadership, variously identified as 'dysfunctional leadership,' 'toxic leadership,'[44] or the 'dark side' of leadership.[45] Others have referred to 'destructive leadership,' described as the systematic and repeated behaviors of a leader who violates the legitimate interests of followers and the organization.[46]

We see that a leader can leverage those defining elements that make transformational or charismatic leadership both effective and ethical, and exploit leadership influence that remains effective but unethical. A clear division between these two models, however, would arise where the motives of the charismatic leader bend toward motivations and values reflecting more self-interest than concern for followers. A charismatic leader, for example, can continue motivating followers by appealing to moral values that the leader appears to embrace, but in reality doesn't. For example, history records numerous instances of charismatic cult leaders inspiring a group of devout followers and motivating them toward an idealistic vision of the future, but ultimately when the enterprise has spun out of the leader's control, the leader influences members all the way into their destruction rather than voluntarily give up power. Even in such a dysfunctional scenario where a charismatic leader – such as cult leader Jim Jones, who became infamous for directing the Jonestown mass suicide – exploits others for narcissistic reasons or self-serving goals, we could still consider the leader's behaviors to be effective and useful.

In contrast, authentic transformational leaders focus on the welfare of followers and the collective good rather than on their self-interest.[47] Logically, the necessary elements that define transformational leadership should preclude an authentic transformational leader from applying leadership influence that is tied to personal motives or self-interest that conflicts with the interests or values of his or her followers.[48]

Ethical implications of transformational leadership

Even if transformational leadership behaviors are useful and effective in achieving results, what makes the behaviors ethical in terms of the outcomes transformational leadership achieves and the way it goes about accomplishing those outcomes? This question has stimulated considerable debate.[49] The answer emerges from the inherent nature of those behaviors that distinguish transformational leaders and also by the positive outcomes such leadership aims to accomplish.

Ethical dynamics of transformational leadership

Given transformational leadership's defining elements, as discussed earlier, we know that this approach relies on leaders engaging in certain kinds of ethical behaviors that inspire, motivate, and encourage people toward higher purposes and goals. Based on four overarching dynamics of transformational leadership, we can reasonably say that transformational leaders engage in ethical behaviors as follows: (a) inspiring pursuit of meaningful goals, higher purposes, and positive change; (b) engaging moral reasoning; (c) relying on strong leader–follower relationships; and (d) developing people through encouragement and support.

Transformational leaders inspire the pursuit of meaningful goals, higher purposes, and positive change. As noted above regarding the components of transformational leadership, such leaders seek to inspire and empower people toward higher levels of motivation and morality.[50] For example, one study showed that leaders who are perceived as being more transformational in their leadership behaviors have more capacity for exercising moral reasoning than leaders who are not seen as transformational.[51] That study looked at followers' perceptions of transformational leadership behaviors and asked employees how often their managers displayed certain behavioral characteristics of transformational leadership. These evaluations were then analyzed against scores each of the managers had received on a test of moral reasoning ability. Managers who scored highest on a moral reasoning test exhibited more transformational leadership behaviors than those who tested lower on moral reasoning. The researchers in that same study concluded that leaders with a capacity for more complex moral reasoning tend to pursue goals beyond self-interest and to seek the collective good. Studies like this demonstrate that the effectiveness of transformational leadership significantly depends on the ethical qualities displayed by a leader.

Another study also examined transformational leadership behaviors as perceived by followers, but this time by considering the moral reasoning capacity of the followers. This study showed that followers' perceptions of transformational leadership depend on the followers' ability to identify and interpret ethical issues.[52] According to this study, the effectiveness of transformational leadership depends not just on the behaviors of the leader, but also on whether followers can recognize, appreciate, and respond to a leader's transformational actions. To be effective in their transformational leadership, leaders must take into account how followers perceive and understand his or her actions.[53]

Similarly, followers' perceptions of the transformational leader's integrity constitute another crucial aspect affecting whether followers view the leader's actions as ethical. Indeed, followers' trust depends significantly on the integrity a leader displays.[54] This study showed that the leaders who demonstrated strong patterns of transformational leadership were perceived as displaying the most integrity.[55] And as perceived leader integrity goes up, so do certain key markers of leadership effectiveness and organizational effectiveness. The same researchers also concluded that the best way to explain why some leaders were perceived as having low integrity arose from evidence those leaders only infrequently displayed or expressed their ideals – one of the defining elements of transformational leadership.

Developmental change as an ethical focus of transformational leadership

Leaders can use influence to serve as active change agents.[56] One can hardly overestimate the crucial importance of leaders having a well-grounded moral view of what constitutes 'good' outcomes in developing people, their organizations, and their communities, and about the means used to achieve those results.[57] Leadership's natural social context and its human impact suggest that leaders should be dedicated to guiding a process that requires reconciling the uniqueness of human cultural diversity and individual human rights with the universal value of promoting global human opportunities.[58] Leaders are vital in developing people and organizations because they have the opportunity to serve as active agents of change – transformation – by influencing people and circumstances in ways that significantly affect human development for individuals and groups.

As observed in the analysis of the four main components of transformational leadership, such leaders focus on the development of people and even of themselves.[59] They actively engage with followers in ways that assist followers in grappling with the challenges of change and personal growth.[60] They also emphasize the need to develop people and positively impact them by encouraging and supporting them – individually as persons and collectively within organizations.[61]

Despite transformational leadership's limitations, it remains accurate to describe the model as a powerful and inherently ethical way for leaders to influence followers. Leaders inevitably face dilemmas in seeking to act ethically while also addressing conflicting demands placed on them.[62] Leaders bear significant potential for driving change in organizations and society, and can profoundly impact the lives of individuals. For example, when a new CEO comes into a company or a new president takes charge of a university, the members of such an organization naturally brace for change – anticipating that some of the members might be hurt as a result of the changes that new leader makes. Yet we can see in the various ways already described, ethical leaders – including transformational leaders – work for the benefit of followers. Transformational leadership emphasizes intentional efforts to transform and develop the people themselves, both individually and collectively. Authentic transformational leaders (as Bass described them) genuinely focus on the growth development of people and strongly emphasize an ethic of developing and supporting them.[63] From an ethical standpoint, transformational leaders legitimately exercise influence from a foundation of genuine concern for developing followers and from an authentic motivation to inspire and support followers in developing them to their fullest potential.[64] There lies at the ethical core of transformational leadership a 'development ethic' that can be viewed as grounded in moral philosophy.

The moral dimension that underlies leadership's ethical imperative fundamentally flows out of the leader's concern for human value.[65] The leader's – particularly the transformational leader's – focus on developing people represents a crucial ethical mandate. This is the reason why transformational leadership is so significant morally; it moves beyond most other leadership approaches in using influence purposefully to drive change and to achieve goals that will enhance (or impair) the human development of followers. A leader who undertakes transformational behaviors to influence people and build organizations essentially creates a moral obligation to be responsible for protecting human value and developing people through that process.[66] These developmental aims and purposes that underlie transformational leadership spotlight the moral responsibilities and practical impact leaders have on people, organizations, and communities.

In sum, we can logically conclude that transformational leadership fundamentally comprises an ethical approach to leadership because of the inherent moral dimensions of its distinguishing behaviors, such as inspiration, encouragement, and support of followers. We also recognize transformational leadership's positive ethical nature in view of such leaders' efforts at balancing results for organizations with developmental outcomes for the people who comprise those organizations. Even so, other ethical leadership approaches reflect similar others-focused behaviors and purposes. This suggests that in the next section we need to consider the distinguishing aspects of transformational leadership and compare them with key aspects of certain other leadership approaches, including other ethical leadership approaches.

Five component analysis

Transformational leadership's central focus on the quality of the relationship between a leader and a follower is a major reason this approach is so widely recognized and accepted.[67] Transformational leadership readily fits within the view of leadership as a process by which leaders and followers develop a relationship and work toward a goal(s) within a context shaped by culture.[68] Accordingly, we may also view transformational leadership and its distinguishing dynamics through the lens of the Five Components Model that serves within this book as our broad framework for analyzing the various leadership approaches. We turn now to the five components to consider how each relates to the transformational leadership approach.

By applying the Five Components of Leadership Model, we see the most important aspects of transformational leadership are the leader, follower, and the goal as well as the relationship between the leader and follower and their means of achieving the goal (see Figure 15.2). As we analyze the leader component of the model, we are looking directly at a leader's own development.[69] Transformational leadership's view of a leader–follower relationship

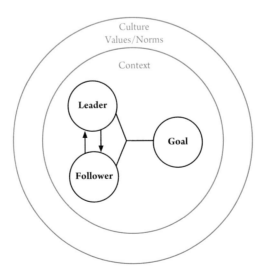

Figure 15.2 The Five Components of Leadership Model applied to transformational leadership

that engages a mutual development exchange readily affirms the importance of the leader. This component depends on what virtues, that is, what values the leader personally embraces and how he or she externally manifests those virtues within his or her relationships with followers. Tying this component to our overview of moral philosophies, we can recall seeing how this focus on the leader as a person required us to consider ethical issues relating to moral virtues. Particularly, in regard to transformational leaders, we see how important 'authentic' transformational leadership is in our understanding of the leader's values underlying efforts to transform and develop one's followers, and of the true 'goodness' of his or her intentions in seeking to inspire and motivate followers toward particular goals. Further, regarding this focus on the transformational leader individually, we can see how Kant's philosophy emphasizing the leader's moral duty also strongly relates to what obligations a transformational leader owes followers in inspiring, motivating, and developing them.

From our discussion of transformational leadership so far, we have seen that such leaders actively engage in building relationships with followers, which ties strongly to the follower component of the Five Components Model.[70] Ethical leaders engage followers in ways that assist others in grappling with the challenges of change and personal growth.[71] We can see this dynamic in the transformational approach. As James MacGregor Burns originally articulated the concept, leaders who engage this distinctive approach to leadership seek to engage with followers in a mutual process of social influence in which both parties are positively changed and developed.[72] We have also seen that transformational leaders emphasize the need to develop people affirmatively and to positively impact them – supporting them both as individuals and collectively within organizations.[73] Accordingly, we understand that authentic transformational leaders engage followers, individually and collectively; seek to inspire and motivate them in ethical ways; and encourage them to achieve meaningful goals, higher purposes, and positive change.

Transformational leadership's significant emphasis on followers means that our analysis is most directly exploring a leader's role in developing others.[74] Because of transformational leadership's priority on developing followers both as individuals and collectively, we already have observed how ethical issues arise concerning what practical effects the leader–follower relationship will have on followers. This means that the leader–follower relationship inherently raises significant ethical issues involving a leader's treatment of followers, especially a leader's sense of justice and fairness toward a follower. As we may observe in regard to the development of followers, John Rawls' moral philosophy of distributive justice specifically seeks to achieve a person's human development by ensuring access to the resources and social goods that allow every person to meet a threshold of human functioning and human capability.

Among the key components we can clearly apply here to our analysis, goals remain essential within transformational leadership. The five component analysis may suggest that within a leadership approach that emphasizes goal achievement, a leader might tend to apply his or her leadership influence in ways ethically guided toward results that are utilitarian, seeking 'good' outcomes for the greatest number of people involved. We may recall that studies show that leaders who demonstrate transformational leadership behaviors generally prove effective in influencing, motivating and enabling others to achieve goals.[75] While it remains accurate to say that transformational leaders seek to be and generally are effective organizational leaders, authentic transformational leadership behaviors genuinely focus on developing people to their fullest human capability and encouraging them to work together to achieve higher-purpose objectives. In the ways discussed earlier, transformational leadership involves a mutual exchange process that drives how development is accomplished. In an organizational context, achieving objectives necessarily involves relating to followers collectively, so the human development dynamic tends to be collective, too.[76] In this dynamic of relating to followers collectively, a transformational leader may sense a need to adopt utilitarian ethical standards by which he or she hopes to achieve organizational goals while also accomplishing the greatest degree of human development for the largest number of organizational members.

The Five Components Model analyzes leadership as applied within a specific context shaped by cultural norms and values. All leadership influence necessarily draws its application and meaning from the particular context in which that leadership actually is being exercised. Transformational leadership's broad acceptance, as noted from the outset of this chapter – as well as the studies discussed earlier – suggests that transformational leadership tends to prove effective within a myriad of different organizational and other contexts. Even though all five of the components remain relevant to transformational leadership, in comparison with the leader, follower, and goal components, the context and also the cultural values/norms components seem to bear less directly on the behaviors that characterize a transformational leader.

Transformational leadership's effectiveness and appeal also may not be tied to particular cultures. By definition within the Five Components Model of analysis, cultural norms and values operate to shape the given context. This observation regarding culture also appears consistent with Bass' observation that transformational leadership's effectiveness tends to cross the boundaries of culture.[77] However, this does not necessarily mean that transformational leadership would always be the leadership approach of choice in all contexts and all cultures. For example, one might logically predict that transformational leadership, with its emphasis on building strong leader–follower relationships, would be an unlikely leadership preference in a highly directive or authoritarian context or in a culture manifesting a wide power-distance gap between leaders and followers.

So far, we have examined in considerable detail the core elements of transformational leadership and have described the characteristic behaviors of a transformational leader. We have also analyzed these leadership elements and behaviors against the template of the Five Components Model as a means of understanding how transformational leaders apply their leadership influence and how their priorities align within the framework of those five components. We are now prepared to examine how transformational leadership emerged in an actual case – Howard Schultz at Starbucks Corporation.

CASE STUDY

Transformational leadership of Howard Schultz, CEO of Starbucks Corporation[78]

Starbucks Corporation remains widely regarded as the world's most successful specialty coffee company and coffeehouse chain. The company rapidly ascended from its founding in 1971 to international recognition. As a result of Starbucks' extraordinary growth and competitive success, it now holds more than 24,000 retail stores in at least 70 countries. In that process, Starbucks distinguished itself as a unique company with a strong people-focused organizational culture. Over the years, Starbucks largely achieved its competitive advantage and its marketplace dominance through the vision and transformational leadership of Howard Schultz, Starbucks' chief executive officer and board chairman.[79]

Schultz shares a poignant personal story about how his father suffered an on-the-job injury and consequently lost his employment. The incident so impacted Schultz when he was young that he determined that if he were ever responsible for employees, he would make sure to protect their welfare and preserve their human dignity. Today, Starbucks under Schultz's leadership has become well-known for strategically leveraging positive human resource policies and benefits – even to the point of shaping human capital into a competitive advantage, and also for demonstrating ethical, sustainable corporate practices. Such a profound and enduring impact on Starbucks clearly affirms the fundamentally ethical grounding of Schultz's approach to leadership.

CASE STUDY *(continued)*

Over the initial decades of growth, Starbucks' shareholders and employees consistently prospered. By the early 1990s, Schultz and the executive team of Starbucks met the challenge of transforming the company from an entrepreneurial startup into a professionally managed corporation operating and expanding across North America and even internationally.[80]

In 2007, Starbucks began confronting the most difficult economic and organizational challenges it had ever faced. Global competitive forces and economic pressures had begun to drag the company's pace of growth. As the company's sales and profits started slipping, its overall financial health declined. To save the company, Schultz and other senior executives had to diagnose the underlying causes of the organizational problems and figure out how to respond. The solutions could only come through difficult choices. Starbucks cut the positions of 1,000 employees ('partners' in the company's vocabulary).[81] Schultz faced the daunting leadership challenge of motivating and ultimately transforming the organization and its people.

Schultz recognized that Starbucks baristas – the partners at the point of direct contact with customers – had lost much of their inspiration and capacity for achieving Starbucks' vision of creating a distinctive Italian-style coffeehouse experience and a welcoming community space. Schultz also saw the need for better training of baristas in espresso-making skills. The situation called for significant organizational change that would refocus on the vision and set people back onto the course that originally had guided Starbucks to success. Schultz persuaded the executives and board members of Starbucks to take a surprisingly bold step – closing all Starbucks stores at the same time to immerse its baristas in an intensive, one-time retraining event. Schultz believed that through careful planning and coordination the company could develop baristas' technical skills to new levels, but also renew and elevate their vision for creating what Schultz calls an authentic 'Starbucks experience.'[82] The renewal succeeded. Starbucks and its people achieved the transformation that laid an even broader foundation for Starbucks' rapid growth and international expansion in the following decade.[83]

Starbucks recently experienced a highly visible problem as a company that serves the public. In early 2018, a Starbucks manager called police into a store in Philadelphia, which culminated in arrests of two black men, a videotape that went viral on social media, and significant accusations of racial bias.[84] Howard Schultz, in his current role as executive chairman, said he felt 'personally accountable' to see that Starbucks addresses the issues. Schultz proposed closing Starbucks' stores for special human resource training for 175,000 members of its workforce as part of the company's efforts to remedy bias in the future and to ensure respectful treatment of all customers.[85]

Five component analysis

We can probe more deeply into the ethical aspects of the Starbucks' case and Howard Schultz's actions as a leader by examining those elements among the five components that most

CASE STUDY *(continued)*

Figure 15.3 The Five Components of Leadership Model applied to Howard Schultz and the Starbucks Corporation case study

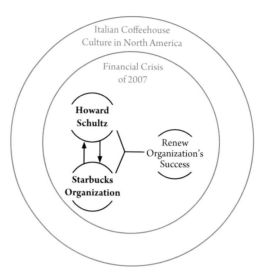

closely relate to transformational leadership. In other words, we can specifically look at the components that appear to strongly shape and drive the actions of transformational leaders. Based on our understanding of transformational leaders, we can reasonably expect that an authentic transformational leader will likely focus on and act consistently with a particular set of priorities. Considering the kinds of priorities that best characterize a transformational leader, we can examine each of the five components of leadership.

Schultz stated that when he joined Starbucks he immediately immersed himself in building the enterprise and surprised even the people at Starbucks with how 'impassioned' he became about coffee and the business.[86] Schultz transparently acknowledged a personal process of leadership development in which he periodically had to reexamine and refocus his priorities as a leader. He became quite purposeful in his role and development.[87] Looking back over the years of Starbucks' growth, Schultz wrote that he had to change as a leader and that he had to reinvent himself at least three times. The nature of his leadership started from his role as a 'dreamer,' moved to an entrepreneur, grew into a professional manager, and emerged as a visionary leader.[88] As we will see in the next component of analysis, much of Schultz's motivation as a leader grew out of not only a desire to achieve financial success and to build a great company, but emerged out of a genuine concern for the long-term welfare and growth of the people within Starbucks.

Applying another of the five components in this analysis of Howard Schultz's leadership, we can observe in this case study that a transformational leader's relationship with followers may be well-grounded in ethical values emphasizing justice and fairness. According to Schultz, one of the most valuable lessons he learned was this: 'There is no more precious commodity than the relationship of trust and confidence a company has

CASE STUDY (continued)

with its employees.'[89] As he wrote, 'Treat people like family, and they will be loyal and give their all. Stand by people, and they will stand by you.'[90] This people-oriented philosophy encompassed not only Starbucks employees (partners) but also the company's customers. In Schultz's view, people – employees and customers – ultimately determine Starbucks' success.[91]

When Starbucks faced the financial crisis triggered by a global economic recession and cut the positions of 1,000 employees, Schultz made a decision that appeared to give priority to achieving organizational goals. This seemed to contradict the corporate values that focused on the welfare of people. After the personnel cuts were completed, many of those who remained questioned whether the company and its people could ever rebuild the organizational trust and recapture the vision on which Starbucks formerly had achieved such success. But Schultz listened to the criticisms, allowed himself to be held accountable to those values, and personally addressed the people of Starbucks in open meetings. He acknowledged a failure to anticipate and mitigate the harm to people, but also reaffirmed in tangible ways Starbucks' commitment to and relationship with employees.[92] For example, Starbucks became one of the first major corporations in the United States to provide health insurance to part-time employees and vested ownership interests to employees as 'partners' in the business enterprise.

Considering the numerous ways in which Schultz actively invests in the people of Starbucks, and recalling the life-changing impact his father's injury and consequent loss of dignity had on Schultz as a boy, we see in Schultz an authentic motivation to assume responsibility for the welfare of the people within his sphere of leadership influence. But beyond just fair treatment and human respect of employees, Schultz has purposefully and consistently sought through Starbucks to improve their lives by creating innovative policies for employees to benefit directly from their efforts that contribute to Starbucks' financial success and by providing training opportunities and career advancement to develop their capabilities as individuals. As an example of the latter, Schultz's memoirs of Starbucks identifies and describes how numerous employees over the years received internal promotions and met the challenges that allowed them to achieve managerial and executive positions within Starbucks. Schultz expressed this developmental priority of Starbucks as 'people growth,'[93] thus capturing succinctly his development ethic as a transformational leader.

Schultz as an entrepreneur was highly motivated toward the goal of building a great commercial enterprise – perhaps at times even personally driven, according to how he described himself. From the beginning, he had envisioned building a great company and leveraged every opportunity to grow the enterprise by increasing the number of stores and expanding its reach with new products in new markets. Yet in this ambitious entrepreneurial effort, he still proved his effectiveness as a transformational leader insofar as this approach to leadership helped him to build and continue to grow a highly profitable corporation that rose quickly to dominate the North American coffee industry. From the beginning, Schultz proved to be results-oriented. He focused on launching a successful enterprise

CASE STUDY *(continued)*

and a great company, building it through discipline and innovation into a nationally recognized brand image, and expanding the number of its sales outlets as rapidly and widely as possible.[94] Schultz's intense drive toward successful achievement, however, remains consistent with transformational leadership's distinguishing elements.

When things are going well in business, Schultz observed, the tendency is to fall into complacency because there is little motivation for change. But Starbucks, like most companies, operates in an industry that rapidly evolves as competition intensifies. Certainly, when a company begins to slip, or even fail, it's far easier to understand the necessity of change – the need for self-renewal. For a company to remain healthy, profitable, and sustainable, it cannot rely on just maintaining the status quo. It is always vulnerable to external forces and must continually reinvent itself to meet the demands of a competitive environment.[95] Thus as Schultz's leadership effectiveness suggests, a transformational approach to leadership seemed to work well in that environment where Starbucks as a business enterprise had to continually reinvent itself to remain competitive and viable, and be able at the same time to remain true to the original core values it still embraced.

Early in launching his business enterprises, Howard Schultz demonstrated a strong sense of the importance of culture. First, he saw the Italian coffee bar culture as a social model for what did not yet exist but could fit well within American society by providing a 'third place' beyond home and work.[96] As he established and grew his company, Schultz recognized the need to infuse it with a distinctive organizational culture based on clear values. Indeed, during Starbucks' crisis in 2007 and 2008, the firmly established core values and corporate culture became the reference point Schultz used in guiding the company's renewal and return to success. As Schultz stated, 'Whatever your culture, your values, your guiding principles, you have to take steps to inculcate them in the organization early in its life so that they can guide every decision, every hire, every strategic objective you set.'[97] The sense of personal accountability Schultz expressed in response to the 2018 incident of apparent racial bias by a Starbucks store manager, plus his subsequent proposal to close Starbucks stores for a day of human resource training to focus on values of respect for all customers, remain consistent with a long-term commitment to reinforce the organizational culture and social responsibility Schultz sought to instill from the outset.

Considering each of the five components, and applying them to the facts of this case of Schultz's leadership at Starbucks, we can readily see how the transformational leadership priorities emerged, impacted Schultz's effectiveness as CEO and as chairman, and reflected ethical leadership values and behaviors in achieving positive change for Starbucks and its people. Taking into account the elements and dynamics applied in the case study and analyzed against the framework of the Five Components Model, we are prepared to offer an answer to the key question with which we launched this chapter.

Summary and concluding remarks

We began this chapter on transformational leadership with a question: 'How can leaders create positive change for themselves, their followers, and their organizations?' The answer starts with a duty to engage in ethical leadership behaviors that are grounded in a moral obligation toward others. Transformational leadership comprises not only an effective approach to leadership across a variety of contexts, but also represents an ethical approach to leadership. The case study of Howard Schultz at Starbucks exemplified this sense of responsibility by a leader toward others and illustrates how the ethical grounding of a transformational leader can manifest in action. At the same time, we can conclude that, as demonstrated by the Starbucks case, transformational leadership proves highly effective in building high-performing teams and successful organizations.

The summation of these leadership principles and dynamics provides strong support that transformational leaders readily inspire, motivate, and stimulate others toward higher goals. Transformational leaders also demonstrate concern for followers and embrace a development ethic toward the people and organizations for whom leaders hold responsibility. This suggests a related question. What kinds of behaviors inspire both leaders and followers to grow as persons and bring about positive change? Transformational leaders are not satisfied with relationships in which leaders only engage with followers to reward or punish them for performance. Instead, these leaders find ways to challenge the assumptions of their followers, connect with them as individuals, and inspire them to action – all while somehow embodying the core values of their mutual organization. To become this kind of leader, one must value long-term development as much as immediate performance. And, one must demonstrate the ability to both clearly communicate core values and live them out on a consistent basis.

? DISCUSSION QUESTIONS

How does a transformational leaders' use of the charisma element make a difference for the performance of members of a team or an organization?

Considering that some observers have questioned transformational leadership's nature as a fundamentally ethical approach to leadership, what are the distinctive behaviors that support the view that authentic transformational leadership constitutes ethical leadership?

What kinds of situations or circumstances might arise that could put a transformational team leader into a dilemma where he or she has to choose between achieving team effectiveness and organizational goals, on the one hand, or promoting the welfare and development of team members, on the other hand? Would the team leader's decision to emphasize one choice over the other choice necessarily make the leader's actions any more or less moral or ethical?

What practical implications or effects emerge for followers from the reality that a given organizational leader can be either displaying an ethical, 'authentic' transformational leadership or a less ethical, 'pseudo' form of transformational leadership? Would it ever be possible for an authentically transformational leader to display a leadership 'dark side'?

What are some of the similarities and differences that characterize the behaviors of a transformational leader and a servant leader? To the extent two leaders in a team or an organization adopt these two different approaches, what would be the potential practical outcomes, if any, for followers and the organization?

According to Howard Schultz's personal story in the Starbucks case study, what was so significant about his father's on-the-job injury that caused Schultz to make up his mind that if he ever held responsibility for employees, he would treat them differently from how his father was treated as an employee?

 ADDITIONAL RESOURCES

B. Bass and B.J. Avolio, The Multifactor Leadership Questionnaire. Online, https://www.mindgarden.com/16-multifactor-leadership-questionnaire.

The MLQ is the survey instrument most typically used for analyzing transformational and transactional leadership.[98]

J. Kouzes and B. Posner, LPI: Leadership Practices Inventory. Online, http://www.leadershipchallenge.com/professionals-section-lpi.aspx.

This is another tool for measuring and evaluating transformational leadership. It follows Kouzes and Posner's model and uses a survey instrument known as the leadership practices inventory (LPI).[99]

P.M. Podsakoff, S.B. MacKenzie, R.H. Moorman, and R. Fetter, 'Transformational leader behaviors and their effects on followers' trust in leader, satisfaction, and organizational citizenship behaviors,' The Leadership Quarterly, vol. 1 no. 2, June 1990, 107–42.

The authors of this study developed a third tool for evaluating transformational leaders, the GTI.[100] The GTI was designed as a short and practical measure in comparison with the longer MLQ and LPI.[101]

NOTES

1 J. Carlin, *Playing the Enemy: Nelson Mandela and the Game That Made a Nation*, London: Atlantic, 2008.

2 *Invictus*, C. Eastwood (Director), Liberty Pictures/Warner Bros, 2009.

3 M. Cleary, 'Nelson Mandela: Francois Pienaar says he never imagined he would be so emotional,' *Telegraph*, December 6, 2013. Online, http://www.telegraph.co.uk/news/worldnews/nelson-mandela/10501078/Nelson-Mandela-Francois-Pienaar-says-he-never-imagined-he-would-be-so-emotional.html (accessed January 15, 2018).

4 R.J. House and R.N. Aditya, 'The social scientific study of leadership: Quo vadis?' *MANAGE Journal of Management*, vol. 23 no. 3, 1997, 409–73.

5 For example, see J.J. Hater and B.M. Bass, 'Superiors' evaluations and subordinates' perceptions of transformational and transactional leadership,' *Journal of Applied Psychology*, vol. 73 no. 4, 1988, 695–702. See also B.M. Bass and B.J. Avolio, *Improving Organizational Effectiveness Through Transformational Leadership*, Thousand Oaks, CA: Sage, 1994.

6 J.M. Burns, *Leadership*, New York: Harper & Row, 1978.

7 W.G. Bennis and B. Nanus, *Leaders: The Strategies for Taking Charge*, New York: Harper Business, 1997.

8 Bennis and Nanus, ibid, pp. 202–3.

9 J.M. Kouzes and B.Z. Posner, *The Leadership Challenge: How to Get Extraordinary Things Done in Organizations*, San Francisco: Jossey-Bass, 1987; J.M. Kouzes and B.Z Posner, *The Leadership Challenge*, San Francisco: Jossey-Bass, 2002.

10 P.M. Podsakoff, S.B. MacKenzie, R.H. Moorman, and R. Fetter, 'Transformational leader behaviors and their effects on followers' trust in leader, satisfaction, and organizational citizenship behaviors,' *The Leadership Quarterly*, vol. 1 no. 2, June 1990, 107–42.

11 Podsakoff et al. 1990, ibid.

12 B.M. Bass, *Leadership and Performance Beyond Expectations*, New York: Free Press, 1985.

13 See Hater and Bass, op. cit.; and Bass and Avolio, op. cit.

14 See Bass, 1985, op. cit.; B.M. Bass and P. Steidlmeier, 'Ethics, character, and authentic transformational leadership behavior,' *The Leadership Quarterly*, vol. 10 no. 2, 1999, 181–217; B.M. Bass and R.E. Riggio, *Transformational Leadership*, Mahwah, NJ: L. Erlbaum Associates, 2006.

15 Bass and Avolio, op. cit.

16 Bass and Riggio, op. cit.; M.E. Brown and L.K. Treviño, 'Socialized charismatic leadership, values congruence, and deviance in work groups,' *Journal of Applied Psychology*, vol. 91 no. 4, July 2006, 954–62.

17 Bass and Avolio, op. cit.

18 Burns, op. cit.

19 See B.M. Bass and B.J. Avolio, *Full Range Leadership Development: Manual for the Multifactor Leadership Questionnaire*, Palo Alto, CA: Mind Garden, 1997; see also B.M. Bass, 'Does the transactional-transformational leadership paradigm transcend organizational and national boundaries?' *American Psychologist*, vol. 52 no. 2, 1997, 130–39.

20 Bass and Avolio, 1994, op. cit.

21 Bass and Avolio, 1997, op. cit.

22 Burns, op. cit.

23 R.J. House, *A 1976 Theory of Charismatic Leadership*, Working Paper Series, Toronto University, October 1976. Online, https://eric.ed.gov/?id=ED133827 (accessed March 11, 2018). Also see R.J. House, *The Theory of Charismatic Leadership: Extensions and Evidence*, Philadelphia: Reginald H. Jones Center, Wharton School, University of Pennsylvania, 1993; F.J. Yammarino and B.J. Avolio, *Transformational and Charismatic Leadership: The Road Ahead*, 10th anniversary edn, Bingley, UK: Emerald, 2013.

24 Bass and Avolio, 1994, op. cit.

25 M.E. Brown and L.K. Trevino, 'Leader–follower values congruence: Are socialized charismatic leaders better able to achieve it?' *Journal of Applied Psychology*, vol. 94 no. 2, 2009, 478–90.

26 Bass, 1985, op. cit.; see also Bass and Avolio, 1997, op. cit.

27 Bass, 1985, op. cit. See also B.M. Bass, *Transformational Leadership: Industrial, Military, and Educational Impact*, Mahwah, NJ: Lawrence Erlbaum, 1998.

28 Bass and Avolio, 1997, op. cit.

29 D. van Dierendonck, 'Servant leadership: A review and synthesis,' *Journal of Management*, vol. 37 no. 4, July 2011, 1228–61; D. van Dierendonck and I. Nuijten, 'The servant leadership survey: Development and validation of a multidimensional measure,' *Journal of Business and Psychology*, vol. 26 no. 3, September 2011, 249–67.

30 D. van Dierendonck, D. Stam, P. Boersma, N. de Windt, and J. Alkema, 'Same difference? Exploring the differential mechanisms linking servant leadership and transformational leadership to follower outcomes,' *The Leadership Quarterly*, vol. 25 no. 3, June 2014, 544–62.

31 A.G. Stone, R.F. Russell, and K. Patterson, 'Transformational versus servant leadership: A difference in leader focus,' *Leadership & Organization Development Journal*, vol. 25 no. 4, June 2004, 349–61.

32 van Dierendonck, op. cit.

33 van Dierendonck, op. cit.

34 J. Parolini, K. Patterson, and B. Winston, 'Distinguishing between transformational and servant leadership,' *Leadership & Organization Development Journal*, vol. 30 no. 3, May 2009: 274–91.

35 Kouzes and Posner, 1987, op. cit.

36 B. George, *Authentic Leadership: Rediscovering the Secrets to Creating Lasting Value*, San Francisco: Jossey-Bass, 2004; B. George, *Discover Your True North*, Hoboken, NJ: Jossey-Bass, 2015.

37 Bass and Steidlmeier, op. cit.

38 See Parry and Proctor-Thomson, op. cit.

39 Bass and Steidlmeier, op. cit.

40 Burns, op. cit.

41 Bass and Riggio, 2006, op. cit; Bass and Steidlmeier, op. cit.

42 Parry and Proctor-Thomson, op. cit.

43 Parry and Proctor-Thomson, op. cit.

44 J. Lipman-Blumen, *The Allure of Toxic Leaders: Why We Follow Destructive Bosses and Corrupt Politicians – and How We Can Survive Them*, Oxford: Oxford University Press, 2006.

45 J.A. Conger, 'The dark side of leadership,' *Organizational Dynamics*, vol. 19 no. 2, September 1990, 44–55.

46 Einarsen, Aasland, and Skogstad, op. cit.

47 A. Christie, J. Barling, and N. Turner, 'Pseudo-transformational leadership: Model specification and outcomes,' *Journal of Applied Social Psychology*, vol. 41 no. 12, December 2011, 2943–84.

48 Bass and Riggio, 2006, op. cit.

49 K.W. Parry and S.B. Proctor-Thomson, 'Perceived integrity of transformational leaders in organisational settings,' *Journal of Business Ethics*, vol. 35 no. 2, January 2002, 75–96.

50 Burns, op. cit. Also see M.Z. Hackman and C.E. Johnson, *Leadership: A Communication Perspective*, 6th edn, Long Grove, IL: Waveland, 2013.

51 N. Turner, J. Barling, O. Epitropaki, V. Butcher, and C. Milner, 'Transformational leadership and moral reasoning,' *Journal of Applied Psychology*, vol. 87 no. 2, 2002, 304–11.

52 A.M. Naber and R.G. Moffett, 'Follower moral reasoning influences perceptions of transformational leadership behavior,' *Journal of Applied Social Psychology*, vol. 47 no. 2, February 2017, 99–112.

53 Naber and Moffett, ibid.

54 R.B. Shaw, *Trust in the Balance: Building Successful Organizations on Results, Integrity, and Concern*, San Francisco: Jossey-Bass, 1998.

55 Parry and Proctor-Thomson, op. cit.

56 P.F. Buller, J.J. Kohls, and K.S. Anderson, 'The challenge of global ethics,' *Journal of Business Ethics*, vol. 10 no. 10, October 1991, 767–75.

57 B.P. Dean, 'Emerging leadership ethics in an interdependent world: Human capabilities development as a global imperative for moral leadership,' N.S. Huber, M.C. Walker (eds), *Emergent Models of Global Leadership*, College Park, MD: International Leadership Association, 2005, pp. 17–33.

58 A. Safty, *Leadership and Global Governance*, Irvine, CA: Universal Publishers, 2003.

59 B.M. Bass and P. Steidlmeier, 'Ethics, character, and authentic transformational leadership behavior,' *The Leadership Quarterly*, vol. 10 no. 2, 1999, 181–217.

60 J.B. Ciulla, *Ethics, The Heart of Leadership*, Westport, CN: Quorum Books, 1998; R.A. Heifetz, *Leadership Without Easy Answers*, Cambridge, MA: Harvard University Press, 1994.

61 Bass and Riggio, op. cit.

62 S. Einarsen, M.S. Aasland, and A. Skogstad, 'Destructive leadership behaviour: A definition and conceptual model,' *The Leadership Quarterly*, vol. 18 no. 3, June 2007, 207–16.

63 Bass and Steidlmeier, op. cit.

64 B.J. Avolio, B.M. Bass, and D.I. Jung, 'Re-examining the components of transformational and transactional leadership using the Multifactor Leadership,' *Journal of Occupational and Organizational Psychology*, vol. 72 no. 4, December 1999, 441–62. See also Bennis and Nanus, op. cit.

65 R.N. Kanungo and M. Mendonca, *Ethical Dimensions of Leadership*, Thousand Oaks, CA: Sage, 1996. See also, R. Bergman, 'Why be moral? A conceptual model from developmental psychology,' *Human Development*, vol. 45 no. 2, April 2002, 104–24.

66 Kanungo and Mendonca, op. cit.

67 Bass and Riggio, 2006, op. cit.

68 R.M. McManus and G. Perruci, *Understanding Leadership: An Arts and Humanities Perspective*, New York: Routledge, 2015, p. 15.

69 McManus and Perruci, ibid. p. 16.

70 For further discussion of the crucial role of followers as viewed through the Five Components Analysis, see here in Chapter 14, which addresses how followers can crucially impact ethical leadership behaviors and also reviews the emerging body of knowledge relating to 'followership.'

71 Ciulla, op. cit.; and R.A. Heifetz, op. cit.

72 Burns, op. cit.

73 Bass and Riggio, 2006, op. cit.

74 McManus and Perruci, op. cit.

75 House and Aditya, op. cit.

76 Even taking into account individualized consideration as a key component of transformational leadership, an organizational leader's focus on and interactions with members tends to be collective, and thus somewhat less individual. This dynamic could constitute another difference between transformational leadership and other leadership approaches, such as servant leadership, if an organizational leader using another approach relates to followers more as individuals.

77 Bass, 1997, op. cit.

78 The case study derives its background facts from Howard Schultz's two books. See H. Schultz and D.J. Yang, *Pour Your Heart Into It: How Starbucks Built a Company One Cup at a Time*, New York: Hyperion, 1997. See also, H. Schultz, *Onward: How Starbucks Fought for Its Life Without Losing Its Soul*, New York: Rodale, 2011.

79 While the focus here is on Howard Schultz as an exemplar of transformational leadership, he also has articulated publicly his belief in the importance of servant leadership. See H. Schultz, 'Howard Schultz: America deserves a servant leader,' August 6, 2015. Online, http://www.nytimes.com/2015/08/06/opinion/america-deserves-a-servant-leader.html accessed (November 19, 2016).

80 Schultz and Yang, op. cit., p. 201.

81 Schultz, op. cit.

82 Schultz and Yang, op. cit., p. 251.

83 Schultz, op. cit.

84 Jargon, Julie, and Aisha Al-Muslim. 2018. 'Starbucks Chief Vows to Learn From Philadelphia Arrests.' *Wall Street Journal*, April 26, 2018, sec. Business. https://www.wsj.com/articles/starbucks-revenue-tops-estimates-maintains-outlook-1524777273 (accessed June 1, 2018).

85 Scheiber, Noam, and Rachel Abrams. 2018. 'Can Training Eliminate Biases? Starbucks Will Test the Thesis.' *The New York Times*, April 18, 2018, sec. Business Day. https://www.nytimes.com/2018/04/18/business/starbucks-racial-bias-training.html (accessed June 1, 2018).

86 Schultz and Yang, op. cit., p. 47.

87 Schultz and Yang, op. cit., p. 200.

88 Schultz and Yang, op. cit., p. 200.

89 Schultz and Yang, op. cit., p. 57.

90 Schultz and Yang, op. cit., p. 127.

91 Schultz and Yang, op. cit., p. 157.

92 Schultz, op. cit.

93 Schultz and Yang, op. cit., p. 131.

94 Schultz and Yang, op. cit., p. 322.

95 Schultz and Yang, op. cit., pp. 215–16, 241.

96 Schultz and Yang, op. cit., pp. 51–3.

97 Schultz and Yang, op. cit., p. 81.

98 Bass and Avolio, 1997, op. cit.

99 B.Z. Posner and J.M. Kouzes, 'Development and validation of the leadership practices inventory,' *Educational and Psychological Measurement*, vol. 48 no. 2, April 1988, 483–96.

100 Podsakoff et al., op. cit.

101 S.A. Carless, A.J. Wearing, and L. Mann, 'A short measure of transformational leadership,' *Journal of Business & Psychology*, vol. 14 no. 3, Spring 2000, 389–406.

16

Adaptive leadership

Stephen C. Trainor

 **FRAMING QUESTION**

How should both leaders and their followers adapt their thinking to solve complex challenges?

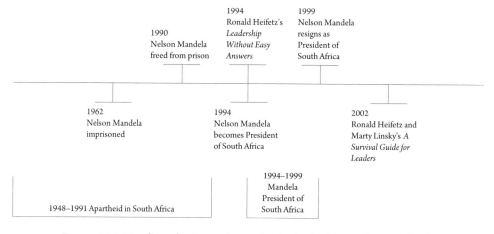

Figure 16.1 Timeline of major works on adaptive leadership in relation to the chapter case study

Albert Einstein famously observed, 'Problems cannot be solved with the same mindset that created them.'[1] His fundamental premise, that a change in thinking is the key to solving the most difficult and complex problems, serves as the organizing principle of the subject for this chapter: the adaptive leadership framework. Adaptive leadership shows us how leaders change the way they frame problems, how leaders support and mobilize their followers to change problem-solving approaches, and how leaders bring about change for good in their organizations and beyond.

Much has changed in the world since Einstein argued for a new way of thinking about problems, but the challenges facing individuals, organizations, and societies today are no less serious, and the stakes still include survival and success. In fact, the interrelated and increasingly globalized nature of the world has resulted in new categories of challenges, the most vexing of which are 'wicked' problems. Those problems are considered wicked because they are incredibly difficult, if not impossible, for any single organization or single leader to solve.[2] Prolific management theorist Peter Drucker goes even further to suggest that the challenges of the twenty-first century cannot be solved by implementing more sophisticated economic, political or managerial plans and policies.[3] Instead, Drucker argues that future problems are rooted in outdated assumptions about how things ought to work and can only be solved when, together, leaders and followers begin to think differently.[4] Adaptive leadership challenges some of those assumptions and provides a framework for leaders and followers to think differently about the problems they face.

As we have done in the previous chapters, we will first examine the history of adaptive leadership, apply the theory to a five component analysis, and finally examine how the theory works in the context of a specific case study, in this instance, Nelson Mandela's leadership of South Africa post-apartheid.

History

Abraham Kaplan observed, 'Give a small boy a hammer, and he will find that everything he encounters needs pounding.'[5] Likewise, while history shows us that leaders have always sought better ways to master the art of solving problems, it also demonstrates that our perspective is often limited. The adaptive leadership framework, first described by Harvard University lecturer Ronald Heifetz in the 1994 book *Leadership Without Easy Answers*, suggests that it isn't merely about finding *a* way to solve problems, but *a different and more effective way* to think about solving problems.[6] As the book's title implies, adaptive leadership emerged from the personal stories of leaders who were increasingly frustrated by an inability to solve organizational problems.[7] A closer study of the framework highlights the connections to key shifts in leadership and management thinking and associated social, political, economic and technological trends of the past century.[8] The most influential of those ideas, trends and connections are described below.[9]

Problem-solving has always been a key concern of organizational leadership, but the leader's approach to that role has changed over time.[10] One of the earliest modern sources on leadership and problem-solving is Frederick Winslow Taylor's study of work and the ensuing field of scientific management.[11] This approach to problem-solving shifted the focus of management from the external challenges of securing capital and resources to an internal focus on efficiency and the productivity of workers.[12] At the same time, the 'Great Man' and trait-based views of leadership suggested that the primary job of leaders was to make decisions and solve organizational problems through an unemotional process of analysis and design.[13] The primary assumptions of this early management perspective were that problems had predictable, rational and technical solutions and only certain types of leaders possessed the ability to effectively deal with those problems. This approach to organizational management and problem-solving contributed much to the dramatic growth of Western industry and society in the early twentieth century. However, by the Second World War, the mechanistic and leader-centric paradigms of problem-solving proved incapable of dealing with challenges of expanding scale, scope and impact.[14]

A new form of management thinking emerged from research that began in the Great Depression and came into prominence during the massive expansion of industrial power in the U.S. during the Second World War. In stark contrast to the deterministic and rational methods of scientific management, the human relations perspective confirmed that the person was a key variable in organizational problem-solving.[15] Research conducted prior to and during the Second World War studied the relationships between leaders and followers and discovered important effects of those relationships on group dynamics and organizational performance.[16] The follower was no longer merely a tool that leaders applied to a problem, but part of a unique social system and a direct and important contributor in the problem-solving process.[17] Leadership theory in this period sought the right conditions and the right behaviors to effectively motivate followers toward the leader's goal. But human relations theory also challenged leaders to consider, for the first time, the effects of their actions on followers as they shaped organizational systems to solve complicated problems. For example, the classic Hawthorne studies of group dynamics sought to understand how leaders could make work groups more productive, but discovered that leaders merely paying attention to workers influenced their motivation and productivity.[18] By mid-century, it was clear that leaders were responsible both for the roles of followers in problem-solving and for fostering an ethical imperative related to the follower's well-being.[19]

As the operating environment for many organizations expanded in the post-war period, so too did the need for effective problem-solving. And a new leadership perspective emerged that highlighted the interconnections and relationships of the organizational environment.[20] The organization was no longer static, but a dynamic, evolving and almost-living organism.[21] While the leader remained at the center of the organization, leadership and problem-solving was increasingly dependent, or contingent, on other factors like technology and communication that made the world smaller and expanded the nexus of problem-solving to the internal and external environments.[22]

The explosive impact of information technology in the 1960s and 1970s contributed to a new wave of thinking about leadership and an equally dramatic shift in the problems that organizational leaders faced. The leader's responsibilities in the information age expanded well beyond the confines of traditional organizations, to include larger interconnecting systems and various other entities. Along with the change in scope and scale of responsibility, approaches to leadership, like transformational, authentic and servant leadership, focus less on roles and activities and more on purposes and forms of leadership.[23] And finally, when we think of leaders in the information age, the image is no longer just of an executive directing an industrial operation from the corner office, but also includes images of people and purposes beyond the traditional organization. Leaders and leadership exist everywhere and range from aid workers helping to bring clean drinking water to a distant community to parents working on a coalition of families, teachers and local businesses to improve student access to learning resources. In each case, leadership extends beyond the factory walls to focus not only on problems of complicated production processes, but increasingly on complex interdependencies, like quality, effectiveness and satisfaction, which cannot be easily or even fully controlled. Unlike earlier times when leaders faced predictable, manageable tasks and plans, information-age leaders must respond to a growing number of problems they are incapable of solving with the expertise and knowledge they alone possess.[24] As a response to increasingly complex problems faced by leaders, adaptive leadership offers an approach to mobilize and leverage the interconnecting systems of people, knowledge, culture, and capabilities to solve the most wicked of problems. The adaptive leadership framework rejects the classical, technical and mechanical solutions, like Taylorism, recognizing that leaders need more metaphorical tools than just a hammer.

Major concepts of adaptive leadership

The previous section highlighted significant changes in management thinking and different approaches to leadership problem-solving. We now turn to adaptive leadership, which is the practice of mobilizing people to tackle tough challenges and thrive.[25] While leaders have always concerned themselves with solving problems and seeking opportunities, it seems that a growing number of leaders struggle in an increasingly turbulent environment, punctuated by macro trends like globalization, demographic shifts, and technological innovation.[26] On one hand, this turbulence might be a product of wickedly unsolvable problems, discussed previously, or it may be that a more turbulent world is one where the pace, size, and nature of problems has expanded beyond the leader's current capability to solve.[27] Whatever the reason, the capability gap, also known as an 'adaptive challenge,' demands more of leaders than traditional approaches to problem-solving can deliver. Two assumptions about leadership help to explain this capability gap. The first assumption is that an increasing number of problems and crises lack simple, straightforward solutions. The second assumption is that many leaders do not recognize that they must change the way they think in order to build the adaptive capacity needed to recognize and solve those problems.[28] Or, as former US Secretary of State George Shultz observed, 'There are problems you can solve, and problems you can only work at.'[29]

The saying, 'building a bridge while you cross it' exemplifies how the problems leaders face today are very different from the ones leaders expect or are traditionally prepared to solve. Instead, leaders in a complex world need a different way of thinking and acting. For example, community service leaders very often find themselves in situations of simultaneously 'building and crossing' this metaphorical bridge. While many community leaders come to their role with a passion to serve and meet needs like nutrition, housing, and healthcare, they soon experience the broad impact of political and regulatory complexity on the achievement of their mission.[30] To be successful in complex environments such as this, leaders must realize the need for new knowledge, ability and relationships. For instance, effective community leaders must often exercise political influence or networking skills with business and governmental organizations.[31] These and other activities are inherently risky because they are outside of the individual's core capability of helping and supporting, and the leader's need for partners and collaborators diminishes their ability to fully control the mission.[32] However, the upside to building and crossing the bridge simultaneously is the possibility of seeing a problem in a new light and accomplishing a previously unimaginable goal. The metaphor of 'building and crossing' simultaneously serves as an example of the distinctions of thinking and activities of adaptive leadership that help leaders solve complex adaptive challenges and goals.

Central to the practice of adaptive leadership are a series of key distinctions of thinking, or differing perspectives, and corresponding activities of adaptive leadership found in Table 16.1. These distinctions and activities form the

Table 16.1 Keys to adaptive leadership

Leadership Distinction	Adaptive Activity
The illusion of the broken system	Get on the balcony
Technical problems are the problem	Identify the adaptive challenge
Authority isn't leadership	Give the work back to the people
What's precious and essential vs. expendable?	Protect leadership voices from below
Live in disequilibrium	Regulate distress
Leadership is an improvisation	Run experiments and learn fast

core of adaptive leadership and distinguish it from other models and theories of leadership presented in this text. The adaptive leadership framework runs on the idea that leaders first need a change in thinking, or perspective, before they can adopt new practices to solve the complex problems of the world. The key idea within Table 16.1 pictured here is that mindset, or thinking, drives activity. In other words, a change in leader perspective enables the work of adaptive leadership. While the work of Heifetz and colleagues presents these and other ideas in greater detail, the following paragraphs highlight six of the most important distinctions, or shifts in mindset, and the associated activities of adaptive leadership.[33]

Get on the balcony

While surveys of leaders from around the globe consistently list dealing with change as one of the most important challenges they face, the reality is that few deal with it effectively.[34] One of the biggest reasons for this shortfall is a narrow and outdated belief that organizational problems are a result of internal design and process, rather than impacts or changes in the environment. Adaptive leadership suggests that an explanation for this shortfall is a flawed mindset around the *illusion of the broken system*.[35] Because of this illusion, leaders often fail to understand the full nature of important challenges and miss profitable opportunities to adapt to new realities. Adaptive leaders deal with this distinction by *getting on the balcony* to truly understand the situation.[36] This figurative activity shows how a change in leader perspective affects the way one views the problems they face. It might be as simple as seeking input from someone outside of a leader's direct reports, or it could involve a physical move, like a strategic offsite meeting to create both time and distance from the everyday activities of leadership. In professional athletics, coaches often move higher in the stadium to see the entire playing field. Adaptive leaders engage in this activity to help them see the broader operational context. A move to the balcony and a shift in perspective also helps leaders recognize where followers may be struggling or who may be better suited to solve difficult problems.[37]

Identify the adaptive challenge

The critical shift to the balcony is necessary for another important reason. Adaptive leadership framework contends that most leadership failures are due to adaptive challenges being treated as if they were technical problems.[38] Adaptive leadership framework suggests that technical problems differ from adaptive challenges because leaders rely on known solutions and current capabilities to solve them, whereas adaptive challenges are undefined and leaders are incapable of solving them alone.[39] While stability and predictability are common and desirable organizational needs, the associated tendency to misidentify technical problems and the resulting costs are undesirable. Outright failure aside, organizations waste precious time and resources in unproductive searches for technical solutions, when they should be learning and developing adaptive capacity.[40] Leaders who move to the balcony see past this illusion and position themselves to *identify the adaptive challenge,* the second key adaptive leadership activity.[41] This adaptive activity is a critical shift in leadership perspective from expert decision maker to the role of diagnostician, searching for clues and causes.

Give the work back to the people

Traditional thinking about leadership holds that formal role authorities are designed to handle any challenge, but another key leadership distinction argues that *authority is not leadership* because today's adaptive challenges require leaders to do more than their roles typically provide.[42] Formal authority structures promote order and protection and work well for technical challenges with known solutions. However, leaders and followers also opt for stability and control out of fear for what is at risk and what might be lost because of change.

Adaptive leaders respond to this resistance by testing and stretching the limits of authority and organizational control to discover values, behaviors and deeply held assumptions that are at odds with the purpose and emerging needs of an organization.[43] The adaptive activity that helps leaders mobilize change this way is by seeking opportunities to *give the work back to the people.*[44] Adaptive leaders see that those closest to the action have unique insights and relevant experience to help solve the challenge and so they look outward for differing perspectives and for those who are willing to see evolving needs and uncover unknown threats to the mission.[45]

Protect leadership voices from below

While the risks associated with change are often programmatic and financial, they often are individual and personal as well.[46] Consequently, another important leadership distinction is to clarify what is really at stake by helping others see what is *precious and essential versus expendable in their culture*.[47] When faced with change it is quite normal for people to fear the loss of things that are central and important.[48] People tend to adopt avoidance behaviors to delay or minimize the loss that comes from change.[49] To overcome this tendency, adaptive leaders highlight core values and look for ways to uncover dysfunctional behaviors and norms to help followers embrace the change rather than avoid it.[50] One way that adaptive leaders uncover norms and behaviors that prevent progress on adaptive challenges is by *protecting leadership voices from below*.[51] They do this by seeking out marginalized and minority voices to build a bigger perspective and mobilize the team even further.[52] Adaptive leaders recognize that it is not enough for them to say they welcome the perspectives of others, they must act to remove the fear and barriers that prevent marginalized voices from being heard.

Regulate distress

Removing the fear of loss and marginalization that comes with change enables people to focus on important decisions about what is essential in an adaptive challenge. But that alone is not enough to facilitate adaptive work. Even technical problems create distress for people, but adaptive challenges present more unknowns, which leads to stress of greater duration and intensity.[53] While stress may spike when a university president calls for budget cuts, adopting customer service as a university value creates waves of distress that move back and forth across the institution over time. To deal with distress, adaptive leaders distinguish what it means to *live in the disequilibrium* of adaptive work, rather than avoiding the situation. While it sounds like something unpleasant, disequilibrium is a state of tension where higher stress promotes deeper learning and growth needed for change.[54] Adaptive leaders accomplish this by *regulating distress*, which describes applying just enough pressure to maintain momentum toward the goal.[55] Similar to setting the temperature of an oven to create the conditions for ingredients to combine and change state, regulating distress creates the conditions for people to learn and accomplish new things. Unfortunately, the levels of stress needed to learn and act adaptively pose risks for followers if not effectively managed.[56] Adaptive leaders regulate distress by 'creating a holding environment' where new learning, conflicts and stress are addressed rather than spilling over to other parts of the organization.[57]

Run experiments and learn fast

While technical problems have finite and well-practiced solutions, adaptive challenges unfold in real time. Consequently, adaptive leaders share a different mindset that allows them to acknowledge, and even welcome, conflicting perspectives and different approaches to time and other contextual factors associated with adaptive work.[58] In other words, while traditional authority produces largely scripted actions, *adaptive leadership is an improvisation*.[59] That distinction enables leaders to see the future not in straight lines or tidy boxes, but as an interacting system of experiments and tests.[60] Sometimes leaders need to go 'off book' in order to manage the adaptive work and distress of others in real time.[61] Just as professional jazz musicians apply methods and practices to improvise a song, adaptive leaders do not just 'wing' their approach to adaptive challenges. Within the structure of the holding environment, they methodically *run experiments and learn fast*, an activity that leaders use to assess how assumptions hold up in the real world.[62] Whereas linear approaches to organizational change have predetermined end states, adaptive leadership is an ongoing and iterative process where leaders observe, interpret, and design interventions with the goal of increasing adaptive capacity in an organization.[63] Each jazz performance is unique, but it relies on common keys and tempo. Just as in the earlier example of building a bridge while crossing it, it demands experimentation, but also relies on principles of mechanics and tools to do the work.

Another way that adaptive leaders improvise their work is by seeing themselves as a system within a system.[64] Like any other person, a leader has unique needs, values and loyalties, but we often forget that both leaders and followers work inside an organizational system with its own array of needs, values and loyalties.[65] Just the thought of calculating the many interactions between and among systems underscores the complexity and demands of adaptive leadership. One way adaptive leaders make sense of the complexity is by regularly changing perspective, or by moving from the balcony to the dance floor, where the work occurs, and then returning to the balcony to assess what has changed.[66] Shifting between the balcony and the dance floor helps leaders see the larger system, the interactions among people, as well as their own influence on the action.[67] A leader who stays in one place cannot see the complex interactions and outcomes that result from systems interacting with and influencing the other systems. In fact, the leadership distinctions and adaptive activities described in the preceding paragraphs are neither scripted nor sequential steps in a model. Rather, the adaptive leadership framework consists of perspectives and practices that change and evolve constantly. Before putting the framework into practice and evaluating its ethical implications, it is necessary to highlight the most important theoretical and practical critiques and ethical considerations of adaptive leadership framework.

Critiques of adaptive leadership

Adaptive leadership first came to prominence in 1994 with the publication of *Leadership Without Easy Answers*, and the framework has played an influential and compelling, but unorthodox, role in the leadership literature ever since. The framework is influential and the book presents volumes of cases and compelling examples illustrating how the various concepts and practices of adaptive leadership bring about real change, for real people, facing real challenges. These factors contribute to the wide appeal and popularity of the framework. However, those same factors are what make adaptive leadership appear unorthodox when compared to other models of leadership. As a result, the framework has many fans and supporters, but it also has its share of critics. This section will highlight the most common critiques of the adaptive leadership framework.

Theoretical disconnect

The practical examples and activities found in adaptive leadership work on the assumption that the concepts are generalizable to the larger framework.[68] The authors accomplish this by drawing heavily on consultation, interviews and observations of organizational leaders, especially those who expressed frustration with problems that prevented them from achieving goals and objectives. However, the overall validity of adaptive leadership suffers because the larger framework is not grounded in theory or the product of a testable model of organizational behavior.[69] While the authors argue that the framework has empirical foundations, which means there is evidence to support their arguments, they also acknowledge that they have not yet developed the framework into an empirical theory.[70] The reader is left to judge the merits of the framework on the weight of historical cases and anecdotal examples alone. The authors do cite a number of influences on the development of adaptive leadership, such as evolutionary biology, systems theory, service orientation, and psychiatry, but the framework has limited connections to other research or relevant theory.[71] Likewise, some concepts of the adaptive leadership are cited in other models of leadership, such as complexity leadership theory, but little more has occurred.[72] In the end, adaptive leadership remains conceptually attractive because it highlights the challenges that real leaders face, whereas some theoretical models of leadership struggle to bridge the gap from theory to practical relevance.

Leader-centric

At the start of this chapter we discussed how perspectives on leadership have shifted over time from *who a leader is*, and the 'great man' or trait-based approaches, to *what leadership is*, or the interactional and systems approaches to leadership.[73] While research still considers characteristics of leaders and individual outcomes, the focus of the field has largely moved beyond the person, or the role, to the activity and outcomes of leadership interactions.[74] At a conceptual level, adaptive leadership highlights a similar shift and focus on the activity of leadership as a means to solve adaptive challenges, but most of the literature on adaptive leadership presents the concepts and describes the activities through a leader-centric lens.

The authors suggest that adaptive leadership exists anywhere, but much of the framework is oriented towards traditional leaders in organizational settings.[75] In fact, the prescriptive set of adaptive activities seems, at times, more like a checklist for leaders to enact than a conceptual framework about how leadership works.[76] While clearly not the intent of the authors, this unintended bias may limit the ability to transmit these important ideas about distinctions, shifting mindsets and adaptive activities to those who don't see themselves as leaders in the traditional sense. Regardless of how narrow the voice and perspective of adaptive leadership may appear, the framework calls out the broader purpose and service of leaders everywhere is to improve conditions and engage people to solve complex challenges and achieve goals.[77]

Practical limitations

Management scholar Peter Senge suggests 'practicing a discipline is different from emulating a model,' and a framework like adaptive leadership must have utility to be of real value for those who practice the discipline of leadership.[78] As a framework developed from real-world cases and the experiences of actual leaders, adaptive leadership offers a set of tools and practices and multiple examples to illustrate central components and outcomes. However, an important shortcoming of adaptive leadership is the absence of deeper conceptual definitions, more precise descriptions of the interrelationships to which it refers, and more complete explanations of outcomes associated with the framework.[79] Without greater clarity and precision, leaders run the risk of misinterpretation or misapplication of the adaptive activities.[80] The authors try to compensate for this problem by providing numerous examples of leaders using the concepts in a variety of situations, but a good set of descriptions and explanations would add practical value to this framework.

Another hazard of this conceptual gap is that some readers, not seeing a coherent whole in the framework, may focus on certain aspects that resonate or seem relevant to the problem at hand at the exclusion of other aspects of the framework. Selecting and applying individual components may offer a practical solution in the moment, and it may contribute to important shifts in a leader's approach to problem-solving. However, it may also lead to 'partial learning' where leaders grasp one or two key adaptive activities, but fail to integrate the broader concepts of the framework, leaving themselves at risk in other important areas.[81] The lack of integration between ideas and actions may result in greater emphasis on certain behaviors and activities, at the expense of other distinctions that provide the conceptual power of adaptive leaderships. Without that conceptual foundation, adaptive leadership risks becoming just another problem-solving tactic.

Ethical implications of adaptive leadership

Adaptive leadership has much to say about what is wrong with leadership, but even more to say about what is right and what can be better if leaders embrace the thinking and actions of the framework. Does that make the framework an ethical approach to leadership? In some ways yes, and in other ways, it depends. Like other models in this text, adaptive leadership suggests an important shift away from leader behaviors and styles to the very character of leadership itself. In fact, authors using adaptive leadership do not write about the framework in an abstract sense (a prior critique), but speak directly to leaders and for leaders – instructing, guiding and motivating them to tackle the difficult challenges in their world. While other approaches like transformational and authentic leadership focus on the leader's values, adaptive leadership speaks to the normative purpose of leadership, which the framework suggests is the condition of thriving, or achieving shared aspirations and goals.[82] From these claims, one might conclude that adaptive leadership has an ethical foundation.

So, what does it mean to thrive and how is that ethical? The authors of adaptive leadership clearly state that thriving is much more than attaining personal or material success, but rather it is about improving the well-being of people's lives, whether in an organization, a community or a society at large.[83] In addition to improving well-being, adaptive leaders assume personal and professional risk by taking on adaptive challenges, both of which highlight a distinct ethical perspective of serving others in the common good, as discussed in Chapter 11.[84]

Adaptive leadership argues that it would be wrong for a leader to pursue selfish values or seek personal gain, but it also assumes that leaders have a sense of what is right from where they stand on the balcony.[85] How are we to know if a leader's pursuits are ethical, and how does a leader ensure their perspective is right? While the framework assumes a leader's motives are pure, leaders must confirm their intentions by asking themselves what is non-negotiable in support of their values.[86] This outcomes-based ethical orientation uses three basic assessments to help adaptive leaders view the impact of their actions: (1) the harm it might cause others; (2) the risk it poses to self and personal values; and (3) the rationalizations, or explanations used to justify it.[87] While adaptive leadership does not offer a measure or test of goodness to judge a leader's values, it assumes that leaders are self-knowing and fully reflective. This approach may not guarantee ethical behavior, but it provides a way for leaders to self-assess the ethics of their actions.

Another question of ethics emerges in the methods and practices of adaptive leadership. The specific focus on the ethics of an action is a strong point of adaptive leadership, but the framework's lack of conceptual clarity (a prior critique) may create conditions of 'motivated blindness' where people have a vested interest to ignore the ethical concerns of an act or 'overvaluing outcomes,' where people see the ends of surviving an adaptive challenge as justifying the means.[88] Vague terminology and lack of clarity may create enough space for leaders to see how surviving and thriving justifies things that could be ethically questionable.

For instance, adaptive leadership places immense value on the distinction between authority and leadership, but is it ethical to encourage leaders to 'exceed their authority'?[89] The framework highlights the importance of pushing oneself and the organization beyond the status quo, but offers little insight into ethical considerations of ignoring the authority limits granted to leaders. While the framework assumes pure motives, the lack of clarity around ethical considerations might suggest resistance, disobedience and rationalizing of the ends to justify the means. The ethical exercise of authority and responsibility build trust in an organization and leaders who disregard the limits of authority may erode that trust.

Another potential ethical issue surrounds the idea's concept of 'disequilibrium.' Living in disequilibrium is an important distinction of adaptive leadership that seeks to establish the conditions necessary to learn and change. While the framework makes it clear that heightened stress facilitates learning and growth in key areas, there may be ethical concerns with encouraging leaders to 'turn up the heat.'[90] The framework describes how pressure and distress move people into the zone of discomfort and learning, but offers little insight into what methods and what limits of inducing stress are healthy and which produce harm. Without offering more specifics, the framework's recommendation to 'adjust the heat . . . and test how far you can push people to stimulate the changes you believe are necessary' could produce negative outcomes or lead to lasting harm.[91]

Finally, the distinction that leadership is an improvisation shows how leaders are not bound by scripts. Instead, they have the flexibility to shape and influence complex situations to encourage adaptive work. However, this distinction leads to questions about the ethical considerations of taking risks and running experiments in an organization. Adaptive leaders observe, interpret and intervene to gather knowledge and feedback needed to learn. However, the framework does not discuss the ethical limits to testing and experimentation, given the natural human fear of loss and distress in response to change. In fact, the framework suggests that in certain situations, if it is 'the only way to get people on board' it is acceptably right for leaders to calm followers' fears by suggesting that an experiment is actually a 'solution.'[92]

Concerns and issues like these are increasingly important in a world where collaboration and relationships between leaders and followers are essential to success, but where most organizational structures are hierarchical and working relationships are still based on impersonal transactions. The adaptive leadership framework seeks better relationships, but it does not provide a concrete collaborative means to reconcile differences in values and practices between leaders and followers. The framework encourages leaders to 'give the work back to the people' but that very act assumes a change in the leader's privileged status of defining the challenge, the goal and the means.[93] Connections with other leadership approaches, such as how leaders ethically empower followers or when leaders share authentic values and shortcomings to build greater trust and respect, may mitigate some of the ethical concerns. The framework may gain ethical strength by building bridges between other theories and approaches that close the gap in some of the ethical concerns and practical shortcomings of adaptive leadership.

The adaptive leadership framework closes with a discussion on the leader's purpose and heart.[94] For a leader to survive and thrive, the framework argues that they must not 'lose heart,' or sacrifice their innocence, curiosity and compassion, which the authors suggest are the attributes that makes each of us distinctly human.[95] The authors continue to stress that without a focus on purpose and heart, leaders are susceptible to 'cynicism, arrogance, and callousness' that can be rationalized in ways to protect the leader instead of serving others.[96] The attributes of heart and the impacts on character taken up by adaptive leadership show distinct connections to virtue ethics, presented in Chapter 4, as well as self-awareness for authentic leadership presented in Chapter 12. Additional connections to other theories and concepts of ethics, like virtue, duty and utility, would strengthen the conceptual and practical value of adaptive leadership.

Five component analysis

As in other chapters of this text, we now turn to the Five Components of Leadership Model to help integrate and synthesize the learning about adaptive leadership. Adaptive leadership emerged in response to the experiences and needs of real leaders in actual organizations.[97] The framework was not designed in a psychology lab, and it was not proposed as a grand theory of human behavior. Instead, it was offered as a prescriptive framework that leaders could use to solve actual problems they faced. The Five Components Model also helps us see leadership as a process where 'individuals come together and develop a relationship with a purpose in mind.'[98]

As you can see in Figure 16.2, the context is the most important aspect of adaptive leadership. This context, however, affects all other aspects of the Five Components Model. The leader alone must 'get on the balcony' and move back and forth to the dance floor to survey the landscape sufficiently to understand where the actual gaps are and what those gaps mean. In today's complex world, leaders can ill afford to miss the strategic gaps

Figure 16.2 The Five Components of Leadership Model applied to adaptive leadership

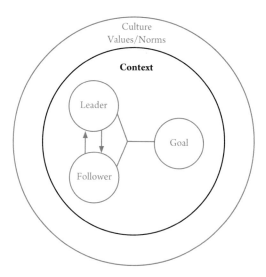

and opportunities they face and must rely on group strategies and team-work to actively move between the balcony and the dance floor. Leaders who change perspective and leverage the capabilities of their teams as 'early warning sensors' gain a much better understanding of the multiple dimensions of a situation. Moving to the balcony is a key first step to finding and assessing the gaps that exist in the leadership situation addressed by the model.

According to adaptive leadership framework, the most common failure of leadership is when leaders misidentify adaptive challenges as technical problems. A second key concern is when leaders 'lose heart' or become overconfident and arrogant in their ability to solve an organization's problems, when, in fact, they do not have all the answers.[99] Without 'heart,' or character and humility, leaders become unable (or unwilling) to truly see the challenges they face, and thus rely on technical solutions instead of adaptive ones.

While 'getting on the balcony' is a leader-centric act, that does not mean adaptive leadership focuses on the leader's efforts alone. One of the chief responsibilities of the leader is to engage followers to assess and address the situation. A leader with 'heart' understands that traditional authority and expertise alone will never solve an adaptive challenge and so they seek ways to 'give the work back to the people' to close the existing capability gaps.[100]

Leaders often speak of empowering followers, and this model requires leaders do exactly that. Here, leaders must let go of their desire to control the situation, and instead allow followers to own the process. For followers, this model can become especially challenging because they want clarity from their leader – but clarity often implies the application of technical solutions that adaptive leadership rejects. To accommodate and manage the stress that followers experience because they lack a clear solution, the leader creates a 'holding space' where followers are able to work through the uncertainty of adaptive challenges.

Adaptive leadership is not about solving technical problems with linear solutions. Rather, it is a different choice about how to solve tough problems that lack clear answers. What makes this approach special is the ability to view adaptive challenges in a new light, and see alternatives that were invisible with traditional, technical methods of problem-solving. To access these new insights and alternatives, adaptive leaders 'run experiments and learn fast' and often go 'off book,' or improvise their work in response to emerging circumstances.[101] Thus, the goal is not only accomplishing an objective, but also how that objective is achieved.

The leader moves between the balcony and dance floor to assess and understand the gaps, but eventually they must search the context to identify the adaptive challenge. In many ways, the context is what demands adaptive leadership. While adaptive leadership does address the leader, follower, and goal triad, it is the context itself that dictates when adaptive leadership is needed. Something in the environment has changed that makes the old way of doing things no longer work and adaptive leaders and their followers must find a different answer.

Even when leaders can see the gaps and understand what the adaptive challenge is, there is no guaranteed easy solution. Adaptive work is hard, it takes time and it always demands change. Sometimes there is a change of perspective, quite often a change in plans and almost always a change in organizational culture. To help their followers understand what is truly essential, adaptive leaders highlight important values, 'protect leadership voices from below' and eliminate dysfunctional norms that prevent progress.[102] Because of the more egalitarian orientation of adaptive leadership, highly authoritarian cultures may struggle with this model.

We will now follow the methodology used by Heifetz and others to better understand adaptive leadership and its ethical implications by applying the theory to a specific case study.

CASE STUDY

Nelson Mandela's use of adaptive leadership – the emergence of democracy in South Africa

With a thorough understanding of adaptive leadership and the Five Components of Leadership Model as our guide, this next section turns to a leader who overcame incredible personal, social and political challenges and united a nation. Adaptive leadership does more than try to explain or describe how leadership works. Instead, adaptive leadership prescribes how leaders should lead and provides a specialized way to solve the most difficult challenges of organizations and society. The case of Nelson Mandela and the emergence of a fully inclusive democracy in South Africa is not only an incredible story of a leader's courage and determination, but it is also a compelling example of how a change of thinking, actions and goals can solve a seemingly intractable and complex problem and transform a nation. In his book on the South African National Peace Accord, Peter Gastrow describes South Africa's change and transition as a 'negotiated revolution.'[103] While negotiation might occur following a revolution, or a breakdown in negotiations might precede a revolution, those two things are not ordinarily viewed together. However, the world we live in is growing increasingly complex and adaptive challenges like negotiated revolutions are more likely to occur.

CASE STUDY *(continued)*

Nelson Mandela's election as President of South Africa in 1994 is one of the most unlikely, yet significant, political and moral triumphs of the modern world, and it cast Mandela forever as one of the greatest leaders of the twentieth century, if not all time. However, Mandela attributed none of the amazing achievement to himself, to fate, or even to divine intervention. Instead, he described the African concept of *ubuntu*, a relational mindset which means 'we are human only through the humanity of others.'[104] It is through this mindset of *ubuntu* that Mandela suggested, 'If we are to accomplish anything in this world, it will in equal measure be due to the work and achievements of others.'[105] The core value of *ubuntu*, or relationship and humanity, provides a foundation on which to view Mandela's work as an adaptive leader. But to fully understand Mandela's role in the transformation of South Africa, you must first know some of the violent history of the nation and how it shaped Mandela as a leader.

History

The nation of South Africa formed in 1910 following a struggle for control between European settlers and British colonial rulers, punctuated by the Boer War of 1899–1902. After establishment, the post-colonial state continued a system of domination, looking inward to continue White minority rule over the majority African population.[106] The Dutch-Afrikaner National Party gained political control in the period following the Second World War and formalized the cultural system of implicit oppression into a national policy of racial discrimination and segregation called apartheid.

Resistance movements like the African National Congress (ANC) became more actively opposed to the government's racial policies and harsh treatment of the majority African population. Around the same time, a young Nelson Mandela moved from a rural region of South Africa to the city to begin training as a lawyer. There in Johannesburg he experienced, first-hand, the extent of apartheid's social and political discrimination.[107] As a result, Mandela joined the ANC and became part of the organized opposition, but he believed the group's strict policy of non-violence was ineffective. As an increasingly strident voice for action and change in the ANC, he led the formation of the ANC Youth League, which advocated a path of increasing violence to counter the government's growing injustice and suppression of African rights.[108] The cycle of violence and repression in South Africa continued with such events as the Sharpeville Massacre in which the White South African police force opened fire on a crowd of Black South African protesters. In response to the increase in violence against Black South Africans, Mandela was appointed head of the *uMkhonto we Sizwe*, meaning 'The Spear of the Nation' and abbreviated as MK. The MK was an opposition military organization that sought to disrupt and damage government facilities through violence.[109] The situation in South Africa worsened, the violence grew, and the prospects for change seemed unlikely when in 1962 Mandela and others were convicted and jailed for treason and sentenced to life in prison on additional charges in 1964.

CASE STUDY *(continued)*

Mandela eventually ended up in the infamous Robben Island Prison, an isolated island off the coast of Cape Town, South Africa. The prison was later ironically called 'The University', for it was during Mandela's 27 years of imprisonment on Robben Island and in other prisons that he grew as an adaptive leader and transformed into a thoughtful and pragmatic peacemaker.[110] By the 1980s, South Africa's system of apartheid and internal strife left the nation isolated internationally and criticized globally.[111] The South African government and opposition leaders were deadlocked in an armed social and political struggle with no foreseeable solution. What happened next many considered a miracle. In 1990, the government freed Nelson Mandela and other political prisoners from prison and, a mere four years later, a racially united South Africa elected Mandela as its first democratically elected President. The extraordinary success of this political and social revolution is due to many factors, but key among them was Nelson Mandela's exercise of adaptive leadership.

Five component analysis

Let's look at Mandela's work as an adaptive leader through the lens of the Five Components of Leadership Model.

Nelson Mandela became a national figure through his activist role and imprisonment for opposing the South African government's policy of apartheid. So it seems odd that his

Figure 16.3 The Five Components of Leadership Model applied to Nelson Mandela's leadership of South Africa case study

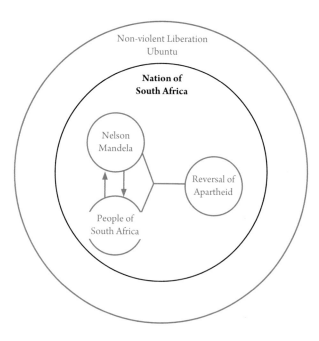

CASE STUDY *(continued)*

growth and development as an adaptive leader would occur while in prison, but that is exactly what happened. In many respects, Mandela's move to Robben Island prison prefaced his move to the balcony as an adaptive leader. By the 1960s, Mandela was an established leader of the opposition movement, but the shift to prison placed him apart from both the formal leadership structure of the ANC and the center of tension in the South African cities and townships. In prison, Mandela was removed from all of this and had nothing but his interactions and relationships with his fellow prisoners and the prison staff, many of whom were abusive and violent to Mandela and the other prisoners. From the balcony, Mandela could see and begin to understand the effects of individual interactions among prisoners, warders and even the effect of his own relationships. During this period of separation, Mandela saw, understood and diagnosed the systemic complexity of prejudice brought on by the policy of apartheid. While apartheid was evil, Mandela came to believe that everyone on Robben Island, prisoner and warder alike, was subject to the cycle of power, domination and harm brought about by apartheid. Mandela determined that changing the cycle of apartheid was the adaptive challenge every South African faced.[112] Mandela moved often between the balcony and the dance floor, seeking ways to treat prisoners and warders with respect and kindness. From this experience, he learned that, even in the darkest of places and across race and role, *ubuntu* could free people from hatred and prejudice.[113] It was at this 'University' that Mandela learned the first lesson of adaptive leadership, the system of *ubuntu* was not broken.

By the late 1980s, Nelson Mandela had been in prison for more than twenty years, but he was now more influential than ever. He held no official role, carried no formal title in the ANC, and had no authority to act, but his face led a protest that crossed the globe in opposition to South Africa's apartheid policy. Here, we see people doing the work for change while the leader was not in a position to do the work directly. This exponential example of giving the work back to the people shows how the story of Nelson Mandela stirred the world to turn against an oppressive regime.

Adaptive leaders do more than just encourage and inspire others, they actively create and sustain a holding environment where the adaptive work takes place. Sometimes they provide structure and protection so conflicting values can be addressed, but Mandela expanded the holding space for adaptive work by secretly writing a letter to the President of South Africa. A man imprisoned with no authority sought a conversation with his sworn enemy and that conversation ultimately ended apartheid. The end of apartheid did not come about because of savvy negotiating skills or special leverage. They achieved the impossible by focusing on the precious values desired by all South Africans while considering both majority and minority perspectives.

In 1990 Mandela was released from prison, and in 1994 became the first democratically elected President for all South Africans achieving the goal of ending apartheid and transforming the government. However, as is often the case, reaching goals does not signal the end of an adaptive challenge, just a new cycle of observation, interpretation and intervention.[114] For the new President, reconciliation and partnership between Black and

CASE STUDY (continued)

White South Africans continued as a long-term obstacle to lasting justice and freedom. But if 27 years in prison teaches anything about leadership, it is that adaptive work operates on a different principle of time and needs continual effort.[115]

As President, Mandela's mission became 'binding the wounds of the country, of engendering trust and confidence.'[116] While he sought unity, Mandela recognized that many South Africans were troubled by the change and feared what the future of South Africa might bring. Adaptive leaders understand the need to regulate the anxiety of followers to ensure the learning and change of adaptive work happens. Mandela was quick to say 'the liberation struggle was not a battle against one group or color, but a fight against a system of repression.'[117] One very symbolic and powerful way Mandela helped calm people's fears was by inviting the very jailers who imprisoned him to sit among important guests at his Presidential inauguration.[118] The image of Mandela welcoming his captors and treating them as equals set the norms for respect and forgiveness for all South Africans.

But examples alone still may not close the gap in adaptive work and leaders must be willing to improvise and test new alternatives to succeed. Despite strict norms and obligations agreed to in the National Peace Accord of 1991, when the government allowed political activity and the return of exiled opposition groups, an unanticipated increase in violence emerged between the main opposition parties of the ANC and Inkatha Freedom Party (IFP).[119] Relationships and trust among the government, the ANC and the IFP plummeted and progress and negotiations broke down several times. Tests do not always go as planned, but adaptive leaders continue the process of experimentation to overcome the challenge. In the end, it was not Nelson Mandela, but one of his Robben Island comrades who drafted a controversial but innovative proposal for a five-year transitional national unity government, which bridged the gap to majority rule democracy and helped end the era of South African apartheid.[120]

The separation and isolation of Robben Island forced Mandela to consider the situation between the government and opposition parties from a different perspective. Imprisoned on the balcony, as he was, Mandela watched both sides of the conflict pursue paths of continued violence that offered no hope of resolution. The government held onto an unjust policy, but had overwhelming power, while the opposition held the moral high ground, but was intent on making the country 'ungovernable.'[121] Both sides approached the situation as a technical problem and used traditional solutions of violence and separation that led to stalemate. From the balcony, Mandela scanned the environment and saw the gap between the ANC's current capability and plans and their ultimate goal to end apartheid. Mandela realized that achieving the goal to end apartheid and bring peace to South Africa would not happen unless they reconciled with the enemy and partnered in the transition to full democracy.[122] From his vantage point, Mandela could see that the adaptive challenge of negotiated revolution demanded that each side abandon its position and take a different path toward a new end-state. Mandela knew what must change, but he was incapable of such change on his own from where he was. He needed to engage others, even his enemies, to solve this intractable problem.

CASE STUDY *(continued)*

We solve adaptive challenges when people open their eyes to what is precious and essential and learn what must change in order to survive and thrive. Although criticized by others, Mandela showed forgiveness and even kindness to his jailers, because he saw them as victims of the same system that reinforced and rewarded hatred and violence toward Africans.[123] Mandela often spoke of his vision for all of South Africa that 'the oppressor must be liberated just as surely as the oppressed. A man who takes away another man's freedom is a prisoner of hatred, he is locked behind the bars of prejudice and narrow-mindedness.'[124] Mandela offered a vision for all South African voices, equally precious and valued. By focusing on the value of *ubuntu* – a cherished African virtue – Mandela helped everyone see that reconciliation and partnership was the adaptive challenge on the path to freedom and peace for South Africa.

Summary and concluding remarks

To conclude this chapter, let us return to the framing question, 'How should both leaders and their followers adapt their thinking to solve complex challenges?' Adaptive leadership offers us three major changes in how organizations view leadership. The first change occurs between leaders and followers, as leaders realize they can only solve these unfamiliar problems by shifting responsibility from the centralized manager to those closest to the problems. The second change emerges in the practices and behaviors of leaders who no longer directly deal with the problem at hand, but nonetheless still bear responsibility for the organizational outcomes. The third change is a shift of organizational focus, from internally held goals and culture to the dynamic interplay between goals, culture and the external environment that holds the keys to unfamiliar problems and opportunities.[125] To prepare both leaders and followers for these changes in thinking, organizations will benefit by training leaders to 'go to the balcony' when problems arise, as well as providing resources to help both leaders and followers navigate the inevitable stress that comes with adaptive changes.

The adaptive leadership framework is a set of choices: tested practices and relevant principles to guide leaders who need to build organizational capacity. The challenges facing today's leaders demand abilities far greater than any leader has alone. Like Mandela, leaders must do many things at once. They must adapt and execute simultaneously, or 'develop "next practices" while excelling at today's best practices,' which is quite similar to crossing and building the bridge at the same time.[126] But like Nelson Mandela in South Africa, the world needs adaptive leadership to survive and thrive.

DISCUSSION QUESTIONS

What are the most common technical challenges facing your organization and where in the environment is an adaptive challenge likely to emerge?

What are the most key factors leaders should consider when facing adaptive challenges?

What types of organizations are best suited for adaptive leadership? What types are least suited?

In your view, what aspect of practicing adaptive leadership is most difficult?

Adaptive challenges quite often present higher risks and greater potential returns. Does this impose any greater expectations or higher ethical standards on the decisions and actions of leaders?

How often do you reach outside of your organization, while overlooking veteran wisdom and experience closest to the problem? Regularly going to the bench is the smart and effective way for leaders to stay in the game and 'do' organizational change.

What ethical concerns do you see with leaders inducing stress in an organization to deal with an adaptive challenge?

 ADDITIONAL RESOURCES

R.A. Heifetz and D. Laurie, 'The work of leadership,' *Harvard Business Review*, vol. 79 no. 11, 2001, 131–40.

The authors make the case that the business of leadership is to solve problems, but many of the problems no longer have easy answers. The authors argue that the work of leadership is to help followers deal with both a changing environment and the demanding work of change.

R.A. Heifetz, A. Grashow, and M. Linsky, 'Leadership in a (permanent) crisis,' *Harvard Business Review*, 87 July–August 2009, 62–9.

In this Special *Harvard Business Review* issue on Leadership in the New World, the authors of the Adaptive Leadership Framework suggest that crises like the global economic downturn in 2008 provide even more evidence that traditional approaches to leadership are no longer relevant in a complex, globalized world.

R.A. Heifetz, A. Grashow, and M. Linsky, *The Practice of Adaptive Leadership: Tools and Tactics for Changing Your Organization and the World*, Boston: Harvard Business School Publishing, 2009.

This text is a comprehensive overview of the adaptive leadership framework and a resource book for leaders to practice and reflect on the journey to become an adaptive leader.

S.D. Parks, *Leadership Can be Taught: A Bold Approach for a Complex World*, Boston: Harvard Business School Press, 2005.

This text provides an overview and assessment of the teaching and learning method associated with the Adaptive Leadership course offered at the Harvard Kennedy School of Government.

NOTES

1 The original quote by Albert Einstein in 1946 was written as part of the debate on the development of thermonuclear weapons published in the Russell–Einstein Manifesto of 1955. 'A new type of thinking is essential if mankind is to survive and move toward higher levels.'

2 See H.W. Rittel and M.M. Webber, 'Dilemmas in a general theory of planning,' *Policy Sciences*, vol. 4 no. 2, 1973, 155–69. The idea of 'wicked problems' was first addressed in the context of systemic social policy issues that, because of interdependencies and uncertainties, were beyond the capability of any one individual, program or institution to solve.

3 P.F. Drucker, *Management Challenges for the 21st Century*, New York: Harper Business, 1999, p. x.

4 Drucker, ibid, p. xi.

5 A. Kaplan, *The Conduct of Inquiry: Methodology for Behavioral Science*, 4th edn, New Brunswick, NJ: Transaction Publishers, 2009, pp. 28–9. Abraham Kaplan's 'law of the instrument' critiqued a narrow-minded, parochial approach to behavioral science problem-solving.

6 R.A. Heifetz, *Leadership Without Easy Answers*, Cambridge, MA: The Belknap Press, 1994.

7 Heifetz, ibid, pp. 16–27. Ronald Heifetz developed the Adaptive Leadership framework after listening to the stories of executives attending programs at Harvard University.

8 E. Schein, *Organizational Culture and Leadership*, 3rd edn, San Francisco: Jossey-Bass, 2004; C. Argyris, *Overcoming Organizational Defenses: Facilitating Organizational Learning*, Boston: Allyn & Bacon, 1990; P.M. Senge, *The Fifth Discipline: The Art and Practice of the Learning Organization*, New York: Doubleday, 1990; R. Kegan and L. Laskow Lahey, *Immunity to Change: How to Overcome It and Unlock Potential in Yourself and Your Organization*, Boston: Harvard Business Press, 2009; R. Martin, 'How successful leaders think,' *Harvard Business Review*, vol. 85 no. 6, 2007, 60–7; P.F. Drucker, *Managing In a Time of Great Change,* New York: Talley Books/Dutton, 1995; and Drucker, 1999, op. cit.

9 For descriptions of the major trends influencing leadership in organizations see: Drucker, 1995, op. cit.; Drucker, 1999, op. cit.; Kegan and Laskow Lahey, op. cit.; Martin, op. cit.; Argyris, op. cit.; Senge, op. cit.; T.W. Malone, *The Future of Work: How the New Order of Business Will Shape Your Organization, Your Management Style and Your Life*, Boston: Harvard Business School Press, 2004; P.F. Drucker, *The Age of Discontinuity: Guidelines To Our Changing Society*, New York: Harper & Row, 1969; and P.F. Drucker, *Managing in the Next Society*, New York: Truman Tally Books, 2002.

10 H. Mintzberg, *The Nature of Managerial Work*, New York: Harper & Row, 1973.

11 G. Morgan, *Images of Organization*, Thousand Oaks, CA: Sage Publications, 1997, p. 22.

12 Drucker, 1999, op. cit., p. 136.

13 Drucker, 1999, op. cit., pp. 136–7; Heifetz, 1994, op. cit., pp. 16–19.

14 Morgan, op. cit., pp. 26–7.

15 M. Anteby and R. Khurana, *A New Vision*, 2007. Online, https::www.library.hbs.edu:hc:hawthorne:anewvision.html (accessed September 4, 2017). See Anteby and Khurana's essay for an introduction to the dramatic impact of The Hawthorne Studies on changes in organizational research and leadership.

16 The American Soldier Studies, a four volume series of research conducted for the U.S. Army, is considered by many to be the foundation of modern understanding of group dynamics and leadership, as well as many core theories of social psychology and social science research methods. See S.A. Stouffer et al., *The American Soldier: Adjustment During Army Life*, New York: Science Editions, 1965.

17 Anteby and Khurana, op. cit.

18 Anteby and Khurana, op. cit.

19 Anteby and Khurana, op. cit.

20 Morgan, op. cit., pp. 31–7. Morgan describes the notion of 'sociotechnical systems,' a term that originated in the Tavistock Institute in England, to highlight the interdependencies between the work, the people and the environment. This early work contributed to the fields of organizational design and contingency theories of leadership that took hold in the 1960s.

21 Morgan, op. cit., p. 33.

22 Morgan, op. cit., p. 56. Contingency approaches to organization and leadership theory emerged in the 1950s and 1960s in response to research that showed how organizational variables interacted in a dynamic environment to influence performance and outcomes.

23 B.J. Avolio, 'Pursuing authentic leadership development', in N. Nohria and R. Khurana (eds), *Handbook of Leadership Theory and Practice*, Boston: Harvard Business Press, 2010, pp. 739–68.

24 D. Kahneman, *Thinking, Fast and Slow*, New York: McMillan, 2011; Argyris, op. cit.; Drucker, 1999, op. cit.; Senge, op. cit.; Kegan and Laskow Lahey, op. cit.

25 R.A. Heifetz, 'Anchoring leadership in the work of adaptive progress,' in F. Hesselbein and M. Goldsmith (eds), *The Leader of the Future 2: Visions, Strategies and Practices For the New Era*, San Francisco: Jossey-Bass: 2006, pp. 75–6.

26 World Economic Forum, *Insight Report: The Global Risks Report* 2017, 12th edn. Online, www.weforum.org (accessed February 25, 2017); Drucker, 1999, op. cit.

27 K. Lawrence, *UNC Executive Development White Paper: Developing Leaders in a VUCA Environment*, 2013. Online, www.execdev.unc.edu (accessed February 25, 2017). The modern leadership environment is often described as increasingly volatile, uncertain, complex and ambiguous and the term VUCA as been used to describe both the environment and the kinds of challenges that emerge from this sort of environment. VUCA was originally used to describe the operational military environment, but it is often used to describe the context and challenges that many organizational leaders face.

28 Heifetz, 1994, op. cit., p. 2; Heifetz, 2006, op. cit., pp. 76–7.

29 Quoted in G. Hamel and B. Breen, *The Future of Management*, Boston: Harvard Business Press, 2007, p. 38.

30 P. Auspos, and M. Cabaj, 'Complexity and community change: Managing adaptively to improve effectiveness,' The Aspen Institute Roundtable on Community Change, September 24, 2014, p. vi. Online, https://www.aspeninstitute.org/publications/complexity-community-change-managing-adaptively-improve-effectiveness/ (accessed September 8, 2017).

31 Auspos and Cabaj, ibid.

32 R.A. Heifetz and M. Linsky, *Leadership On The Line: Staying Alive Through the Dangers of Leading*, Boston: Harvard Business School Press, 2002, pp. 2, 13.

33 Heifetz and Linsky, ibid; Heifetz, 1994, op. cit.; R.A. Heifetz, A. Grashow and M. Linsky, 'Leadership in a (permanent) crisis,' *Harvard Business Review*, vol. 87 no. 7/8, 2009, 62–9.

34 W.A. Gentry, R.H. Eckert, S.A. Stawiski, and S. Zhao, *The Challenges Leaders Face Around the World: More Similar Than Different*, Greensboro, NC: Center for Creative Leadership, 2016.

35 Heifetz et al., 2009, op. cit.

36 Heifetz et al., 2009, op. cit.

37 Heifetz, 2006, op. cit., pp. 76–7. For an example, consider how Keneddy handled the Cuban missile crisis. See M.T. Hansen, 'How John F. Kennedy changed decision making for us all,' *Harvard Business Review*, November 22, 2013. Online, https://hbr.org/2013/11/how-john-f-kennedy-changed-decision-making (accessed September 8, 2017).

38 Heifetz, 2006, op. cit., p. 77; Heifetz and Linsky, 2002, op. cit., p. 14.

39 Heifetz et al., 2009, op. cit.; Heifetz, 1994, op. cit., Heifetz, 2006, op. cit.

40 Kegan and Laskow Lahey, op. cit.; Heifetz, 1994, op. cit.; Heifetz, 2006, op. cit., p. 75.

41 Heifetz et al., 2009, op. cit.

42 Heifetz et al., 2009, op. cit.

43 Heifetz et al., 2009, op. cit.

44 Heifetz, 2006, op. cit., p. 77.

45 Heifetz et al., 2009, op. cit.

46 Heifetz et al., 2009, op. cit.

47 Heifetz, 2006, op. cit. p. 78.

48 Kegan and Laskow Lahey, 2009, op. cit.

49 Kegan and Laskow Lahey, 2009, op. cit.

50 Heifetz et al., 2009, op. cit.

51 Heifetz et al., 2009, op. cit.

52 Heifetz et al., 2009, op. cit.

53 Heifetz, 2006, op. cit., p. 80.

54 Heifetz et al., 2009, op. cit; Heifetz, 1994, op. cit.

55 Heifetz, 2006, op. cit.

56 Heifetz, 2006, op. cit.

57 Heifetz et al., 2009, op. cit.

58 Martin, op. cit.

59 Heifetz, 2006, op. cit., p. 80.

60 Heifetz, 2006, op. cit., p. 79.

61 Heifetz et al., 2009, op. cit.; HBR Spotlight on Leadership Lessons from The Military, 'You have to lead from everywhere: Interview with Admiral Thad Allen, USCG (Ret.),' *Harvard Business Review*, November 2010, 76–9: pp. 77–8.

62 Heifetz, 2006, op. cit., p. 79.

63 Heifetz et al., 2009, op. cit.

64 Heifetz et al., 2009, op. cit.

65 Heifetz et al., 2009, op. cit.

66 Heifetz et al., 2009, op. cit.; and Heifetz, 1994, op. cit.

67 Heifetz et al., 2009, op. cit.

68 R. Angelmar, G. Zaltman, and C Pinson, 'An examination of concept validity,' in M. Venkatesan (ed.), *Proceedings of the Third Annual Conference of the Association for Consumer Research*, Chicago: Association for Consumer Research, 1972, 586–93, p. 586.

69 S.D. Parks, *Leadership Can Be Taught: A Bold Approach for a Complex World*, Boston: Harvard Business School Press, 2005, p. 251; and P.G. Northouse, *Leadership: Theory and Practice*, 7th edn, Thousand Oaks, CA: Sage, 2015, p. 275.

70 Heifetz, 1994, op. cit., pp. 7–8.

71 Heifetz, 1994, op. cit., p. 4; and Heifetz et al., 2009, op. cit.

72 Parks, op. cit., p. 251; and M. Uhl-Bien, R. Marion, and B. McKelvey, 'Complexity leadership theory: Shifting leadership from the industrial age to the knowledge era,' *The Leadership Quarterly*, vol. 18 no. 4, 2007, 298–318, p. 300.

73 Uhl-Bien, Marion, and McKelvey, op. cit., p. 298.

74 Uhl-Bien, Marion, and McKelvey, op. cit., p. 298.

75 Heifetz and Linsky, 2002, op. cit., p. 236.

76 Heifetz and Linsky, 2002, op. cit., p. 5.

77 Heifetz and Linsky, 2002, op. cit., p. 236; and Heifetz et al., 2009, op. cit.

78 Senge, op. cit., p. 11.

79 Parks, op. cit., 251–252; and Northouse, op. cit., p. 276.

80 Northouse, op. cit., p. 276.

81 Parks, op. cit., pp. 251–2.

82 Heifetz, 2006, op. cit., pp. 81–2.

83 Heifetz et al., 2009, op. cit., p. Kindle Loc 98.

84 Parks, op. cit., p. 256.

85 Heifetz, 2006, op. cit., p. 83.

86 Heifetz et al., 2009, op. cit., p. Kindle Loc 7418.

87 Heifetz et al., 2009, op. cit., p. Kindle Loc 7418.

88 M.H. Bazerman and A.E. Tenbrunsel, 'Ethical breakdowns,' *Harvard Business Review*, April 2011, 58–66, p. 63.

89 Heifetz et al., 2009, op. cit., p. Kindle Loc 8246.

90 Heifetz et al., 2009, op. cit., p. Kindle Loc 8261.

91 Heifetz et al., 2009, op. cit., p. Kindle Loc 8273.

92 Heifetz et al., 2009, op. cit., p. Kindle Loc 8168.

93 Heifetz et al., 2009, op. cit., p. Kindle Loc 6321.

94 Heifetz et al., 2009, op. cit., p. Kindle Loc 8046.

95 Heifetz and Linsky, 2002, op. cit., pp. 225–6.

96 Heifetz and Linsky, 2002, op. cit., pp. 225–6.

97 Heifetz, 1994, op. cit., p. 7.

98 R.M. McManus and G. Perruci, *Understanding Leadership: An Arts and Humanities Perspective*, New York: Routledge, 2015, p. 17.

99 Heifetz et al., 2009, op. cit.

100 Heifetz et al., 2009, op. cit.

101 Heifetz et al., 2009, op. cit.; and HBR Spotlight, op. cit.

102 Heifetz et al., 2009, op. cit.

103 P. Gastrow, *Bargaining for Peace: South Africa and the National Peace Accord*, Washington, DC: United States Institute of Peace, 1995, p. vii.

104 R. Stengel, *Mandela's Way: Fifteen Lessons on Life, Love, and Courage*, New York: Crown Publishers, 2008, p. Kindle Loc 17.

105 Stengel, ibid.

106 Gastrow, op. cit., p. 3.

107 L.S. Graybill, *Truth & Reconciliation in South Africa: Miracle or Model?* Boulder, CO: Lynne Rienner Publishers, 2002, p. 12.

108 Graybill, ibid, p. 13.

109 Graybill, op. cit., p. 15.

110 Graybill, op. cit., p. 17.

111 Gastrow, op. cit., p. 4.

112 N. Mandela, *Long Walk to Freedom,* New York: Little, Brown and Company, 2013, p. x.

113 Mandela, ibid, p. 623.

114 Heifetz et al., 2009, op. cit., p. Kindel Loc 4186.

115 Heifetz, 2006, op. cit., p. 78.

116 Mandela, op. cit., p. 619.

117 Mandela, op. cit., p. 619.

118 Graybill, op. cit., p. 19.

119 Gastrow, op. cit., p. 93.

120 Mandela, op. cit., p. 606.

121 Gastrow, op. cit., p. 4; and Stengel, op. cit., p. Kindle Loc 485.

122 Mandela, op. cit., p. x.

123 Graybill, op. cit., p. 16.

124 Mandela, op. cit., p. 623.

125 Heifetz, 2006, op. cit., pp. 74–5.

126 R.A. Heifetz and D. Laurie, 'The work of leadership,' *Harvard Business Review*, vol. 79 no. 11, 2001, 131–40, p. 133.

17
Conclusion

Once again, we return to our central question in this book – 'What is ethical leadership?' We hope that by now readers realize there is no single ethical or leadership model that answers the question in every situation, because of the many layers involved in leadership. Therefore, we encourage readers to see themselves as ethical leaders who are developing a suite of tools for handling complex leadership issues with a variety of ethical concerns. As our previous chapter reminded us, 'If your only tool is a hammer, then everything looks like a nail.' As a counter to the leader who reduces every leadership dilemma to one technical solution, we want our readers to have a full toolbox.

Review is the mother of learning. As we conclude our text, let's spend some time reviewing the work we've done so far in order to internalize it. After that, we can get to yet another question, and this is the one that should be at the heart of any educational endeavor – 'So what?' We will do that here by first summarizing the content of our chapters on ethics and leadership. Then we will make some general observations based on those summaries. Finally, we will dig into the 'so what' for our text, with the hope that we can provide our readers with some final insights that will last even longer with the tables and figures we developed to help readers synthesize and remember key content for each chapter.

Review

As we come to the conclusion of *Ethical Leadership: A Primer*, we offer this helpful table to help sort through information that might be new for the majority of our readers. In our book, we have attempted to describe ethical leadership by examining how a variety of ethical models highlight various pieces of the five components of leadership. Table 17.1 provides an overview of the ethical models we considered in Section I – starting with the framing question, highlighting how those models draw attention to various pieces of the Five Components Model, and listing the accompanying case example.

Table 17.1 Summary of ethics models

Model	Framing Question	Emphasis	Case Example
Kantianism	'What is the moral duty of leaders and followers?'	The Goal, regardless of the Context	Apple and Foxconn
Utilitarianism	'How do leaders create the greatest good for the greatest number?'	Both the Goal and the Context	Vaccinations
Virtue Ethics	'What virtues should a leader possess to act ethically?'	The Leader	Greg LeMond vs. Lance Armstrong
Ethical Egoism	'What is self-interested leadership?'	The Leader	International conflicts over petroleum
Universal Ethics	'How can universal standards guide leaders and followers in any context?'	Universal Values and Norms	Muslim immigrants in France who wear head coverings
Cultural Relativism	'How do culture and context impact leadership?'	Cultural Values and Norms	The use of ultrasound technology for sex-selective abortions
Divine Command Theory	'What does The Divine require from leadership?'	The Divine's Values and Norms as well as The Divine's Commands applied in the Context	Evangelical response to Syrian refugee crisis
Social Contract Theory	'What obligations do leaders and followers have to each other?'	Leaders, Followers, and Goal	DACA
Justice as Fairness	'How can leaders and followers together create a just society?'	The connections between Leaders, Followers, and Goals	Mental health reform
The Common Good	'What does the common good demand of leadership?'	All five components	The Paris Agreement

Likewise, the next table provides a list of the leadership models we considered in Section II, the framing question for each model, the leadership component(s) emphasized, and the case example for each chapter.

Now for some observations

In the same way that our introductory chapters began with a serendipitous discovery in the special collections at the library, we would like to offer

Table 17.2 Summary of leadership models

Model	Framing Question	Emphasis	Case Example
Authentic Leadership	'How can I lead with integrity?'	Leaders	Steve Jobs revitalizing Apple Inc.
Servant Leadership	'How can leaders serve their followers and organizations?'	Leaders serving followers	Leymah Gbowee in Liberia
Followership	'How can followers partner with their leaders?'	Followers partnering with leaders	Wells Fargo scandal
Transformational Leadership	'How can leaders create positive change for themselves, their followers, and their organizations?'	Leaders and followers with a transforming goal	Howard Shultz's leadership during a crisis at Starbucks
Adaptive Leadership	'How should both leaders and their followers adapt their thinking to solve complex challenges?'	Adaptive challenges in the context	Nelson Mandela moving South Africa away from Apartheid

some unexpected observations made at the end of the writing process. Once the editors had assembled all the material for these chapters three themes revealed themselves:

1. How ethical and leadership models seem to pair with each other.
2. What seems to be required for ethical leadership.
3. Specific behaviors for promoting ethical leadership.

How the models pair with each other

One fascinating finding occurred as we developed the visual representation of the five components of leadership for each ethical model. These models often 'paired' themselves by having similar or inverted areas of emphasis. These similarities became the final organizing scheme for the order of chapters. For students who want to understand better the nuances of these different models, we suggest they pay attention to the similarities and differences of these pairings. While all models of ethical leadership may ask a fundamentally similar question – 'What is the right thing to do?' – the nuanced differences in how these models frame the question – and where they seem to focus on the five components of leadership – is worth noting (see Figure 17.3).

Table 17.3 Models with mutual areas of concern

Leadership Component	Ethical Models	Leadership Models
The Leader	Egoism and Virtue Ethics, Justice as Fairness, Social Contract	Authentic Leadership, Servant Leadership
The Follower	Justice as Fairness, Social Contract	Followership
The Goal	Justice as Fairness, Social Contract, Utilitarianism, Kantianism	Transformational Leadership
The Context	Utilitarianism	Adaptive Leadership
Cultural Values and Norms	Universal Ethics, Cultural Relativism, Divine Command Theory	
All Components	The Common Good	

Distribution of components and emphasis

When first thinking about 'ethical leadership,' it is easy to slip into the mind-set that it is all about the individual leader, and that if individual leaders can simply develop enough strength and personal character everything will take care of itself. If our analysis of the ethical models is correct, then ethical and effective leadership will require leaders to tap into components that go far beyond themselves. Also, note how three of the five leadership models also looked beyond the individual leader for their primary emphasis. This observation is consistent with how the last few decades of leadership studies have continued to push academics to see leadership as something that is larger than simply individual leaders or the 'great people' of history.

Egoism, virtue ethics, and authentic leadership

What an irony that our egoism and virtue ethics chapters both emphasize the same component. At first glance, it can appear that these two models are pointing in opposite directions. However, both models emphasize a leader's self-awareness. For egoism, the leader must be reflective enough to determine what is genuinely in the leader's self-interest in the long term versus the short term. Likewise, a virtue approach that explicitly emphasizes humility requires self-awareness that accurately assesses the leader's actual strengths and weaknesses, as compared to what the leader might imagine those traits to be. This emphasis on a self-aware leader is also at the heart of authentic leadership. And it is no surprise that our table places it on the same line as egoism and virtue ethics. Authentic leadership emphasizes being true to oneself in a manner that could parallel well with egoism, as well as an emphasis on living consistently with core values, which correlates with virtue ethics.

Kantianism, utilitarianism, and transformational leadership

Kant focused on an immutable goal – the 'leader's duty always to do what is right' no matter what the consequences. In a different manner, utilitarianism also emphasizes the goal, but with a specific assessment of the consequences of that goal. As we now reflect on transformational leadership and note its emphasis on the goal as well, we can note that it is also concerned for the consequences of the goal – transforming both the organization and the members of that organization toward 'higher levels of motivation and morality,' as James MacGregor Burns would say.[1]

Utilitarianism and adaptive leadership

Both of these models look to the context of a leadership event. In the case of utilitarianism, it considers the impact of the leaders, followers, and goal upon the context. In an inverse of this, adaptive leadership recognizes how the context impacts leaders, followers, and goals.

Universal ethics, cultural relativism, and divine command

These are the ethical approaches that often ignite the 'culture wars.' And, as we consider some of the different claims from these ethical models, we can understand why there could be tension between adherents to these different ethical positions. Those claiming to follow a 'universal ethic' are attempting to root themselves in a tradition that respects religion, yet does not look toward religion as an ultimately authoritative source. Instead, it often looks toward the values of a secular, and often a Western model of liberal 'freedom granting' values. Cultural relativism also appreciates religious values, but it places different religious systems all on an equal footing, asking 'What can we learn?' from each system, rather than claiming that one system is 'right.' In contrast, divine command theories are founded upon a particular religious tradition and look both toward the divine and how the will of the divine has been expressed in written tradition. Nonetheless, all three models value the role of reason in the application of their various claims. Thus, you might see why those holding to these particular ethical traditions might run into conflict with each other.

The common good

In our analysis of ethical leadership, the common good seemed to work almost like a 'superlayer' over the top of our whole schema. We need to be careful with that representation – especially in light of the concept of 'culture wars' mentioned above. We believe that the common good is distinct among the ethical models because it is equally concerned with leader, follower, goal, context, and cultural norms – striving to find actions that benefit all those layers of the model.

Requirements for ethical leadership

After considering the various questions asked by our chapters and the answers provided, we observe a few components that seem to be a *sine qua non* for ethical leadership:

- Humility expressed as a realistic sense of self – both strengths and weaknesses. Humility shows up in a number of chapters as an essential quality for leadership. In virtue ethics, we saw how humility was prized in Hinduism, Buddhism, Judaism, Christianity, and Islam, as well as how the Greek tradition warned against hubris. It was also a necessary characteristic for dealing with the challenges of cultural relativism. Additionally, we can argue that humility is beneficial for applying the leadership models in our text. For example, those who wish to practice servant leadership must accurately assess their genuine motives for leadership. A similar self-awareness must also be applied to determine how both the leader and follower are impacted by their mutual goals to practice transformational leadership. For authentic leadership, self-awareness is the fundamental trait required. Humility also expresses itself when adaptive leadership takes place, because the leader must give up the desire to be the 'problem solver' and allow followers to do the work. Regarding followership, leaders will not be willing to receive honest feedback from followers who act as 'partners' and not just 'implementers' unless those leaders also demonstrate humility.
- While practically impossible to make decisions completely free of self-interest, ethical awareness often calls the leader to something beyond self-interest. Note how often the emphasis on an ethical or leadership model was on the followers, the goal, the context, or the culture instead of just the leader. One could even argue that the humility we just discussed is necessary for leaders to appreciate the lack of leader-centricity in these models. Certainly, what leaders do matters – but for them to operate effectively as ethical leaders, they must assess themselves in light

of how they impact the other spheres of the Five Components Model. Even something as leader-centric as egoism requires leaders to be aware of their impact on the other spheres – and to assess how that impact is or is not in the leader's self-interest. We suggest that for leaders to be truly ethical, they must be accountable to something outside of themselves. Our discussion of ethics and the five components of leadership confirms this.

Action steps for ethical leadership

So, if we take these observations from our text and once again think about the five components of leadership, we can understand the journey of the ethical leader. It begins with the self-awareness that leads to an accurate assessment of the self and one's place in the world. This awareness also continues to consider how one relates to others and their impact on others as they work together to achieve a common goal. Then the perspective continues to broaden by reflecting on how the work that they do together impacts the context in which they work to reach their goals. Finally, one considers how all of that either corresponds with the prevailing values and norms of the culture or challenges those same values. Such self-awareness is the journey of a lifetime, so we now suggest some very practical action steps readers can take on their journey as an ethical leader:

- Note how we framed each of our chapters with reflective questions. Asking such questions is not just an activity for academics. Rather, these questions are intended to promote self-awareness. As you strive to be an ethical leader, consider it to be a journey that works from the inside-out and a mix of self-aware thinking with self-aware action. (So once again, we return to the definition of leadership as *purposeful interaction*.)
- Take time to assess yourself as a leader. Which ethical models or leadership models are your default? How would you benefit from drawing on additional models?
- When trying to lead others ethically, we invite you to ask these questions of your peers and followers. Try questions like, 'How do we promote the greatest good for the greatest number?' 'How can followers partner with leaders in this situation?' 'How can we work together to transform our organization?' By using these questions to frame your goals and interactions with others, you can purposefully move yourself and your organization to consider how specific ethical frameworks and leadership models impact your work.
- Studying and teaching leadership with case examples has become standard practice. Use these case studies and stories when you want to educate

and inspire those you work with and continue to look for more examples that can help you and others continue to understand the implications of these ideas better.

Summary and concluding remarks

In our introduction to the book, we mentioned the need to connect ethical thinking and ethical doing. One can still 'ace' an ethics exam in the classroom by cheating. Therefore, the real test of an ethics class is not how students do on a classroom exam or essay, but rather how they act ethically in day-to-day life. So while our book has encouraged readers to look beyond the scope of the individual leader, we will now return to considering their personal leadership.

Sacrifice and ethical leadership

During graduate school, one of the editors studied great American leaders such as George Washington, Abraham Lincoln and Dr. Martin Luther King, Jr. He observed the overwhelming sadness that seemed to saturate their time as leaders – particularly Abraham Lincoln and Dr. King's assassinations. His professor paused the class discussion on this point and commented with a soft and slightly trembling voice, 'If you really want to know if you are ready to be a leader, you have to know what you are willing to suffer.'

On a similar note, we're convinced that the real test of our ethics, or 'values,' is what we are willing to suffer to maintain those values. In other words, for a thing to truly have 'value,' we must be willing to pay something in exchange. As another example from our case studies, Greg LeMond was willing to risk his success as an athlete rather than use performance-enhancing drugs. We also saw multiple examples of how businesses should have made financial sacrifices to meet the various standards of the ethical models in our text. We saw cases where individuals may have to forego personal advantages that may have been allowable by law in order to benefit a larger population. Sometimes, pro-secular or pro-religious adherents will need to find a way to accommodate the other for the sake of common interests. The humility necessary for cultural relativism will require leaders to abandon the comfort of adhering to the faultlessness of their own cultural assumptions and accede where others are correct. Leaders who genuinely want partners in their organizations will have to share their power with others, and in some cases drop their defenses so they can receive critical feedback from subordinates.

As with our text, leadership studies often use case examples to help illustrate a point. And numerous stories about ethical leadership or character-based leadership feature the tales of individual leaders. While some of our case studies may have drawn attention to and celebrated those who have made difficult decisions at personal or organizational cost, we also recognize that on a daily basis numerous leaders make intentional decisions that have personal costs – sometimes *great* personal costs – and they do so without fanfare. Instead of 'no guts, no glory' it's 'all guts and still no glory.' No wonder humility showed up in our earlier analysis of themes for ethical leadership. As a consequence, a fundamental question for knowing where you are ready to be an ethical leader is to ask yourself, 'For what am I willing to suffer?' If you want an ethical organization, ask your team, 'For what are we willing to suffer?' To the extent that you and your organization can have that conversation genuinely, you've taken a positive step forward. We must remember, ethical leadership is about both using ethical theories and models to facilitate ethical decision-making, and for leaders to use their positions of leadership to create positive change. We now call you, and ourselves, to rise to both of these challenges.

DISCUSSION QUESTIONS

Which of the ethical theories and models presented in this book resonated most with you and why?

Which of the leadership theories and models presented in this book resonated most with you and why?

What do you view to be the largest obstacles to ethical leadership?

How can you apply the insights of this book in your own leadership roles?

For what are you willing to suffer to be an 'ethical leader'?

ADDITIONAL RESOURCES

J.B. Ciulla (ed.), *Ethics, the Heart of Leadership*, 2nd edn, Westport, CT: Praeger, 2004.
This compilation is often referenced when studying leadership and can be a helpful next step in a journey of thinking about the connections between leadership and ethics.

T.L. Price, *Leadership Ethics: An Introduction*, Cambridge: Cambridge University Press, 2008.
Price's book is an introduction to ethical theories and their relevance to leadership that also emphasizes psychology and Kantianism.

C.E. Johnson, *Meeting the Ethical Challenges of Leadership: Casting Light or Shadow*, 6th edn, Los Angeles: Sage, 2018.
Johnson's book introduces ethical theories and models, and their relevance to leadership and also has a focus on the implications of the 'dark side' of unethical leadership.

NOTE

1   J.M. Burns, *Leadership*, New York: HarperCollins, 1978, p. 20.

Index